D1593894

JEWS &
GENTILES
in EARLY
AMERICA

1654–1800

William Pencak

THE UNIVERSITY OF MICHIGAN PRESS   ANN ARBOR

E
184.3512
.P46
2005

Copyright © by the University of Michigan 2005
All rights reserved
Published in the United States of America by
The University of Michigan Press
Manufactured in the United States of America
⊗ Printed on acid-free paper

2008   2007   2006   2005   4   3   2   1

No part of this publication may be reproduced, stored in a retrieval system,
or transmitted in any form or by any means, electronic, mechanical, or otherwise,
without the written permission of the publisher.

A CIP catalog record for this book is available from the British Library.

Library of Congress Cataloging-in-Publication Data

Pencak, William, 1951–
    Jews and gentiles in early America : 1654–1800 / William Pencak.
        p.   cm.
    Includes bibliographical references and index.
    ISBN-13: 978-0-472-11454-2 (cloth : alk. paper)
    ISBN-10: 0-472-11454-9 (cloth : alk. paper)
        1. Jews—United States—History—17th century.   2. Jews—United States—
    History—18th century.   3. Antisemitism—United States—History. 4. Judaism—
    Relations—Christianity—History.   5. Christianity and other religions—
    Judaism—History.   6. United States—Ethnic relations.   I. Title.

E184.3512.P46   2005
305.892'4073'0903—dc22   2005014440

CONTENTS

PREFACE & ACKNOWLEDGMENTS

$\mathcal{S}$OMETIME IN THE WINTER OF 1998–99, I was chatting with my friend, then the head of the Penn State Department of History, A. Gregg Roeber. He asked me out of the blue if I knew anything about colonial Pennsylvania Jews. I said no and asked him, "Does anybody?" The conversation was the inspiration for a paper I delivered at one of several conferences Gregg has organized bringing German and American scholars together to study the interaction of the German-speaking world with colonial America. Entitled "Jews and Pietists in Dialogue in Enlightenment America," it produced the first installment of the present project, "Jews and Anti-Semitism in Early Pennsylvania," which was published in the *Pennsylvania Magazine of History and Biography* in July 2002.

Thanks to the article's reception, I decided to write similar essays on the other four major Jewish communities in mainland British North America: New York; Newport, Rhode Island; Charleston; and Savannah, to put them in order of Jewish settlement. Although historians of early American Jewry, notably Jacob Rader Marcus, have been studying colonial Jews throughout the twentieth century, my approach has been different. I was interested in placing each Jewish community in the context of the history of the five cities and colonies. When were Jews welcomed, and despised, and by whom? Why did anti-semitism or its converse, philo-semitism, occur when it did? Why did Jewish communities grow, decline, remain stable, and quarrel among themselves? What was the role of Jews in the American Revolution and the politics of the early republic?

My main conclusions are that a strain of popular anti-semitism appeared intermittently before the American Revolution, largely derived from traditional European prejudices. There were few Jews in early America, but a good number of those were closely associated with the gentile elite. Opposition to the Jews came from the very populist or "democratic" elements who were themselves contending for liberty against governors or leading merchants. In consequence, the revolutionary era witnessed increased anti-semitism along with increased popular participation in civic life, as the Jews were linked with the local elites even though they, too, sought political privileges they had lacked (except in New York) during the colonial era. Political anti-semitism exploited popular anti-semitism as the status of the Jews in a republic, and a predominantly Christian republic, became an item of debate far out of proportion to the minuscule number of Jews (about three thousand) in the new nation as of 1790. The nature of anti-semitism changed, too: Jews were no longer greedy, dishonest, and comic although inconsequential; now their intelligence made them a real threat to lead other negatively signified ethnic groups—Germans, Irish, French, and African Americans—and undermine the republican experiment.

Politicians used anti-semitism in an effort to secure votes. Until 1793 the Jews were supported by and supported the Federalists, who had worked with them at the highest levels of revolutionary government. They were attacked by the Anti-Federalists, or Democrats, or Republicans, or Democratic-Republicans, or Jeffersonians. But when the French Revolution gave the Jews complete equality, the parties switched their attitudes. The Federalists became more narrow minded, insisting on a Christian, largely Anglo-Saxon America; the Jeffersonians for their part welcomed Jews—both ethnic and practicing, for even Jews who converted or were the gentile children of mixed marriages were tarred with anti-semitism. Each party's version of anti-semitism reflected its political ideology: Anti-Federalists and Republicans viewed Jews as wealthy, conspiring with merchants and speculators to impose aristocracy; Federalists focused on poor Jews who they thought were trying to foment a second revolution and rise to power and wealth on the ruins of the nation. My story ends in 1800, with a few excursions into the nineteenth century, by which time the Federalists' anti-semitism had proven to be a failure.

Some scholars have questioned the existence of anti-semitism in early America. There were no pogroms, and probably no murders of Jews because they were Jews, with the possible exception of a Jewish loyalist in

Rhode Island. Southern Jews who were insulted fought duels on equal terms with their antagonists, a practice of which both law and society approved. Yet the extent to which Jews and Judaism, and their role in what either was or was not to be a Christian nation, was a lively subject of debate in the last quarter of the eighteenth century. At this time, the United States set a precedent of which it ought not to be proud: for the first time in modern history, democratic politicians, with varying degrees of sincerity and cynicism, exploited popular anti-semitic prejudices in an effort to gain votes. Others, such as Presidents Washington and Adams, who personally expressed the highest admiration for Jews both individually and collectively, did not challenge prejudices uttered by their supporters. Jews and their defenders, in an atmosphere where abuse rarely went beyond the verbal, in turn were able to articulate powerfully their patriotic contributions to the new nation and their worthiness of full equality.

Despite tiny numbers, early American Jews played important roles in commerce, frontier expansion, the American Revolution, and the partisan battles of the early republic. The degree to which continental European and English Jewish behavior patterns were successfully transferred to the colonies was frequently manifested in the extensive correspondence between Jews on both sides of the Atlantic. Small communities that sometimes fell below the critical number of ten men, the minyan required for religious services, struggled to maintain Judaism while at the same time interacting with gentiles in cities, rural areas, and on a frontier that attracted Jewish traders. As with others who populated British North America, the tiny number of Jewish immigrants hailed from an astonishing range of places in both the Christian and Islamic worlds, and encompassed rich and poor, Ashkenazi and Sephardic Jews who assimilated to, accommodated, and antagonized the greater gentile population as well as their own. The integration of elite Jews into a transnational enlightenment culture through the Masons and other associations of well-off colonists threatened Judaism even more than it did the Protestant Christian denominations, for only a Jewish mother could produce a Jewish child. It was easier for Jewish men to renounce their faith— especially given the shortage of both minyans and Jewish women—than for Christian women to convert to Judaism. Between 1790 and 1840, all the American Jewish congregations combined only accepted twelve converts, a figure dwarfed by the 28 percent of Jews who intermarried.[1]

Studying the Jewish experience in early America will strike many chords familiar to students of European Jewry in the early modern world. By the eighteenth century, both European and English Jewry included a mixture of Sephardic and Ashkenazi elements. Because of persecution, many Spanish (Sephardic) Jews had moved to Italy (where the popes after the Counter-Reformation for the most part protected them), the Near East or North Africa (where Islam was even more tolerant), and the Netherlands (the most tolerant of all). German Jews first were pushed eastward toward Poland during the Reformation, but as would occur time and again after persecutions and wartime devastation, they returned, prospered, and were for the most part tolerated from the time of the Thirty Years War into the early twentieth century. Although many adopted the Christian religion, they soon found that they could not shed their ethnic identity as easily, for anti-semites continued to use their Jewish heritage against them. For instance, although the fathers of Felix Mendelssohn and Karl Marx converted to Christianity, and the former was a Protestant and the latter an atheist, their enemies accused them of writing "Jewish" music and philosophy. (Gustav Mahler and Sigmund Freud suffered a similar fate.)[2]

Visibly concentrated in ghettoes or particular neighborhoods, and wearing distinctive clothes, Jews in Europe outside England and the Netherlands lived precarious lives. They could easily be attacked by Christians who dared not directly oppose the aristocracy under whose regimes elite Jews prospered. From time to time, rulers such as Philip II of Spain, Louis XIV of France, and Maria Theresa of Austria joined in the persecution, putting religious zeal ahead of the financial interests of their kingdoms, but these were exceptional. Elites found Jews economically useful, whereas the general population that confronted them as tax farmers and moneylenders in western Europe or estate agents in eastern Europe tended to blame Jews for their problems. At the same time, some Jews themselves reacted against assimilation, which became more pronounced as the Enlightenment progressed. Like the Protestant Great Awakening in Britain and North America in the 1740s, the Hasidim emerged in eastern Europe at this time and also questioned an increasingly secular, rational, and cosmopolitan society. No Hasidim, however, are known to have come to America before the mid-nineteenth century.[3]

The history of English Jewry, too, was initially marked by persecution.

No Jews were allowed to live openly in England from the time Edward I expelled them in 1290 until 1655, when Menasseh ben Israel of Amsterdam arrived and successfully pleaded for their readmittance and naturalization. His efforts enabled a secret Jewish community that lived in London's East End to reveal itself. Thereafter, English Jews joined their Dutch counterparts in their immunity from formal persecution if not popular anti-semitism. Beginning in 1655, England "naturalized" Jews, permitting them to stay, do business, and own property without granting them political rights.

English Jews Christianized more rapidly than those on the continent. This "radical assimilation" occurred, historian Todd Endelman notes, because there was no long-standing Jewish cultural community in England—its rabbis came from abroad—and the Jews endured neither the isolation in ghettoes nor the persecution endured by Jews on the continent. With these liabilities had come a tradition of limited self-rule and the defense of tradition that comes from persecution. In England, Jews had most of the rights of gentiles except political participation, an exclusion that encouraged conversions, especially among upper-class Jews, notably Isaac D'Israeli, father of the great prime minister. British elite relations with Jews were sufficiently friendly that the term *philo-semitism* has been commonly used by scholars to describe the interaction of well-to-do English Jews and gentiles who shared a philosophical commitment to the Enlightenment.[4]

The great mobility of early modern Jews did not reflect a rootless people, but rather the tight connections maintained between the mainland communities of Newport, New York, Savannah, Charleston, and Philadelphia with those in Europe and the West Indies. International connections came into play when London Jews appealed successfully to their American brethren for funds to aid their fellow religionists in Palestine, a major, repeated destination of European Jewish charity.[5]

Such transatlantic ties were not peculiarly Jewish: Rose Beiler has demonstrated similar networks among Pennsylvania German Christian sectarians, many of whom could understand their fellow Jewish immigrants, since Yiddish is a dialect of German. Quakers and Anglicans, among others, also supported each other across the ocean.[6] But Jewish ties were among the closest. Historian Nuala Zahedieh has found that in seventeenth-century England, Jews, along with Quakers, were disproportionately represented in the colonial trade because "their religious belief sys-

tems allowed community leaders to enforce conduct and insure information flow." In short, Jews and Quakers could trust each other as members
of more numerous Protestant faiths could not. Examining business practices two hundred years later, in nineteenth-century America, scholar
Rowena Olegario observes that Jewish merchants in the United States stood
apart from gentiles, who used the services of credit-reporting agencies to
determine the reliability of their clients: instead, the Jews continued to rely
on personal contacts among themselves. In the intervening eighteenth century, tight connections among the Jewish traders of British North America
were the product of Jewish integrity (despite stereotypes to the contrary),
the Franks family and its numerous connections, and habits of mutual
assistance that grew out of the experience of persecution on the continent.
In the exceptional national diversity of their population, in their role in
occupying borderlands, and in their desire to prove themselves worthy
members of the body politic, Jews exemplified trends found among ethnic
groups on the cultural margins of the British world.[7]

I could not have written this book without the financial and moral support
of a host of people and institutions. I hope anyone I omit will forgive me.
The Jacob Rader Marcus Center, which holds the American Jewish
Archives at Hebrew Union College in Cincinnati, Ohio, offered me a
Wiener-Lowenstein fellowship for a month in the summer of 2002. I stayed
in a dormitory with a group of rabbinical students, and was extraordinarily
moved by their willingness to pursue their scheduled studies in Israel
despite an exceptionally brutal spate of terrorist activity at the time.
Camille Servizzi, Elise Nienaber, Kevin Proffitt, Fred Krome, and Gary Zola
were the most congenial of hosts, as was all the staff in the library. And of
course there is the debt I, and everyone who studies American Jewish history, owes to the late Jacob Rader Marcus. By collecting available materials
from all over the globe, he made it possible to do research in American Jewish history with exceptional ease and thoroughness. He also left to the
archives his many publications during his long lifetime, which fell just a
year short of a century.

Mark Häberlein and Michaela Schmölz-Häberlein, whose fine work on
the Jews of Lancaster appeared in the same issue of the *Pennsylvania Magazine of History and Biography* as mine, were especially helpful to me at the

conference. My article, "Jews and Anti-Semitism in Early Pennsylvania," appeared in *PMHB* 126, no. 3 (July 2002): 365–408. I thank the editors, Shan Holt and Tamara Miller, who helped me write a much better essay, for permission to reprint parts of it in altered form. I also presented a preliminary version of the article at the McNeil Center for Early American Studies, where Daniel Richter, Michael Zuckerman, Susan Klepp, Miriam Bodian, Brendan McConville, and George Boudreau belonged to another fine audience that helped me refine my work. Along the way, Natalie Zemon Davis, Leonard Dinnerstein, John B. Frantz, Alison Olson, and Adam Sutcliffe also read the article and offered both criticism and encouragement.

My department head at Penn State, A. G. Roeber, and Dean of Liberal Arts Susan Welch, persuaded me to cut down drastically on historical editing, take a sabbatical, and write this book. I didn't know I had another book in me, but they had more confidence in me than I did in myself. Several of my colleagues, especially Baruch Halpern, Paul Rose, and Brian Hesse from our Department of Jewish Studies, which works closely with History at Penn State, were unfailingly helpful and encouraging to someone who is, after all, a colonialist poaching on their territory. I hope some of my insights will partially repay them. Sally McMurry, our department head, offered both friendship and a semester's leave when I became seriously ill. The Penn State Department of History—staff, faculty, and graduate students—is the most congenial imaginable, and if I can't remember who helped me how and when, may I simply offer a hearty "thank you" to everyone. The department's Robert Haag Research Fund paid for the reproduction of the maps and illustrations.

I should also like at this point in my career to reiterate my thanks to all my teachers who nourished my love for history, beginning with Mrs. Tropper in the sixth grade, Mrs. Laird and Mr. Haken in junior high school, Messrs. Passy, Chiarello, Karp, and Pleven, and Mrs. Reichmann, Santor, and especially, Mrs. Gottlieb in high school. At Columbia, I will always be indebted to Alden Vaughan, William Leuchtenburg, Marcia Wright, J. M. W. Bean, Peter Onuf, the late Eric McKitrick and Leonard Krieger, and especially, Chilton Williamson Sr.

I was also fortunate to receive the Mellon Bank Fellowship for 2002–3 from the Huntington Library in San Marino, California. Everyone there—most notably research director Roy Ritchie, Susi Krasnoo, and Paul Zall, the legendary discoverer and editor of Benjamin Franklin's "real" *Autobiography*—made that year one of the most productive and enjoyable of my life, especially given that weatherwise it was among the most balmy in California history, and one of the stormiest on the East Coast. I was able to write nearly the entire book there, and even make a significant dent in my next one (a study of John Jay and his family) despite the fact the library was only open until 5:00 p.m., an hour at which I am usually just shifting into full gear. While in California, I presented some of my research to the Huntington Library Seminar and the Bay Area Seminar in Colonial History, and also at California State University, Long Beach. Special thanks to my friends Edith Gelles, Brent Mizelle, Peter Mancall, Jack Rakove, Dee Andrews, and the late, wonderful Jackie Reinier for their incisive questions and warm hospitality.

While at the Huntington I made the acquaintance of several excellent historians. Joshua Piker of the University of Oklahoma provided invaluable information on Native American relations on the southern frontier. Hermann Wellenreuther and Claudia Schnurmann brought to the Huntington their pathbreaking research in German and Dutch sources along with their stimulating personalities. Their transatlantic approach to early American history has caused me to rethink a subject I have been studying for thirty-odd years now. Gene Fingerhut and Joe Tiedemann made me a silent partner in their new book on the American Revolution in New York, an innovative study that looks at the nature of the Revolution in the different counties and regions of the state. I would especially like to thank Mark Stern, piano tuner and amateur historian extraordinaire, for sharing his excellent research on David Franks and the Franks family with me. I hope to see it in print before this book appears. Mark also arranged a meeting with Leo Hershkowitz, scholar of New York Jews, who not only told me most of the stones in the Chatham Square burial ground were moved (without the bodies) from an earlier site, but corrected me (as I hope to correct others) in the misapprehension that Asser Levy (of Vilna in eastern Europe, as he had signed his name in Amsterdam) was one of the twenty-three original New York Jews who came from Brazil, meaning none of them stayed and the real community was begun by Levy and other Dutch Jewish merchants.

By sheer chance, for the first time several scholars are working on large topics in early American Jewish history simultaneously. They are also splendid people who share their work gladly and whose sense of community approaches the level of a mutual admiration society. We all gave papers at the Omohundro Institute's Annual Meeting in New Orleans in the summer of 2003. Holly Snyder's book on the Jews of Savannah, Newport, and Jamaica, based on her 2000 Brandeis University Ph.D. dissertation, will appear about the same time as mine. There is little overlap: she probes the psychology of individuals and the nuances of social life as I never could, whereas I focus more on the public realm and the political relationship of Jews and gentiles. If I occasionally present a different interpretation, hers is always worthy of at least equal consideration. Frederic Cople Jaher's *The Jews and the Nation* appeared as I was writing my book: his comparison of how Jewish civil rights developed in France and the United States will provoke thought about the paradox that the instantaneous formal equality Jews achieved with the French Revolution was a mixed blessing as it linked Jewish rights with left-of-center politics in Europe until the Holocaust. Fred's critique for my publisher was a model of both courtesy and incisiveness, and the book is much better because of his criticisms and suggestions. Edith Gelles is working on colonial Jewish women, especially Abigaill Levy Franks of New York: she brings to the study of this simultaneously orthodox yet Enlightened woman the beautiful prose and profound insights of her work on Abigail Adams. And Heather Nathans has incorporated into her pioneering work on early American theater the most incisive work yet on Jewish stereotypes in early American intellectual and cultural life. If this book does not examine images of Jews or commercial and family networks as thoroughly as it ought to, this is because Holly and Heather are in the process of doing a far better job than I could with these specialized topics. Thank you all for a great session and your collegial friendship!

Mary Kelly, wonderful historian and an equally good friend, persuaded me to publish this book with the University of Michigan Press. I was extremely fortunate to work with Jim Reische, Amy Anderson, and Kevin Rennells of the Press in bringing the book to publication.

Mary Miles, Eileen Gallagher, Mattie Scott, Jason Kelly, Kristen Cooper, and my nephew Patrick Pencak spent a great deal of time with me in California so I could enjoy the whole experience rather than simply do research. I'll never forget the Pasadena Ritz, the Descanso Camelia Garden, the Getty, Universal Studios, and the trips to Santa Barbara, Berkeley, and the bottom of the Grand Canyon for champagne lunch. My mother was always ready at the other end of the phone, encouraging me not to work too hard and have a good time. Her moral and financial support and that of my late father is the only reason I have been able to live my dream of being a historian who writes what he wants rather than what pays the bills.

I initially intended to dedicate this book to solely the memory of the late Pamela Manzi, M.A., History, New York University, 1965, whose friendship during my year in California represented more than she could ever suspect. However, between completion of the manuscript and publication, I suffered from spinal meningitis that nearly cost me my life. So I include in the dedication all of the doctors, nurses, and staff at Long Island Jewish Hospital, the Parker Jewish Institute for Rehabilitation, and Mount Nittany Hospital for exemplary care and what I hope will be a full recovery by the time this book sees the light of day. And also my mother, my brother, and Vincent Andrassy, who continued that care and gave me more love and hope than I have ever deserved.

CHAPTER 1

INTRODUCTION

WHEN IN 1782 THAT FIRST great apostle of American exceptionalism, Hector St. John Crèvecoeur, proclaimed that in British North America the typical European, "leaving behind him all his ancient prejudices and manners," was "melted into a new race of men," he listed as examples the "English, Scotch, Irish, Dutch, Germans, and Swedes."[1] He left out the Jews, but can hardly be blamed. They comprised an almost infinitesimal proportion—less than one-twentieth of 1 percent—of the population of eighteenth-century British North America. Perhaps thirteen hundred to three thousand Jews, out of over three million people, lived in the new United States at the time of the first national census in 1790. One credible estimate of the size of the two largest Jewish communities, in Charleston, South Carolina, and New York City, is 188 and 242 members, respectively.[2]

Nevertheless, Jews were far more important in the history of early America than their numbers suggest. New England Puritans considered themselves a "New Israel" and tried to model their society on the ancient Jewish republic that existed under the judges; during the American Revolution, both statesmen and ministers wrote and preached that the new nation had succeeded both Massachusetts and Israel as God's chosen, republican people. The Hebrew Bible comprises over half the Christian Bible, and contains almost all the relevant discussions of government and the moral mission of a nation specially favored by God.[3]

Moreover, America's real Jews played an important role in its early history. It is easy to overlook anti-semitism in America before the 1820s, a decade when immigrants primarily from German-speaking lands increased the Jewish population from about three thousand in 1820 to fifteen thousand in 1830. But whether Jews were fit for citizenship was a major subject of debate in both colonial and revolutionary America. Like other groups on the North American continent, Jews encountered opposition to their settlement, denial of equal rights, and criticism of their general character in the press. What Jews did not find, however, were the pogroms or ghettoes of continental Europe. Nothing occurred like the 1739 riot against the wealthy Jews of Speightstown, Barbardos, the second largest city of that West Indian colony. In that case, the notorious confidence man Tom Bell caused the trouble by claiming to be a son of the late Governor Burnet of Massachusetts. Bell moved easily among the island's elite both Jewish and gentile until he was caught stealing from the Lopez family at a Jewish wedding. When a member of the family beat him up, Bell professed outrage and sued him for ten thousand pounds. After the assault, the Jews' gentile business competitors protested the Jews' "daring insolence . . . toward the Christians," thereby instigating a crowd that drove them out of town to Barbardos' capital, Bridgetown. Here, the colony's elite and British officials supported the Jews, "they being generally pretty rich, 'tis reported they will be protected by one of the greatest men of the island."[4]

Yet the absence of personal violence does not mean anti-semitism was either nonexistent or trivial. It took different forms, but this tiny segment of the population was disproportionately scrutinized, and either condemned or praised as a race or nation—terms largely used interchangeably—by the gentile population to determine the role of Judaism in colonial society and then the new Republic. Stereotypes of the Jews as shrewd, mercenary, industrious, grasping, intelligent, ambitious, and sly persisted in England and America from the Middle Ages until at least the 1930s.[5] In early America, the most visible, and violent, evidence of anti-semitism was the desecration of Jewish graveyards in each of the five major communities. Although the Jews had placed these cemeteries on the periphery or well outside the edge of urban settlement—Jews in Newport, the only city located at the base of the hill, built theirs at its top—the graves were attacked nevertheless. Furthermore, they were locked and surrounded with high metal fences (Newport and Savannah) or walls (New York, Charleton, and Philadelphia). This meant that the vandals were not merely drunks, rowdies, or boys who might have committed their actions on a whim: whoever went from town to a Jewish cemetery had to make a deliberate decision to go there (see maps). Jews also maintained a low-key institutional presence in that none of the synagogues built by 1800 exhibited a Star of David or any exterior proclamation of the Jewish faith. The buildings in New York, Philadelphia, and Newport resembled houses or public buildings, the one in Charleston a Georgian, Protestant church. In New York and Newport, simple facades hid elegant interior settings for worship.[6]

Anti-semitic prejudice was so much a part of gentile cultural baggage that it would casually be mentioned even where no slur was intended. For example, the *Pennsylvania Gazette,* which, following founder Benjamin Franklin's retirement in 1748, continued his philo-semitic bent when explicitly discussing particular Jews or the overall quality of the Jewish people, occasionally used language and humor that would appeal to general prejudices. On June 10, 1731, the twenty-five-year-old Franklin pleaded with his readers not to be upset if particular remarks in the paper upset them, since "they who follow Printing [are] . . . scarce able to do any thing in their way of getting a living, which shall probably not give offence to some." As a counterexample, Franklin wrote that "the merchant may buy and sell with Jews, Turks, Hereticks, and infidels of all sorts, and get Money by every one of them, without giving offence to the most orthodox." Franklin was here alluding to the popular trope that linked these groups as undesirables, with the Jews usually mentioned first.

Over a half century later a writer in the *Gazette* asked, "Is not the gravity which retains Jupiter in his orbit, the same gravity which operates on a grain in the scales of a Jew?" This offhand statement appeared in a satirical article of August 21, 1782, that argued that trees had as much right to vote as some of the lower-class elements who were insisting on the suffrage. The thrust of the question, however, was to brand the weight in the Jewish merchant's scales as the smallest conceivable body of matter—that is, lighter than other merchants' and thus fraudulent—thereby reinforcing the stereotype that Jews were overly concerned with milking every sale for the last penny.

The first anti-semitic joke in the *Pennsylvania Gazette,* operated by Benjamin Franklin's partner David Hall after the former's retirement in 1748, appeared in 1753. It was reprinted from a New York source. In two paragraphs it managed to present four popular stereotypes about Jews: they were greedy, dishonest, uncouth, and lusted after Christian women. A peddler came to a woman's house and exchanged a piece of calico "upon Condition of giving up her Charms to him": she could not pay him as her absent husband had the key to the money-box. Shortly thereafter, the peddler encountered the husband and told the man he had sold the calico to his wife on credit. Claiming that he could not afford the cloth, the husband returned with the peddler and insisted his wife give it back. She did, but put a piece of burning coal inside. The Jew "march'd off, pleas'd with Thoughts of His Success; but for his Sweet Meat he soon found Sour Sauce." He then encountered a man, who upon noticing the flames in his pack, asked him where he came from. "From Hell," replied the peddler, to which the man responded, "so I perceive." Seeing his goods on fire, the Jew began to "stamp and rave like a mad Man, and curse his Folly in cuckolding the poor Man."[7] This brief anecdote is rich with meaning. The Jew is presented as completely immoral, both seducing a woman and then thinking nothing of cheating her husband. "Hell" is suggested as the appropriate place for the Jew, and only his symbolic sentencing to the flames makes him see the error of his ways. When he finally does, his "cleverness" is shown to be inferior to that of a Christian woman.

However, it is also worth noting that anti-semitic jokes and stereotypes, while present in the colonial era, were far less numerous than those against other groups such as the French, Spanish, Scots-Irish, Germans, and Roman Catholics in general, all of whom posed serious international or domestic problems for colonial societies. For example, in the fifty-odd pamphlets that emerged during the Paxton Boys' march on Philadelphia in 1764 and 1765, the targets were the Germans, the Scots-Irish Presbyterians, and the Quakers.[8] Early Americans held negative views about various minorities, but the Jews were usually distinguished from others. They (like Quakers) were frequently criticized for their cleverness and wealth. Germans, in contrast, were fat, stupid, and drunk, Scots-Irish violent and drunk, and French, Spanish, and other "papists" slaves of their tyrannical rulers and the Catholic Church, although hot-blooded and overly amorous as individuals. All had to give up such alien behavior to be good British subjects before 1776, and good Americans thereafter. Like African Americans and women who struggled for full citizenship, the right to vote, and to hold public office in the nineteenth century, Jews had to prove themselves morally, a task the gentile, propertied, white male population did not share.

Still, American popular anti-semitism was generally far more benign than in Europe. There were far fewer Jews, and the diverse religions found in colonial seaports ensured that no established church or shared religious fanaticism could mobilize the relatively small populations effectively against an impotent scapegoat. (Philadelphia's twenty to thirty thousand people made it the colonies' largest city on the eve of independence.) On the European continent, peasants in the countryside and the poor in the cities resented their financial dependence on Jews, who turned to loaning money at interest when Christians barred them from other occupations. But the English-speaking world lacked the prejudices against commerce found on the continent: if Jews were usurers, they could only be accused for bettering the English trading class at its own game. Yet even in Britain, the "Jew Bill" of 1753, which merely granted to immigrant Jews the same naturalization privileges already held by native Jews, unleashed a wave of protest from country members of Parliament and the opposition press. This so stunned the pro-Jewish Newcastle administration that the law was repealed.[9]

Popular anti-semitism similarly existed in early America as a prejudice that required some catalyst to bring it to the surface. Otherwise, some leaders would not have scapegoated a handful of Jews as responsible for major political problems in the quarter century from 1775 to 1800, which in retrospect appears completely absurd. Before the Revolution hostility only surfaced occasionally, since there was so little popular literature in which anti-semitism could appear. The major site of American publishing was Philadelphia, tiny compared to London's Grub Street. The colonial elites of Newport, New York, Philadelphia, Charleston, and Savannah, although sometimes divided among themselves, were in general philo-semitic and dominated colonial political life, especially at the urban and provincial levels, without much popular input before the third quarter of the eighteenth century.

As a result, colonial anti-semitism tended to be populist, a word I prefer to democratic, for the term *democracy* raises complex problems of political theory as to whether a majority that denies civic participation to minorities can in fact be democratic. Furthermore, colonial political factions opposed to the governor claimed they were more "popular" even when they were a minority in colonial legislatures. Ethnic minorities, such as the Germans in Pennsylvania and Georgia, Presbyterians in South Carolina, and rural-based groups that opposed royal authority and mercantile elites in New York and Rhode Island were the principal anti-semites before the Revolution. These alignments explain why New York and Rhode Island Jews were deeply divided during the Revolution—roughly equally between loyalists and patriots, like the elites of Newport and New York City—whereas nearly all the Jews in the other three states were enthusiastic revolutionaries. In the two southern colonies and Pennsylvania, Jews were politically united with the revolutionary elites. Jacob Rader Marcus is correct in noting that Jews taken collectively were patriots, but his judgment should be qualified so as to note that different patterns of allegiance emerged in the five cities as a result of late colonial politics.[10]

Political anti-semitism—the calculated appeal to popular anti-semitism to influence public opinion and elections—only appeared with the popular politics that accompanied the American Revolution against both Britain and conservative colonial governments that refused to incorporate hitherto excluded minorities. Paradoxically, despite the fact that only in New York could Jews legally vote, the association of a large proportion of the Jews with the merchant elite meant that more moderate revolutionaries—the forerunners of the Federalists—supported extending Jewish rights, whereas what historians have called the more "democratic" elements (although they rarely showed concern for individual rights) supplied almost all the known instances of anti-semitism in the 1770s and 1780s. That about half the Jews in New York and Newport, although not in the other three cities, were loyalists did not help their cause.

With the Revolution, the nature of American anti-semitism changed. Jews were no longer seen, as in popular jokes and culture, as mendacious but essentially harmless and comic; after 1776, they received backhanded compliments for their economic success and intelligence, which made them the potential ringleaders of more numerous and less intelligent groups such as French, Irish, and German immigrants, and African Americans, who also supposedly lacked the virtue required for a republic to survive. Given the importance of Jews in Christian doctrine—they were not only the forerunners of the true religion, but had to be converted before the Second Coming of Christ—the question of whether a Jew, and by extension anyone who was not a Protestant Christian, could be a good American became an item on the national political agenda. That the role of Jews in the

Republic was a subject of debate at all is worthy of mention, for most early American Jews resembled their fellow countrymen in both dress and speech, and their institutional presence was minimal. It did not extend beyond cemeteries in the five cities, and only New York had a synagogue before the 1760s, when Newport and Philadelphia built theirs. In Charlestown and Savannah, until after the Revolution, Jews worshiped in people's houses—perhaps one reason anti-semitism was less pronounced in those cities than in the North.

Political anti-semitism in the early Republic was not confined to any one political ideology or allegiance. As the question of whether Jews morally deserved full citizenship in a purportedly virtuous Republic was periodically debated, politicians, newspaper writers, and clergymen passed the torch of prejudice from one to another as circumstances changed. From 1776 until 1793, anti-semitism was the weapon of "populist" elements, radical revolutionaries, Anti-Federalists, and their successors, the Democratic-Republicans, who feared that irreligious Jews would lead the nation into atheism and immorality, anger God if the Republic admitted them to citizenship, and, in tandem with the wealthy speculators and members of the elite who supported them, inflict the yoke of aristocracy on a virtuous people. After 1793, when revolutionary France granted the Jews full political equality and the Federalists became hostile to the French Revolution, the two nascent parties' attitudes toward the Jews were almost immediately reversed. Now it was the Federalists who feared that the nation's small number of Jews would combine with "Jacobin" intellectuals and use their superior intelligence to lead the unwashed masses of Irish, German, and Scots-Irish to overthrow the men who had successfully guided the Revolution and forged the nation, reducing an orderly Republic to the tumult they observed in France. Federalist anti-semites did not perceive Jews as wealthy, but rather as poor, scheming men seeking to raise their fortunes on the ruins of the Republic, or men who had through chicane acquired wealth for this purpose. Since America had both poor and wealthy Jews—the former mostly post-1760 Ashkenazi immigrants from eastern Europe, the latter well-established Jews who interacted comfortably with the upper classes—each party could find appropriate scapegoats for the evil it feared the most.

To be sure, it is impossible to know whether most rank-and-file Federalists and Democratic-Republicans had anti-semitic attitudes. There were simply too few Jews, other issues were far more pressing, most people left no record one way or the other of their opinions, and the election of 1800 proved the futility of such appeals outside New England. But it is significant that leaders of neither political party repudiated partisan newspapers that used anti-semitic rhetoric to win adherents, even if they themselves publicly supported Jewish equality to various degrees.

Among the most virulent anti-semites on both sides, however, were men whose own credentials as revolutionaries were questionable, or who were newcomers to America or to a particular city. Printers such as Englishmen James Rivington and William Cobbett and New Englanders John Fenno and Thomas Greenleaf who moved from place to place in search of founding a profitable press were especially culpable. Outsiders and the very image of the stereotypical wandering Jew, they projected their own rootlessness and questionable dedication to revolutionary principles onto Jews who were, for the most part, well established in American society and who had vigorously supported the Revolution. Other prominent anti-semites were Christian clergymen who belonged to minority or beleaguered groups, such as Lutheran Henry Melchior Mühlenberg in Pennsylvania, and Anglicans Samuel Frink and Haddon Smith in Georgia, all of whom favored the loyalists.

Postrevolutionary anti-semitism also took on a racist dimension. That some anti-semites tarred Christians with Jewish ancestors (especially John Israel in Pittsburgh and Israel Israel in Philadelphia) with all the usual stereotypes transformed these anti-semites into the unwitting heirs of the Spanish and Portuguese, who expelled converted Jews on the grounds many of them were still secret practitioners of their former faith; in the Iberian peninsula, they were. People who were ethnic Jews, this variety of anti-semitism implied, could not shed inherited characteristics that made them undesirable citizens. Historian Jonathan Sarna has perceptively noted that by the early Republic, Jews usually referred to themselves as belonging to a religious "society," rather than constituting a separate "race" or separate "nation," as Europeans had traditionally regarded them and American anti-semites hoped to brand them. They thereby claimed equality with the various Christian denominations that used similar terminology.

Before the mid-1790s, leading Republicans were openly anti-semitic.

Thomas Paine, Thomas Jefferson, and Benjamin Rush favored toleration philosophically while expressing their distaste for Jews who failed to follow in their Enlightenment footsteps. Paine, America's most famous radical and democrat, condemned the Jews scathingly. Dismissing the biblical Jews in his 1776 tract *Common Sense* as merely another group of people who foolishly sought a monarch, he let loose his thunder in *The Age of Reason*, published at the height of the French Revolution. Here he contrasted the works of genius by the ancient Greeks with the "horrid" character of Moses and the impossible occurrences of the Book of Genesis, such as Joshua stopping the sun in the sky. When challenged by the conservative, anti-revolutionary British bishop of Llandaff, who defended the biblical Jews as worthy forebears of both Christian society and praised modern Jews as valuable members of civilized society, Paine turned his wrath on contemporary as well as historical Judaism. "As to the Jews, there is not one single improvement in any science or in any scientific art that they ever produced. They were the most ignorant of all the illiterate world," for if they were correct in their belief that "the Lord had given them a special message for the rest of humanity, why did he withhold the gift of printing which only came much later, and from the gentiles."

Even the Jews' support of the French Revolution failed to change Paine's mind, as it did for most of his democratic associates, who applauded its gift of Jewish equality. Instead, he branded them as a secret, invidious cult much like the reactionaries who looked to such mythical groups as the Elders of Zion and the Bavarian Illluminati as the sources of rebellion. Citing the medieval Jewish philosopher Maimonides, who wrote that anyone who could discern the hidden meaning of the Book of Genesis ought to keep it secret, Paine deduced that this wisdom "must be something which the Jewish nation are afraid or ashamed the world should know." Although Paine was also critical of Christian bigotry, he went out of his way to single out the Jews as especially backward, ignorant, and superstitious, traits they had passed down since biblical times. He did not, for instance, bring up their resistance to tyranny in both the days of Moses and the kings. Another famous democratic writer, Philip Freneau, was also notoriously anti-semitic.[11]

Pennsylvania's Dr. Benjamin Rush, a Jeffersonian Republican, for his part, accepted Jews as citizens primarily because he thought the better they were treated, the more likely they would convert to Christianity and thus usher in the millennium. Since the United States was God's chosen nation, the conversion of the Jews, a stipulated precondition of the Second Coming of Christ in the Book of Revelations, would begin in the United States. Rush echoed, or may even have been, the newspaper correspondent who explained in 1784 that full citizenship for Jews "would tend to the propagation of Christianity, by impressing the minds of the Jews, from this generous treatment; with sentiments in favor of the gospel."[12] Thus, on the one hand, Rush could observe with joy "the Rabbi [actually, hazan] of the Jews locked in the arms of two ministers of the gospel" in Philadelphia's Fourth of July parade for 1788. There "could not have been a more happy emblem" of "that section of the new constitution which opens all its power and offices . . . to worthy men of every religious sect." Yet on the other hand, Rush lamented what he considered the Jews' excessive concern with earthly advancement, their anticipation of "a mere temporal instead of a spiritual kingdom."[13]

Rush corresponded with Thomas Jefferson on the subject of whether Jews were fit citizens for a Republic that required exceptional virtue, or devotion to the common good, to survive. Early American Jews were mostly city and town dwellers; many were involved in commerce and currency exchanges. For Jefferson, virtue rested in the yeomen farmers, many of whom, like Jefferson himself, were in debt to merchants. To be sure, Jefferson was also critical of Christian "superstition," especially Catholicism, but like Thomas Paine he singled out the Jews for special censure. The statesman who wrote Virginia's statue of religious freedom considered Jews "repulsive & anti-social, as respecting other nations," their ideas of God "degrading and injurious," and their "ethics . . . often irreconcilable with the sound dictates of religion and morality."[14] Despite having observed at firsthand the Jews' loyalty and sacrifices during the struggle for independence, Jefferson and Rush had internalized the stereotypes that Jews were greedy and dishonest. Jefferson stood the Jews' justifiable solidarity in protecting themselves from persecution and assimilation on its head, claiming that the Jews took the initiative in isolating themselves in a gentile world.

Jews thus joined blacks and Native Americans in Jefferson's mind as people who lacked the moral character required to participate in the republican experiment. In all three cases, he ignored empirical evidence before his very eyes in reaching these sweeping judgments. He observed the efforts of the black community in Philadelphia to fight yellow fever in 1793 and the flourishing of the assimilated Cherokee nation. Jews did not only fight in the Revolution; refuting the stereotypes against them, some of them gave substantially to Christian churches and civic charities, demonstrating a pattern of interdenominational cooperation that was at least as prevalent in eighteenth-century Europe and America as hostility between Jews and gentiles. But for Jefferson, unlike blacks and Indians, whose racial qualities were ineradicable, Jews could convert and cease to be Jews. Whereas Jefferson believed blacks and Indians had to be forcibly removed for both their own and the national good to Haiti and the Louisiana Territory, respectively, Jews could shed their ethnicity. But they had to renounce both their religion and the cultural traits associated with it to gain his favor.[15]

In contrast to the Republicans, some Federalists initially made explicit the philo-semitism prerevolutionary elites had adopted toward their Jewish connections. Just as congressmen and army officers of different religions, sections, and ethnic backgrounds began to feel solidarity with those who had shared their eight-year ordeal as architects of a nation, it was impossible for the forgers of the nation to ignore the presence of Jewish soldiers, merchants, and financial brokers in furthering the cause. Jews fit the profile of Federalists: they were cosmopolitans, with nationwide and international connections, accustomed to dealing with different sorts of people, unafraid of diversity, and requiring a strong national government to facilitate their commerce. In addition, as Jack Foner has noted, from the beginning of the nation, no effort was made to exclude the Jews from military service (as were blacks at first in the Civil War and immigrants in World War I), thereby giving them a significant claim to citizenship.[16]

Appropriately, no one gave more support for full Jewish equality than George Washington himself. Upon his ascension to the presidency, he turned the office into a forum praising Jews and urging their full acceptance in American society—as Jews. In 1789, he not only responded separately to various congratulatory addresses from Jewish congregations throughout the states, as he did to those of Roman Catholics and small Protestant sects, he had all of his replies published in the *Gazette of the United States* to circulate throughout the new nation. One of several responses he penned to the nation's Jewish communities was, "I rejoice that a spirit of liberality and philanthropy is much more prevalent than it formerly was among the enlightened nations of the earth, and that your brethren will benefit thereby in proportion as it shall become more extensive." In fact, as though he could have imagined the culture wars two hundred years in the future, Washington specifically endorsed and distinguished diversity from tolera- tion: "It is now no more that toleration is spoken of, as if it was by the indulgence of one class of people, that another enjoyed the exercise of their inherent natural rights." Washington never referred to the Christian God in his speeches, letters, or proclamations, preferring nondenominational terms such as the Supreme Being or Providence, thereby deliberately hop- ing to integrate all elements of the population into a secular Republic.[17] John Adams, his successor as president, also thought that "the Hebrews have done more to civilize men than other nations," and never changed his mind and uttered anti-semitic remarks as did other members of a Federal- ist Party that changed its tune in the mid-1790s. Still, neither Adams nor Washington insisted anti-semitic Federalist printers cease their attacks.[18]

Adams was not typical of his fellow New Englanders. This region, whose Puritan founders paradoxically modeled their society on the ancient Hebrews, lacked any Jewish community outside sectionally deviant Rhode Island until the nineteenth century. Here anti-semitism appears to have been more general than in other parts of the country. In 1796, the *Litchfield Monitor,* an organ of the High Federalists, printed the false story that as a result of the spread of French revolutionary ideas to Italy, the Jews of that country had agreed to shave their beards and observe the Sabbath on Sun- day. Three years later, the *Monitor* unintentionally illustrated some of the contradictions and hysteria in Federalist ideology at the time of the Alien and Sedition Acts. On the one hand, it branded "The Jew," in a poem of that title, as a primitive and superstitious being, but on the other as a hyp- ocrite who did not even practice his own religion. "The Jew" was linked instead to scientific rationalist, British refugee, and Republican enthusiast Joseph Priestley, a very different yet equally undesirable character:

> Once upon a time, a Jew, a wretched sinner,
> Had got a *spare rib* (nicely cook'd) for dinner;
> And as he took a bit—a clap of thunder
> (Such as would make e'en Dr. Priestly wonder)

Began to roll, and it began to lighten,
In such a way as half mankind might frighten:
"Zounds (quoth the Jew—as down he laid his knife)
I never knew the like in all my life
Heavens!—he exclaim'd—straight dropping down his fork
What horrid, dreadful, terrifying work!
And all—*because I ate a bit of pork.*"[19]

Unlike their fellow partisans elsewhere in the nation, New England Republicans were equally anti-semitic, even after Jefferson's victory in 1800. Baptist clergymen such as Isaac Backus and Nehemiah Dodge were themselves representatives of a predominantly lower-class minority in a region where Massachusetts, Connecticut, and New Hampshire continued to support both the Federalists and the established Congregational churches. Dodge concocted the interesting if implausible idea that this "connection between church and state" was a "Jewish plan" in which "high-toned federalists" and "Catholics had also joined." He urged New Englanders, "[end] your standing in the Jewish church and [cease to] constantly pay your money to support these Judaizing teachers who are constantly trying to gull you out of your inalienable rights."[20]

While anti-Jewish prejudice did not die out, those who held to it in the first two decades of the nineteenth century usually had the intelligence to refrain from using this counterproductive ploy in public debate. A prime example is John Quincy Adams, who became a Republican during the first decade of the nineteenth century, but retained the anti-semitic attitudes of his Federalist past when he changed political allegiances. Unlike his father, he had never worked with Jews during the Revolution and could not appreciate their contributions at first hand: his first adult experiences with Jews came in Europe in the 1790s, and they were unfavorable. A Jewish Dutch moneylender tried to cheat him in a currency exchange, and when he visited Frankfurt, Germany, he wrote that "the word filth conveys an ideal of spotless purity in comparison with Jewish nastiness." Yet John Quincy Adams did not utilize anti-semitism in his political rhetoric.[21]

As anti-semitism changed in the revolutionary era, so did the nature of quarrels in the Jewish communities themselves. Despite, or perhaps because of their small sizes—for the most part, the same handful of Jews had to attend synagogue with each other for the requisite ten men to gather and services to occur at all—four of the colonial Jewish congregations, Savannah Philadelphia, Charleston, and most severely, New York, were severely divided. By the 1760s, Ashkenazi newcomers were resenting elite Sephardic services they could not understand and the domination of established upper-class Jews (who included both Sephardim and Ashkenazim) who they thought had assimilated far too much to gentile ways in both thought and appearance. (In Savannah, this quarrel had occurred in the 1730s and ended when the Sephardic Jews left in 1740; Newport Jews were predominantly Sephardic and elite.) In this regard, the eighteenth-century English Jewish community, concentrated in London, set the pattern that reappeared in the colonies: it was both divided within itself and yet united when necessary against gentile hostility. Despite arguments between Sephardic and Ashkenazi Jews, all of London's three synagogues—one Sephardic, one traditional Ashkenazi, and one friendly toward the Enlightenment—were located within a block of each other.

In the third quarter of the eighteenth century, the division in North American Jewish communities corresponded to a large extent to the split between recently arrived Ashkenazim and well-established Jews, both Sephardic and Ashkenazim, who dominated the existing congregations. (In New York this was complicated by a feud between the Franks and Levy families similar to, and overlapping with, the larger provincial political battle of the Livingstons and Delanceys.) These inter-Jewish ethnic conflicts sometimes took the form of struggle over who was to rule the congregation, resulting in two separate minyans in Georgia in the 1730s, Philadelphia by the late 1760s, and Charleston by the 1780s. Individual merchants from the two groups also quarreled, and sometimes sued each other, over their respective reputations for honest dealing.

Internal Jewish tension also reflected class differences. More established Ashkenazi and Sephardic Jews, who were physically indistinguishable from Christians, united in all the cities to avoid confusion with a number of poor, predominantly eastern immigrant European Jews of distinctive appearance who were committing crimes and endangering their reputation. Prominent Jews applied the same stereotypes of greed, dishonesty, and unattractive appearance to the newcomers that anti-semitic gentiles applied to Jews in general. In Philadelphia, Matthias Bush asked London Jews not to send over poor Ashkenazim, and Benjamin Nones criticized

Jewish newcomers for their beards and ignorance of English as well as dishonesty. In his memoirs, New York Jew Naphtali Phillips blamed Shearith Israel's quarrels not on family struggles among older congregants who took the lead, but on Ashkenazi newcomers.

After the Revolution, like Americans who worried about whether their public virtue was adequate to maintain the Republic, the Jews' quarrels, although to some extent incorporating preexisting ethnic and class divisions, also became matters of keeping the faith sufficiently pure to survive in a New World in which assimilation and conversion were seductive. Hessian soldier Johan Conrad Dühla, observing Jews in Newport and New York during the American Revolution, noted that Jewish women who could afford it "go about with curled hair and in French finery such as is worn by the ladies of other religions." Intermarriage, business partnerships, and mutual respect among Jews and the gentile elite were common. Dühla noted that American Jews "are not like the ones we have in Europe and Germany, who are recognizable by their beards and their clothes, for they are dressed like other citizens, get shaved regularly, and also eat pork, although that is forbidden in their Law. Also, Jews and Christians intermarry without scruple." The question now was who was a Jew, and whether people who did not strictly observe Mosaic law could retain their faith. But even where the law was violated, congregations were too small to expel people without reconciling and readmitting them shortly thereafter.[22]

Jews who dominated the existing synagogues tried to cling rigorously to the forms of their religion as many Jews blended into and flourished in a Christian world. In 1784, Philadelphia's Manuel Josephson gave the following reason for building the required ritual bathhouse for women who had given birth: "should it be known in congregations abroad that we had been thus neglectful of so important a matter, they would not only pronounce heavy anathemas against us, but interdict and avoid intermarriages with us, equal as with a different nation or sect, to our great shame and mortification." The next year, Mikveh Israel placed the question before Amsterdam's Rabbi Saul Lowenstamm whether the daughter of a Cohen, a descendant of the priests of ancient Israel, could marry outside the faith. The issue, the congregation claimed, "touches the roots of our faith, particularly in this country where each acts according to his own desire." The elders complained that too many American Jews were "completely irreligious," yet it was impossible to prevent these "evil people" from coming to the synagogue, as there was no effective power to discipline members and "the usage of the land" permitted people to attend any service of worship they chose. (She married him although the rabbi was opposed.)[23]

If they could not discipline the living, Jewish elders could control who was buried in Jewish cemeteries. David Franks, for instance, although he had done much for Philadelphia's Mikveh Israel, was not allowed burial in 1794 in its cemetery. (He died of yellow fever and was nearly interred in the potter's field before some friends rescued his body and buried it in Christ Episcopal churchyard.)[24] Two of the twelve probable American converts to Judaism between 1790 and 1840 were respectively denied burial in the cemeteries in Philadelphia and Richmond because their conversions were deemed improper (America lacked genuine rabbis who were required to sanction these changes of faith).[25] In 1801, Charleston Jews came to blows and a lawsuit over who had the right to participate in a burial service. In a telling incident, in 1785, Mikveh Israel only allowed Moses Clava, a New Jersey Jew married to a gentile who did not belong to any congregation, burial in a corner of the ceremony without a shroud, ceremony, or ritual washing. Equally telling, Mordecai Moses Mordecai, who had been rebuked by the congregation the previous year for performing a ceremony marrying a Jewish man and a Christian woman, went ahead, washed Clava's body, and prepared his shroud.[26]

Maintenance of respectability before other congregations at home and abroad was essential, as the very survival of American Jewish communities was threatened by prohibitions against intermarriage with gentiles. Still, devout Jews refused to compromise their principles even after the Lancaster and Newport congregations went out of existence in the early Republic. In a case that became famous throughout the English-speaking world and inspired an episode in Sir Walter Scott's *Ivanhoe*, Philadelphia's Rebecca Gratz remained single her entire life rather than either marry her beloved Samuel Ewing or renounce her faith. Yet many Jews ate pork, worked on the Sabbath, married gentiles, and by the early nineteenth century could choose to belong to more liberal congregations.

In the years immediately following 1800, anti-semitism died out in the public debate. While Jefferson's victory ended threats of persecution and foreshadowed the general acceptance of Jews in the United States, the partisan smears of the preceding quarter century anticipated an undercurrent of intolerance that has frequently resurfaced. The debate in revolutionary and Federalist America over the role of Jews in the Republic fused for the first time in the United States two strains of anti-semitism—one popular, one elitist—that served to scapegoat Jews in the political life of the new nation. Similar thinking would resurface again in the 1820s, significantly, in schoolbooks and missionary tracts. These were mostly published by New Englanders and Midwestern migrants from that region. People who were, or would have been, Federalists switched from electoral politics to social and religious reform movements.[27] In 1800, the overwhelming victory of Thomas Jefferson's party, a man whom the Federalists had grouped with Jews and atheists as a threat to the Republic, demonstrated the futility of political anti-semitism outside of New England. To be sure, the attitudes Jefferson, Freneau, Paine, and Rush harbored indicated that while they accepted assimilated individual Jews as citizens, they did not accept Judaism as a worthwhile element in America's diverse ethnic and religious montage. Still, things undoubtedly would have been worse had the Federalists won the election of 1800. It is easy to applaud the peaceful transition of power that year and forget what near a thing it was. Had the High Federalists been able to raise their army during the Quasi-War with France and eliminate their opponents—much as the administration of William Pitt the Younger did in contemporaneous Britain—the United States would have been significantly less open to immigrants, significantly more intolerant than it became.

In the process, the Revolution of 1800 implicitly repudiated an anti-semitic strain that otherwise might have become far more prominent in American life. Outside of New England, Federalists who supported the Alien and Sedition Acts troubled the country far more than the people they targeted as public enemies. Anti-semitism was simply irrelevant in much of the country, as most Jews continued to congregate in a few cities and only three new synagogue buildings were erected between 1794 and 1840. Jews were converting to Christianity, and their numbers were growing slowly if at all; as a percentage of the rapidly burgeoning Republic, Jews decreased between 1790 and 1820.

Yet signs of anti-semitism that remained in popular culture and New England elite thought persisted, to be resurrected in the second quarter of the nineteenth century when Jews became more numerous. Yet by 1825—when heavily Catholic Maryland finally acted—all the states where Jews visibly lived had either formally or in fact granted them full citizenship. Anti-semitism has always been present in the United States, but it has been far less prevalent and influential than in Europe, where Jews (except in Holland, and, to a lesser extent, in Britain) confronted a single, overwhelmingly dominant Christian faith. Rather, the history of Jews in the United States is best compared to that of other ethnic and religious groups. Historian Jonathan Sarna has noted that "throughout the nineteenth and twentieth centuries, American Jews collectively embraced the idea that the dynamics of American culture presented a historically unique opportunity to synthesize Jewish and American identities."[28] America's cultural pluralism held forth the possibility of acceptance in an overwhelmingly gentile society.

Ironically, as Frederic C. Jaher has noted, although Jews obtained full political equality in France and elsewhere in Europe thanks to the Revolution before all the American states had granted it, both Jews and their rights thereby became inextricably linked with left-wing politics and hostility toward traditional religion of all sorts on the European continent. There anti-semitism became more virulent, the tool of conservative, radical nationalists and reactionary politicians who did not respect the liberal national governments associated with tolerance, secularism, or pluralism. In the United States, on the other hand, while anti-semitism did increase in response to the expansion of Jewish rights, the Jews were one element of many in a complex ethnic, religious, and predominantly moderate political culture rather than a negatively signified other for a society's ethnically and religiously homogeneous conservative elements. American Jews have led a less controversial, albeit by no means untroubled, existence as one of the Republic's many legitimate constituents.[29]

CHAPTER 2

NEW YORK

$\mathcal{F}$AMOUS AS THE LARGEST JEWISH community and most important
Jewish cultural center in the modern United States, New York was making
Jewish history well before the mass migrations from Germany and eastern
Europe of the nineteenth century. In 1654, even before the city acquired its
present name, twenty-three Jewish refugees from Dutch Brazil joined a few
merchants who had arrived previously in New Amsterdam, briefly forming
the first Jewish community in territory that later became part of the United
States. Almost immediately, they were threatened with expulsion. They
fought back with a successful campaign to acquire the rights and privileges
Jews held in the more tolerant parts of Holland. Dutch Jews thereby set a
precedent for Jews in colonial America and later the United States by refusing to accept anti-semitic remarks or legislation without vigorously defending themselves. Under British rule, colonial New York Jews were the only
Jews in the empire who enjoyed the right to vote and hold public office. In
1777, the newly independent state of New York confirmed this status. New
York was the first state to adopt a constitution granting Jews full political
equality with Christians, and the first government in the modern world to
do so. From the beginning, special circumstances in the city on the Hudson
offered the Jewish population opportunities not only to survive, but to
flourish and pave the way for its sister communities.

New York Jews were also characteristically New Yorkers. That is, much
like the "factious people" described by historian Patricia Bonomi, they
quarreled among themselves and with their gentile neighbors far more than
did the other Jewish congregations of British North America. Insults,
assaults, and court cases by members of the community against each other
plagued this small group throughout much of its colonial history. Yet when

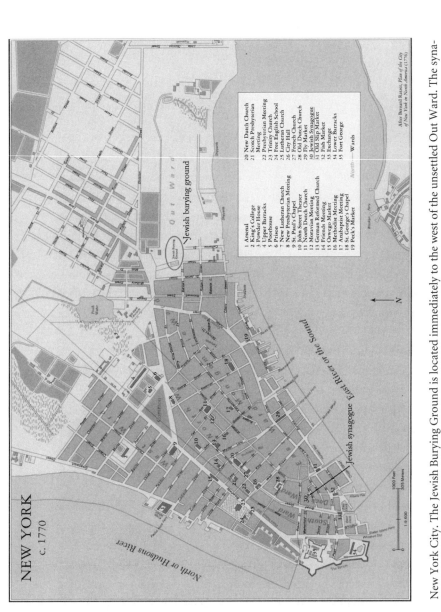

NEW YORK
c. 1770

1 Arsenal
2 King's College
3 Powder House
4 Upper Barracks
5 Poorhouse
6 Prison
7 New Lutheran Church
8 New Presbyterian Meeting
9 St. Paul's Chapel
10 North Dutch Church
11 Moravian Meeting
12 German Reformed Church
13 Friends Meeting
14 Oswego Market
15 Methodist Meeting
16 Anabaptist Meeting
17 St. George's Chapel
18 Peck's Market

20 New Dutch Church
21 Scotch Presbyterian
   Meeting
22 Presbyterian Meeting
23 Trinity Church
24 Free English School
25 Lutheran Church
26 City Hall
27 French Church
28 Old Dutch Church
29 Fly Market
30 Jewish Synagogue
31 Old Slip Market
32 Fish Market
33 Exchange
34 Lower Barracks
35 Fort George

— Wards

After Bernard Ratzer, *Plan of the City
of New York in North America* (1776)

New York City. The Jewish Burying Ground is located immediately to the west of the unsettled Out Ward. The syna-
gogue on Mill Street is four blocks up Broad Street between the West and the East Dock.
(After Bernard Ratzer, "Plan of the City of New York in North America" [1776]. Map adapted from Lester J. Cappon,
Atlas of Early American History: The Revolutionary Era, 1760–1790. © 1976, Princeton University Press, renewed 2004.

it was all over, New York Jewry emerged in the early Republic as a united community, its synagogue governed by a democratic constitution. While all five synagogues had changed their government, New York paved the way in achieving harmony.[1]

FROM OSTRACISM TO ACCEPTANCE, 1654–1730

New Amsterdam Jews were in a position to demand expanded rights because in seventeenth-century Holland a variety of bodies held substantial but overlapping power in a loosely united federation. In religious matters, the Synod of Dordrecht in 1619 ended a civil war between the predominantly rural, strict Calvinists and the more urban "Remonstrants," who sympathized with the less intolerant teachings of Jacobus Arminius that permitted human beings to earn their salvation through good behavior. Although the Calvinists won and many Remonstrant preachers were exiled, to maintain the United Provinces' still-threatened independence from Spain, communities and provinces enforced religious conformity in the manner their own political constituents determined. In Amsterdam itself, practices were inconsistent. The Classis, Amsterdam's leading religious body, was staunchly pro-Calvinist, but the civil authorities and merchant class were considerably more tolerant. The city council permitted the erection of a Jewish synagogue in 1612, but popular opposition—encouraged by Catholic Spanish secret agents who hoped to provoke religious turmoil—forced construction to stop halfway. When the Amsterdam Jews did build their first synagogue in 1639, public worship by those who were not Reformed Christians was still technically illegal.[2]

By the mid-seventeenth century, there were perhaps ten thousand Jews in Amsterdam, comprising about 6 percent of the population.[3] The Jews received their strongest support from overseas commercial circles. In Holland, Jews were excluded by law from domestic retail trade and craft manufacturing, and by custom from established local trading networks, but they were indispensable in new commercial ventures in Africa, the Iberian peninsula (clandestine and conducted under assumed names), and America. Since many Jews were recent immigrants from Spain or Portugal (ruled by Spain from 1580 to 1640), where their earlier, nominal conversion to

Christianity ceased to be acceptable and they were expelled, they had the connections and knowledge of both Iberian countries and their territories to prosper in colonial business.[4]

Jews invested heavily in the Dutch West India Company, Holland's means of fighting Spain and establishing colonies in the New World. At various times they numbered between 4 and 11 percent of the stockholders: in 1674, an accounting of principal stockholders listed five Jews who had invested at least thirty thousand guilders each.[5] Founded in 1621, the company conquered northeast Brazil from the Portuguese between 1630 and 1654. The company stipulated that there "the liberty of . . . Jews will be respected," encouraging Portuguese conversos to abjure their nominal Christianity and Jews from the Netherlands—where they could not worship publicly except in Amsterdam—to emigrate. By 1644, Jews numbered between a third and a half of the 1,450 white settlers in the colony. The capital of Recife, its principal thoroughfare named the Rua dos Judos, boasted two synagogues and a rabbi for each.[6] Jews specialized in the exportation of sugar and tobacco and the importation of provisions and slaves; others owned plantations and sugar mills. The richest Jew was Jorge Homen Pinto, who had 370 slaves and owned nine sugar mills in the mid-1640s.[7]

In turn, the processing of colonial exports became an important source of Jewish prosperity in Holland. Jewish tobacco and chocolate acquired international reputations for high quality. From 1625 to 1651, the number of Jewish depositors in the Amsterdam Exchange Bank rose from 76 to 197, from 6 to 10 percent of the total, largely thanks to the wealth of Brazil.[8]

Nevertheless, in spite of, or perhaps because of, the Jews' wealth, the Brazilian Christian majority, many of whom were conquered Portuguese Catholics, periodically demanded their expulsion. Johan Maurits, Brazil's governor from 1637 to 1644, on the other hand, was such a friend to the Jews that they augmented his salary by three thousand guilders per annum to persuade him to stay after 1642, and offered him six hundred thousand guilders when he left to turn his residence into a synagogue, a move prevented by the Christians. As in so many instances, grassroots prejudice was countered by a cosmopolitan elite's appreciation for the Jews' contributions.[9] Even the inquisitor-general of Spain, recognizing in 1639 that "one of the things which permit the Dutch to sustain with such force and obstinacy the wars in Brazil are the contributions of the Nation [of Jews]," proposed that they be pardoned for their past offenses if they agreed to return to Spain and live inoffensively as Catholics. The proposal interested neither the king nor the Jews.[10]

While Jews had been tolerated in Brazil, they were not welcome in the Dutch West India Company's poor relation of a colony, New Amsterdam. As historian Evan Haefeli writes: "Contrary to its popular and scholarly reputation, New Netherland was not a haven of religious toleration and diversity. It was a stronghold of Reformed orthodoxy from the moment it began as a colony of the West India Company, an explicitly Calvinist enterprise aimed at undermining Spanish Catholic hegemony in the Americas. Throughout the history of New Netherland, only one religion was allowed, that of the established Reformed Church."[11] Founded in 1624, the colony only had some 750 inhabitants in 1652. The company originally hoped that furs—especially the famous beaver pelts from which the hats of Rembrandt's "Dutch Masters" were made—would prove a bonanza approaching sugar, but within a decade it became clear that New Netherland could not compete with the French at Quebec, who commanded a far vaster hinterland as well as thicker pelts thanks to a colder climate. So the directors recast the colony as a source of fish and grain for Brazil: as with other sugar-growing colonies, soil suited for the New World's most lucrative export was so scarce that it made economic sense to import food from thousands of miles away.[12]

To attract the strict Calvinists who comprised much of Holland's rural population, the company not only promised land, but a spiritually pure environment: New Netherland's charter of 1640 stated in no uncertain terms that "no other religion shall be publicly admitted in New Netherland, except the Reformed, as it is at present preached and practiced by public authority in the United Netherlands."[13] Ironically, Jews were forbidden public exercise of their religion in a colony that was maintained primarily to supply a much more important one where Jews who possessed that freedom were essential to the colony's success. The difference was that Brazil was a prosperous commercial colony whose wealth depended on a Jewish presence, whereas New Netherland could only service Brazil if it attracted impoverished rural farmers who were virulently anti-semitic, anti-Catholic, and anti-everything except Dutch Reformed. Significantly, while New Amsterdam's Reformed minister, Johannes Megapolensis, frequently criticized the Jews in his letters home, Johannes Polhemus, the minister at Midwout in Breucklyn (Midwood in Brooklyn) who arrived from Brazil at the same time as the first Jews, "in all his correspondence keeps himself free from the persecuting spirit of his fellow ministers," having experienced firsthand the Dutch Jews' importance and loyalty to the South American venture.[14]

Still, New Netherland's 1640 charter was ambiguous: Jews, like other non-Reformed people, were barred as in the Netherlands (despite the synagogue recently built in Amsterdam) from public worship, but could the colony admit those who practiced their faith privately? And what was the "Reformed" religion? Governor Peter Stuyvesant and Predikant Johannes Megapolensis not only tolerated the English settlers who constituted the majority on eastern Long Island, but encouraged their immigration as providing much-needed farm labor for the colony, whose population more than doubled from 1652 to 1664. Stuyvesant and the company concurred that both Presbyterians and Puritans from New England agreed "in Fundamentals" with the Dutch Reformed Church.[15] When New Netherland conquered some five hundred Swedes and Finns living on the South or Delaware River (the Hudson was the North) in 1655, the terms of capitulation stipulated that "those who will then remain here and earn their living in the country, shall enjoy the freedom of the Augsburg Confession [Lutheran Church, established in Sweden], and one person to instruct them therein." Yet they had to stay there, for the Lutheran faith could not be exercised publicly in New Netherland proper.[16]

The status of Jews was equally ambiguous. Stuyvesant, who arrived in 1647, had served the West Indian Company in South America from 1630 until he lost his leg in combat in 1644, and was thus familiar with Jewish toleration in Brazil. But he also knew that toleration varied depending on locality in Holland, and he was the son of a Reformed minister, a firm supporter of that faith, and a believer in its stern morality.[17] More recently, while Stuyvesant was dividing his time between New Netherland and the West Indies in the early 1650s, the company had permitted two groups of Dutch Jews to found settlements in Curaçao. The first scheme only attracted twelve men, the second a larger number who engaged in illegal trade with Holland's rivals in the Caribbean by smuggling horses and timber instead of planting sugar or tobacco. Both failed miserably by the spring of 1654 since slavery, the foundation of the Caribbean region's prosperity, was forbidden. Firsthand observation of these futile experiments with Jewish toleration undoubtedly contributed further to Stuyvesant's prejudices.[18] Still, "some Jews," according to Megapolensis, among whom were the merchants Asser Levy, Jacob Bar Simon, and Solomon Pietersen, arrived in New Amsterdam from Holland shortly before the twenty-three Jews from Brazil, without protest from either Stuyvesant or Megapolensis.[19]

The Brazilians, however, were another matter. New Amsterdam was not their destination, for the majority of Brazilian Jewish refugees, some two hundred families, returned to Holland, while the rest tried their luck in the Antilles, for the most part in Curaçao and Surinam. Only one group appeared in New Amsterdam purely by accident because they were captured by a Spanish vessel, freed by a French one, and then escorted to the northern Dutch colony. Stuyvesant's letter to the West India Company, written on September 22, 1654, within three weeks of their arrival, asked for permission to expel them. He stressed that if allowed to remain, the Jews, "hateful enemies and blasphemers of the name of Christ," would soon practice "their customary usury and deceitful trading." They had immediately made themselves "very repugnant" to the town's "inferior magistrates" (the *schout* or sheriff, *burgomeister* or mayor, and *schepens* or aldermen) and would "infect and trouble . . . your worships' most affectionate subjects."[20]

The New Amsterdam records make clear why the aforementioned magistrates found the Jews repugnant. Having only been constituted as the colony's court that February, they spent most of September and part of October 1654 dealing with the legal hassles arising from the Jews' journey. Two suits involved Asser Levy, a merchant of Vilna who had arrived from Amsterdam just prior to the refugees, and a Jewish woman named Rycke Nounes, who sued each other: he claimed to have advanced her money, she countered that she had paid his way. But the major problem was that Captain Jacques de la Motthe, who had transported the Jews aboard the *Ste. Catherine,* claimed he had not been paid the large sum of 2,500 guilders he had coerced them into accepting as the price of their passage. Almost immediately upon his arrival, September 7, he won a judgment that the Jews' remaining possessions should be auctioned off to pay a shortfall of some 1,600 guilders. To ensure payment, he insisted that two of their number be held in prison until the money was raised, which the court agreed to as long as de la Motthe footed their expenses while in jail. On October 26, with his ship idling in port and still 495 guilders short, he sailed away, having accepted the word of the Jewish community that they would send for the remaining funds from Holland, which ends all record of the matter.[21]

In Stuyvesant's letter to the company, therefore, the Jews became the scapegoats for the legal trouble caused by the Frenchman who had rescued them. Stuyvesant was also projecting onto the Jews blame for the very same deed his own court had authorized under the cloak of legality: instead of nullifying an exorbitant contract extracted under duress, the officials took advantage of the newcomers' misfortune to direct that the Jews' goods be sold at auction. To add insult to injury, Stuyvesant claimed that the Jews were so poor that "owing to their indigence they might become a charge in the coming winter."[22] Like many anti-semites, he was more interested in piling up the stereotypes than in the consistency of his argument. Apparently these Jews, impoverished by the New Netherland court's verdict, somehow would acquire money to lend at high interest and cheat the Christians even though they were incapable of supporting themselves, all the while becoming impoverished in the process! The director thus combined contradictory anti-semitic stereotypes: to adherents of the Reformed Church he stressed the polluting presence of "blasphemers"; to those with less troubled consciences, he presented the specter of a drain on the company's treasury and a threat to public order through the Jews' litigious behavior.

On November 11, Predikant Megapolensis seconded Stuyvesant's claims in a letter to the Amsterdam Classis. Megapolensis, although he did not like the Jews, offered them help, but they paid for it with his scorn. He claimed that they "came several times to my house, weeping and bemoaning their misery," and out of pity he gave them several hundred guilders. In fact, Megapolensis insisted that it was the responsibility of the "Jewish merchant," presumably Bar Simon, to care for his people, but he "would not lend them a single stiver," the Dutch equivalent of a penny. The cleric had also heard rumors that more Jews were on their way from Holland, and that they were planning to build a synagogue, which "causes a great deal of complaint and murmuring." He then lambasted the Jews as "godless ras-

cals," who "have no other God than the mammon of unrighteousness, and
no other aim than to get possession of Christian property and to overcome
all other merchants by drawing all trade towards themselves."[23]

Like Stuyvesant, Megapolensis reversed the situation: the New Amsterdam Christians, by settling the lawsuit in favor of the French captain, were
able to obtain the Jews' property at rock-bottom prices, although historians
sympathetic to the Dutch claim, without any evidence, that many of the
"good hearted" New Netherlanders gave back the items and only bought
them to aid the Jews. However, it is much more likely that a not particularly
wealthy and predominantly anti-semitic population would have eagerly
paid low prices because so many goods were a glut on the market. That
almost all the Jews needed relief during the winter and most of them soon
left New Amsterdam suggests the populace was not charitably inclined. So
does the fact that the next year, the town council refused Jews admission
into the militia "owing to the disgust and unwillingness of the trainbands to
be fellow soldiers with the aforesaid nation."[24] It seems Megapolensis, who
supplied what relief there was, dwelled to such an extent on the Jews'
propensity for sharp dealing to soothe his conscience and justify why
Christians could take comparable advantage of Jews.

In the conclusion to his letter, Megapolensis hit upon the real reason so
many in New Amsterdam feared the Jews. The small Dutch colony was surrounded by much more powerful French, English, and Native American
societies. By the 1650s, "Papists, Mennonites, and Lutherans" had migrated
into New Netherland, not to mention "Puritans or Independents" from
New England and others Megapolensis termed "atheists and various other
servants of Baal . . . who conceal themselves under the name of Christians."
Here he undoubtedly referred to the Anabaptists and militant Quakers who
were preaching throughout the colony.[25] Thus, while using stereotypes
associated with Jews to argue for their expulsion, New Netherland's leaders
were not so much singling out the Jews for persecution as grouping them
with a veritable invasion of Christian sectarians whose religious principles
they perceived, correctly, as threats to the tiny colony's existence.
Stuyvesant termed the Quakers "heretical and abominable," identified the
Anabaptists as "libertines," and even wrote once that the real problem with
admitting the Jews was not so much the Jews themselves, but that "giving

them liberty, we cannot refuse the Lutherans and the Papists," far more substantial threats to both the Reformed religion and the Dutch state that supported it.[26]

Stuyvesant lived in a world in which each form of religion mandated a particular political order, a fact recognized by the Treaty of Westphalia that in 1648 ended the Thirty Years War by granting each sovereign the right to enforce religious conformity in his realm. One could even argue that the director's hostility to Jews was less than that toward other deviants: Quakers were beaten and imprisoned, and Lutherans and Anabaptists expelled from the colony without any hint of the "friendly" admonition Stuyvesant gave the Jews and without the formality of a comparable request for permission to the West India Company. We can only speculate why Stuyvesant did not act unilaterally to expel the Jews. Did he sympathize with the refugees, was he afraid of the wrath of Jewish investors in the company, or did he care less about whether the Jews remained than he did about supporting them out of his meager public funds? In Stuyvesant's absence on March 1, 1655, his deputy, Sheriff Cornelis van Tiefhoven, and the rest of the city court in fact did command the Jews to leave, after they fined Abram de la Sina the considerable sum of six hundred guilders for engaging in retail trade on a Sunday. However, their judgment was not enforced; perhaps it was simply grandstanding for the righteous Calvinist majority. Or perhaps Stuyvesant countermanded it. Or perhaps the fact that most of the Jews did leave in short order was good enough.[27]

Further, Stuyvesant was not being singularly cruel by sending the destitute back from whence they came—in this case Holland—or passing them along to where they would be tolerated. This was standard operating procedure in early modern society. Removal would have been especially tempting when twenty-three poor people suddenly imposed themselves on a colony of about 150 families. In the eighteenth century, the twenty-odd men who belonged to Shearith Israel, New York's synagogue, had no difficulty in dealing with poor Jewish migrants exactly as Stuyvesant had. The congregation's Constitution of 1728 ordered the parnas, or president, to use his utmost endeavors to dispatch poor transients "to some other place as soon as possible assisting them with necessaries." This provision was enforced consistently: for example, in 1751, "the widow Abrams" and her family were ordered "shipt away" at a cost not to exceed fifty pounds; in 1768, the congregation remanded Jacob Musqueto, who had arrived from St. Eustatia in the Dutch West Indies and wished to go to Barbardos, to the Jews of Philadelphia, and only offered to put up three or four pounds if the latter could not pay for his trip. In 1774, Aaron Bosqualo received full passage to Curaçao, the largest Dutch Jewish community in the New World, while a "Dumb Man" was sent back to Philadelphia. As with Christian colonial churches, the congregation was much more generous to its own members who fell on unfortunate times than it was to strangers. Members of the Lousada family are listed as significant contributors to Shearith Israel in the earliest minutes that survive, beginning in the late 1720s. By the late 1750s, the impoverished widow Hanah Lousada tried to find a home (at the synagogue's expense) in Lancaster, Pennsylvania, and then "the Jerseys" while the synagogue put up the money to raise her son and pay her debts. During the winter 1764–65, however, she was back in New York, one of four poor women allowed between three and five pounds each year to pay for firewood.[28]

Given that the pre-1654 presence of merchants Levy, Bar Simon, and Pietersen did not attract their anger, it seems plausible that Stuyvesant and Megapolensis objected less to the Brazilian Jews as Jews and more to their poverty, potential charge to the government, and the sudden visibility of yet another sizable non-Reformed community in the small and beleaguered colony. When Stuyvesant's request to expel the Jews reached Amsterdam, however, the Jewish merchants in the West India Company argued powerfully against him, insisting that barring Jews from New Netherland would not only "result to the great disadvantage of the Jewish nation," but be "rather damaging" to the company itself. Recalling that the Jews of Brazil had "at all times been faithful and have striven to guard and maintain that place, risking for that purpose their possessions and their blood," their brethren in Holland insisted that they would in no way jeopardize the stability of New Netherland. As would the Jews in the new American nation over a century later, Dutch Jews argued for citizenship not on grounds of equality, but because of their exceptional patriotism and economic contributions.

The Jews also argued, making a true but not especially relevant point, that Holland's "States-General have in *political* matters always protected

and considered the Jewish nation as upon the same footing as all the inhabitants and burgers" (emphasis added). The Jews did enjoy political rights in
those Dutch states and cities that allowed them to live there, but nowhere
were they allowed to practice the mechanical and retail trades that com-
peted with Christians, trades to which the poor Jews of New Netherland
would have had to resort unless they moved to the countryside. Hence, the
Amsterdam Jews argued that given such an "extensive and spacious land,"
in which the company had already "consented that those who wish to populate the Colony shall enjoy certain districts of land gratis," Jews as agrarian settlers would increase both trade and "payment of various excises and
taxes."

But the clinching argument was not justice but power. The Amsterdam
Jews did not hesitate to tell the company to "please consider that many of
the Jewish nation are principal shareholders."[29] The company's response
suggests that this argument was decisive, for the directors' letter to
Stuyvesant shows considerable sympathy with his position, but argues that
their hands were tied by Jewish pressure. (An alternate interpretation is
that they were pretending to empathize with Stuyvesant to appease the
capable although irascible governor.)

> We would have liked to effectuate and fulfill your wishes and request
> that the new territories should not be allowed to be infected by people
> of the Jewish nation, for we foresee therefrom the same difficulties
> which you fear, but after having further weighed and considered the
> matter, we observe that this would be somewhat unreasonable and
> unfair, especially because of the considerable loss sustained by this
> nation [the Jews], with others, in the taking of Brazil, as also because of
> the large amount of capital which they still have invested in shares of
> this company.[30]

Interestingly, the company made no mention of land grants to the
Jews—predominantly an urban people in Holland whom the future would
show had little desire to take up farming in New Netherland and New
York—but instead directed Stuyvesant to let them "travel and trade to and
in New Netherland and live and remain there." But Stuyvesant won some
points, too. He not only received the company's approbation of his fear
that the Jews would "infect" his colony, but the Jews' right to remain was

subject to the condition that "the poor among them shall not become a burden to the company or to the community, but be supported by their own nation," which was probably his primary concern. In one of many examples of such intercontinental solidarity, the wealthy Amsterdam Jewish community offered to subsidize their poor brethren overseas, a customary procedure in both Holland and New Netherland, in which the members of a particular religious group cared for their own poor.[31]

The status of Jews in New Netherland thus marked a compromise between their privileged situation in Brazil and the restrictions sought by the Dutch Reformed majority of the colony. Nowhere in Stuyvesant's instructions were the Jews granted the right to own land or to worship publicly; nor were the conditions under which, or places to which, they could travel and trade specified. Juggling various constituencies—the Dutch Reformed Church in both Old and New Netherland, who objected to the exercise of the Jews' "blasphemous" religion; a hostile governor, yet the first one to bring a modicum of order and prosperity to New Netherland; and a powerful lobby of Jewish merchants whose investments were critical to the company's survival—the company constructed a document that allowed the Jews to remain in New Netherland provided they were self-sufficient; otherwise, their status was left ambiguous.[32]

All of the twenty-three refugees from Brazil left New Amsterdam in short order, for with the exception of Levy and Bar Simon, the Jews who signed a series of petitions in the late 1650s—Abraham de Lucena, Salvador d'Andrada, Jacob Cohen (sometimes with Henriques added), Joseph d'Acosta, and David Frera—were well-to-do merchants from Holland who arrived after 1654 and soon formed the nucleus of a thriving Jewish trading community that persisted into the era of English rule.[33] By 1658 a series of company rulings granted the Jews the right to participate in the militia, own land, trade outside of New Amsterdam, exercise their religion in private, and obtain burgher status in New Amsterdam. At the same time, the company forbade the local government from inflicting discriminatory taxes on Jews, as they were originally taxed more heavily than Christians with the justification that they were not required to perform military service.[34]

Of the signatories to the several petitions, members of the Bar Simon (or Simson), Lucena, and d'Acosta families remained in New York and were active in Shearith Israel in the eighteenth century. Asser Levy, an exceptionally litigious man who died in 1682 worth what historian Cathy Matson terms the "great sum" of fifty-seven thousand guilders, also stayed. By 1664 Levy was the only Jew summoned by Stuyvesant among the city's wealthiest taxpayers to lend money in the face of an English invasion. Two blocks of Avenue A in lower Manhattan bear his name today,[35] and a Jewish battalion in World War II adopted him as their patron.

Yet despite the Jews' important contacts in Amsterdam connected to their economic rise, victory was not total. In 1656 the directors rebuked Stuyvesant for having disobeyed orders dated February 15, 1655, by not allowing the Jews to trade at either Fort Orange or on the South (Delaware) River or to purchase real estate. (Since these orders are the only major document concerning Jewish rights in New Amsterdam that does not survive, it is at least plausible Stuyvesant never received them and could have argued that he was acting according to a reasonable interpretation of his previous instructions.) The company insisted that as a rule he should have governed his behavior by permitting the Jews what "is allowed them here in this country without any difficulty . . . only so far as civil and political rights are concerned."[36] Acting on that principle, the company forbade Jews to engage in retail trade or mechanical (craft) occupations but granted them the other privileges requested.

Following Old World precedent also had drawbacks as well as privileges, and the company concluded this set of directions to Stuyvesant with one to the Jews themselves: they were to "peacefully carry on their business . . . and exercise in all quietness their religion within their houses." The company further stipulated that "they must without doubt endeavor to build their houses close together in a convenient place on one or the other side of New Amsterdam—at their choice—as they have done here." The company specifically denied "the said Jews a claim to the privilege of exercising their religion in a synagogue or gathering," which they enjoyed in Amsterdam.[37] The voluntary proclivity of Dutch Jews to live together—there was no formal ghetto—became a prescriptive order for those in New Amsterdam that they were to segregate themselves from the gentile population, yet another compromise the company tried to negotiate between its Jewish financiers and its overseas colonizers.

Whether New Amsterdam Jews also lived close together or the order was ignored became moot in 1664 after New Amsterdam surrendered to an English fleet. When the articles of capitulation stated that "the Dutch here shall enjoy the liberty of their consciences in divine worship and church discipline," it is doubtful the colony's handful of Jews were much on the minds of either conquerors or conquered. A great variety of religions were practiced in New York—"the Church of England, several Presbyterians and Independents, Quakers, Baptists of several sects, some Jews," wrote Governor Edmund Andros in 1678—but the Dutch Reformed were the great majority. As late as 1682, the Church of England had no minister and was obliged to hold its services in the Dutch church. Historian Joyce Goodfriend has persuasively shown that the Dutch culture and language remained dominant until between 1730 and 1750.[38]

Between 1664 and 1682, the Jews only came to public attention as individuals. Asser Levy instituted a spate of lawsuits before he died as one of the wealthiest men in the province.[39] Jews were allowed to participate in retail trade—Jacob Lucena receiving this privilege in 1678 upon payment of twelve pounds, which may have simply been the required license fee rather than a special burden imposed on a Jew.[40] Other Jews surfaced occasionally in records: "Moses the Jew" paid a tax of one pound, two shillings, six pence in 1676, Isaac Abrams four shillings the following year. Also in 1677, "Jacob the Jew" was grouped with "Frederick the shoemaker and John the glass maker" as men who were forbidden to build chimneys, which could prove to be fire hazards. In 1678, Asser Levy received permission to build a slaughterhouse, which facilitated the preparation of kosher meat required by Jewish law.[41]

Paradoxically, it was the Charter of Liberties that the local population coerced in 1683 from the Duke of York—basically by going on a tax strike—that again put Jewish rights in question, forbidding them once more from worshiping in public. As the first surviving notice of a synagogue was recorded by Dutch minister Henricus Selyns in October 1682, it may have been a recent grievance. As under Dutch rule, autocratic elite intervention from overseas was required to protect the Jews from colonists asserting their rights. Historian John Murrin has pointed out that it was primarily the English and Anglicized Dutch members of the trading community minority who insisted on the charter. Both this colonial elite and the agrarian Dutch Reformed majority had reasons to resent the Jews: they were commercial competitors for the wealthy and a non-Christian presence for the pious.[42] Governor Thomas Dongan, himself a Catholic, tried to pass off the blame for enforcing this aspect of the charter by referring the Jews' 1685 petition for public worship to the mayor and common council of New York, comprised of a majority of Dutchmen, who turned them down. Jews were also again barred from retail trade (although allowed to participate in wholesale commerce if the governor permitted). Nor, thanks to a law clearly passed to appeal to devout Reformed worshipers, could they work, travel, or amuse themselves publicly on the Sabbath.[43] The Charter of Liberties for Christians meant that the local majority relegated Jews to the position they had held before the English Conquest.

New York practice under the Charter of Liberties from 1683 to 1685 subjected Jews to liabilities absent from England itself. Whether from a sincere belief in the benefits of religious diversity or in the hopes of winning allies against the Church of England as a prelude to promoting Roman Catholicism, both King Charles II and his brother the Duke of York—as of 1685 he was James II—promoted toleration of Jews, Quakers, and Catholics. In 1673 and 1685, they respectively stopped court proceedings by London authorities against Jews for worshiping publicly in their synagogue. This royal policy was transferred to the New World in 1685, when New York lost its assembly and Sir Edmund Andros arrived as governor-general of New England as well as New York. On May 29, 1686, King James sent instructions to Dongan, who remained as Andros's deputy in New York, both nullifying the Charter of Liberties and mandating, "you shall permit all persons of what religion soever quietly to inhabit within your government . . . provided they give no disturbance to ye public peace, nor do molest or disquiet others in ye free exercise of their Religion."[44]

This toleration proved short lived. After the English overthrew James in the "Glorious Revolution" of 1688, New Englanders and New Yorkers followed suit in 1689 by ousting Andros and Dongan. Almost immediately, Jacob Leisler, head of the interim government, which represented the Dutch Reformed majority, drew up a plan requiring each inhabitant to swear an oath "to maintain and defend to the utmost of my power with my person and estate the true Protestant Religion against Popery and all Papist

Superstition, Idolatry, or Innovation." While King James's Catholicism was clearly the main target, New York's Jewish population was thereby either thoughtlessly or consciously excluded from civil society. In an ordinance made on May 13, 1691, the Leislerians were more explicit: they specifically forbade public worship by Jews and Catholics. Leisler's militia demonstrated the zeal associated with Parliamentary soldiers during the English Civil War by hoping to rid the land of non-Protestants. At least one specific case of Leislerian anti-semitism survives: Jacob Melyan, a leading Leislerian who hoped to obtain money to send his son to Harvard College, rented his house to a Jew although he equated "a Jew" with "a crook" as two people he "never esteemed." Pointing to the tendency of Jews to do business with each other, he also complained that the Jews' "keeping it [money] in their own hands . . . is not good to me, and mine, but a great wrong."[45] In effect, Melyan blamed Jews for doing business with each other as compelled to in an anti-semitic milieu exemplified by his own remarks.

The Leislerian restriction on Jewish worship, however, lasted less than a year, assuming it was enforced at all. Leisler's troubled administration never received English approval. Leisler was executed and his supporters ousted, unlike the revolutionaries in Massachusetts who were recognized as legitimate for following in the mother country's footsteps. New York chief justice William Atwood wrote later that Leisler was opposed by "some Englishmen, French, Jews, and some few Dutch who all assumed the name of the English party"—that is, the province's wealthier, commercially inclined inhabitants who were influential in Europe and succeeded in having Leisler replaced and tried. His successor, Governor Henry Sloughter, arrived in 1692 and executed his leading opponents but restored freedom of worship for the Jews. For the third time, a European elite had compelled New Yorkers to accept toleration. Given the situation of William III, the former stadtholder of the Netherlands who had just become king of England, no other outcome was possible. William would rely until his death in 1702—as his successors would throughout the eighteenth century—heavily on Jewish financial support for the armies that defended his territories against the intolerant Louis XIV of France.[46]

Jewish loyalty to the Crown in New York appears to have transcended partisan politics. Sloughter and his successor, Governor Richard Coote, the Earl of Bellomont, were on opposite sides of New York's sharp political fence. Bellomont was generally supported by the Leislerians and opposed by New York's commercial elite, especially for his campaign to end their involvement with pirates, including the notorious Captain Kidd. Two Jews, however, supported the antipiracy campaign. Benjamin Franks had originally relied on Kidd to take him to India, where he hoped to reestablish his fortune—wiped out in the Port Royal earthquake on that West Indies island in 1692—by buying and selling jewelry. Franks later deserted Kidd and testified to his piracy in 1698, by which time Bellomont was in New York. Bellomont also relied on Jewish jeweler Joseph Bueno to ascertain the value of pirates' spoils.[47]

Jews and the imperial administration mutually supported each other at the turn of the century. Bellomont, who had trouble collecting a salary in New York as the legislature was pro-pirate and opposed to English control, wrote that "had it not been for one Dutch merchant, and two or three Jews that lent me money, I should have been undone."[48] Between 1696 and 1701, grand juries brought in several indictments against Jewish merchant Isaac Rodrigues Marques for altering the weigh-house books, but none of the four men who acted as the province's attorney general—all of them anti-Leislerians—prosecuted them. Also anti-Leislerian was New York's Anglican priest John Sharpe. In 1712, he suggested that New York was a good place for people to migrate to, for among other advantages they could meet a diverse variety of the world's population. Among the many languages they could learn was "Hebrew, there as well as in Europe, there being a synagogue of Jews, and many ingenious men of that nation from Poland, Hungary, Germany, etc."[49]

All of these nations were the home to Ashkenazi Jews. They were setting a pattern in British North America where at times the two sorts of Jews intermingled and intermarried, with class and personal tensions mattering more than the traditional distinction of eastern and western European Jews. This new union was not well understood elsewhere: when in 1729 the hazan at Curaçao agreed to contribute to building the second New York synagogue, he sent a warning along with the money. He suggested that the Sephardic Jews persuade the "asquenazim"—who were a majority in New York—to have "no votes nor authority," but still allow their brethren to establish worship after the model of "Portugal, London, and Amsterdam" for the sake of peace. But without excluding the Ashkenazim, New York

Jews in fact had already adopted the Sephardic worship, indicating that a desire for these supposedly more genteel services appealed as well to elite Jews of both sorts who governed the New York synagogue.[50]

How many Jews Sharpe meant by "many" must remain a matter of speculation, but they included at least the ten men or minyan required for synagogue services. Jews were known to worship publicly as early as 1682. In 1695, the first known Jewish synagogue in New York, a small building on Mill Street, appeared on a map of the city. It took the name Shearith (Remnant of) Israel. It must have had at least three hazans by 1710, for in that year Abraham de Lucena successfully petitioned Governor Robert Hunter for exemption from holding office or serving in the militia, and "other duties and services" on the grounds that his "predecessors, ministers of the Jewish Nation" had been so exempted "by reason of their ministerial situation." He thereby obtained that form of equality with the town's Christian clergy. The original building was replaced in 1730: the fund-raising drive was probably the reason for establishment of a synagogue minute book that still survives, as almost all early entries list contributions, pledges, and shortfalls for this purpose. According to tax assessments, the size of the Jewish community ranged between twenty and thirty-one households in the 1720s (when New York City had ten thousand people). Although not numerous, New York Jews had come a long way since they were unwelcome refugees on the shore of New Amsterdam.[51]

FACTIOUS PROVINCIALS, 1730–1776

New York's Jewish community did not grow at the exponential rate of the colonies' population as a whole. Forty-nine men signed the synagogue covenant in 1746, when New York had some fifteen thousand inhabitants. The city's enumerated Jewish population in the federal census of 1790 was 242. Solomon Simson counted seventy-two men in the synagogue in 1795, although many shared households with family members.[52] Fifty-two Jewish men were naturalized in New York under English law between 1688 and 1769: added to the handful of Jews who previously lived in New York, the Jewish population clearly grew much more slowly than the gentile. Two reasons for slow growth were outmigration (the Levy and Franks families, for instance, sent representatives to handle family business in Philadelphia, lesser colonial urban centers, and on the frontier), and the fact that Jews either remained unmarried or else frequently married gentiles and converted to Christianity.[53]

Jewish marriages were retarded both by devout Jews unwilling to marry outside the faith and quarrels within a small community whose members found each other unacceptable. New York's Jewish congregation was plagued by contention, a "factious people," the term historian Patricia Bonomi has used to describe colonial New Yorkers in general. Jewish connections with the New York elite ensured that Jewish and gentile factionalism overlapped. At the center of the Jewish troubles stood Abigaill Levy Franks (1696–1756), supported by her husband Jacob (1688–1769), New York's wealthiest Jewish merchant, the largest contributor to Shearith Israel, and an active member of that congregation. Franks's brother Isaac was one of the richest Jews in England, worth some three hundred thousand pounds when he died in 1736.[54] Although Jacob represented the family interests in the synagogue, Abigaill's extensive letters to her son Naphtali in England show that behind much of the feuding was Abigaill's belief that no one else was good enough for her family. Thanks to her snobbery and quarreling, a good deal of anti-semitism in New York between the Glorious and American Revolutions centered around the Franks family. In fact, it is even questionable whether much of the hostility was anti-semitism at all, or whether that served to hide the personal vendetta of Oliver Delancey against his estranged in-laws. In addition, the respective adherents of Abigaill and her stepmother Grace Mears were in large part responsible for initiating Shearith Israel's persistent turmoil, which after various permutations ultimately played itself out in the Jewish community from 1735 until the congregation closed for seven years under the British occupation in 1776.

Abigaill Franks's letters reveal that she was a very intelligent and literate woman (despite being completely ignorant of punctuation). She read and quoted Pope and Shakespeare, purchased some of Hogarth's caricatures, eagerly awaited new issues of the *Gentleman's Magazine* from England, and ordered copies of scholarly books from London, including one on the history of Poland.[55] But she was also extremely critical of everyone around her, frequently in contradictory ways that made satisfying her impossible.

For instance, she and Jacob sent her eldest son, Naphtali, to London to go into business with his paternal uncles, only to demand that he never eat anything at her own brother's house (where Naphtali lived), "Unless it be bread & butter nor noe where Else where there is the Least doubt of things not done after our Strict Judaicall method." Abigaill Franks was probably only too aware of a practice noticed by Swedish traveler Peter Kalm in the late 1740s, that while New York Jews "commonly eat no pork, . . . I have been told by several men of credit that many of them (especially among the young Jews, when traveling) did not make the least difficulty about eating this or any other meat that was put before them." In 1757, Shearith Israel itself complained of "severall of our brethren, that reside mostly in the country and . . . dayly violate the practice of our holy religion, such as trading on the Sabath, Eating of forbidden Meats, and Other Heinous Crimes." Abigaill was determined that no such backsliding would occur in her family.[56]

In the same letters, Abigaill condemned the English upper class for the very sort of elitism she practiced with regard to her own family: they "will not allow any thing right but what has the Advantages of being bred amongst" them. Yet she had no use for either the "ignorant Dutch" or the "Stupid set of people" she thought comprised New York's Jewish community, which she in turn criticized for practicing the same religious scrupulousness she enjoined on her own children: "I Must Own I cant help Condeming the Many superstitions wee are Clog'd with & heartily wish a Calvin or Luther would rise among Us . . . I don't think religeon should Consist in Idle Cerimonies & works of Superogations wich if they Send people to heare wee & the papists have the Greatest title too."[57]

One would imagine these remarks would have come from a religious woman, but Abigaill's letters, aside from urging her son to behave himself, show no interest in what she termed "Our Little Congregation," about which, she frankly admitted to Naphtali, she was "never" concerned, unlike her husband. Instead, she sought social status and took a great deal of "secret pleasure to Observe the faire Character our Familys has in the place [New York] by Jews & Christians." (She was probably more accurate concerning the Christians.) Franks was a fervid devotee of the "baubles from Britain" historian T. H. Breen demonstrates American consumers began to devour at precisely this time. She took great delight in the family portraits, jewels, gowns, musical instruments, books, and Scotch snuff Naphtali sent her, and in return shipped him native flora (flowers, plants, and food) and fauna (birds that sometimes died). Although she wanted her son to shine in England, she kept reminding him of the natural bounty from America he was missing. One can only speculate whether Abigaill, whose letters contained astute and well-expressed comments on contemporary society and politics, would have been happier and less caustic had a literary circle of women existed in New York high society, like the one in the Philadelphia area about which Carla Mulford has written so eloquently.[58]

Abigaill Franks exhibited in extreme form the competing yearnings and conflict of identity endured—if that is the right word, for she lived very well—by America' provincial elite. On the one hand, she looked to Britain to provide the wealth, the influence, and the occasional presence of members of its upper class to give her the social validation she craved. On the other hand, she criticized the mother country's snobbery and neglect of colonial rights, exhibited by Governor William Cosby and his supporters, all the while sending her son to live in England, expecting him to succeed economically while eschewing the cosmopolitan sociability required to achieve this success. She brought up her children in America to be genteel but demanded that they, despite her own negative example, be good Jews. Her daughter Phila went to school with the elite to learn French and Spanish, her daughter Richa played the harpsichord, her son Moses painted and played the flute.[59]

Peter Kalm also noticed Anglophilism, elitism, and class consciousness among New York Jews. He met in New York "a rather good natured and polite man," whom "it would scarcely have been possible to take . . . for a Jew from his appearance." His gentility appeared in the instruction he gave Kalm on how to prevent a porcelain bowl from cracking when warm water was placed in it—boil some corn husks in it first. Observing synagogue services on November 1, 1748, Kalm commented that "both men and women were dressed entirely in the English fashion. . . . During prayers the men spread white cloth over their heads . . . but I observed that the wealthier sort of people had a much richer sort of cloth than the poorer ones." That it was more important to make an appearance, and a good one, at synagogue than take a deeper interest in matters religious appears in Kalm's observation that the "rabbi" [actually the hazan] "spoke so fast as to make it impossible for any one to understand what he said." Similarly, Naphtali Phillips recalled that New York's leading Jews "were surrounded with all sorts of affluence and wealth" and when they attended synagogue "had their slaves walking behind them through the streets carrying their prayer books and shawls." Attendance at synagogue for this secularized, commercial group was primarily a matter of maintaining ethnic and elite solidarity rather than either moral instruction or theological enlightenment. Europeans noticed the secular and exceptional nature of America's Jewish population. Such observations underlie Jacob Rader Marcus's insight that "Jews in America looked upon themselves, unconsciously at least, as an ethnic, rather than a purely religious community."[60]

Elite Jews also took an interest in colonial politics. Abigaill Franks's astute commentary about the "Perfect war" in New York between two elite factions from the 1730s to 1750s is an excellent source for studying the conflict. Although she favored the Morris/Livingston clique rather than the Cosby/Delancey, her approval of the "Town side" she supported was by no means unconditional: "Patriots Generly act Oppon a Private Peek but always blend theire intrest with the Weall of the Commonwealth," she wrote to her son, a sensible account of why many people oppose those in power. Franks socialized almost exclusively with partisans of the Morrises and Livingstons, along with visiting British notables, and despite repeated pleas from the wife of Governor Cosby, refused to visit her husband, a man she termed "very much disliked—I think they are best who have nothing to doe with him."[61]

Nor was New York's Jewish community itself the "best" in the eyes of Abigaill Franks. Their politics did not agree with hers. In keeping with New York's past history, most Jews rejected the populist faction of Lewis Morris and his printer, John Peter Zenger, favored for the most part by the province's Dutch ethnic majority, and supported the more cosmopolitan Anglican Delancey faction allied with Britain and the Crown. Five Jews had contributed to the building of Anglican Trinity Church in 1711, a good indication that they believed their protection lay in their connections with the local elite and the Crown.[62] In 1737, Cornelis Van Horne, the Morris faction candidate for a New York City seat in the colonial assembly, lost a close election to Adolph Philipse, who sided with the recently deceased Cosby and his successor, Lieutenant Governor George Clarke. In an attempt to reverse the verdict, Van Horne challenged the legality of both nonresident freeholders who voted, notably military officers and Jews, who favored Philipse. In a dispute that dragged on for exactly a month, from September 12 to October 12, Philipse was finally confirmed: the assembly allowed the nonresident freeholders and soldiers to vote, but "unanimously" rejected the Jews, still giving Philipse a narrow margin of victory. The House also ruled that Jews could not testify concerning irregularities during the election.[63]

But the assembly's apparent unanimity was deceptive. The vote on the Jews only came under scrutiny after several other disputes concerning electors' qualifications had been raised. First, on September 6, voters in Ulster and Orange Counties questioned the results there. Only on the twelfth did "a great Number of the Inhabitants" of New York City complain of the "Extraordinary Injustice of the Sheriff," who ruled on which voters were qualified—and he was William Cosby Jr., son of the late controversial governor. They petitioned that neither Van Horne nor Philipse be seated "till the Justice of the Sheriff's Action and Judgment be examined into and determined." Philipse was finally elected. Prior to Philipse's election, the house also ruled that New York City's sheriff, William Cosby Jr., had not committed "a great number of extraordinary injustices," as supporters of Van Horne had charged. The upshot was that despite the high level of contention, Philipse and Van Horne managed to agree on which votes should be allowed. It seems likely both factions in the House struck a bargain to seat some of each other's candidates to enable business to continue. Also in dispute was whether James Alexander of the Morris faction could serve as a member of the House since his opponents alleged he had acted as a councilor (he denied he had and was seated in the lower chamber).[64]

Another reason for the unanimous verdict against the Jews appears in eighteenth-century historian William Smith Jr.'s account of the "memorable debate" between lawyers representing Philipse and Van Horne. Even decades later, he claimed, "auditors . . . never mention[ed it] . . . without the highest encomiums upon the art of the orator." The only speaker Smith Jr. identified by name as entitled to such praise was William Smith Sr., who represented Van Horne. His opponent, one Murray, Smith Jr. noted, "dryly urged the authority of the [New York] election law, giving a vote to all freeholders of competent estates, without excepting the descendants of Abraham." Murray thought the law was enough and he did not need to do more. He was wrong. In an argument that combined praise for his father's oratorical skills and disdain for the use to which he put them, the younger Smith noted that the legislature "with astonishment heard a reply, which captivated the audience into an opinion that the exception [to Jewish votes] must be implied for the honor of Christianity and the preservation of the constitution." One can only hope that Smith was exaggerating the effects of his father's speech, for if his description is true, no greater heights of rhetorical anti-semitism were reached in colonial British North America: Smith Sr. "so pathetically described the bloody tragedy at Mount Calvary that . . . the unfortunate Israelites were content to lose their votes, could they escape with their lives." Had not some of the Philipse supporters interposed, "the whole tribe in this dispersion would have been massacred that very day, for the sin of their ancestors in crucifying Jesus."[65]

Smith was at a loss to understand how his father, who had supported the assembly's assertion of the people's rights and printer John Peter Zenger's right to publish criticism of Governor Cosby, could take such a stand: "His religious and political creed were both inflamed by the heat of the times," the younger Smith guessed, and because the speech was delivered extemporaneously, "perhaps . . . he was not conscious of the length to which his transition, from the impolicy of a Jewish interposition in the legislation of a Christian community, to the severity of exercising it, would carry him." But there was no inconsistency at all. The assembly gave as its justification for Jewish disfranchisement that "Persons of the Jewish Religion have no Right to be admitted to vote for Parliament men in Great Britain," and "unanimously" disallowed the Jewish electors. At this time, the New York assembly, to enhance its power with respect to the governor, was claiming equality with the British legislature like its sister bodies throughout British North America. The language of the assembly's journal does not mention the Jews' collective guilt or refer to Smith's religious attack: it instead suggests that whether anti-semitic or not, New York's assemblymen felt obliged to act like Parliament itself.[66]

Whatever the law was in England, New York's provincial agent, who was himself a Jew, informed Representative James Alexander, "I will not take it upon myself to say Jews can vote for Parliament men in England, however, it is my poor opinion if they take the oaths they may [do so in New York]."

It was ironic that the New York assembly that denied the right of Jews to vote in 1737 had in 1731 appointed Jewish merchant Rodrigo Pacheco to represent the colony in England. He told Alexander that he had appeared before Parliament as Jew, that no one objected, and that a colonial law that prevented Jews from voting would "be no more difficult to overset . . . here, than buying a truck of Callicoes fit for Madam Alexander's shop." Whether Pacheco was being honest we cannot tell, for Jews were not formally enfranchised in England. Associating the Jewish franchise with his own mercantile partnership with Alexander was a none too subtle way of pointing to the influence of leading Jews in an empire that valued commercial expansion more than religious affiliation.[67]

The New York election of 1737 shows that New York was well ahead of its neighbors in pioneering the spirited elections between two competing factions that more and more resembled modern political parties and were marked both by coalition building and the active recruiting of ordinary folk. Less progressively, at least on this occasion, this political maturity was accompanied by the fusion of elite and populist anti-semitism that would only become general in the revolutionary era. Smith Sr. had appealed to a latent prejudice that paradoxically was only able to manifest itself precisely because the Jews had been exercising full political rights in New York since the English Conquest; evidence shows them voting at least as early as 1701.[68]

The election of Jews to political office by New Yorkers was yet another paradoxical variety of anti-semitism that could only appear where they had full political rights. New Yorkers usually elected Jews to offices far beneath their social station, compelling them either to pay fines or hire deputies to avoid serving. The first such election seems to have been in 1718, when Nathan Simson and Samuel Levy were chosen constables of the North Ward. Choosing them for the position listed last in the town records of the five offices for which New Yorkers voted (after alderman, assistant alderman, assessor, and tax collector), the electors were demeaning the Jews by choosing prominent merchants to be what we would call policeman, an onerous job in which both popular anti-semitism and class antagonism would make itself felt in the unlikely event they indeed exercised this office. Simson and Levy appointed deputies (whom they doubtless paid) to take their places. In 1719 the merchant Moses Levy paid a fine of fifteen pounds rather than serve as constable of the South Ward, an option also exercised the following year by Jacob Franks, New York's most prominent Jew, when the Dock Ward elected him to police it. Constables Samuel Myers Cohen (1730), Baruch Judah (1732), Abraham Myers Cohen (1744), and Isaac Hays (1748) would also avail themselves of deputies. (It should be noted that gentiles frequently did the same thing, suggesting that the voters would elect to office unpopular but well-to-do people to humiliate and get some money out of them.)[69]

Proof that anti-semitism rather than desire for Jewish public service motivated these choices appears in the fact that more Jews were elected to public office in 1736 than in any other year, just before the handful of Jewish voters were disqualified in 1737. No less than seven Jews were elected that year to city office: four constables, one assessor, and two collectors. Only Judah Hays, constable for the Montgomerie Ward, was actually sworn in. The Jews were off the hook for the next several years, but in 1742 five were again chosen to office, and only one, Abraham Myer, took his place as assessor of the South Ward, a post in which he could do some damage to his enemies if he wished. In other cases, Jews elected to office, as with Samuel Myers Cohen, sometime parnas of Shearith Israel, in 1730, and Isaac Seixas of the South Ward in 1747, successfully claimed exemption on the grounds they were neither freemen nor freeholders.[70]

Some Jews did accept office, although whether from a sense of duty, a desire to demonstrate Jewish citizenship, or because they could not pay a fine or hire a substitute remains unknown. Mordecai Gomez seems to have been the first, as collector of the East Ward in 1723; Abraham Hays followed as constable of the South Ward in 1725. By the mid-1750s, New Yorkers seem to have stopped using elections as a means to demonstrate anti-semitism; from 1756 to 1766 no Jews were elected to office. After 1767, the South Ward elected one Jewish constable annually until the Revolution: first Isaac Moses (1767–69) and then Michael Hays (1770–75), both of whom served.[71]

The disqualification of Jewish voters in 1737 was thus a political ploy rather than a permanent decision. No effort had been made to disfranchise the Jews since the brief triumph of Leisler's Rebellion in 1691, and in short order the Jews were voting again. They were elected to office in 1742, which, whatever its negative connotations, at least acknowledged their citizenship. Swedish traveler Peter Kalm noted in 1748 that "there are many Jews settled in New York, who possess great privileges. They have a synagogue and houses, and great country seats . . . they have likewise several ships . . . in fine, they enjoy all the privileges common to the other inhabitants."[72]

Unless the theft of a valuable plate from the synagogue in 1740 is counted—the culprit was caught in Stratford, Connecticut, and his captors rewarded financially by the congregation[73]—the next bouts of anti-semitism to be suffered by New York Jews after the 1737 election came from the Delancey rather than the Morris faction. Again, these episodes are highly problematic since Abigaill Franks herself provided a powerful reason for the Delanceys' anger. Instead of being a struggle between religious groups, the quarrel may perhaps be better described as one between the Franks and Delancey clans.

In the 1740s, the immovable object of Abigaill Franks was confronted by the irresistible force of Oliver Delancey, whose elder brother James led the family's political party, served as chief justice of the New York Supreme Court, and intermittently acted as governor in the 1750s and 1760s. Governor George Clinton (1743–53), the brothers' bitter political opponent, made frequent references to Oliver's "riotous manner, bidding defiance to everybody," hoping to "incite tumults and sedition." Oliver apparently nearly murdered one Dr. Colhoun in a tavern brawl, and among the "abusive and injurious" remarks he made about Clinton were "damned Rogue," "Villain and Scoundrel," and the "Worst Governor that ever was in this Province." When brother James could not persuade people to vote for him and "against their conscience" through "artful condescention and dissimulation," he "had his two Bullies, Peter [another brother] and Oliver to frighten them." The most dominant faction in eighteenth-century New York politics, according to Patricia Bonomi, the midcentury Delanceys were so powerful that Clinton commented that "if Oliver could but set up his Four Coach Horses, they would be elected." It was no wonder that "no Lawyer will undertake to prosecute him" for his violence, even though he and his friends "committed all sorts of riots and abuse, for which they would be hang'd in England"—or so Clinton claimed.[74]

Something in macho bully Oliver must have attracted the genteelly raised Phila Franks, for she and her other siblings rebelled against the schizophrenic upbringing Abigaill had inflicted on them. Phila married Oliver in Philadelphia—where her brother David lived—on September 8, 1742, and kept it a secret for six months: besides being an Anglican and a

roustabout, Oliver was a member of the family that led the political opposition to the Franks' friends. Only several months later did Jacob Franks
agree to see his daughter, and he made it clear in a letter to his son Naphtali
in England that he was less than delighted with Phila's choice: "If you concede wee live in a Small place & he is Related to ye best family in ye place &
though yr sister has Accted so very UnDutyfull yet It would give Me & family a great Deall of Trouble was she to be Ill Used by her husband or Relations." Jacob was not referring to spousal abuse, but to the question of one
thousand pounds, to which Oliver as Phila's husband was lawfully entitled
as her inheritance from her uncle Isaac upon reaching her twenty-first
birthday. While Jacob chose not to tackle the powerful Delanceys over the
money, neither he nor Abigaill ever spoke to their daughter or son-in-law
again.[75]

The Franks' second son, David, who had moved to Philadelphia and
taken charge of the family business there, followed his sister's example in
December 1743, marrying Margaret Evans, daughter of the Quaker recorder
of the City of Philadelphia and his wife Mary. They had met through the
auspices of Frances Moore, one of Abigaill's best friends. Abigaill again
banished a child from her life for marrying outside the faith: "if I can't
throw him from my heart I will by my conduct have the Appearance of it."
But what choice did the Franks children have? David Gomez, who belonged
to the second wealthiest Jewish family in New York, at least if the synagogue
assessments were just, was interested in Richa Franks, a second daughter.
But Abigaill found him "such a Stupid wretch that if his fortune was much
more and I a begar noe child of Mine . . . Should Never have my Consent."[76]
Richa responded by becoming the third Franks to marry a Christian: her
departure for London was one of the specific things about New York that
Peter Kalm reported in his journal in 1748: "A daughter [Phila] of one of the
richest Jews had married a Christian after she had renounced the Jewish
religion. Her sister [Richa] did not wish either to marry a Jew, so she went
to London to get a Christian husband."[77] Only Naphtali's choice of a bride
met with his mother's full approval, but she was a cousin, a British Franks
whose first name (Phila or Bihlah) was also Abigaill's, although she preferred not to use it. A third son, Moses, was only married in 1765 at the age
of forty-six, again to a Franks cousin with the same name as his mother, by
which time he lived in London, his mother had been deceased for nine

years, and his father was in his late seventies. Another daughter, Rebecca, never married.[78]

The Franks' marriage patterns were not unusual for New York or colonial Jews in general. Historian Robert Cohen has shown that an astonishing 45 percent of New York Jewish males and 41 per cent of females were unmarried when they reached the age of fifty. (By contrast, only 16 percent of colonial Quakers, another group noted for a large single contingent, remained unmarried.) The story of New York's Hays family may be added to the Franks saga to explain why this was so. In 1763, a year before he died, Judah Hays disinherited both his son Michael—"having frequently taken very just offence at . . . [his] general and disobedient conduct"—although he forgave him a debt of three hundred pounds and the interest thereon, and his daughter Rachel, "to whom I give only give five shillings as she married contrary to my will and desire." (Her husband was Jewish fur trader Levi Michaels, who did business at Montreal.) The other children and his wife shared in his considerable estate. In fact, Cohen has argued that "without the enormous influx of immigration in the nineteenth century, the Jewish community of New York would have ceased to exist," a fate that in fact befell the eighteenth-century Jews of Newport, Rhode Island, and Lancaster, Pennsylvania.[79]

At the same time Abigaill Franks was inadvertently laying groundwork such that none of her American grandchildren would be brought up in her faith, she and her stepmother managed to start a quarrel that divided Shearith Israel for decades. In 1718, at the age of fifty-two, Abigaill's father Moses Levy married the twenty-four-year-old Grace Mears (Myers), who was only two years older than his daughter. Abigaill detested her stepmother, calling her "a base Vile woman," the "plague My father has intailed opon Us here in New York." Grace was Abigaill's equal when it came to carrying a grudge: although left well-off by her husband, who died in 1728, she refused to pay for his coffin and instituted a lawsuit in which she claimed Abigaill's brother Nathan had promised to pay the four pounds, six shillings, and eleven pence. In 1735, seven years after Moses Levy died, Grace in turn married David Hays, who did not die until 1778, and played a big role in synagogue politics. Abigaill made their union the subject of a vicious pun: "I doe think my grace full mothers marriage disgracefull," commenting "noething but a madman would Marry a Woman with Seven child[ren]."[80]

Both colonial New York's anti-semitism and internal Jewish factionalism arose from the complicated animosity among the Franks, Mears, Hays, and Delancey families. In 1742, Oliver Delancey, his brother Stephen, and a friend William Montague were indicted for attacking Judah Mears, Grace's brother, who in yet another spat had been quarreling with Jacob Franks as early as 1734 over the ownership of a ship's cargo.[81] The reason for the attack is unknown: perhaps Mears had learned of Delancey and Phila Franks's secret marriage and made some comments about it. In any case, after his marriage was announced, Delancey continued his bad behavior, arguably in response to the cold shoulder he and Phila received from their relatives and perhaps other Jews. In May 1743, a related news item appeared in Peter Zenger's pro-Morris/Livingston paper, the New York Weekly Gazette. The writer reported that "one who by his dress I should have thought to be a Gentleman seem'd to Head a Mob" that tormented the city's Jews while they were burying one of their dead, a procedure that required a long procession to the burial ground on the outskirts of the city. This news item appeared only in Zenger's paper, not the administration organ, the New-York Weekly Post-Boy, which suggests that the "gentleman" was a member of the Delancey faction. Given Oliver Delancey's past and future conduct, he was the most likely "gentleman" in town to do such a thing. The story continued that the "Gentleman . . . held out an image (which I fear he is too fond of)"—probably a crucifix—"and Mutter'd in Lattine I suppose his Pater-Noster [Lord's Prayer]." Zenger's observer, who claimed to have attended the ceremony out of "curiosity . . . with little thought of returning the better Friend to that [Jewish] Nation which was so much despised and ridiculed by ours," "saw nothing but decency on their part" as they "with difficulty" interred the corpse in the face of a "Rabble" of "unthinking Wretches," a bunch of "Brutes" led by someone who was a "Scandal to Mankind to Christianity in particular."

If we assume the most likely scenario, Zenger relied on the general prejudice against the Jews among the ethnic Dutch—which his writer admitted or pretended to hold—to show that even Jews were models of civility compared to the political opposition who "are nominated and pass for Christians [but] deserve not the name of men." If the writer's account of the crowd's behavior is accurate, by noting that Oliver carried a crucifix and was "supposed" to have said the Lord's Prayer in Latin, he was also attempting to associate the Anglican Delanceys with Catholicism or popery. This was a frequent tactic of colonial Dissenters in criticizing Church of England supporters of the Crown, for British Americans despised Roman Catholicism far more than Judaism. (In 1742, the British Empire was at war with Catholic Spain.)[82]

The news item also suggests that there was enough sympathy and toleration for Jews in the city that Delancey's action would be more likely to arouse a backlash than approval. That the general public of New York did not share the Delanceys' attitude also appeared when in early January 1743, a fire began in a bakery near the synagogue and consumed part of its roof. Although the timing of the fire suspiciously coincided with the high-water mark of the Delanceys' hostility, the fact that it began elsewhere strongly implies that even they did not resort to arson. But thanks to "the never-too-much to be commended diligence of the inhabitants," the "engines [were] brought very speedily" and "the flames were soon extinguished, with very little other damage."[83]

It would be tempting to dismiss Zenger's story that Delancey harassed a Jewish funeral as political propaganda were it not for his general reputation and at least three more incidents of anti-semitism that followed in relatively short order. In 1746, Jacob Franks offered a reward of five pounds in the *New York Weekly Post-Boy* for discovery of those responsible for damage to the walls and fences of the Jewish burial ground, an act of vandalism requiring that somebody leave the settled area of the city and consciously seek out the cemetery. Five years later, both of the city's newspapers printed the synagogue's elders' renewal of the five-pound reward and their "urgent request to desist from further vandalism in the Jewish cemetery."[84]

Whether Delancey was involved in these desecrations we do not know, but in 1749 he was definitely concerned in another incident of anti-semitism. Governor Clinton reported that on February 2, Delancey "and several others, with their faces black'd and otherwise disguised," attacked the house of a "poor Jew and his wife, who lately came hither from Holland, where they had lived in a very handsome manner even to keeping their coach, but were reduced by misfortunes." Since 10 to 15 percent of New

York City's population was black and fear of black disorder greatly troubled the white majority—in 1741 a number of blacks and poor whites had
been executed in the belief they were planning to burn down the city—
Delancey's disguise implied an added measure of intimidation: he was
identifying himself with the group perceived as the most dangerous and
violent in the city. Yet the disguise was also clearly transparent, or Delancey
would not have been identified, suggesting he wanted to associate himself
with the image of violence run amuck. In any event, the crowd "broke all
the Jew's windows" and afterwards "broke open his door, enter'd his house,
and pulled and tore every thing to pieces, and then swore they would lie
with the woman." Clinton added that "Oliver swore she was like Mrs. Clinton," his own wife, "and as he could not have her, he would have her like-
ness, and used very indecent language."[85]

Three months later, a peculiar anti-semitic letter appeared in Zenger's
paper that was perhaps related to this incident. Someone addressed "the
Israelites of the tribe of Juda," blaming them for not telling a new Jewish
family they were raising the general level of rents by paying an exorbitant
amount to lease their house. The author related the renter's extravagance to
the "Appearance and Haughty spirit of your Consort," and predicted that
the family would soon be bankrupt. The only Dutch Jews known to have
arrived at that time were Isaac and Charity Adolphus, who recovered their
former prosperity before dying in 1771 and 1774, respectively. Adolphus was
a voting freeman in 1761 and as a merchant did well in partnership with his
nephew Benjamin Etting.[86]

Delancey's hostility toward Jews seems to have run its course in the
1740s. By the 1760s, the aged Jacob Franks, his sons Moses and David, and
David's son Jacob (known as Jack) were among his principal business associates. The letters of John Watts, Delancey's partner, to Moses Franks, who
lived in London, reveal genuine friendship as well as a successful business
partnership. From 1760 until 1783, Moses belonged to a consortium of
extremely wealthy merchants charged with supplying the British army in
North America. He delegated that business in New York to Delancey and
Watts, in Pennsylvania to his brother David and to Joseph Simon of Lancaster. Moses Franks also helped Watts raise money for New York's King's
College, and Watts in turn trusted Moses to buy and sell stocks on his
behalf on the London Exchange. The two men exchanged coded informa-

tion about business rivals they feared might learn of their plans; Moses warned Watts about his neglectful agents in Philadelphia thanks to information from David and Jack, who lived and traded there, and Watts sent Moses extensive letters criticizing British impositions on the colonies such as the Sugar and Stamp Acts in the hopes he would use his connections to facilitate their repeal. Such cordial relations between elite Jews and gentiles were common in New York. Jews joined Masonic lodges, formed business partnerships with gentiles, and after the Revolution would participate vigorously in political associations such as Tammany Hall.[87]

Only once was there a slight problem on account of religion: that during the Jewish High Holy Days of 1763, Jacob Franks's observance of "the Sabbaths & Holidays of the Sons of Israel" forced Watts to advance some money for business transactions out of his own pocket. But this seems more like a joke than a criticism, since of course Franks paid him right back. Watts's expressions of "Friendship [from] almost time immemorial" with "good old" Jacob Franks, ring true, as does his thanks for Moses's letters, "so explicit and full of Confidence," based on "a well grounded Friendship" in which each man wishes the other "all the Happiness you wish." Watts's elegant congratulations on Moses's marriage at the belated age of forty-six conveys the warmth of their friendship: "By this Time I suppose you must be in Fetters [married], may they set easy upon you, tho' they have galld some poor mortals confoundedly. . . . but to be serious, believe that I wish you both all the Happiness the State [of matrimony] Affords."[88] Similarly, the fact that David Franks of Philadelphia was that city's only prominent (if reluctant) Jewish loyalist and that Peter Delancey, brother of the notorious Oliver, praised his loyalty in the highest terms, securing him a pension of one hundred pounds a year, suggests that the Franks and Delanceys made their peace after Abigaill's death.[89]

But there was no peace in Shearith Israel. After the 1740s, internal conflict was a more persistent problem for New York's Jews than antisemitic threats from gentiles. By the 1760s and 1770s, the feuding had reached such a height that members of the congregation resorted to two extreme devices: they kept secret minutes that detailed the nature and names of people involved in disruptive behavior, and they placed their differences before Christian judges in secular courts for arbitration. In his nineteenth-century memoirs, Naphtali Phillips blamed the trouble on "a large addition of Ashkenazim" in the 1750s and 1760s, but of the rival faction's leaders, only Manuel Josephson was a newcomer at this time. The Hayses, Levys, Simsons, and Cohens had all been around for many years: Phillips was probably simply projecting the Sephardic stereotype against central European Jews, which was enhanced after large numbers of them began to come to New York in the nineteenth century, a century earlier. Phillips's analysis attributing the difficulties to the synagogue's traditional, authoritarian structure is more accurate: "the trustees . . . were absolute masters of the life and liberty and fortunes . . . of everybody who was a member of the community. In New York they endeavored to perpetuate that idea, but it did not always work. . . . There never was a time, whether it was the spirit of the new country or not, when there was that implicit obedience from the congregation to these edicts that there had been in Amsterdam."[90]

Shearith Israel's 1728 constitution had rules to keep order, maintaining that "if any person or persons whatsoever shall offer to give any affront or abuse, either by words or action to any person or persons within the said Sinagog," they would be fined twenty shillings.[91] This proviso became inadequate by the mid-1740s, when feuding among the Delanceys, Franks, and Mears was in high dudgeon. In 1746, the fine was raised to five pounds, it being "necessary for the peace of our said Congregation that something must immediately be done" against "aggressors" who were causing "disturbances." The men of the synagogue collectively pledged that they would all forfeit ten pounds "if each of us do not assist all in our power" to collect the fines due from troublemakers.[92]

A few years after the Delancey-Franks troubles seem to have subsided, new animosities surfaced. In 1755, the congregation's elders and officials expelled "S . . . H . . ." "for the frequent disturbances he has occasioned in the Sinagoge & the scandalous things he has reported of us about the city." (Use of initials rather than a full name was how the record symbolized a person's expulsion.) Members were forbidden to "communicate or converse" with him "till such time as he has given proper satisfaction." Among his other sins, S. H. had instituted a lawsuit against Shearith Israel, which required it to hire a lawyer and defend itself." S. H. was probably Solomon Hays, a dry goods merchant who on September 6, 1756, advertised in the *New York Gazette or Weekly Post-Boy* that he would pay one hundred pistoles to anyone who revealed to him the identity of "several scandalous

Jews" who were "defaming his character and hurting his credit." In 1756, another disturber of the peace arose, the wealthy fur trader and merchant Hayman Levy, whom the officials "unanimously" fined "the sum of twenty Shilling for the indecent and abusive language he gave the Parnass in the Synagogue yard." At the same time, much like New York gentiles had formerly done to annoy Jews, they voted Levy himself parnas for the succeeding year. Since he immediately turned down the job and was thereby subject to a fine of ten pounds, it seems probable he was chosen in the knowledge he was too angry to accept the post. Levy made amends a year later, and thereafter held office in the synagogue on a regular basis.

Despite a plea for peace read in synagogue on March 28, 1758, in which the leaders proclaimed it an "indispensable duty . . . to invite & cherish week [sic] Brethern" to return, the strife continued. Struggle over who was to sit in the front of the *banca* in the women's gallery upstairs became an issue to determine the most prominent family in the synagogue. Since observers noted that the front of the gallery was "a breastwork as high as their chins," so only the women's heads appeared over it "like a hen coop," this was more than a symbolic issue. Except for the women in front, any exceptionally tall ones behind them, or those willing to stand, they were obliged to listen to the service—which went on for several hours—without the privilege or diversion of viewing it.[93]

The word *banca* was used to designate the seat of the presiding parnas, but whether a comparable seat of honor would automatically be given to his wife, the "lady parnas," as she was sometimes called, began to cause controversy. On June 24, 1760, Judah Hays complained that Judah Mears had entered the women's gallery of the synagogue and physically expelled his daughter Josse Hays "from the seat, claimed by Miss Mears." The congregation fined Mears forty shillings "to prevent for the future any person assuming to themselves the authority of determining the property of seats in the Sinagogue." In an effort to "pacify" Hays, one of the two parnassim, none other than Hayman Levy, proposed "lengthening the bench on which Mrs. Hays sits in the synagogue." Hays agreed in principle, but on inspecting the new bench found it was not long enough. The parnassim (Levy and Benjamin Gomez) called for a new meeting, but Joseph Simson, Naphtali Hart Myers, and Jacob Franks refused to come, insisting that "their first resolve [the forty shilling fine] was not complied with." Hays was ordered to place his daughter in the seat designated for her, and until he did and paid a fine of forty shillings, he would "not be looked upon as a Member of our Society." Hays refused to comply, his name was never mentioned in the records again, and Mears died in 1762. The offending *banca,* which women of the Gomez family eventually occupied as a matter of custom, was removed in 1796, "having been the cause of much dissatisfaction," as Naphtali Phillips recalled in his history of the synagogue.[94]

When he published *A Concise Account of North America* in 1765, Major Robert Rogers of Ranger fame singled out the colonies' Jews as a particularly obnoxious people. Speaking of New York, he wrote, the Jews "who have been tolerated to settle here . . . sustain no very good character being many of them selfish and knavish (and where they have an opportunity) an oppressive and cruel people."[95] Whatever their behavior toward non-Jews, the members of New York's small Jewish community had little love for each other and, it seemed, could not agree on anything. The political divisiveness that troubled the province in the 1760s found its reflection in Shearith Israel. Of the five Jewish freemen in New York City who voted in February 1761 for the city's four legislative representatives, none voted the identical ticket despite the fact that the Livingston and Delancey factions had campaigned against each other and their candidates were easily identified. Isaac Adolphus, the probable object of Oliver Delancey's ire a decade earlier, was one of two Jews who did not vote for Oliver's nephew James, who finished last in the polls of the six candidates. Benjamin Moses Franks not only voted for Delancey, indicating that he probably supported Rebecca in her quarrel with her late mother Abigaill, but for Philip Livingston as well, who received four out of five Jewish votes. Winners John Cruger and William Bayard also received four Jewish votes each, while winner Leonard Lispenard received two. A Livingston supporter who lost, attorney John Morin Scott, received one vote. (The aged Jacob Franks did not vote.)[96]

Whether quarrels among the Jews had anything to do with the imperial crisis is not known, but the two escalated together. On October 16, 1765, "H. . . . L. . . ."—Hayman Levy again—was fined twenty pounds "for an abuse given by him to the hazzan." In June 1767, it was hazan Isaac Cohen De Silva himself who was in trouble: Parnas Moses Hays "at two difficult times" had to pay off debts owed by De Silva to deliver him "from the

Hands of a Bailiffe: and keep him out of jail." De Silva, however, had other creditors, and confined himself to his house to keep from being arrested. Thus, he was unable to perform his duties. The congregation was not sympathetic: his petition to "vindicate his character and conduct" from his "indiscreet and scandalous behavior" was rejected by a vote of eleven to one, with six elders abstaining.[97]

In 1767, Hayman Levy was once more at the center of a serious quarrel. On June 28, Joseph Pinto was fined forty shillings for "abusing Mr. Hayman Levy (acting Parnass) in the street going from the synagogue."[98] This seems to have been part of a larger brouhaha, for the deleted minutes for the same day note that "Mr. Abraham Isaac Abrahams made acknowledgment and confession for striking Mr. Abraham Seixas in synagogue." New names kept joining those who already had reputations as troublemakers. In the deleted minutes for 1768, Moses M. Hays, Samuel Hart, Daniel Gomez, Joseph Simson, and Hayman Levy met and criticized the "scandalous behavior" of Manuel Josephson, Hilel Judah, and Uriah Hendricks during services. The next year, the elders, by a vote of eighteen to three, determined that Solomon Hays, Manuel Josephson, Hilel Judah, Moses Judah, Andrew Hays, and Barak Hays had been "for a Considerable time . . . tending to subvert the Laws & Rules made for the Good order, and support of our Congregation." The miscreants were given one month to reconcile with the majority upon pain of expulsion.

In 1770, Josephson and various members of the Hays family could no longer contain their wrath within the walls of the synagogue. They took one of their adversaries to court and enlisted the aid of Daniel Gomez and his family. Their resentment seems to have partially stemmed from young men who resented their elders, partially from factional strife between those families who controlled the synagogue and those who felt slighted. On September 23, 1770, the father of Samson Simson, "Old" Joseph—who was eighty-four at the time but did not die until seventeen years later—was called to read from the Torah at High Holy Days services.[99] Manuel Josephson (in company with Judah Hays) allegedly laughed at him because of his appearance. According to different witnesses, either his prayer shawl fitted poorly or dragged on the ground. One witness revealed the majority's presumption that Josephson's gestures and speech were directed against Simson, claiming (as the minutes for 1768 and 1769 had previously attested), "he is very often offensive at Synagogue, laying at the Elders and at the persons who give out the Honors of the Synagogue." In any event, Josephson appeared to be shaking his head and "making a face of defiance and impudence" when other members of the congregation flashed him glances of rebuke and reminded him "he was in a house of worship." "Look at how they make game of daddy," Solomon Simson complained to his brother Samson, a remark Samson used to criticize Josephson for mocking a man "who is old enough to be your grandfather." Then, according to Benjamin Etting, Samson Simson called Josephson "a mean dirty scoundrel . . . for I brought you from Carolina when you was starving out of compassion," and mentioned "that he [Josephson] had been taxed [charged] with theft in public and hadn't spirit to resent it." Etting managed to separate the men, but Josephson swore to Simson that he'd "take the law of him . . . to the utmost extent." In any event, witnesses for both sides, who heard different fragments of the dispute, agreed that "a great deal of noise" and "much abuse passed between them."

Josephson's witnesses countercharged that he had behaved properly in synagogue whereas Simson had falsely called him a thief and threatened to expose his dishonesty "in the public coffee house." A good deal of testimony was spent determining whether Simson had challenged Josephson's integrity or merely his honor and masculinity. Simson's defenders stated that he only alleged that Josephson did not have the courage to defend himself when accused of theft rather than actually accusing him of theft itself. Josephson also claimed that Simson threatened to expose publicly his "low-liv'd" origins, used colorful words such as "footman," "shoeblack," "shoe-maker," and "dirty dog" to describe him, and threatened to "drub him" as well.

Josephson sued Simson for one thousand pounds, a huge amount that reflects anger rather than any measurable damages. Part of Josephson's lengthy charges included "contriving and maliciously intending the same Manuel not only into Scandal, Trouble, Vexation, and Infamy among his Neighbors and other faithful Subjects . . . but also to subject him to the manifest Danger of Losing his Life on September 23, 1770." Josephson claimed such large damages because he was "greatly hurt, injured, prejudiced, and damnified in his good Trade, Name, Fame, Conduct, and Reputation" by Simson's threats.[100] Even wilder than Josephson was his witness

Solomon Hays, who had entered the dispute with his own sarcastic remark that the synagogue had ignored decency in that "the sexton should be called up" to read the Torah "before the Honorable Daniel Gomez." Hays added that he and Josephson had done nothing unusual, since "the Elders [themselves] were always quarreling in the synagogue." Moreover, "the rulers were all of one Family," and Hays thought they were a bunch of murderers: "when the Word was said they would kill people," and "if it was not for the Christian Law they would kill many." Hays claimed that this "parcel of strangers and vagabonds" had already killed his father (although he had kept this a secret for several years). He stated that the only synagogue members in good standing who had contributed for the burying ground were himself, his brother, his brother-in-law, and the snubbed Daniel Gomez.

In the midst of all this, Hays had a point. In 1771, with the exception of Daniel Gomez and Hayman Levy, the congregation's other six officers were all named Myers or Simson. The fourteen elders who elected them—half of them belonging to the Simson or Myers clan—specifically chose this slate because they were "apprehensive of great disorders arising from the want of Rulers" after four of the outgoing officers—not surprisingly considering what was going on in the synagogue—were unwilling to exercise their powers.

Hays and Josephson were so angry that they were willing to appeal to an anti-semitic stereotype—that Jews secretly committed murder—and to enlist the aid of Christians in their effort to seize power in the synagogue by setting their grievances before a secular court. The court would have none of this, sharply dismissing Hays's extreme remarks as having "no concern . . . directly or indirectly with the evidence in the cause depending . . . he said it for no other purpose, but to make the congregation appear odious to the court and audience, and that he has absurdly imposed on the court by setting forth many things which can be proven false." Elite Christian magistrates thus supported elite Jews in opposing a challenge from those whom the record reveals resented both the age and class bias of the synagogue, the very biases that in colonial society at large would shortly persuade young and poor New Yorkers—although not only them—to revolt against Britain.

Much of the testimony in the Josephson/Simson case—aside from who said what nasty things about whom in the synagogue—concerned the truth of whether Josephson was really a thief and whether he in fact possessed a reputation for honesty worth destroying. Witnesses disputed whether about six years previously, Josephson was merely examining some silver buttons belonging to John Franklin, the man who "taxed him with theft," at a public sale or had actually stolen them. Franklin himself showed up to testify that he "was as sure as he could be of any thing," that "the Plaintiff did take the Buttons." Simson also presented a witness trying to show that Josephson possessed no reputation worth destroying. Daniel Jacqueri explained how at Pensacola, in the new British colony of East Florida, in August or September 1766, Josephson had cheated a group of Spaniards by offering an "extravagant rate" for provisions in return for Campeche logwood, which he had bought at an extremely low price. As did his opponents, Simson appealed to the Christian court using an anti-semitic stereotype—that Jews were miserly and dishonest—in an effort to win his case against his coreligionist.

Shearith Israel took the precaution of consulting Judge Whitehead Hicks before yet another case came to trial. Unfortunately, no record survives as to whether the same people were involved; the letters A through D are used to identify the principals. However, given the synagogue's small membership, the problems of seating, and the possibility of another lawsuit, it appears that once again the Hayses and Josephson were challenging the established elite. In writing to Judge Hicks, the elders noted that two members, "C and D," "have in contempt" seated themselves contrary to the regulations of the synagogue and refused to "move unless it be by force." The elders inquired whether "the Law of the land will not protect the Rulers' agents [identified as A and B] if they displace those that take Seats without their Consent by calling Constable and taking them out if they will not yield peaceably," and asked "the best way to do it . . . to prevent their Sueing any person concerned for an assault." Hicks responded on November 21, 1770, that "if the synagogue is not Incorporated the Orders and regulations of the Rulers I Conceive are not Obligatory on the Society"—and the synagogue was not incorporated until 1784. However, Hicks added that "if any persons, make a practice of behaving so disorderly as to disturb the Society in their Religious Worship, it is a breach of good behaviour, and I am of opinion they may be prosecuted by indictment." Hicks's opinion would be most useful to the synagogue in yet another case.[101]

That Jewish law required ten men (a minyan) for services to be conducted contributed to the feuding in Shearith Israel. Otherwise, it is hard to imagine the Hayses and Josephson returning repeatedly to the fold or the elders' reacceptance of them. By 1772, they were back at it, now having acquired allies from the Levy family. That year, "B . . . H . . ." (identified as Barak Hays in the deleted minutes) and Manuel Josephson were accused of unruly behavior, along with Samuel Eleazar Levy and Michael S. Hays. All were required to apologize, but only Samuel Levy did.[102] Barak Hays, on the other hand, was expelled. He proceeded to institute lawsuits against Solomon Simson and Benjamin Seixas, the principal malefactors he claimed had "turn'd [him] out" of the synagogue "for disturbing our holy worship."

The circumstances of this case were complicated. In addition to all the troubles previously mentioned, a division had developed within the Hays family after Judah Hays's 1764 will had disinherited his son Michael and daughter Rachel. Furthermore, Michael's brothers looked upon his subsequent marriage as illegitimate. On September 20, 1772, Michael brought his child into the synagogue to be named. His estranged brother Solomon, according to witnesses, uttered the word "bastard" and seemed to be "in a passion." Referring to what Michael's enemies thought was an improper ceremony, brother Barak said something such as "D—— what the Scoundrels do." Moreover, he made a spectacle of himself by loudly stating, "Father, what can you expect from a parcel of Scoundrels," looking up at the ceiling (was he invoking God the Father or his own deceased parent?), "which he repeated several times so as to disturb our reader who was obliged to stop." When Parnas Hayman Levy asked "what he meant by calling him scoundrel," Barak replied in no uncertain terms, "I mean scoundrel." Levy then instructed the sexton (to clarify the issue for the jury, the Christian word was used rather than *shammash*) to remove Hays, and Hays responded by "unbuttoning his waistcoat and attempting to put off his coat as he intended thereby to prepare himself for fighting within the said synagogue." Even more explicitly, he offered to "fight any scoundrel that should dare to touch him." (Witnesses differed as to his exact words but agree on the gist.) At this point, Solomon Simson and Benjamin Seixas, rather than Sexton Benjamin Gomez, provided the principal muscle that ejected Hays, as they were the men he sued "for coming with Force and Arms . . . against the Peace of Our Lord the now King and also the wound-

ing above." Barak indeed put up a fight, not only shouting "Murder" as he
was being thrown out, but demanding that his brother—whose child he
had just called a bastard—"command the peace, as he was a constable," do
his public duty, and come to his assistance!

Barak Hays's case was based on the fact he did not—he said—hear Hayman Levy order his removal, and that in any case the men had "without
cause . . . made an assault and him did beat, wound, and evilly treat." Hays
claimed he was seized by the collar, shoved against the rails, struck in the
breast, and kicked in the shins by Joseph Myers's "boy" as the other men
heaved him out the door. (Simson, in turn, insisted that he only "softly put
his hands" upon Hays.) Hays thus contended that he was not only never
properly ordered out the synagogue, but that in any case "more force was
used than was necessary" to evict him. John Tabor Kempe, the province's
attorney general who also had a private practice, served as Hays's lawyer
and argued "the Jewish religion was not established here and in no Christian Church would he have been turned out" for what he did.[103]

Solomon Simson, in turn, countersued Hays, charging that he "did most
indecently and irreverently behave himself and with a loud Voice and abusive, opprobrious, and scurrilous language did then and there talk so loud
and make so great noise that divine service could not be celebrated with
due solemnity." Simson also summoned witnesses who attested that Hays,
although he had formerly belonged to Shearith Israel, was no longer a
member and thus had no right to be there at all. On the night of October
21–22, 1772, after deliberating from four in the afternoon until five in the
morning, a jury finally accepted Judge Robert Livingston's charge, which
echoed Judge Hicks's opinion of 1770, and decided for the defendants: "if
Barak Hays disturbed the worship of the Almighty God, what he did was
a nuisance, and as such any of the members had a right to turn him out."
"For the said offences and many others," Hays and his brother Solomon
were expelled from the congregation. As might have been expected, when
the vote came, the Judah and Hays families united against the Simsons,
Myers, Seixas, Levys, and Benjamin Etting. Two Gomezes supported the
Hayses, one the elders.[104]

Fresh contention arose in 1773 concerning the funeral of Baruch Judah
on Rosh Hashanah. Moses Lazarus insisted on preaching over the objections of one of the two parnassim, either Manual (sic) Myers or Solomon

Myers Cohen. Manuel Josephson backed up Lazarus, stating that "if you are Parnass over the Bog House, you are not Parnass here." Lazarus for his part "most maliciously and wickedly cursed the Parnass to which the said Josephson was most wickedly heard to say *Amen.*" Lazarus and Josephson were suspended from membership until they would "at least promise to behave better" and paid fines of ten pounds each (Isaac Moses paid for Josephson). To make sure this decision stood, the elders ordered that if any future parnas let the two miscreants back in before the fine was paid, that parnas himself would have to cough up the money![105]

One has to look to Protestant communities distinguished for exceptional contentiousness—Salem before 1692 or Jonathan Edwards's Northampton flock—to find anything approaching Shearith Israel's divisiveness in the 1760s. On the eve of the American Revolution, New York Jews were divided in two factions much like the Livingstons and Delanceys. On one side stood the more established Simson, Seixas, Myers, and Cohen families, on the other the Hayses, Gomezes, and Manuel Josephson. Feuding within the congregation had split families, caused children to leave the faith, retarded population growth by discouraging marriage, and led to both litigation and physical violence. It was no surprise that the American Revolution divided New York Jews as much as any other group on the continent.

FROM REVOLUTION TO CONSENSUS, 1776–1800

While New York's Jewish community split drastically during the Revolution—at least sixteen identifiable Jews were loyalists, although not all went into exile, as opposed to twenty-some patriots—it is difficult to account for the pattern.[106] In 1770, six Jews, Samuel Judah, Hayman Levy, Jacob Moses, Jacob Myers, Jonas Phillips, and Isaac Seixas, were among the more radical merchants who urged that the current nonimportation agreement be stringently enforced rather than disbanded.[107] Barak Hays became a loyalist along with the merchant Uriah Hendricks and shopkeeper Samuel Myers, as did two Gomez brothers, Abraham and Moses Jr. By the 1770s the brothers were wealthy merchants, but Hayman Levy and Manuel Josephson, also merchants, and like loyalist Barak Hays troublemakers in the congregation, were fervent revolutionaries, as was the Simson family. It would be fascinating to know if Josephson and the Simsons ever made peace.

The Simson family's revolutionary ardor appeared when in 1784 prominent revolutionary Arthur Lee met the ninety-nine-year-old Joseph Simson. Lee described the old man as having blue eyes and a fair complexion, "both of which are uncommon among Jews." A medical miracle, "in all his life" Simson "had not kept his bed two days from sickness, . . . had never observed any particular regimen, had used spectacles for forty years, until of late he could see without them." Lee observed that "he walked well, ate well, slept well, and talked well. His voice was strong." "A very warm Whig" who "quitted the city when the British took it," Simson "believed General Washington was the greatest warrior in the world and ought to be called Joshua." When he and Lee discussed some Jews who were about to purchase land in the "back part of Georgia for the purpose of establishing a colony of Jews exclusively," Simson made the sociologically astute comment that "it would not do, for that the Jews prospered most when intermixed with other nations."[108]

Another New York Jew showed exceptional qualities during the Revolution, although politically on the opposite side. New York loyalist merchant Abraham Wagg (1719–1804), a recent immigrant from Britain, had married into the Gomez family in 1770. Wagg wrote two letters, the first to the peace commissioners Britain sent to America in 1778 to negotiate a settlement with Congress, the second in 1782 to the prominent British Jewish merchant Solomon Henry, in which he hoped to employ the close transatlantic ties between the Jews to influence the peace settlement. Wagg suggested that the British simply withdraw their forces from North America and direct their attention to their traditional French and Spanish enemies. Paraphrasing the Declaration of Independence, Wagg argued that "the law of Nature and Nature's God intitles America to enter into treaties and be perpetual allied with Great Britain by the nearest ties of consanguinity, being of the same religion, speaking the same language, and remembering the former intercourse of good offices &c." Whether his writings influenced the Shelburne ministry's decision to pursue a separate peace with the United States is doubtful, but Wagg was one of a growing chorus of voices supporting this course, which eventually was taken. He correctly predicted that "the republican spirited Americans" would jump at an opportunity to end the French alliance that "clogd" their "favorite hopes"—independence, peace, and a boundary at the Mississippi—and would lead to "the evil Consequence of introducing the French Nation among them, which must corrupt their youths and endanger their Religion."[109]

With parts of the Carolinas and Georgia, New York, like the other middle colonies, had a substantial loyalist minority. Its Jewish community containing the rich and the poor, the prominent and the obscure, split roughly down the middle, reflecting similar divisions in New York as a whole. Occupied by the British army from 1776 to 1783, New York was a haven for loyalists, including Jews such as members of the Lucena family of Charleston and the Lousadas, who returned from Bound Brook, New Jersey. New York Jewish loyalists were sufficiently influential—Naphtali Phillips singled out Lyon Jonas, Barak Hays, and Olivier Zuntz—that they were able to prevent the synagogue from being turned into one among several "hospitals, riding academies, barracks, and things of that kind," as were "most of the other churches." The British did remove the metal from one of the Jewish graves to make bullets, but in general respected the cemetery as well. Two British soldiers who stole the synagogue's valuable ritual items were caught and severely flogged, one of them dying as a result of the punishment.[110]

While we can identify the prominent Jewish loyalists, the sixteen Jews (out of 944 people of all sorts) who pledged their loyalty to General William Howe in 1776 included several obscure folk about whom nothing is known. As with the colonies in general, New York contained many people who only rose to historical notice, if at all, in criminal records or under other extraordinary circumstances. Some of these were Jews. As early as June 1727, New York City's Mayor's Court convicted one Moses Sousman for burglary and sentenced him to death, although no goods were found in his possession. In August, the Common Council paid to have a gallows erected for his execution. We know nothing else about Sousman, nor anything about "Jew Nell"—even whether she was Jewish—except that in 1755 she was charged, along with Elizabeth Collier, as leading a "Base and very Lewd Life as a common Bawd" who "Harbored also some of the worst Strumpets and Vile Adultermen."[111]

Also typical of New York, as historian Judith van Buskirk has shown, is that the allegiance of many people, especially among the wealthy, was a choice made only reluctantly. People on both sides of the political fence retained friendships, visited each other across the lines, and were relatively forgiving of their opponents once the war was over. David Hays, who signed the oath of loyalty to Howe in 1776, lived in Westchester, as did his brother Michael. David changed his allegiance—perhaps, like many, he signed the oath under duress—and supplied the Continental army with cattle: his house was burned by loyalist raiders. Michael and his brother Barak were deeply hostile to each other, but neither renounced King George. The reconstituted Shearith Israel that reopened in 1783 included erstwhile loyalists Moses Gomez, Abraham Abrahams, Uriah Hendricks, and Alexander Zuntz, a civilian in charge of supplying the Hessian army who had served as interim parnas of the congregation during the occupation. Zuntz was briefly exiled, but returned to New York as a prominent member of the synagogue and became a founder of the New York Stock Exchange. Hazan Gershom Seixas, who fled to Connecticut and then Philadelphia, risked capture by returning to the city to perform the marriage ceremony of Samuel Lazarus, great-grandfather of Emma Lazarus, whose poem adorns the Statue of Liberty. Abraham Florentine, a loyalist refugee from New Jersey, left New York in 1783 but then returned and became a street inspector after the British turned down his claim for nine hundred pounds in losses.[112]

Quantitatively, the New York Jewish community was as divided as the state and city in general. A reconstituted Shearith Israel had twenty-eight men present at a meeting in 1786—perhaps a few others were absent—only two of whom had signed one of the two manifestoes of loyalty to General Howe. Since eighteen Jews had signed either or both manifestoes, although some of those about whom nothing is known were probably not New Yorkers, it is best not to interpret the various numbers too precisely but to regard them as exemplifying not only a community, but many individuals, whose allegiances were divided and in flux. But it is safe to conclude that unlike the Jews of Philadelphia and Charleston, New York Jews were "flattering" themselves indeed when in 1783 Shearith Israel addressed Governor George Clinton, writing, "tho the Society we belong to is but small, when Compar'd with other Religious Societies . . . we flatter ourselves, that none has manifested a more Zealous attachment to the Sacred cause of America."[113]

The Revolution also changed the economic destiny of New York Jews. At least two were examples of the upward mobility and opportunity for newcomers that the turmoil of revolution made possible. Isaac Moses, a shoemaker, was one of the artisans who began to challenge New York's elite political factions in the 1760s. Chosen a constable in 1766, his election was annulled as he was "neither a freeman nor freeholder." Eight days later he took the freemanship oath and exercised the office. Given the riotous times, Moses must have sought this post rather than spurned it, perhaps either to put down or tolerate political turmoil. Similarly, Haym Salomon was a Polish newcomer imprisoned by the British for his revolutionary activities, but he had earned the esteem of state leaders such as merchant Leonard Gansevoort and General Philip Schuyler both for supplying the army and for providing information on the British in New York, an activity that nearly cost him his life.[114]

In any event, when New York State drafted its first constitution in 1777, the granting of full political equality to Jews was not in question, as it was in every other state. Because the province had at first belonged to the Duke of York, and his policy of toleration was confirmed by William III, the right of New York Jews to vote and hold office seems only to have been questioned once since the 1690s, during the fluke election of 1737. With a good number of New York's Jews serving the revolutionary cause, it would not have served the patriots well to disfranchise its loyal supporters at a time when other states were courting previously excluded groups. Still, it is noteworthy that the original clause in the state constitution proclaiming "free Toleration be forever allowed in the state," drafted by John Jay, contained words that were ultimately removed: "to all denominations of Christians without preference or distinction and to all Jews, Turks, and Infidels, other than to such Christians or others as shall hold and teach for true Doctrines principles incompatible with and repugnant to the peace, safety and well being of civil society."[115]

Such thinking appears to have been bipartisan, at least among New York's cosmopolitan elite. William Smith Jr., a loyalist, also insisted that all religious bodies ought to be treated equally. In 1774 as a member of the Governor of New York's Council, he opposed his colleagues John Watts and Oliver Delancey, who argued that a Dutch church in Schenectady ought not to be allowed to possess more than two hundred pounds of wealth since Parliament had rejected a comparable petition from Presbyterians in England. Smith insisted, "I would consent if it was asked for by a Jewish synagogue or a Turkish Mosque," and urged "this Liberality of Sentiment as approved by sound Philosophy and Experiment, and especially in the colonies." He then mentioned the rapid Growth of Pensilvania."[116]

The hypothetical threat of Jews, Turks, and infidels that so vexed Pennsylvania was trivial in New York compared to the real threat of Roman Catholicism. From the Glorious Revolution until the last royal instructions given to Governor William Tryon in 1771, Catholics could not practice their religion openly in the province. John Jay—who until the end of his life retained his anger that Louis XIV had exiled his Huguenot ancestors from Catholic France in 1685—introduced an amendment that would have excluded Catholics from the state by denying them the right to own lands or enjoy civil rights until they would appear in the supreme court and "solemnly swear" that they would owe no allegiance to any "pope, priest, or foreign authority on earth," renouncing as well the "false and wicked, the dangerous and damnable doctrine," that the "pope or any earthly authority" could either absolve men from sin or "from the obligation of this oath." Jay's anti-Catholic amendment was defeated nineteen to ten after it was debated "at great length." If toleration of Catholics was granted by a nearly two to one vote after a century of exclusion provided they did nothing "inconsistent with the peace and safety of this state," it is understandable that New York would not take from patriotic Jews the rights for which they were fighting.[117]

Although Jewish political rights were a nonissue in New York, Jay made the case for them even stronger in "An Address of the Convention of the Representatives of the State of New York to Their Constituents." This important proclamation of 1777 encouraged the people to fight fervently for the Revolution. Jay singled out the Jews as a people especially devoted to freedom, favored of God, and therefore worthy models for the new American nation. He told his countrymen: "You were born equally free with the Jews, and have as good a right to be exempted from the arbitrary domination of Britain, as they had from the invasions of Egypt, Babylon, Syria, or Rome." God only permitted tyrants to subdue his chosen people "when they forgot the smiles of their benevolent creator," in which instances "they were severely chastised." Jay, however, was not concerned with showing that the Jews were justly punished when they lacked moral fiber. Rather, he used their example to demonstrate that the appearance of a tyrant could lead to the reformation of a people and reestablishment of freedom. In the long run, the biblical Jews persisted, and "those tyrants themselves, when they had executed the vengeance of Almighty God, their own crimes bursting on their own heads, received the rewards justly due to their violation of the sacred rights of mankind." Americans ought to profit by the knowledge that "the Jews were under His peculiar direction, and you need not be informed of the many instances in which he took the crown from such of their kings as refused to govern according to the laws of the Jews." Jay concluded: "If we turn from our sins, He will turn from His anger. Then will our arms be crowned with success, and the pride and power of our enemies, like the arrogance and pride of Nebuchadnezzar, will vanish away." Whether Jay was thinking of American Jews who at that very moment were proving their patriotism remains unknown. His father, Pierre, who limited his lucrative trade to a few correspondents, had done business early in the century with Daniel Gomez and strongly vouched for the solvency of Abraham Moses when he was being hounded by creditors. His son John, in turn, used the biblical Jews, rather than the Romans or English defenders of freedom, as the prime example of a virtuous people the revolutionaries should imitate.[118]

Despite granting Jews full political equality, eighteenth-century New York was no more liberal than its sister states when it came to demanding that business and pleasure cease on the "first day of the week," "commonly called Sunday." A law to that effect passed the state legislature by the overwhelming vote of thirty-four to five, but it is interesting that its principal opponent was Egbert Benson, a Federalist who later became a state supreme court judge. A graduate of Columbia College, the state's attorney general from 1777 to 1789, and a lifelong friend of John Jay, Benson argued that the bill was "repugnant to the [state] constitution . . . as the same principle that would establish any particular day for the worship of the Deity might also describe the mode, and this would lead to intolerance and persecution." Benson especially noted that "a Jew, to be consistent with himself, is obliged to keep holy the 7th day of the week, which is Saturday, and to prohibit him from working on a Sunday would be taxing him one sixth part of his time. This was not equal liberty, one of the boasted blessings of our government." The bill's supporters replied that America was "a country professing Christianity," and since "it was on the first day of the week . . . that Jesus Christ descended on the apostles and instructed them to produce a church," "justly therefore is the first day of the week consecrated to the honor of that divine person, to whom we owe both our being and our new being." Some supporters of the bill allowed that Jews could be permitted to work in their houses on the Sabbath, but this half-measure did not satisfy Benson. "Suppose a Jew should say, you offend me by working on Saturday, and for which he will say he has a positive command. Why has he not as good a right to a law. . . . Suppose there was a majority of Jews in the state."

Other supporters of the bill could not see its unconstitutionality, and argued that both traditional practice and the need for some agreed-upon day of worship to preserve public morality—preventing "horseracing, etc. to disturb the serious part of the community, and to the great corruption of their morals"—required some day to be set aside. As most New Yorkers were Christians, Sunday was the logical choice. Benson's retort was that the bill's main concern was not "sports and idle diversions"; it granted practitioners of Christianity both economic advantages and formal recognition as the cult of the state. The only other man identifiable of the four who supported Benson was John Dongan of Staten Island, an Anti-Federalist, but also the descendant of Catholic governor Thomas Dongan, who was sent to the colony by the Duke of York a century earlier to promote religious toleration.[119] Yet this bill was a minor fly in the ointment. New York's Jewish leader Solomon Simson bragged to the Jewish community in Cochin, China—the United States began trading with the Far East after the Revolution—"We here in America in New York and other places, live in great security. Jews sit in judgment in civil and criminal cases just as do Gentiles."[120]

What the Jews did not have when the Revolution ended, however, was their own agreed-upon form of public worship. Referring especially to his own state, New Yorker Manuel Josephson, probably the most learned American Jew in rabbinic law at the time, wrote to Moses Seixas, parnas of Newport's declining congregation, that America represented an extreme case of what was occurring in Judaism throughout the world: "with regard to ceremonial customs, these have been established in different ways in different congregations according to the fancy and opinion of the head men that were amongst them at the time of framing their several constitutions." If Sephardic Jews in Amsterdam and London, or even several Ashkenazi communities within London, could not agree on a minhag (or service), was it any wonder that "our North American congregations . . . have no regular system, chiefly owing, in my opinion, to the smallness of their numbers and the frequent mutability of the members from one place to another." "Unpolished" European newcomers, especially, were apt to be "narrow minded" and adopt "arrogant language" in dictating to their American brethren, supposing it "next to impossible any knowledge can be obtained out[side] of Europe." As a result, "every newcomer introduced something new, either from his own conceit and fancy, or what is more probable, from the custom of the congregation where he was bred, or the one he last came from." Such "transient" people Josephson termed the "men of yesterday." He looked forward, like other Jews and, indeed, Americans of different religions, for a more settled, democratic religious order appropriate to the diversity of the new nation.[121]

New York Jews were equal to this challenge. The year after George Washington's inauguration, following the letters he circulated throughout the nation commending the Jews' patriotism, Shearith Israel, "in the most solemn manner in the Presence of the Almighty and of each other agree[d] to form such rules to serve for, or be considered, a constitution" clearly inspired by that of the United States. It began with the preamble,

> In a state happily constituted upon the principles of equal liberty Civil and Religious, the several Societies, as Members of that Government, partaking of that Blessing, being free to adopt the best means for Preserving their Privileges and for entering into such Compact for regulating and well-ordering the Internal Institutions for the Administration of affairs of their several communities,

before enumerating a series of rules and regulations. First was the right of every man over the age of twenty-one "except a bound or hired servant . . . professing to be and living a Jew" to join the congregation as long as he behaved himself. Then followed a list of rules governing election of officers and penalties for violating them.

Next, again modeled on the United States Constitution, came a bill of rights. "Whereas in free States all Power Originates and is derived from the People who always retain every right necessary for their well-being Individually . . . a declaration of bill of Rights in like manner the Individuals of every Society in such a State are entitled to and retain those several rights which ought to be preserved inviolate." First among these rights was a reaffirmation of the inclusiveness found in the main body of the constitution: "Every free person professing the Jewish religion is entitled to worship the God of Israel in the synagogue, by purchase or gift of a seat, and to be treated in all respects as a Brother and as such a Subject of every fraternal duty." The congregation was fundamentally democratic: every member could propose changes in the constitution or other rules, which then had to be publicized two Sabbaths consecutively before a vote was taken on the third. While measures were under consideration, every adult man had a "full right to speak his sentiments freely on any such proposal on any occasion whatsoever." But membership required good behavior, both "decency and decorum" in the synagogue and adherence to Jewish law in personal life. Any person who would "heretofore marry a Goiah [gentile] or otherwise contrary to our custom" without the approval of the parnas would no longer be "considered or hereafter admitted as a member of our Society."[122]

Shearith Israel had to work hard to preserve this "decency and decorum," not to mention democracy, as the eighteenth century ended. Some members sought special privileges: in 1801, Isaac Moses, who was among the writers of Shearith Israel's constitution, was himself turned down for additional land in the cemetery on the grounds that "if we admit the principle others are equally entitled to the same privileges . . . and thereby our Beth Chaim [cemetery] would be divided among a few families." Some of the by-laws the congregation adopted in 1805 sought to curtail other special privileges. A number of members had attempted to distinguish themselves through their loud singing, for one bylaw stated, "Every member of this congregation shall previous to the singing of any psalm or prayer remain silent until the Parnass shall signify the tone or key, in which the same is to be sung, and those who are so inclined may then join therein with an equal voice, but neither higher or louder than then the Parnass." Those attending were also enjoined not to bring children under the age of three to the service, and to restrain themselves from going in or out during services (which lasted several hours) in groups, which were apt to be disruptive. Clearly,

New York's Jews in the 1790s, as a half century earlier, were still using the synagogue as a space in which to assert their status and to socialize, remaining indifferent to those members who might have wished to pay close attention to the proceedings.[123]

Historian Gad Nashon has pointed out that Shearith Israel's "new, liberal constitution" was "exceptional in the Jewish world." Yet without comparable fanfare, the Jews of Philadelphia in 1782, Savannah in 1791, and Charleston in 1793 would also begin to choose their officials by adult male suffrage rather than the congregational elders. Isaac Moses, nephew and son-in-law of Hayman Levy and a very wealthy merchant, and Solomon Simson drafted Shearith Israel's constitution. Like several of their coreligionists—as the document's use of the words of "fraternal" and "brother" make clear—they were Masons who took seriously that society's proclamations of Enlightenment and toleration. Further, they would soon become ardent supporters of the French Revolution and members of Aaron Burr's Democratic party.[124]

For at least three members of the congregation, however, the new constitution was not democratic enough. Four years earlier, in 1786, the Judah sisters Abigail, Becky, and Sally—the diminutives suggest they were fairly young—had denied the right of Shearith Israel's men to govern them without their consent. Exactly what they had sought to do is unclear. Perhaps in the flush of excitement following a Revolution that maintained women had to be moral guardians of republican virtue, they had sought to participate in rather than merely attend services. In any case, they did something to get themselves expelled, a ruling they refused to accept. In a note handed to the trustees, since they could not speak in the synagogue, the sisters protested that "when the gentlemen trustees can convince us that we are subject to any laws they chance to make which is to hinder us from attending Divine Worship, they may endeavor to exercise their authority." The trustees were not impressed: after what they regarded as the women's persistent and "obstinate" refusal to "have the case determined by [their] own law," they sued them for trespass in a New York court to keep them out of the synagogue. The court supported the trustees, and fined the women a nominal sum (six pence) plus court costs. The aftermath, however, was significant. Becky and Sally were forgiven for "the sake of peace," as the trial established the right of the synagogue's officials to govern. No mention, however, is made of Abigail's readmittance. She must have rejoined, however, for two years later she was one of two women (the other was Rachel Myers) who applied, unsuccessfully, to be the synagogue's shammash, or custodian.[125]

Despite Shearith Israel's democratic constitution, the fact that anti-semitism in New York remained a political tool in the hands of the Anti-Federalists and their successors, the Democratic-Republicans, into the early 1790s, suggests most New York Jews were initially Federalists. With the national capital still in New York, the leading opposition newspaper singled out wealthy Jews as members of the elite especially liable to profit from the economic program advanced by Secretary of the Treasury Alexander Hamilton in 1790. Hamilton's proposal that current holders of the debt—mostly wealthy people who had bought large numbers of securities at greatly depreciated prices from farmers, soldiers, and other ordinary folk who desperately needed hard money—be repaid at the face value of the certificates, which had been issued in greatly inflated currency, generated the ire of the *New York Journal.*

Publisher Thomas Greenleaf first broached the topic. Greenleaf, like his anti-semitic Federalist counterpart in Philadelphia, John Fenno, was an outsider, a former inhabitant of Massachusetts whose own career had exhibited the transience of the wandering Jew. He had published the *Independent Chronicle* in Boston before moving to New York in 1787, where he soon became a sachem of Tammany Hall, Aaron Burr's political machine. Like Fenno, he brought New England style intolerance to the press of the Middle Atlantic.[126]

On April 26, 1790, Greenleaf printed the letter of "A CITIZEN" who accused the speculators as having descended to a level beneath the Jews themselves. Taking for granted the stereotype that Jews were greedy, he charged: "The ****** [penises] of these people may be unmutilated, and may be in the original State, but their minds are far gone in *Israelitish* avarice." At least for Shakespeare's Jewish moneylender Shylock, a central figure in the play *The Merchant of Venice,* his mixture of "avarice and bigotry," could be excused by his religion, "the malignant effects of his holy rage." But with some of "our Christians, who tamper with the distress of their fellow soldiers . . . Shakespeare's Jew . . . is surpassed in avarice, by the real character of these Christians." Greenleaf at best paid Jews a back-handed compliment by saying that Christian speculators were even worse.

In the May 11 issue of the *Journal* "A. B." sarcastically turned against Hamilton his statement that "prudential considerations" ought not to be overlooked by the government in paying off the debt to those who held it now on the grounds the original holders would be impossible to locate. Real prudence "might excuse, might even instigate a breach of contract" against the "Jews or Usurers" whom the author implied held the debt at present, rather than against the soldiers and ordinary folk who had sold them apparently worthless certificates. The current holders, A. B. stated, "had taken advantage of the national distress, and had rendered government tributary to their extortion, and had bowed down the shoulders of the people with the heavy impositions of their unlimited avarice."[127]

As late as January 1793, Dutchess County Republicans used anti-semitism to attack the Federalist candidate for the state assembly, in this instance James Kent (later the famous chancellor). A "Farmer" wrote that 90 percent of the public securities were held by "brokers, speculators, Jews, M[embers] of C[ongress] and foreigners," while farmers were earning the necessary cash to pay them off, "digging it in the earth by the sweat of their brow." Kent narrowly lost the election and relocated to New York City.[128]

Then "the French Revolution had burst forth and party sprit ran high," reported Mordecai Myers (1776–1871) in his memoir: "the Federalists went so far as to invent a black cockade as a distinctive badge, and the Democrats, or anti-Federalists not adopting it, were often insulted and even pushed off the pavement." Myers, upon reaching his majority, "became an active politician to put a period to the despotic reign of John Adams," who was supported by the "old Tories" of the Federalist Party.[129] After the French Revolution granted the Jews complete civic equality, many New York Jews—including Isaac Gomez, Isaac Levy, and Isaac Seixas, and Naphtali Judah, a merchant and printer—joined the Democratic Society, Aaron Burr's Tammany Society, or both. Myers explained how Tammany became the first modern political machine, "dividing the city into small districts with a committee appointed to each, whose duty it was to canvass its district and ascertain the political opinion of each voter by going from house." In the election of 1800 it brought down the "despotic" "reign of terror" instituted by the "hydra-monster Federalism" with the Alien and Sedition Acts. Most prominent among New York's Jewish politicians was Solomon Simson, who had fled New York in 1776 to support the Revolution in Norwalk, Connecticut. He served as president of Shearith Israel in 1789, 1790, and 1791, was the original second vice president of the Democratic Society formed in New York in 1794, and rose to be first vice president (1795–1796) and then president by 1797. His political connections led to his election as a city assessor in 1794 and 1795.[130]

Simson's principal antagonist was James Rivington, a British-born printer who had remained in New York during the British occupation to publish his loyalist newspaper. Although Rivington's two sons went into exile and received pensions from the British government, Rivington remained in postrevolutionary New York and in the printing business. He served as a deeply undercover spy for George Washington, who surprised his officers by greeting Rivington in a friendly way after the occupation and speaking to him in private. A supporter of the Federalists and very pro-British, in 1795 Rivington printed a novel written by Britain's poet laureate Henry James Pye, a mediocre versifier who received his appointment because he had strongly supported William Pitt's administration in the House of Commons. It bore the cumbersome title *The Democrat: or Intrigues and Adventures of Jean Le Noir, From his Inlistment as a Drummer in General Rochambeau's Army, and arrival at Boston, to his being driven from England in 1795, after having borne a conspicuous Part in the French Revolution, and after a great variety of Enterprises, Hazards and Escapes during his stay in England, where was sent in quality of Democratic Missionary.*

Rivington, however, added a preface, drawing a parallel between the spy Jean Le Noir, sent by the French to disseminate subversive ideas in England, and the Jewish members of the recently formed Democratic Society of New York, especially vice president Solomon Simson. The American subversives were an "itinerant gang." Rivington begins by invoking the stereotype of the wandering Jew, who is a citizen of no land, and adding to that the word *gang*, signifying a group of people who gather to produce mischief. They "will easily be known by their physiognomy: they all seem to be, like their Vice-President, of the tribe of Shylock: they have that leering underlook, and malicious grin, that seem to say to the honest man—*approach me not*." For Rivington, the Jews, equated with greedy upper-class speculators by the Anti-Federalists only two years before, were still dishonest, only now they had adopted "the political cant of LE NOIR, and his propensity to equalize the property of anyone he has anything to do with."

The name "Le Noir" itself links the Jews with New York's lower-class black population, some of whom had just arrived in America with their former masters fleeing the Haitian Revolution. As in the cartoon "A Peep into the Anti-Federal Club" prepared in New York for Philadelphia in 1793, probably by Rivington, Jews are placed at the head of a conspiracy in which non-Anglo-Saxon Americans (blacks, Jews, Germans, French, Irish) are joined by intellectuals who conspire against the government and hope to appropriate the property of the respectable sort.[131]

Rivington did not go unanswered. Ironically, the responses appeared in Thomas Greenleaf's *New York Journal,* the very organ that had been bashing Jews two years previously when they were generally associated with the Federalists. "J-m-s R-v—gt-n" was identified as the author of the preface and marked as the real traitor to his country. He was an anti-semite who projected his own disloyalty onto Solomon Simson: "If, by the appellation Shylock, you mean a Jew, from my knowledge of the Vice-President, I dare say he would think himself honoured by the appellation, Judaism being his religious profession, as Democracy is his political creed." If having a "peculiar leer" or a "countenance resembling a Creole or African" were signs of a traitor, none fit the bill better than the Federalist businessmen who ran the New York Chamber of Commerce. A class stereotype was used to refute an ethnic one. Nor did Rivington's respondent forget to remind his readers of the printer's overt behavior during the Revolution: "While the British fleets and armies were wantonly burning out towns . . . did not your zeal then, and does it not still continue to represent them as the bravest and most gallant people on the glove terrestrial." Rivington had termed Washington and his army "banditti" and supposedly identified for the British patriots living in New York City during the Revolution, causing "many brave Americans to be confined in the Provo, and Jersey prison ship." Nor did Simson's defender hesitate to argue that Rivington's remarks were irrelevant and absurd: "It is a good maxim not to ridicule religion, or the natural defects of the human body. The first shows depravity of the head, the latter the malignity of the heart."[132]

Although anti-semitism subsequently occupied a back burner in New York's hot political climate, New York's Jews continued to espouse the French cause even when it was least popular. After President John Adams proclaimed May 8, 1798, a day of fasting and prayer as war with France loomed, New York's hazan and de facto rabbi Gershom Mendes Seixas preached perhaps the nation's only sermon that called for peace rather than preparation for hostilities against a godless enemy. He began his sermon, "Behold how good and how pleasant it is for brethren to dwell together in unity"—suggesting that for nations, like individuals, the best course of action was inaction—"that every man sit under his own vine and under his own fig tree." Seixas then recommended that "thou shalt love thy neighbor as thyself," quoting Moses's statement in Leviticus rather than its more familiar reiteration by Jesus in the New Testament, implicitly calling attention to the fact that a Jewish rabbi was urging peace when his Christian counterparts were calling for military preparedness. To be sure, he did rebuke the French. After calling attention to France's services during the American Revolution "when we were oppressed by the ravages and devastations of an enraged enemy, who sought to deprive us of our invaluable rights and privileges," he noted that "we are threatened with all the horrors of war by a great and conquering nation, who but few years past was looked upon to have been highly instrumental in procuring liberty and Independence for the United States of America." Still, citing the civil war that tore the Jews apart and led to the Roman destruction of Jerusalem in 70 C.E., he urged the Adams administration not to pursue divisive policies, such as fight a controversial war or enforce the unpopular Alien and Sedition Acts, which had just passed the House of Representative by votes as narrow as forty-four to forty-one. Instead, the government ought to "promote unity in society." At this critical juncture Seixas's was "the only sermon [in the nation] that was published by a democratic printer, for a democratic bookseller, [and] advertised in democratic papers."[133]

Naphtali Judah printed the sermon, advertised it—although this stopped after three days because of fear of the Sedition Law—and arranged for it to be sold at his "Book and Stationery Store" at the "Sign of [Thomas] Paine's head." The sign itself was an act of defiance, if not courage, at a time the Federalists were trying to root out supporters of the French Revolution, among whom Paine was prominent. Judah was a Mason and a sachem (1803–9) and councilor (1816–20) of Tammany Hall. Another example of his zeal for Democratic politics occurred in 1802. New York's Democratic boss Aaron Burr, who had intrigued with the Federalists in 1800 in the hopes of becoming president, disapproved of John Wood's extreme attacks against the Federalists in *The History of the Administration of John Adams, Esq., late President of the United States.* In December 1801, Burr and his Tammany Hall supporters (in which Judah was "Sachem of the Foxes") persuaded the original publishers Barlas and Ward to suppress the entire edition. The following June, however, Judah advertised the tract for sale.[134]

Another sermon by Seixas, this time offered in 1799 for a Thanksgiving when the war crisis abated, may also have been a coded critique of Federalism."[L]et those who are on the Lord's side," he urged, "continue and cheerfully associate to suppress this hideous monster, who has reared his gigantic head . . . and is endeavoring to tread down and trample everything holy." Although he had previously referred to "sin" as the "monster" in question, both Federalist and Republican writers had frequently used such language to identify their political enemies.[135]

The Federalists went down to defeat in 1800 as Jews were being elected to public office. Solomon Simson in 1798 had added to his previous offices the post of election inspector of New York City's Second Ward. A fitting coda to the Federalists' futile attempt to use anti-semitism to preserve their power and stigmatize their enemies was the lawsuit filed in New York by Pennsylvania Jeffersonian Dr. Benjamin Rush against William Cobbett. Cobbett had printed Federalist newspapers in Philadelphia, where he had (incorrectly) criticized Rush's medical treatment for yellow fever as increasing rather than decreasing mortality. In December 1799, Rush won a Philadelphia judgment for five thousand dollars. Moving to New York, Cobbett wasted no time publishing the *Rush-Light,* in which he focused his ire on Moses Levy, one of Rush's four attorneys. Like Philadelphia's Israel Israel, the principal brunt of Cobbett's anti-semitism in Philadelphia, Levy was not Jewish. Cobbett claimed that "Levy" suggested "that because Cobbett was a *royalist,*" he "hoped, by discrediting the Doctor's [Rush's] practice, *to increase the mortality amongst the republicans.*" "Such a diabolical thought," Cobbett insisted, "never could have been thought but in the mind of a Jew." "But honest Moses seemed to have forgotten, that I could not possibly want to kill MYSELF."[136]

Cobbett was an Englishman who had moved from New York to Philadelphia and back again. Like many printers in the early Republic he fit the stereotype of the wandering Jew, concerned with making a living in a precarious trade. He insisted that although a staunch Federalist, he too was a republican, that is, a supporter of republican government. He was hoping to use anti-semitism in order to restore his much-tarnished patriotic credentials. In any case, Cobbett concluded that he regarded "a poor devil like Moses" with contempt rather than anger: "he did not believe a word that he said: he vash vorking for de monisy, dat vash all." The prominent attorney Levy was identified with un-Americans who could neither speak English nor provide the virtue requisite for citizenship.[137]

By denying the sincerity of his "Jewish" opponents, Cobbett exemplified the sorry decline from the general consensus of the Founding Fathers, for whom Washington had spoken for 1790, that the "liberal sentiment towards each other which marks every political and religious denomination of men in this country stands unrivalled in the history of nations."[138] But were the Federalists in general, as opposed to the printers who worked for them, really anti-semitic? The case of Alexander Hamilton shows the difficulty in answering this question. An entry in his papers, unfortunately undated, cites the "*progress of the Jews . . .* from their earliest history to the present time" as "entirely out of the *ordinary course* of human affairs" and the result of "some great providential plan." Hamilton also served as the attorney for Moses Franks, Haym Salomon, Isaac Gomez, Abraham Rodrigues Rivera, and Moses and Joseph Gomez. Had Hamilton publicly entertained the same opinions as Cobbett, Rebecca Gratz, visiting New York in 1804 from Philadelphia at the time of the Hamilton-Burr duel, could not have written her sister Rachel of "the melancholy and heartrending information" of Hamilton's death. Having known Hamilton during the 1790s, the pious and perceptive Gratz—who refused to marry a Christian with whom she was deeply in love—would not have expected her sister to share in her grief at the demise of an anti-semite. But Hamilton and his friends were willing to tolerate if not encourage a prejudice in which they themselves did not believe—and persuade at least some Jews that there was "nothing personal" about it. Hamilton had no problem comparing two men to "Shylock the Jew" at the height of the Alien and Sedition crisis in 1799 to make a point in court, for which he was castigated by the *New York Journal* for giving "vent to the most scurrilous language against two citizens." The Federalist leaders must be numbered among those who either cynically or unthinkingly sacrificed the reputations of Jewish people they admired, or at least on the surface flattered, in a futile effort to obtain the support of lower-class anti-semites they despised.[139]

Or, perhaps, looking back on the eighteenth-century Jewish experience from the perspective of 1800, New York Jews, like Rebecca Gratz and many gentile Americans, were simply prepared to forgive and forget the partisanship that had marred the late colonial period and the struggle for the new Republic. One of the speeches at the Columbia College graduation ceremony in 1800 was written by the Reverend Seixas, who had been named a regent (later trustee) of Columbia College when it was incorporated by the state legislature in 1784, a position he would hold until 1815, the year before his death. Seixas was the only Jewish trustee of Columbia before the twentieth century.[140] Reciting the speech in Hebrew, Joseph Simson, the son of the Republican leader, drew a veil over the three great ordeals Americans in general and American Jews in particular had survived in the eighteenth century. First, he noted that in 1730 "our regular synagogue was built, where we have been serving Almighty God unmolested for upwards of seventy years." Not quite true: there were incidents of anti-semitism, as well as rows within the synagogue itself, not to mention disruption of services for seven years when most of the congregation left during the Revolution. Second, he claimed that "in the year 1776 . . . the people of this country stood up like one man in the cause of liberty and independence and every Israelite that was among themselves rose up likewise." Seixas surely remembered New York's substantial loyalist minority among both Jews and Gentiles, and his own hazardous infiltration of enemy lines to perform a marriage ceremony, yet chose to ignore all this. Instead of providing accurate history, Seixas was reaffirming the main point of George Washington's Farewell Address, that partisan strife for or against other nations threatened the Republic, and anticipating Thomas Jefferson's famous remark upon his inauguration in 1801: "we are all Federalists, we are all Republicans." He urged patriotic unity, "free of any allegiance to any other [government] whatsoever, monarchical or republican, and we exclaim in the language of King David 'Redeem us, O Lord!, from the hand of the children of the stranger, whose mouth speaketh vanity and whose right hand is the right hand of falsehood.'" Recalling his own Fast Day speech two years earlier, Seixas urged both Jewish and gentile Americans to "beat your swords into ploughshares and your spears into pruning hooks." Inventing a comforting but inaccurate consensus history for Shearith Israel, Seixas could only hope that the future might live up to his mythical past. However, given that New York's Jews had united against Federalist anti-semitism, which the election of 1800 had crushed, and transformed Shearith Israel into a democratic synagogue in 1790, there was reason for hope indeed.[141]

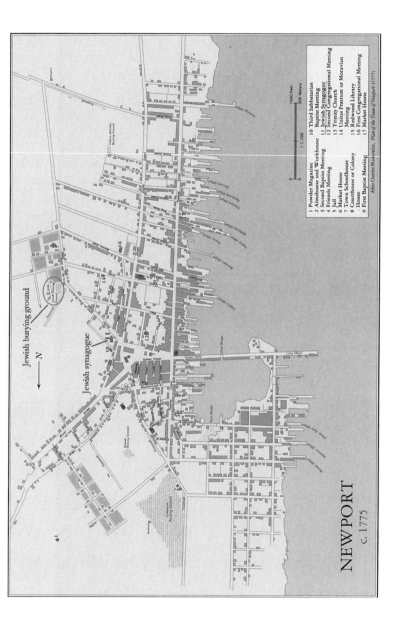

NEWPORT
c. 1775

Jewish burying ground

← N

Jewish synagogue

1 Powder Magazine
2 Almshouse and Workhouse
3 Second Baptist Meeting
4 Friends Meeting
5 Jail
6 Market House
7 Town Schoolhouse
8 Courthouse or Colony House
9 First Baptist Meeting
10 Third Sabbatarian Baptist Meeting
11 Jewish Synagogue
12 Second Congregational Meeting
13 Trinity Church
14 Unitas Fratrum or Moravian Meeting
15 Redwood Library
16 First Congregational Meeting
17 Market House

1:7,700
0   1000 Feet
0   305 Meters

After Charles Blaskowitz, *Plan of the Town of Newport* (1777)

Newport, Rhode Island. The Jewish synagogue is located at the intersection of Bull, Ann, and Griffin (now Touro) Streets on a hill overlooking the town. The burial ground is a very long block uphill on the outskirts of the city, on what was then known as Jew Street.

(After Charles Blaskowitz, "Plan of the Town of Newport" [1777]. Map adapted from Lester J. Cappon, *Atlas of Early American History: The Revolutionary Era, 1760–1790.* © 1976, Princeton University Press, renewed 2004. Reprinted by permission of Princeton University Press.)

CHAPTER 3

NEWPORT, RHODE ISLAND

Newport's jewish community had been in existence for over a hundred years before it mustered the resources to construct a synagogue. Fifteen obscure families founded a congregation in or around 1658. The best evidence suggests they came from Barbardos and maintained close ties with that island, sailing back and forth. Another possible origin is Brazil, perhaps via New Amsterdam, which all of the twenty-three Jews who arrived in 1654 left in short order. Since ten men were required for services, Newport's Jewish congregation in all probability antedates New York's as the first on mainland British North America. In 1677, the congregation purchased a burial ground, and three years later opened a school.[1]

Jews remained in Rhode Island for the reason they failed to remain in New York: religious toleration. Historians have shown that the colony's founder, Roger Williams, was not "the first American democrat," as was once thought. Rather, he sought to preserve the church from worldly corruptions: because he denied Puritan New Englanders' claims that they could identify likely "visible saints," the only way to preserve the church's purity was to separate it completely from a profane and godless world. The desire to keep the church pure and the evidence of a history dominated by unbelievers demonstrated that "t'is the will and command of God, that . . . a permission of the most Paganish, Jewish, Turkish, or Antichristian consciences and worships, be granted to all men in all Nations and countries." Therefore, "God receiveth not an uniformity of Religion to be enacted and enforced in any civil states: which uniformity . . . denies the principles of Christianity and civility." Only persuasion ought to wean the godless to the true church, Williams believed, because history had shown that the "persecutor which hunts or persecuteth a Turk, a Jew, a Pagan, an anti-Christian" was in "greater error than any of the four, because he hardens such consciences in their errors by his persecution."

Still, Williams lumped Jews with Turks, Pagans, and anti-Christians as "briars"[2] amid the roses of the true Christians, and never gave any indication that they ought to be granted full political rights as opposed to the right to live peaceably under Christian authorities. If he admired biblical Jews before the coming of Christ, he denounced those of New Testament times who "stand for Satan" because they killed Christ and refused to repent. He also warned that "their known industry of enriching themselves in all places where they come" would impoverish Rhode Island Christians. The royal charter he negotiated for Rhode Island in 1663 only guaranteed the inhabitants "that liberty in the true Christian faith and worship of God which they have sought with so much travail."[3]

Jews were tolerated and lived in Rhode Island without incident until 1684. They were obscure people who did not appear in the colony's records before that date. Historian Carl Bridenbaugh notes that over half the colony's small population, which he estimates at about a thousand adults at that time, belonged to the Society of Friends, or Quakers. Like Williams, they denied forcible conversion and supported mutual toleration among the tiny colony's diverse population. Rhode Island was spurned by the Puritan colonies (Connecticut, New Haven, Plymouth, Massachusetts, and New Hampshire) and excluded from their confederacy. Rhode Island Jews were lumped with the colony's other settlers by Massachusetts Rev. Dr. Cotton Mather as "the common receptacle of the convicts of Jerusalem and the outcasts of the land." Rhode Island's toleration of Jews was one of its many transgressions, according to the neighboring colonies that paradoxically based a good deal of their church and state polity on Jewish examples from the Old Testament.[4]

Neither Rhode Island nor its Jews could escape the crisis caused by the British government's efforts in the early 1680s to tighten control over the colonies. Rhode Island hoped to maintain its virtual independence by pledging voluntary conformity to British law, thereby distinguishing itself from the intolerant and obnoxious Puritan colonies that had proven recalcitrant. In 1682, the General Assembly promised obedience to the Acts of Trade and Navigation. On June 24, 1684, the colony's governor, William Coddington, perhaps inspired by a recent, similar action in New York, seized the goods of Jewish merchants Simon Mendez and David Brown on the grounds Jews had never formally been granted the right to trade in Rhode Island. Yet the colony's assembly, aware perhaps that King Charles II and his brother, the Duke of York, favored religious toleration, overruled him on that very day. The legislature responded positively to a petition of Mendez and Brown: "They may expect as good protection here as any strangers being not of our nation residing amongst us, in his Majesty's colony, ought to have, being obedient to his Majesty's laws." The first explicit mention of Jews in Rhode Island's official records thus granted them equality with other "strangers," yet defined them as a special "nation" within the British nation, and thus not fully entitled to political rights.

Perhaps Coddington's failure encouraged William Dyer, whom the Duke of York had appointed surveyor of customs in the American colonies in 1685, to try to exclude the Jews again. Dyer's mother Mary was the famous Quaker preacher executed by Massachusetts in 1660 after she had repeatedly returned to the colony after several expulsions. (She is now commemorated with a prominent statue in front of the State House in Boston.) William Dyer was no radical agitator, but a firm supporter of royal authority and an associate of Edmund Randolph, the most notable imperial official sent to investigate and plague the colonists in the late seventeenth century. The equally zealous Dyer had been accused of treason by New York's colonial assembly for attempting to enforce the Navigation Acts and collect the required duties. As might have been expected, he was exonerated in England and returned to America. An anonymous satire promptly burlesqued him: "Well might his cursed name with D begin, / Who was a Divell in his heart for Sin, / And currently did pass, by Common Vogue, / For the devilish wretch and greatest rogue."[5]

What Dyer learned or whom he talked to in England between his departure from New York and arrival in Rhode Island remains unknown, but his actions in 1685 seem to have been coordinated with those of Englishmen who also began persecuting the Jews that same year. Historian David Katz has described how British opponents of King James used the Jews as pawns in their effort to weaken the king. Among the king's problems was that he favored both strengthening royal authority at the expense of Parliament's and local governing bodies' privileges, and the rights of non-Anglican minorities at the expense of the Anglican Church. Both policies alienated some of the most powerful people in the kingdom, for exactly at the moment Parliament was debating the suspending power—which allowed the king to exempt individuals and groups from statute law—the lord mayor of London and other members of the city corporation resurrected a previously unenforced law of 1581. In December 1685, they suddenly insisted that the wealth of a number of Jewish merchants be taken away to fulfill the confiscatory twenty pounds per month penalty stipulated for failing to attend Church of England services. In theory, this law could be enforced against any non-Anglican, but by focusing on the Jews the litigants deliberately placed the king in a difficult position. If he let these proceedings stand, his policy of toleration could be exposed as a sham on the grounds that he only intended to apply it to the unpopular Catholics. Yet if he suspended the Jews from the law requiring they attend Anglican services, he could be depicted as both an advocate of arbitrary power and a friend of the Jews, whom many of the English public despised.[6]

It is easy to understand why the lord mayor of London, that city's corporation, and the Whigs who opposed James also opposed toleration. They had held this position since the beginning of the reign of James's brother Charles in 1660, for wealthy Londoners feared both royal power and the competition of Jewish merchants who flourished under royal protection. All corporate privileges in the kingdom—including those of the city of London, Anglican Church, and the Jews—had to be confirmed with a new reign, and James was following in his brother's footsteps of prosecuting "corporations" (broadly defined) that failed to obey their charters—notably colonies that insisted on self-government while violating the Navigation Acts and persecuting the established church. At the same time, James was using the suspending power to exempt subjects from certain laws, allowing Catholics, Dissenters, and Jews to engage in trade, serve in the army, and practice their religion in public.

Earlier in 1685, colonial officials Samuel Hayne and William Dyer had employed exactly the same tactic against the Jews of Rhode Island that the city of London would shortly employ. Hayne, an impoverished customs official at Falmouth, Massachusetts (now Maine), seems to have been motivated more by the need to pay his creditors than by political or religious convictions, since soon thereafter he was imprisoned for debt. Perhaps Dyer too simply looked for an opportunity to make money, since he fell out even with Randolph and earned the contempt of Massachusetts' governor Simon Bradstreet, a conciliatory, elderly official, for collecting customs duties himself instead of merely appointing and supervising those charged with this task, as his job required. That Dyer appears to have invited a disabled French privateer to repair itself in Boston harbor before seizing it as a pirate ship did not help his reputation as a greedy crook who broke the law he was supposed to enforce.[7]

Why Dyer, whose career had flourished under the tolerant James, would follow in the footsteps of his master's opponents is hard to understand. Possible reasons besides pure greed were that he had changed political sides, or he thought his patron would be too preoccupied with the Duke of Monmouth's Rebellion and other troubles at home to notice his shenanigans in Rhode Island. At any event, in March 1685, Dyer charged seven Rhode Island Jews with being "aliens" who did not have the right to trade in the colony under the Navigation Acts and thus had forfeited their estates. Since there were at best fifteen Jewish families in Newport at the time, Dyer's list reveals that about half of the colony's Jews belonged to a well-to-do and established community, for his action implied these Jews were merchants and shopkeepers whose estates were worth seizing. Governor Coddington, conforming to his action the previous year, complied with Dyer's requests, and ordered the Jews' estates confiscated. Rhode Island's judges were willing to dodge the legal question and dismiss the case on the grounds that Dyer had not brought suit in the proper manner, but the Jews insisted on a jury trial, which the court then granted. The jurors, following the assembly's recent declaration, ordered the Jews' estates restored and insisted that Dyer pay court costs.[8]

It was well that Rhode Island supported Jewish rights, for Jews were among those willing to turn out in a heavily Quaker colony when in 1690 a French fleet attacked Block Island. Three years later, Rhode Island's tolerance and the presence of an established Jewish community combined to encourage immigration, when some ninety Jews from Curaçao chose the tiny colony as their home. (New York, the only other option, was still in turmoil from Leisler's Rebellion, in which the ethnically Dutch minority had clearly displayed its anti-semitism.) Sephardic Jews all, the families that arrived included several that would become leaders of the community, the Touro, Gomez, Rodrigues, and Henriquez (later Hendricks) clans. But

most of the 1693 arrivals did not stay. As prejudice eased in early eighteenth-century New York, most Newport Jews left, although some of their
relatives remained behind to carry on the family business. By 1700, Newport's congregation could no longer muster a minyan, and only resumed
services in 1754. Until then, Newport Jews could be found worshiping in
New York when business called them there.[9]

Those Jewish families who remained in Newport, however, were flourishing by the mid-eighteenth century. Newport's Congregational minister,
the Reverend Dr. Ezra Stiles—future president of Yale College who
befriended and wrote a great deal about Newport's Jews—was the most sta-
tistically minded and intellectually curious clergyman in colonial America.
(Stiles befriended and admired individual Jews, but he did so despite rather
than because of their religion, which provoked in him a "natural disgust.")
He counted fifty-six Jews in ten families in 1761, estimated them at eighty
souls in fifteen families in 1764, and recorded twenty-five families in 1773.[10]
In 1772, at the height of Newport's commercial "Golden Age" just before
the American Revolution, nearly all of its Jewish heads of household ranked
among the town's top 135 taxpayers (total number approximately 1,200).
Aaron Lopez paid twice the tax (£37 11s. 10d.), based on twice the assess-
ment of anyone else in town (the Wanton brothers were next at £18 11s.).
Other wealthy Jews included Lopez's father-in-law, Jacob Rodrigues
Rivera, ranked fifth at £13 11s., members of the Polock family, ranked
twelfth at £10 3s., Moses Levy, twenty-second at £8 9s. 10d., and five mem-
bers of the Hart and two of the Levy family. On a less savory note,
Rodrigues was the town's fourth leading slave-owner with twelve (George
Rome had twenty, two men had thirteen, and Lopez five). Lopez,
Rodrigues, and Moses Levy were three of the thirty-four Newporters who
owned all or part of at least one slave ship.[11]

Lopez was not only Newport's wealthiest inhabitant, he was the most
prominent slave trader in the city that dominated the business in British
North America. A refugee who in 1752 escaped from Portugal's Inquisition,
he was brought over by his brother Moses, and in turn arranged for another
brother, Abraham, to escape in 1767. He was well connected by marriage
and trade with New York's Gomez family and took Rodrigues Rivera's
daughter for his second wife. Rodrigues owned a slave ship in partnership
with gentile William Vernon as early as 1753, but the first Lopez-Rodrigues

venture left Rhode Island in 1761, reaching Charleston, South Carolina, after a multipurpose transatlantic voyage on January 25, 1763, with 134 slaves. Lopez, either alone or with his father-in-law (usually at a ratio of two to one) invested in at least ten more slave ships between 1764 and 1774: a typical ship was worth between six hundred and one thousand pounds sterling, could carry twenty thousand gallons of rum, and could transport between 100 and 250 slaves. The six voyages out of twenty that the two men outfitted between 1761 and 1774 for which statistics exist brought 951 slaves to South Carolina, Jamaica, Barbados, St. Kitts, and St. Christopher: if their cargoes were typical of their other ships, the two men probably brought over 3,000 slaves from Africa to the Western Hemisphere in this period. The three ships for which mortality statistics exist reveal 96 of 108, 230 of 257, and 90 of 101 slaves captured arrived alive. This suggests that either the Jewish merchants were more careful with their cargo than their gentile counterparts, or that historians who estimate the death rate on the voyages at what is considered a low 10 percent may use Lopez and Rodrigues to support their theory. Other Newport Jews who invested in one slave ship each were Isaac and Moses Elizer (1762), Naphtali Hart Jr. (1764), and Moses Levy (1765). Slaves and free blacks also figured prominently in Newport maritime life: Aaron Lopez's account books frequently mention the sale and employment of Negroes.[12]

Yet slavery was only a small part of the Newport Jews' extensive trade, and Newport Jews themselves were responsible for only a small part of the trade. The canard that the slave trade was primarily Jewish is a lie fostered by the anti-semitic Nation of Islam.[13] Jewish merchants offered manufactured goods from London, sold rum, and exchanged currency. They manufactured "Scotch Snuff," introduced the manufacture of soap (in 1705) and potash (in 1753), and worked as silversmiths and tailors.[14] Especially notable were the Massachusetts and Rhode Island partnerships formed in 1761 to monopolize the manufacture and sale of candles and oil from the thriving whaling industry. Twenty-six people representing nine partnerships joined, six of them Newport Jews: four members of the Hart family, Aaron Lopez, and Jacob Rodrigues Rivera. Lopez joined up with Henry Collins, a non-Jewish partner for this venture. And it was the three firms containing Jews (Collins and Rodrigues, the Harts, and Lopez) who had the dubious satisfaction of complaining that their gentile counterparts were the ones conforming to the Jewish stereotype by cheating their colleagues and selling below the stipulated price. Thus, a new, stronger agreement was signed in 1763, this time by the four reshuffled Jewish partnerships now in this business—Aaron Lopez and his brother Moses (as two separate firms), the Harts, and Rodrigues—which fixed the proportions each firm could enjoy of the trade as well as the prices for buying and selling the valued "head matter" from the sperm whales. The four Jewish firms were allotted 33 percent, precisely a third, of the business, although interlopers soon made the agreement unenforceable.[15]

Close Jewish-gentile relations in Rhode Island also appear in a mutual willingness to flout British trade regulations. When in 1758, two of Naphtali and Isaac Hart's vessels were seized for illegal trade, gentile merchant Obadiah Brown offered him "every assistance in my power" in an unsuccessful attempt to recover them. (In 1763, the Harts' ships were carrying Dutch as well as British papers on illegal voyages to Spanish Hispanola and Dutch St. Eustatia.) In January 1769, Aaron Lopez warned his friend and fellow whaler Nicholas Brown "that our Man of War's Tender [small boat] is this day to visit your river." In May, Brown returned the favor. Newport and Providence merchants could thus keep each other informed of the activities of itinerant British customs inspectors and thereby avoid detection.[16]

While cooperating with gentile merchants, Newport's Jews, like their brethren in New York and Philadelphia, quarreled among themselves and took their disputes to the courts and newspapers in an effort to obtain vindication and keep themselves respectable in the eyes of gentile society. In 1763, Myer Polock was arrested on the complaint of fellow merchant Isaac Howland on the grounds that he "uttered scandalous words about Isaac to wit 'that he [Isaac] was a damned rogue and he could prove it'" and that he had cheated one Levy about some tea. Naphtali Hart provided bail for Polock. While the case's outcome is not known, it shows Jewish merchants were greatly concerned about their business reputations and did not hesitate to sue each other to protect their image in the eyes of the larger community.[17]

Another Polock, Isaac, ran afoul of Isaac Elizer by failing to return to him thirty-four hundred pounds of Spanish candles that Elizer had posted to secure a debt of Polock to Jacob Isaacs. Polock attempted to influence the jury determining the case by publishing his side of the story in the _New-_

port Mercury, leading at least one juror to change his mind and affirm that Polock was an "honest man" rather than a "villain." Elizer in turn sued Polock for trying "to ruin and destroy his trade and business and for subjecting him to grievous pains and penalties." In addition to publishing his account, Polock called Elizer "a villain, a rascal . . . a damned thief and a liar" to his face in front of "a large gathering," some of whom restrained the two men from coming to blows. Isaacs and Polock also nearly rumbled when Isaacs told Polock he would rather fight him than take him to court. The cause of the dispute, according to one witness, was that Polock was preparing a ship to sell twenty-four thousand Spanish candles, including Elizer's, in England, but Elizer had received information that Polock "would run away to Holland with the vessel and cargo," and therefore "hindered the voyage" from taking place.[18]

Quarrels among the Jews extended across the ocean as well. The businesses of a number of Newport Jewish merchants failed in 1772, including that of Naphtali Hart Jr., who left for Barbados to seek his fortune. There he found "several Christian merchants who would have readily contributed towards my getting into business could they have proposed any business to my advantage." His real problem was the island's established Jews, who, he claimed, "have ruined the [shopkeeping] trade," selling at artificially low prices for a short time to eliminate new competitors. Nor would any of the Jews help him out: "there is no sincerity in our society, being jealous of each other," he wrote to Aaron Lopez, pleading for any kind of help he could give.[19]

Rhode Island Jews also associated freely and on equal terms with gentiles as participants in Newport's eighteenth-century Enlightenment. Dean George Berkeley, future Anglican bishop and well-known philosopher, arrived in Newport in 1729 and stayed for several years. In 1730 he founded the Philosophical Society for the Promotion of Knowledge and Virtue, By Free Conversation, coincidentally, or perhaps not, about the same time Benjamin Franklin—whose brother James was a Rhode Island printer—was forming the Library Company and Junto in Philadelphia. An observer noted that while the Baptist and Church of England preachers refused to consider Berkeley's radical teaching that we can only perceive ideas directly rather than the external world itself, "the Quaker preacher and the Jewish Rabbi," while "alike tenacious of their rules of doctrine," nevertheless "listened respectfully to the preaching of Berkeley." Jews Abraham Hart, Moses Lopez, and Jacob Rodrigues Rivera were among the founders of Newport's first library, the Redwood. Aaron Lopez and other members of the Hart family joined them in purchasing books for that institution. Rodrigues left all his books except for his copy of the books of Moses to the library, along with "his gold and silver valuables" and "silver-hilted sword." The college that became Brown University was another object of Jewish charity. Aaron Lopez contributed five thousand feet of boards and Rivera ten thousand for its construction, even though the colonial legislature took the site of the college from Newport and gave it to Providence after it had promised the institution to the city that contributed the most. Jews were also prominent among the city's Masons: fifteen belonged to St. John's Lodge in midcentury. In 1780, after the British troops had abandoned the city, sixteen Jews organized King David's Lodge under the tutelage of Moses Michael Hays, who in 1768 had introduced Scottish rite Masonry to British North America in New York, where he had resided at the time. Hays had held the highest post a Mason could in North America—deputy inspector general—and until the Newport Jewish community dissolved in the 1790s most members and officers of King David's Lodge were Jewish. Comparing Stiles's estimate of the number of Jews with the Masonic membership lists, nearly all the town's Jewish males sat as equals beside their gentile brethren in these fraternal, Enlightened lodges.[20]

Newport Jews were also the target of non-Jews who tried to enter the community to claim the charitable services Jews extended to each other. Jews who came to Newport were allowed to join the community. Such people began arriving in the 1760s. In 1767, Aaron Lopez wrote that one Emmanuel Rodrigues, "who I thought might be a Jew, is I suspect a Negro and is related somehow or other as a servant of a client of Abraham Lopez of Jamaica. He seems to be a free man but there is no proof either way." Jacob Jackson, too, who was warned out of town, was another Negro who was trying to pass as Jewish. At the time, southern New England was host to a community of blacks, Indians, and poor whites who lived and intermarried with each other and performed menial labor when they could find employment. This community's existence and solidarity is suggested by the threat accompanying the five-dollar reward Isaac Elizer offered four times in the *Newport Mercury* in May 1769, for his "Negro woman named Bina."

He warned that "those who harbor her may depend upon being prose-cuted."[21]

Assuming that at least some Iberian and Caribbean Sephardic Jews were relatively dark-skinned, it made sense for members of this multiracial underclass to attempt to pass as Jews. If successful, as Rodrigues and Lopez were not—the names they used suggest they hoped to claim kinship with the city's two richest Jewish families—they could avail themselves of the charity Jews generally practiced toward their coreligionists. Otherwise, they would suffer the warning out of town and other hazards of life endured by a marginal community. For poor Jews who were accepted, things were much better. In 1770 Aaron Lopez delivered to a Mrs. Lazarus fourteen pounds of rice, a pound of tea, two pounds of chocolate, and thirty-nine pounds of biscuits on behalf of the congregation. In his will, Jacob Rodrigues Rivera, who died in 1789, left ten pounds to the poor of this city. His charity extended to an African American, but only to one who had per-sonally assisted him. "In consideration of the fidelity of my faithful black servant Grace, and for divers, other good causes and considerations," Lopez freed her and left her ten dollars.[22]

In addition to cooperating with the gentile elite, Newport's wealthy Jews also founded institutions of their own, notably the synagogue that still stands on what is now Touro Street. Even before it was finished, it impressed visitors, such as English traveler Andrew Burnaby in 1760. He found the city in general "handsome," but with "few buildings in it worth notice." Those that were had been designed by the former British sea cap-tain Peter Harrison, who introduced the Palladium style of architecture to British North America. Harrison had already completed the "handsome public [Redwood] Library . . . in the form of a Greek temple" (1748). "The foundation of a very pretty building . . . for the use of the Freemasons" and plans for a "very elegant" public market, although not finished until 1772, were also Harrison's work. But pride of place went to "the Jew's syna-gogue," the only one of eight houses of worship in the city built of brick rather than wood and the only one Burnaby considered "worth looking at." Burnaby praised the incomplete structure as "extremely elegant within" but with an outside destined to be "totally spoilt by a school, which the Jews would have annexed to it for the use of the children." But in fact the facade was not spoiled: because the ark that housed the Law had to face to the east, and Griffin Street was at a thirty-degree angle to due east, Harrison designed the structure so the school remained invisible from the road. (Griffin Street was later renamed Touro Street after the congregation's greatest benefactor.) As with his other projects, all of which may still be viewed in Newport today, Harrison did his work for the Jews without a fee. He could afford it: his wife, Elizabeth Pelham, had inherited some twenty thousand pounds, and Harrison himself was a successful merchant and commercial farmer.[23]

Harrison could forgo his fee, but despite the fact that several Jews were among Newport's most prosperous inhabitants, the congregation's members could not or would not fund the building by themselves. Two appeals to New York's established Jewish congregation and more than four years passed between the laying of the cornerstones on August 1, 1759, and the synagogue's dedication on December 2, 1763.[24]

That Newport's Jews preferred to wait four years and rely on outside assistance to complete the town's most elegant house of worship rather than erect a simple, functional structure—like the Mill Street synagogue in New York—suggests the synagogue was not built merely to honor God, but to establish a symbolic architectural superiority over the Christian churches in the town. Jews, the architecture implied, were Enlightened individuals, worthy of citizenship, not practitioners of an archaic faith. The synagogue on the outside resembled a large private dwelling rather than a church, implying that Jews did not wish to stand out as the "special nation" their enemies considered them. Furthermore, it stood on a hill above the town, next to a smaller Baptist church, with the cemetery even further up the hill. While Jewish cemeteries were traditionally positioned away from Christian population centers to avoid desecration, the synagogue's location was clearly meant to call attention to the building: it both stood above the town and beside the Baptist meeting house, another group persecuted elsewhere but welcomed in Rhode Island. The synagogue also had a trap door, as did the Amsterdam synagogue and many others in Europe as a possible escape from an attack. But the trap door led nowhere, except to a small room in the cellar. The Jews, it seems, were expressing their confidence that that they would never need to use this emergency exit.

The ceremony dedicating the synagogue was as impressive as its beautiful interior. Ezra Stiles observed that "it began with a handsome procession" followed by prayers and "finely sung" psalms. "There were present many ladies and gentlemen" of the town, indicating the integration of Newport's thriving Jewish elite with its gentile counterpart. "The Order and Decorum, the Harmony & solemnity of the music, together with a handsome Assembly of People, in a[n] Edifice the most perfect of the kind perhaps raised in America, & splendidly illuminated, could not but raise in the mind a faint Idea of the Majesty & Grandeur of the Ancient Jewish Worship mentioned in the Scripture." The building itself Stiles considered "superbly finished inside at a cost of £2000 sterling." He was equally impressed that the books of law were three vellum volumes imported from Amsterdam that were over two hundred years old. Establishing such an impressive house of worship prompted Rhode Island's Jews to change their congregation's name from Nephutsé (the Scattered) to Yeshuat (the Salvation) of Israel. Perhaps in keeping with either Harrison's or the congregation's Enlightenment tendencies, the women's gallery, unlike in the New York synagogue, offered an open view of the ground floor.[25]

Along with the synagogue, the first Jewish social club in British North America was founded in 1761, proudly proclaiming the coming of age of Newport's Jews. It also suggested resentment of a Rhode Island government that had just denied naturalization to Aaron Lopez and Isaac Elizer, leading contributors given the honor of laying two of the synagogue's six cornerstones (there were six rather than four due to the annexed schoolhouse). Yet the club's rules established it as a strictly secular association: anyone who brought up synagogue affairs would have to pay a fine of four bottles of good wine, the same penalty for those who would "behave unruly, curse, swear, or offer fight." These penalties, along with annual dues and the requirement members approve of all newcomers, made sure poor Jews had no more chance than gentiles of belonging to the club. Meeting every Wednesday for five hours, the members would play cards (for low stakes, "to avoid the name of a gaming club") and then have a supper and discussion for two hours.[26]

Newport Jews thus insisted on a costly yet architecturally impressive synagogue to impress Christians while simultaneously forming an exclusive social club even though they frequently dined, conversed, did business, and (presumably) played cards with Christians as well. The founding of these two associations illustrates the complicated nature of Jewish ethnic identity in the mid-eighteenth century. Jews wanted total acceptance without total assimilation; they wanted to maintain a distinctive religion and culture while achieving equal status as Britons and later Americans. The gentile community, on the other hand, granted the Jews social acceptance but refused to give them political rights (see the later discussion).

More than anyone else in early America, Newport's Congregational minister, Rev. Dr. Ezra Stiles, not only sought to bring the Jews into mainstream society, but he displayed an unequaled interest in Jewish culture and had an unparalleled personal relationship with both Newport Jews and those who visited them. He frequently attended the synagogue and debated theological subjects with Jews. For instance, he, a visiting rabbi, and Jacob Rodrigues Rivera argued, without reaching a conclusion, whether a man who had been married twice would be married to his first or second wife in Heaven. With another visiting rabbi, Stiles also debated whether Abraham, Isaac, and Moses would still observe Old Testament dietary laws after the Messiah came, and whether circumcision would still be practiced. The rabbi voted yes on both counts, Stiles no. Since the rabbi was also a jeweler, Stiles took advantage of the opportunity to assess the value of some pearls that he owned: he was pleased to discover they were worth about one hundred pounds. Yet even Stiles could write, upon attending a Jewish service, "how melancholy to behold an Assembly of Worshippers of Jehovah, Open and Professed Enemies to a crucified Jesus." Stiles liked Jews, admired them, and socialized with them, but still hoped to obtain their conversion and harbored a deep hostility toward their faith he did not express openly to them.[27]

In most cases, such as membership in the Masons or Redwood library or contempt for religious enthusiasts, class, gentility, and education mattered more in Newport social relations than religion. In 1772, the seventy-three-year-old Jacob Pipels of Shippensburg, Pennsylvania, an Irishman who came to America in 1736, visited Newport and told Stiles about his visions. He claimed that he would live to 218 years of age, that the Jews would return to Palestine, and that he had encounters with angels. A visiting rabbi from Poland and the local hazan Abraham Touro called on Stiles while he was listening to these rantings. When Pipels repeated his visions, the rabbi asked him what color the angel was before assuring him that he had seen no such thing. The "whimsical visionary," as Stiles termed Pipels, was offended by this "humor and sarcasm," which persuaded him to "cross the ferries and return to Pennsylvania."[28]

Yet on the very same day he and his colleagues were making fun of Pipels, Stiles purchased a Zohar, a book of Jewish mysticism, for the considerable sum of twenty-two shillings, six pence. He spent a good deal of time discussing its prophecies and the possible date the Messiah would come with the six rabbis whose acquaintance he was proud to make as they visited Newport between 1759 and 1775, five of them between 1772 and 1775, when Newport Jewry was at its zenith. For instance, in 1773 he and the Reverend Chaim Carigal from Hebron in Palestine talked about whether the Zohar's prediction that Edom should conquer the Israelites really meant "the Russians should conquer the Turks, or whether the pillar of salt that was formerly Lot's wife still stood"—the Turks unfortunately prevented Jews from visiting the site and obtaining verification. When they parted, Stiles assured Carigal of his lifelong "affection" and expressed the hope that "we might after Death meet together in the Garden of Eden and there rejoice with Abraham Isaac and Jacob, and with the Soul of the Messiah till the Resurrection," feelings and wishes Carigal reciprocated. Stiles thought so highly of Carigal that when the rabbi died and Stiles had become president of Yale College, he and Aaron Lopez arranged for Carigal's portrait to hang at the college. Lopez told Stiles that this act "manifest[ed] your unbounded benevolence and most exalted sympathy with the literary world, in which you made so respectable a part."[29]

Unlike many Newport Jews, Carigal took a stand against British violations of American liberty. A sermon he preached at the synagogue in Newport on May 28, 1773, "the Salvation of Israel," which was translated from English into Spanish and published, had two meanings. It could be read by Newport Jews as an exhortation to remain true to their religion and await the Messiah. But the text was addressed to an audience that included the Massachusetts loyalist judges Peter Oliver and Robert Auchmuty; Rhode Island's governor, Gideon Wanton; and other gentiles as well as the Jews. It could just as easily appeal to Americans who feared that apparently minor British encroachments on their rights would only lead to a full-fledged enslavement by those contemplating tyranny. Carigal compared a tyrant's assault on the body politic to the first symptoms of a disease of the human body: "we despise the first attack of the enemy, which working with the

greatest vigilance, and meeting with no opposition, slyly and by impercep-
tible degrees insinuates himself into the fortress of our constitution till at
last taking sufficient possession, doest not fear to show himself in public
with the greatest boldness."

While warning his audience to be vigilant, Carigal also told them God
would punish tyrants: he pointed to the death of the Roman emperor Titus
after only two years on the throne "in the prime of his age" following the
destruction of Jerusalem, and the madness of Nebuchadnezzar, who had
earlier destroyed the first temple, as tyrants who merited divine punishment. Comparing the calamities of the ancient Jews to those that threatened
the present age, Carigal offered advice on the divine meaning of history:

> There have not been wanting some critical men, who, because they
> know something of the ancient histories, think they are able to pene-
> trate the natural causes of the rise, increase, and decline of empires and
> republics. This they dare to utter not thinking at the same time, that
> such public commotions and revolutions are effects proceeding from
> the council of the divine creator, who establishes and destroys king-
> doms and empires for reasons reserved only to his infinite wisdom. . . .
> With the same liberty and arrogance with which these men talk of the
> misfortunes and calamities of other nations, they have been bold
> enough to speak of those of ours.

When Carigal spoke of "our" nation, he could either have been referring
to the Jews or to the British nation, which also modeled itself on Roman
and biblical examples. He was telling Newport's Jews to remain faithful to
their religious roots while at the same time telling British Americans to preserve their constitution. He reaffirmed that both British America and its
small Jewish population had important roles to play in God's plans for
humanity. He need not have worried on the latter score: Newport's Jews,
like many of their Christian counterparts, expected an imminent millennium. As Stiles noted, in "Thunder Storms [they] set open all their doors
and windows for the coming of Messias." During one "amazingly violent"
July hailstorm in 1769 they also "employed themselves in Singing and
repeating Prayers &c for Meeting Messias." The previous year, the Jews of
New York had predicted the Messiah's arrival based on biblical numerol-
ogy suggested by a visiting rabbi.[30]

If Stiles was interested in Jewish mysticism, his efforts to convert the Jews were in vain. Otherwise enlightened and secular Jews resolutely clung to their faith. Stiles would invite visiting Jews to sit in his own pew, a place of honor in his church. A Jew was among the young men who visited him to discuss religion one evening in 1773, but failed to be convinced by Stiles's arguments that the Messiah's duty was to suffer. In 1771, Enoch Lyon spent four hours with Stiles. They examined the Talmud and rabbinical writings they both had studied, along with the Bible. Stiles had no trouble persuading Lyon that sin was both original and "infinitely Evil," and Lyon "allowed Jesus to be a holy and good man." But the Jew did not "see the necessity of Satisfaction or a Messiah's Atonement," reasoning such sacrifice was superfluous, "God being infinitely merciful."[31]

Cupid, however, could succeed where reason failed. In 1771, Stiles reported that a Miss Polock, aged about fifteen, was sent by her family, one of the major Newport mercantile clans, to attend a writing school with Christian girls. As a genteel young lady, she could obtain the necessary social connections and graces in no other way. But the schoolmaster did not confine his instruction to worldly matters, and "often gave religious advice and exhortations to the students." Miss Polock soon expressed the wish to become a Christian, which caused her family to keep her at home. But they could not keep her from hearing the great evangelist George Whitefield on his final trip to America (he died in Rhode Island in 1771) and "greatly admiring his promise of the Gospel of Christ," or from reading the New Testament together with a young Christian who fell in love with her, which "highly displeased" the Jewish community.[32]

Stiles hoped his Savior would accomplish in the next world what he could not in this. He mourned the death of his friend Aaron Lopez, expressing the wish that he would join such "amiable and excellent" characters as Socrates, Pope Clement XIV(!), and seventeenth-century Amsterdam rabbi Manasseh ben Israel in paradise. There, Stiles hoped, "the virtuous and good of all nations and religions, notwithstanding their delusions, may be brought together in paradise." However, this reunion would be based on the "Christian system," where "sincere, pious, and candid" minds would realize "that Jesus was the Messiah predicted by Moses and the Prophets."[33]

An even better friend to Lopez than Stiles was Captain Benjamin

Wright, a New England sea captain who sailed Lopez's ships and managed his commercial affairs in the American South and the West Indies from 1768 until Lopez's death. Wright jocularly called himself "Yankey Doudle" and, when continental paper depreciated during the Revolution, "Redemption Doudle." He and Lopez could joke about religion, especially the Presbyterians, whom neither of them liked. When Lopez was visiting Boston and Wright staying at Lopez's Leicester, Massachusetts, estate, where he removed from Newport to avoid the war, Wright wondered why his friend was inclined "to tarry among a people who by their own confession are strongly attached to the political Laws and government of inferno." Meanwhile, he, Wright, was "living on the fat of the Land," his "attendance fit for a nobleman." Wright chided Lopez that he had taken in so many Jewish refugees "that your family at present are in a number only 99 and still there is room for one more." He tried to make Lopez both smile and return home by warning him that "your family if I mistake not, incline to embrace the Presbyterian Faith, a Religion of All Now Extant [that] is the most Fatal to Humanity and Common Honesty, frought with Superstition and Oppression," adding, as if a revolutionary censor were watching, "whatever I may think I will not say Rebellion." That an elite Jew and an Anglican captain would make common cause against what they considered the sanctimonious piety of Massachusetts and Connecticut, which they termed Presbyterian—they were actually Dr. Stiles's fellow Congregationalists—makes sense given the loyalism or neutrality of most of the Newport merchant community and the revolutionary ardor of its rivals at Boston and New London.[34]

Yet when it came to obtaining full political rights, even the friendship of leading merchants and divines could not help Rhode Island Jews. In 1750, Moses Lopez successfully petitioned the Rhode Island assembly for both naturalization and exemption from taxes on the grounds that he had "for several years past, translated letters and papers from the Spanish into English for the use of the government, which he has declined being paid for." Three years later he introduced potash manufacturing to America. In December 1760, James Lucena was naturalized as well, probably as a prelude to granting him a ten-year monopoly on the manufacture of Castile soap, the "true method" of which he had acquired from the king's manufactory in Portugal, an item that would not only furnish "a great and valuable article of commerce which may be exported to all parts of the continent and, to the West Indies, &c," while "employ[ing] many poor people" to boot. There is no evidence that three Jews who served with the Rhode Island contingent in colonial wars, Jacob Judah (1747), Michael Isaacs (1755), and Isaac Moses (1757), were naturalized.[35]

Rhode Island's denial of Aaron Lopez and Isaac Elizer's petition in 1761 for freemanship, which would have granted them full political rights, is thus easy to understand. No Jew in Rhode Island had previously attained freemanship, as opposed to naturalization, which did not carry political rights, the assembly noted after the Superior Court had dumped the petition in its lap. In a colony founded upon "the holy Christian faith and worship," the lawmakers argued that "the said Aaron Lopez hath declared himself to be by religion a Jew, [and] this Assembly doth not admit him nor any other of that religion to the full freedom of the colony . . . to be chosen into any office . . . nor allowed to give a vote as a freeman." Rhode Island's upper house, the next body to receive the petition, in turn, suggested that Lopez and Elizer apply to the Superior Court for the less encompassing privilege of naturalization according to the 1740 act of Parliament. This they did in March 1762. This privilege would merely confirm the de facto rights all Rhode Jews enjoyed to engage in trade, receive the protection of the law, and exercise their religion.

Here, too, however, Aaron Lopez and Isaac Elizer failed where Moses Lopez and James Lucena had succeeded. The court ruled that the 1740 act of Parliament permitting naturalization of Jews was intended for "increasing the number of inhabitants in the plantations, but this colony being already so full of people that many of his majesty's good subjects . . . have removed," there was no need to attract more people to tiny Rhode Island—not to mention the fact that Lopez and Elizer were already there. Invoking as well the letter of the Charter of 1663 and a law Rhode Island passed to confirm it, the court piously observed that "by the charter granted to this colony, it appears that the free and quiet enjoyment of the Christian religion and a desire of propagating the same were the principal views with which this colony was settled." Thus Lopez and Elizer's request was "absolutely inconsistent with the first principles upon which the colony was founded."[36]

Why were Lopez and Elizer turned downed for naturalization? One possibility is Jews only received this honor when, like Moses Lopez and James Lucena, they had rendered notable service to the colony. Also, although not involved in politics directly, Lopez and Elizer were members of the political faction favored by the mercantile elite and led by Newport's Stephen Ward. The Ward group was usually the minority in a legislature more often dominated by the colony's farmers, who were supported by Newport's commercial rival, Providence. Its leader, Samuel Hopkins, won seven of the ten annual gubernatorial elections he contested with Ward in the 1750s and 1760s. Rhode Island elections, in which all freemen voted for all colony-wide officials, could be extremely close; in 1764 Hopkins won the governorship over Ward by 24 votes. That year, four members of the Superior Court won their seats by 3, and one member by 1, out of 3,960 votes cast. Voters could submit proxies if they did not come to the polls, and it was customary for candidates to question the eligibility of the opposition's voters in close cases. Thus, had the two Jewish merchants been allowed to vote in 1761, they could have swung a major election not only in Newport, but in Rhode Island itself. The right to vote was a matter of money, not just of principle. Elizer and Lopez were two of the ten Jews who complained in 1762 to the Rhode Island General Assembly that a new tax "was very unequally proportioned" and that the men entrusted with rating the taxpayers had done so in a "negligent, careless, and partial manner."[37]

Samuel Ward, leader of an opposing faction, however, was chief justice of Rhode Island when Lopez and Elizer submitted their petition.[38] Thus, Ezra Stiles was undoubtedly correct when he stressed that a populist anti-semitism in colonial political culture was at least one important reason for their rejection. Enough assembly delegates and at least three of five superior court justices regardless of faction were opposed to Jewish rights. Stiles noted that bringing up the question of Jewish rights, even if the practical consequences were trivial, became a symbolic way Christians could assert their religion's superiority. In Britain, Stiles noted, the naturalization act of 1740 produced "such a national disgust towards the Hebrews" that "the Jews themselves joined in petition to Parliament to repeal the act." Stiles also remembered the "tumult at New York" in 1737, when Jews were disqualified in an election where they may have cast the deciding votes. At the time of the application for naturalization and when Newport Jews were having the Touro synagogue constructed, a local poet called it the "synagogue of Satan." Such anti-semitism lay in the back of Lopez's mind when he wrote to John Nazro, nearly two decades later, that "the foolish abuse of determining People's honesty by the bigness of his Thumb should be abolished," with the "thumb" standing in for the stereotypical Jewish nose.[39]

If anything, the setting in which Lopez and Elizer were refused by the Superior Court was even more humiliating than the petition's denial. Whether or not "designedly, or accidental in proceeding upon the business of the court," Stiles observed that the Jews learned "their almost equally mortifying sentence" right after three felons had been tried and found guilty. Stiles could only regret that "Providence seems to make every thing work for the mortification of the Jews, and to prevent their incorporating into any nation."[40]

Rejected in Rhode Island, Lopez and Elizer obtained their naturalization elsewhere. Lopez was well connected to the Boston merchant Henry Lloyd, brother-in-law of attorney Samuel Fitch, who advised him that after residing a short time in Massachusetts he could become naturalized there. Swansea's representative Jerathmeel Bowers, who owed Lopez some money, put him up at his house, and the Massachusetts Superior Court approved Lopez's naturalization after he had lived there for three weeks. In 1763, Elizer in turn obtained his naturalization with no difficulty from the New York legislature, a colony where Jews routinely voted and held office.[41]

Significantly, New York, the mainland colony with perhaps the most Anglicized and conservative politics, was also the only one with an enfranchised community of Jews. Massachusetts had few or no Jews, but its leading citizens who helped Lopez—including Superior Court justices Thomas Hutchinson, Peter Oliver, and province secretary Andrew Oliver—became loyalists, and were at the pinnacle of the colonial elite, whereas Rhode Island's assembly was the hotbed of democratic politics. On the other hand, when it came to protesting the Stamp Act three years later, the leader of the Massachusetts popular party, James Otis Jr., trotted out the familiar trio of "Turks, Jews and infidels" as the driving force behind the "little, dirty, drinking, drabbling, contaminated knot of thieves, beggars, and transports" who were hoping to cure Rhode Island's "radical distemper" by replacing its democratic constitution with a royally appointed governor and council similar to the other colonies. There is no evidence Lopez or any other Jews were in fact associated with the "Newport Junto," a group of merchants and royal officials, including Martin Howard Jr., an Anglican lawyer, and George Rome, a London mercantile agent and Newport's second highest taxpayer. But in defending colonial Stamp Act protestors from Howard's criticism in *A Vindication of the British Colonies Against the Aspersions of a Halifax Gentleman,* Otis tried to make political hay by linking Newport's supporters of royal authority with the unpopular Jews.[42]

Otis's charges were somewhat plausible because unlike their counterparts in New York and Philadelphia, Newport's merchants, including its Jews, in fact showed little support for colonial opposition to British authority. To be sure, like most colonial merchants, they had no problem petitioning against new trade regulations and taxes. In 1764, forty-six Newport merchants, including five Jews, addressed the Rhode Island General Assembly to protest the recent crackdown on illegal trade. Referring to the depression in trade after the French and Indian War, they pleaded "that at this time, when our commerce is restrained and circumscribed within very narrow limits, and under the most discouraging situation, our circumstances are rendered still more deplorable by the grievous exactions of His Majesty's Custom House Office, who without any Pretence of law or Equity have burdened our trade with the most unreasonable and exorbitant impositions." Complaining that the city's commerce was in danger of being "entirely ruined" and that several vessels in the coastal trade had already been forced out of business, the merchants called for the assembly to retaliate on the customs officers by prohibiting them "from taking any greater Fees than they shall be allowed by law under such penalties as shall be thought sufficient to put a stop to this evil." The following year, too, Newport's Jewish merchants joined with Americans throughout the continent in protesting the Stamp Act in writing.[43]

But then things changed. Newport merchants in general remained aloof from the nonimportation agreements that Providence, Boston, New York, Philadelphia, and other seaports implemented to protest the Townshend Acts beginning in 1767. In 1770, Nicholas Brown shared with Aaron Lopez a copy of a letter from the New York nonimportation enforcement committee to the one in Boston, expressing regret that the Rhode Islanders' refusal to attend a meeting to coordinate efforts by the several ports would "give such offence as will do great injury to the cause." By then, Newport's continued importation despite some half-hearted commitments to cease was so obnoxious that these same cities imposed a boycott on Newport itself. Providence merchant Samuel Nightingale, who trusted his correspondent to keep his identity secret, warned Lopez that the Bostonians were preparing to send a committee to "inflame the inhabitants to oblige the importers" to cease their trade. Following in Otis's footsteps, the Bostonians made scapegoats of Newport's Jews for the town's unpatriotic behavior, sending word to newspapers in other cities that "several persons, chiefly Jews," had imported goods from England and failed to warehouse them, contrary to their "plighted promise." Newport's own patriots, such as merchant William Vernon, agreed. He claimed that "the trifle of goods we have Imported here" were brought in "chiefly by Jews this spring and summer," which "caused the resentment of the colonies" to fall once again on Rhode Island's leading port. Ezra Stiles, too, gave "five or six Jews" pride of place over "three or 4 Tories" among Rhode Islanders who had drawn "down [such intercolonial] Vengeance upon" the city, suggesting he, too, scapegoated the Jews for a practice general among Newport merchants.[44]

The Newport Jews' lack of involvement in resistance to Britain and friendliness toward royal officials led Stiles to give credence to a story told to him by a Captain Peck of London. Peck claimed there was "a secret *Intelligence office* in London in the street where the Jews live," containing some thirty clerks who corresponded with and paid agents all over America to spy on the patriots, an "entirely Jew affair." Fortunately, Stiles asked Henry Marchant, Rhode Island's colonial agent and a friend of the Jews, for confirmation. Marchant told Stiles he was "mistaken about the ministerial Jew-store," but it speaks volumes about the political stance of Newport's Jews that Stiles would even consider such a story believable.[45]

Two years later, Stiles was angry that "Mr. Aaron Lopez, a Jew merchant in this town" had profited handsomely by his refusal to participate in the "late combinations of American merchants against importations . . . and against the exorbitant fees of the customhouses." Newport's customs officials supposedly rewarded Lopez by showing him "all lenity and favor," exempting the captains of his twenty-some vessels from swearing that they were paying their duties and importing nothing illegal. Meanwhile, "the oath is strictly exacted of all who were concerned in the non-importation agreement." When some of Lopez's goods were once accidentally seized, he was allowed to buy them back at a price less than the duty he would have paid. Lopez was also guilty by association. Among the guests at his home were the commander of the British ship policing the Newport harbor and Chief Justice Daniel Horsmanden of New York, who came to investigate the burning near Providence of the British customs vessel *Gaspée*.[46]

In 1774, Newport patriot John Collins blamed the town's Jews for violating yet another nonimportation agreement that followed in response to Britain's dumping East India Company tea on the colonial market. Eleven days after the Boston Tea Party, Lopez in the *Newport Mercury* assured his fellow inhabitants that his ship the *Jacob* had imported no tea. Gentile Newport merchants were importing tea, but the special scrutiny suffered by Lopez may be attributed to his past behavior, his religion, and his exceptional wealth. Still, Lopez was a leading culprit. Early in 1774 he had ten chests shipped in from Dutch St. Eustatia. Perhaps it was no coincidence that Newport's Jewish burial ground, located outside the residential area of the town, suffered desecration about this time. In March 1775, it required both substantial repairs and a padlock to keep children and vandals from hurting the monuments. (Boys were important agents of colonial protest, since their "frolics" could be excused as youthful and apolitical.) As late as 1778, Lopez's agents purchased a ship, the *Hope*, in Jamaica, and attempted to import a valuable cargo of sugar, rum, and fruit. Lopez claimed that he took out British papers listing Halifax, Nova Scotia, as the ship's destination merely so it could escape from Jamaica and avoid capture on the high seas. But Connecticut privateers rather than the royal navy captured the vessel. Although the incriminating papers were tossed overboard, the *Hope's* log and location were considered presumptive evidence of trading with the enemy. Lopez made several trips to Hartford and even personally visited Congress in Philadelphia to plead for the *Hope's* return, obtaining testimony from various notables including General John Sullivan, commander of the American forces in Rhode Island, that he "had ever proved himself by the most conspicuous and open conduct to be a warm friend to the rights of America." Yet the case dragged on for five years, and only in September 1783, more than a year after Lopez's death, was the ship freed from the "thieves" of the "government of inferno," as two of Lopez's associates termed Connecticut authorities.[47]

Lopez was not among the six Newport Jews—Nathan Hart, Isaac Hart, Moses Seixas, Hyam Levi (Hyman Levy), Moses Levy, and the Reverend

Mr. (Abraham) Touro—listed by Stiles among the town's twenty-eight "principal and active tories," all of whom who remained during the British occupation that began in December 1776. But Lopez was no revolutionary either. As when he cultivated the friendship of the naval and customs officials who guarded Newport harbor while at the same time contributing to Nicholas Brown's college and other local institutions, he did what was best for business and sought to keep on good terms with anyone who could help or harm his personal affairs. In the summer of 1775, in partnership with Francis Rotch, co-owner of the *Dartmouth,* which had been the subject of the Boston Tea Party, Lopez undertook a major whaling expedition to the South Atlantic that involved twenty ships and cost nearly forty thousand pounds. On the one hand, Lopez had no qualms about seeking American exemption for two of his vessels to depart despite a Massachusetts wartime embargo, obtaining letters testifying that "the whole tenor of Mr. Lopez's conduct as a merchant hath been wholly unexceptionable," and that as a "fair trader" he had "ever from principle paid a strict attention to the resolves of the Continental Congress." On the other hand, when five of his vessels were seized "without any cause" in Britain, he and Rotch petitioned Lord North that they were "innocently and unexpectedly involved in difficulty"—a fine reward for having "employed a considerable capital for the establishment of a branch of fishery" encouraged by Parliament and "producing salutary effects to these kingdoms." It took two petitions and three months (November 1775–February 1776) to obtain release of the vessels, but Lopez and Rotch were successful. To prepare for future contingencies, the partners represented Lopez as a resident of Jamaica (Rotch resided in London) to exempt their ships from further seizures. While successfully escaping both American and British authorities, the whaling vessels were much less fortunate in their dealings with Mother Nature: most of the ships were wrecked. Shortly thereafter, Lopez contributed a whale boat and gunpowder to aid Rhode Island's revolutionary effort.[48]

Lopez, his father-in-law Jacob Rodrigues Rivera, his sons and nephews Moses, Jacob, and Joseph, and his son-in-law Abraham Mendes were among about two thousand Newporters, some 40 percent of the population, who left town to avoid British raids and then an occupation that lasted from December 1776 until the fall of 1779. The Lopez clan moved to Leicester, Massachusetts, where Lopez wrote that in "these times of publick and almost universal calamity," his extended family was able to live "secured from sudden alarms and the cruel ravages of an enraged enemy." Lopez claimed that he "experienced the civilities and hospitality of a kind neighborhood."[49] Indeed, if we add these three Jews to the six Tories, at least nine of Newport's adult Jewish males did not support the Revolution, while only seven favored it: Jacob Isaac, who provided supplies, and Solomon Rophee, David Sarzedas, Abraham Seixas, Samuel Benjamin, and Moses and Abraham Isaacs, who joined the army. Unlike the loyalists and neutrals, no one bearing any of these surnames appeared among the top 10 percent of Newport taxpayers in 1772, although the Seixas family ranked among the intercolonial Jewish elite with members in Rhode Island, Charleston, and New York. The allegiances of Newport Jews suggest a class revolution comparable to that experienced by Rhode Island itself. The populist, rural majority that dominated Rhode Island displaced much of the prewar Newport elite that ultimately sided with the British. Newport would never rise again, except as a late-nineteenth-century resort for the very rich and a twentieth-century historical site, as Providence became the state's leading city.[50]

Lopez and Rodrigues were not the only Newporters to hedge their bets and look out for themselves first. In 1780, after the British left, Moses Levy and Moses Seixas joined many "Citizens, and inhabitants, and Residents" of Newport who pledged to defend the city "to the utmost of our Power and Ability . . . against the King of Britain." Earlier, they had joined with many of the same people, numbering 444 inhabitants, who declared their "Loyal and Dutiful Allegiance to His Majesty George the Third." Like most Newport men, they put preservation over principle. The Reverend Mr. Isaac Touro did not, and paid a price. Having left Newport in 1779 with the British troops and settled in Jamaica, the hazan who gave his name to Newport's synagogue was reduced by 1782 to begging for a twelve-month allowance from Sir Guy Carleton, British commander in North America, in compensation for "the distresses which your petitioner suffered from Persecution for his attachment to government." Had it not been for the "kind patronage" of the former governor of New York, William Tryon, and Brigadier General Marsh, who endorsed the petition, Touro "must have sunk under the weight of his affliction and distress."[51]

The Hart family remained loyal as well. Moses suffered confiscation of his estates for having "with force and arms and against the peace of the state and of the United States of America aided and assisted the enemies of the United States." He fled to the British lines in New York City when they evacuated Newport. His brother Isaac did not, and paid an even higher price for his allegiance, as James Rivington's *New York Gazette* noted on December 2, 1780.

> Mr. Isaac Hart, of Newport, R.I., formerly an eminent merchant and ever a loyal subject, was inhumanly fired upon and bayoneted, wounded in fifteen parts of his body, and beat with their [a crowd's] muskets in the most shocking manner in the very act of imploring quarter, and died of his wounds a few hours after, universally regretted by every true lover of his king and country.

Since many loyalists, as well as patriots, suffered from "lynch law"—the name itself comes from a revolutionary leader in backcountry Virginia—it is impossible to tell if Hart's attackers were motivated by anti-semitism. Still, Hart's slaying was especially brutal. His manner of death suggests Stiles may have been correct when he complained in 1777 that "the Jews are very officious as informing against the Inhabitants" whom they considered sympathetic to the Revolution and "who [were] frequently taken up & put in Goal." As a result, the citizens of occupied Newport lived under a reign of terror, being "cautious and fearful of one another."[52]

Aaron Lopez's fate symbolized what happened to the Newport Jews: they returned from exile only to watch their community dissolve. When hostilities appeared to have ended, he planned his first visit to a devastated Newport in over five years. "Misirable island, what wretched inhabitants has thou to nurich," he mourned. On May 27, 1782, while on the way back from Leicester, he attempted to water his horse in a pond. It was deceptively deep, and Lopez, who was not among the few colonial Americans who could swim, drowned within a few feet of shore as his horrified family watched. Forgiving his friend's past political ambivalence, Ezra Stiles penned an elegant epitaph for his tombstone at the family's request that praised his mercantile abilities, "polite and amiable manners, hospitality, liberality, and benevolence," "an ornament and valuable pillar to the Jewish society, his integrity irreproachable . . . he lived and died, much regretted, esteemed and loved by all."[53]

By the end of the war, Lopez was either firmly in the patriot camp or else pleased that no matter who won, the war was ending. When he learned of the "glorious" victory at Yorktown, he wrote to a South Carolinian that such "happy events cannot but presage much felicity to this continent." Whatever his true feelings, after the war wound down, Lopez ingratiated himself with the revolutionaries by refusing to profit from their misfortunes. He forgave a debt owed to him by Captain John Wiley, allowing "the gallant officer and brave soldier who so deeply has earned those pledges of public faith [government certificates to] retain them, until government shall redeem then out of their own hands for their specie value."[54]

Accounts from Leicester, however, imply that the arrival of a wealthy contingent of Jews may have provoked some resentment on the part of the local farmers. Emory Washburn, nineteenth-century town historian, took his words praising Lopez directly from Stiles's epitaph, his major addition being that "the furniture of his [Aaron Lopez's] house, the plate upon his table, and the retinue of his servants, wore an air of magnificence among his less endowed neighbors." Washburn quickly added that the virtues for which Stiles praised Lopez "disarmed all cavils remaining on their part." Still, a note that survives in the Lancaster, Massachusetts, public library from Horatio Gates Henshaw, whose father knew the Jews, suggests that some cavils remained. While they may not have been speculators, Lopez and Rodrigues, Henshaw sarcastically noted, "were too patriotic to refuse in payment for their commodities, continental bills, the currency of the times, but felt rather scrupulous about holding such treacherous paper over the Sabbath and were careful to pass it off to the farmers in exchange for their grain." That Henshaw would single out the Jews for their desire to get rid of depreciating continental paper money and mention their Sabbath as well shows that once again, wealthy Jews were being blamed for a common practice, since nobody in their senses kept depreciating continental money if it could be unloaded. Lopez must have been less successful in getting rid of it than most: when he died, he held some eighty-one thousand dollars in public securities.[55]

Newport's wartime devastation foretold the end of its Jewish community. Thirteen years after its founding, as a result of the war and the loss of a minyan, America's most beautiful synagogue closed its doors for nearly a century, to be reopened in the interim only to hold funeral services, mostly for Jews from elsewhere who wished to be interred with their families. Like the town itself, its Jewish community enjoyed a brief "Golden Age" in the quarter century before the American Revolution, only to be devastated during the war. Most of the congregation who had not been loyalists left for New York and elsewhere within a decade. The scarcity of Jews allowed a 1798 state law, which purportedly granted Jews full equality, to coexist unquestioned until 1842 with the still-valid colonial charter that limited political privileges to Christians in this most populist of New England states. By 1800, there were only two Jewish families of note left in town, the Seixas and Rodrigues, along with some of their Levy and Lopez relatives. Thanks to the bequests of Moses Levy and Abraham and Judah Touro and the historical sensitivity of the city of Newport and State of Rhode Island, which implemented and supplemented their donations, the synagogue and graveyard were preserved until a congregation was formed again in 1881.[56]

Judah Touro's bequest in his will of 1854 of ten thousand dollars to preserve the synagogue is especially noteworthy. Touro had been reared by his uncle Moses Michael Hays, a Newport Jew who relocated to Boston, and would have been his heir had he not fallen in love with Hays's daughter Catherine. Despite the tiny marriage pool available for practicing Jews, Hays forbade the union and cast Touro out without a penny. (Neither of the lovers ever married, and fate dictated they died only nineteen days apart in 1854.) Touro relocated to New Orleans, where he became one of the wealthiest men in the United States, giving away vast sums of money to philanthropic organizations during his lifetime, and $387,000 on his death. (The greatest part of his estate, estimated at $750,000, went to the man who saved his life during the Battle of New Orleans.) His will included bequests of at least $2,000 to every Jewish synagogue and charitable society in the United States, and many Christian institutions as well. Touro seems to have devoted his life to refuting the stereotype of the selfish, money-hungry Jew. Among his largest gifts were $80,000 to the New Orleans alms house, $80,000 for the poor of New York City, and $60,000 for the relief of Jews in the Holy Land. Born on the eve of the Battle of Bunker Hill, June 16, 1775, he provided the last $10,000 needed for the monument's construction, but only on the condition, which was not fulfilled, that his contribution remain anonymous. Judah Touro's bequests were the final, and one of two great, legacies of the eighteenth-century Newport Jews to the United States.[57]

Their contribution to the cause of religious toleration, however, is perhaps equally important. After George Washington became president, the Jewish and other small religious denominations throughout the nation addressed the chief executive, congratulating him on his election and asking his confirmation of the fact that they could hold services in the United States on equal terms with the more numerous and powerful Christian churches. Washington responded individually, and positively, to each letter. It is the observation of the Newport Jews, however—"behold a Government which to bigotry gives no sanction, to persecution no assistance"—that Washington quoted in his reply that has gone down in history as Washington's own.

Earlier, the handful of Newport Jews, who no longer met in the synagogue but maintained close ties with each other, had refused to join in a more perfunctory address to Washington supported by the congregations of New York, Charleston, Philadelphia, and Richmond, Virginia. They chided these larger groups for the fact that, unlike the Jews of Savannah, who had addressed Washington in May 1789, they took over a year to write to the president. Such "neglect . . . almost amounts to disrespect," they commented. Rhode Island, however, had not yet joined the union, and the Newport Jews thought it inappropriate to write to Washington until they belonged to the United States.[58]

When Rhode Island finally became the thirteenth state and Washington visited Newport in August 1790, the Jews lost no time in presenting their own address, whereas the four larger Jewish communities could not reach consensus on their far less eloquent document until December. To be sure, like the other four cities and Savannah the previous year, Newport praised Washington's achievement in war, his role in the adoption of the Constitution, and his willingness to leave retirement to preside over the new government as essential for domestic peace and prosperity. All the congregations also noted that the hand of God was involved in establishing the new Republic. But only Newport invoked biblical history, comparing Washington to Joshua, David, and Daniel, and comparing delivery of the United States from a British yoke to relief from "the Babylonish Empire." Moreover, the Newport Masons, many of whom were Jews who belonged to King David's Lodge, addressed Washington the very same day, August 17, 1790. They referred to Washington as a "Brother" and to themselves as representatives of an "enlightened people." The address was signed by the Jew Moses Seixas, the master of the lodge, and the gentile Henry Sherburne, who joined him in writing it.

In addressing Washington, Newport Jews alone linked their cause with that of the Masons, the international brotherhood that Washington had joined in Fredericksburg, Virginia, at the age of twenty in 1752. Washington was most at home with the Masonic rather than traditional religious faith, referring to Divine Providence and the "Supreme Architect" of the universe rather than the Christian God. Thus, it was in writing to the Newport Jews that Washington took his preemptive stand in the "culture wars" that his nation would endure two centuries later: "All possess alike liberty of conscience and immunities of citizenship. It is now no more that toleration is spoken of, as if it was by the indulgence of one class of people, that another enjoyed the exercise of their inherent natural rights."[59]

After its congregation dissolved, the Touro Street Synagogue became a site of national remembrance, albeit a curious one. Its deserted, archaic appearance encouraged two eminent poets to reflect on the nature of the Jews and their place in history. In 1836, friends and relatives returned to Newport to bury Slowey Hays, daughter of Moses Michael Hays and an intimate correspondent of Philadelphia's Rebecca Gratz, in the family plot. Henry Wadsworth Longfellow, meditating on the internment, wrote "The Jewish Cemetery at Newport," in which he expressed regret that "what once has been shall be no more." Commenting on the decline and potential extinction of American Jewry in the early nineteenth century—the large German Jewish immigration that began in the 1840s had yet to occur—he remarked that

these sepulchral stones, so old and brown
. . . .
Seem like the tablet of the Law, thrown down
And broken by Moses at the mountain's base.

For Emma Lazarus, a Jewish poet who wrote "In the Jewish Synagogue in Newport" in 1867, the synagogue evoked both the grandeur and sadness of Jewish history, "the patriarch with his flocks . . . a wondrous light upon a sky-kissed mount. . . . midst blinding glory and effulgence rare," on the one hand, "the slaves of Egypt . . . the exiles by the streams of Babylon," on the other.

Both Longfellow and Lazarus called attention to the tragedy of Jewish history from biblical times to modern Europe. But they seemed oblivious to the persecution and exile endured by the Jews of Newport themselves during the American Revolution within a generation after the Lopez family escaped the Portuguese Inquisition. Instead of casting aspersions on the intolerance and persecution the revolutionaries had inflicted on the congregation's loyalists, the poets glossed over the Jewish community's extinction as either "mysterious" or "strange," that is, inevitable or incomprehensible, given the celebratory tradition of a nation claiming to be exceptional in its freedom, toleration, and prosperity. In Lazarus's words, Newport enabled the "weary ones, the sad, the suffering," to find "comfort in the holy place," one group among the "huddled masses yearning to breathe free" her poem at the base of the Statue of Liberty invites to the United States. In Newport, and by extension America, Longfellow wrote, the Jews supposedly found refuge from the "burst of Christian hate / . . . persecution, merciless and blind," that "Drove o'er the sea . . . These Ishmaels and Hagars of Mankind." But he concluded:

The groaning earth in travail and pain
Brings forth its races, but does not restore,
And the dead nations never rise again.

Lazarus ended by describing the synagogue as a "sacred shrine" proclaiming "the mystery of death and God."

The fate of Newport Jewry as the two poets described it permitted Americans to congratulate themselves on their tolerant, open society without remembering how and why the congregation disappeared. But to those willing to admit that the American Revolution was a brutal civil war that ruined much of the economy—over five hundred of Newport's houses were destroyed, about half the town—there is no mystery or cause for nationalistic celebration. The fate of Newport's Jews should remind us that in the United States, too, Jews suffered from anti-semitism and were persecuted, if not for their faith, for their loyalty to the British Empire, which had welcomed them, brought them prosperity, and was overthrown in

America. The lesson of the Touro Synagogue should remind us of the brutality and displacement of the War for American Independence, of the replacement of a tolerant elite by a less attractive populist regime. If the Touro synagogue survived, it was because the British army, which was inclined to spare houses of worship whose congregations remained loyal to the Crown, used it as a hospital.[60]

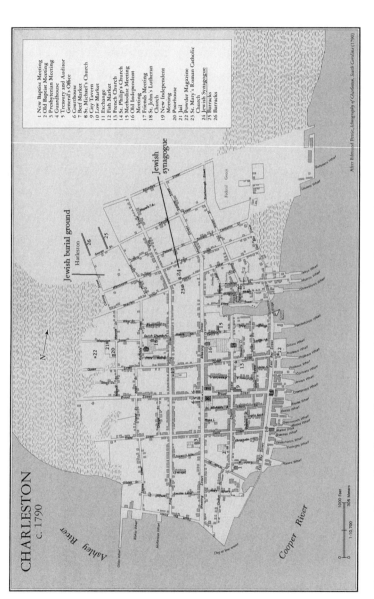

CHARLESTON
c. 1790

Ashley River

Cooper River

N

1000 Feet
305 Meters
1:10,700

Jewish burial ground

Harleston

Jewish synagogue

Federal Green

After Edmund Petrie, *Ichnography of Charleston, South Carolina* (1790)

1 New Baptist Meeting
2 Old Baptist Meeting
3 Presbyterian Meeting
4 Guardhouse
5 Treasury and Auditor General's Office
6 Courthouse
7 Beef Market
8 St. Michael's Church
9 City Tavern
10 Low Market
11 Exchange
12 Fish Market
13 French Church
14 St. Philip's Church
15 Methodist Meeting
16 Old Independent Meeting
17 Friends Meeting
18 St. John's Lutheran Church
19 New Independent Meeting
20 Poorhouse
21 Jail
22 Powder Magazine
23 St. Mary's Roman Catholic Church
24 Jewish Synagogue
25 Barracks
26 Barracks

Charleston, South Carolina. The Jewish synagogue is located on Hasell Street. The burial ground, not shown on the map, was on Comyng Street in the upper-right-hand corner of the map near "Harleston." (After Edmund Petrie, "Ichnography [sic] of Charleston South Carolina" [1790]. Map adapted from Lester J. Cappon, *Atlas of Early American History: The Revolutionary Era, 1760–1790.* © 1976 Princeton University Press, renewed 2004. Reprinted by permission of Princeton University Press.)

CHAPTER 4

CHARLESTON, SOUTH CAROLINA

THE ONLY FOUNDING DOCUMENT OF a British American colony that explicitly mentioned the Jews was the Fundamental Constitutions of Carolina, promulgated in 1669 by proprietor Anthony Ashley Cooper, Lord Shaftesbury, and written in consultation with his friend the philosopher John Locke. To attract diverse settlers to a province that had foundered for six years, they offered freedom of religion to "Jews, Heathens, and other Dissenters from the purity of the Christian Religion" and gave seven people of any group the right to form a religious congregation. Conspicuous by their absence in this broad grant of religious freedom were Roman Catholics, for Carolina was established primarily as a buffer against Spanish Florida. To forestall the religious strife that had led to civil war in England and the Thirty Years War on the Continent, the constitutions also forbade the use of "any reproachful, reviling or abusive Language against the religion of any church or Profession."[1]

America's first law against "hate speech," like the rest of the Fundamental Constitutions, was never accepted formally by South Carolina's popular representatives. As early as 1671, one of Charleston's inhabitants told Cooper, "I Pray God send more thankful spirits and grateful hearts . . . than those stubborn, hard hearted, stiff-necked, and rebellious Jews." This writer, who did not sign his letter, made scapegoats of the Jews for the infant colony's considerable troubles, for the rest of his letter implies that the Jews' presence was the only flaw in a veritable "land of Canaan . . . flowing with milk and honey" that could be "compared with any in the world for either health, pleasure, profit, or delight," a "bowling alley full of dainty brooks and rivers of running waters," a "garden" boasting the healthiest of climates (of all the newcomers, only the eighty-year-old former governor had died).

The letter hides the fact that the present Anglican governor and his Dissenter opponents were locked in a bitter struggle, for none of the other signed documents sent to the proprietors concerning the quarrel either mention Jews or their connection to the unrest. The new governor blamed some malcontents for "inciting the people to sedition and mutiny," whereas his opponents charged he denied them a "Parliament" and was overly partial to the Church of England. Yet one anti-semite sought to blame the whole mess on the Jews, suggesting he hoped that the proprietors would leave the colonists alone except for banishing this "rebellious" group.[2]

Were there in fact Jews among Carolina's earliest settlers? Both circumstantial evidence and the anti-semitic letter suggest there were. Over half of Carolina's first three hundred white settlers came from the West Indies, and residents of Barbados—the most populous, productive, and overcrowded of all Britain's Caribbean sugar colonies—provided the largest contingent. In the island's extremely detailed 1680 census, 54 of 404 households in the capital, Bridgetown, were Jewish, and there were at least 18 other Jewish families on the island, 15 of whom lived in Speightstown. Jews in Bridgeton possessed 163 of 1,325 slaves in the capital, a percentage approximately equal to their share of the population. Since most of the island's wealth was in land and slaves, the Jews' average wealth resembled that of their urban Christian neighbors. On the other hand, in the primarily agricultural parish that included Speightstown, Jews comprised about 7 percent of the population, but only owned 53 out of 2,977, or less than 2 percent of the slaves. Barbardos Jews were primarily urban merchants and tradesman as in England and much of Europe. The only large Jewish planter on the island owned forty-one acres of land and had ten white servants and sixty-one blacks.[3]

Yet the prosperity of Barbadian Jews would have not have prevented their immigration to Carolina. As historian Richard S. Dunn has noted, even island families with considerable wealth were sending their surplus offspring away as land and opportunity became scarce on the tiny island. Early Carolina families, Dunn notes, included scions of some of Barbados' most prosperous clans, such as the Colletons, and provided three of Carolina's seventeenth-century governors. Twelve Jews out of 593 people left Barbardos in 1679 alone, and while none of the Jews gave Carolina as their destination, this by no means precluded immigration there before or after: 38 percent of all migrants that year sailed for Carolina. Proportions of Jewish migrants in 1679, 3 percent for New England (presumably Rhode Island), 1 percent for New York, 2 percent for Antigua, 2 percent for Jamaica, 2 percent for London, 1 percent for Nevis, and 1 percent for Surinam, correspond roughly to the destinations of the emigrant population as a whole.[4]

Thus, it is probable that Barbardian or other Jews were among the earliest settlers of Carolina, especially since Jewish merchants throughout the Atlantic world were quick to seize the main chance and move to new areas. Although the same Barbadian Jewish names appeared wherever they moved, Mendes, DaCosta, DeLeon, Levy, Nunes, Cardozo, Gutteres (Guttierez), Carvalho, and D'Olivera can be found frequently in both Barbardian and South Carolinian records. It is thus likely Jews had lived for a quarter century in Carolina before 1695, when Governor Joseph Archdale, himself a Quaker, used a "Jew for an interpreter" in dealing with Spanish-speaking Indian captives he ultimately returned to St. Augustine in Florida.[5]

At least, and perhaps at most, three Jewish families lived in South Carolina in the 1690s, judging by the number of Jews who in 1697 joined with sixty French Huguenots in a successful petition for citizenship that was approved by the governor, John Blake, and the legislature. The petition arose in the aftermath of the fear, ungrounded as it turned out, that the Jews and Huguenots would be excluded from trade within the empire by the new Navigation Act proposed to Parliament in 1695. Given their high proportion of merchants, both groups were alarmed that the bill initially proposed to limit trade to "native" Englishmen—persons born in lands under English rule, which would have excluded a large proportion of Jews and all of the Huguenots, recent French refugees from Roman Catholic persecution. English Jews took the lead in February 1695 in calling attention to what was probably an oversight in drafting the law: the Huguenot petition followed three weeks later. Defining themselves as "the Hebrew Nation residing at London," a nation who "look upon whatever country they retire to" as "their native country," London Jews petitioned Parliament for the right to trade not only for themselves but "in behalf of their brethren, merchants, and factors in His Majesty's plantations." They offered the argument that they had enjoyed this right in the British Empire for some forty years since their presence in the realm was recognized in 1655. The Jews were making the point that an English Parliament could hardly turn back the clock after the Cromwellian Commonwealth, the Anglican Charles II (not to mention the Roman Catholic James II), and the former Dutch Reformed William III had all tolerated the Jews and their lucrative economic endeavors. As Joyce Appleby has shown, England was beginning to develop a new ideology: that the welfare of the nation rested in government support of the economic endeavors of the capitalist class. An England that abolished internal geographic and cultural obstacles to promote trade did not hesitate to eliminate religious barriers as well.[6]

The debate over the Navigation Act came when Parliament was investigating a "horrid and detestable" conspiracy by French agents against the king and debating increased funding for an ongoing war with France. A second petition by three Jewish merchants thus did not appeal to the right of Jews to practice a religion most Englishmen disliked if not despised. The men instead invoked the Protestant identity no Englishman could publicly repudiate following the Glorious Revolution: the exclusion of "foreigners," the technical status of most Jews as nonnaturalized aliens, would "be the ruin of many families, who by the rigor of the Spanish and Portuguese Inquisitions, were forced to remove from their native countries and shelter themselves under the protection of the English government." England could hardly place itself on a level with its enemies, especially given the aid Jews and Huguenots had provided in the struggle against a common foe. The Huguenots, for their part, explicitly mentioned Carolina and New York as colonies where French Protestant merchants had "transported [themselves] at great expense" and "improved the English colonies by Trade and great Labour."

The complementary arguments of the Jews and Huguenots were successful: the Navigation Act of 1696 permitted naturalized citizens to trade on equal terms with native-born British subjects, and Carolinians of both persuasions eagerly seized on the opportunity to obtain equality. But only three Carolina Jews—Simon Valentine, Abraham Avila, and Jacob Mendes—applied to be naturalized. Avila's papers read that he was "a native of the Jewish nation," indicating the contemporary acceptance of the Jews as an ethnic diaspora, a nation without a state. Mendes was listed as an inhabitant of Barbardos in 1680 and was living in London by 1700: the date of his naturalization suggests that he made South Carolina an intermediate stop.[7]

Not all Carolinians supported the Jewish-Huguenot cause. These minorities were aligned with the aristocratic, British proprietors, and with the colony's Anglican elite, which had known and worked with Jews in the Caribbean and in England. Against them were the Dissenters—mostly Presbyterians, Quakers, and some German Lutherans—who in 1700 numbered about two thousand of the colony's forty-two hundred white inhabitants. Part of the problem was apportionment of the assembly. Most Dissenters lived in Colleton County. Berkeley County, including Charleston, was home to most of Carolina's eighteen hundred Anglicans, whereas the four hundred Huguenots concentrated in Craven County. A law of 1691 gave this county six delegates to the assembly as opposed to seven each for Berkeley and Colleton, virtually assuring the Anglican-Huguenot faction a large majority in the legislature. Had the Huguenots not voted or the apportionment been fairer, the division would have been much closer.

The Dissenters were also disgruntled because beginning in 1701, the year the Anglican Society for the Propagation of the Gospel was founded, South Carolina's proprietors and Anglican community joined in this religious offensive. The assembly passed a law, nullified in 1706 by the Board of Trade, requiring that all members of the assembly take Communion in the Anglican Church. Since the province's Jews were associated in both the naturalization petitions and in business dealings with the Huguenots and Anglicans, in 1703 the defeated Dissenters complained to the proprietors that they had lost the previous election because "Jews, Strangers, Sailors, Servants, Negroes & almost every French Man" had been allowed to vote. Anti-semitism appears in the fact that although only three Jews had been naturalized in South Carolina, they assumed first place on the list. An agent sent to London by the Dissenters, John Ash, confirmed this prejudice by focusing on Simon Valentine, a wealthy Charleston Jewish merchant who also owned a rural estate and was related to New York's Asser Levy, as a key figure in the Anglican-Huguenot camp. Ash argued that one reason the war against Spain and France in Florida and the Caribbean was going badly was that Governor John Moore was a traitor. "Mr. Valentine the Jew" was supposedly a key figure in facilitating his "private trade with the French."[8]

So little information survives about the Carolina Jewish community in the early eighteenth century that we are not even sure whether one existed and, if it did, how it got there. Jacob Marcus maintains that it had dissolved by 1715, whereas James Hagy believes that the handful of Jews naturalized at this time remained to form a permanent community. Hagy also thinks that the Jews who arrived beginning in the 1730s came as individuals, although he admits the legend that they arrived as a group from London might be true.[9]

The official establishment of the Anglican Church in 1704 and the outcome of the struggle between Anglicans and Dissenters did not affect directly any Jews who might have been living in the province. They had no chance of election to office, and their rights to vote and trade were maintained. In 1716, however, the assembly, now dominated by rural Dissenters, limited the right to vote to Christians. That year, the colony's two factions—Huguenots, Anglicans, and Charleston merchants against Dissenting planters—split so violently that three years later the proprietors were overthrown, replaced by a royal government, and Carolina divided into two provinces. Although no explicit anti-semitism can be found in this period of convulsion, any Jews in South Carolina—seven had been naturalized by 1715—probably would have found themselves allied with Anglicans and Huguenots on every important issue. To begin with, if they were mostly Charleston merchants with European connections—as they had been earlier and would be later—they would have opposed the new paper currency supported by the planters, which eased the tax burden of land and slave owners in economic hard times but made it difficult for merchants to acquire hard currency for overseas trade.[10]

Jews were also friendly with the proprietors, whom the majority of the assembly blamed for failing to be prepared for three costly wars against the Tuscarora, Yamasee, and Creek Indians that nearly destroyed the colony. Very possibly, Jews on the Carolina frontier were involved in the back-country Indian trade, as they were in Georgia, Pennsylvania, and New York. At least one prominent trader's name, Isaac Marzÿck, suggests a possible French or German Jewish heritage, although his ethnicity can only be guessed. (If he appeared to be foreign, he might have been considered a Jew even if he was not.) Marzÿck seems to have had a particularly close relation with the governor: he conveyed a gun from him to the Cherokee "king" as a gift and received a bonus for his "conduct with the burdeners," that is, the Cherokees who transported trade goods.[11]

These men, who traded goods such as utensils, whiskey, and guns for furs and slaves, which the Indians captured from their enemies, did not enjoy a good reputation. The assembly blamed them in large measure for the Indian war that nearly destroyed Carolina. In 1716, it passed new bills to control the traders, who were "notoriously infamous for their wicked and evil actions." Although Jews continued to be naturalized without difficulty, which enabled them to engage in commerce, the assembly on several occasions limited political rights to Christians and (redundant for a colony frequently at war with Catholic Spain) in 1759 to Protestants.[12]

Jews were probably not the object of the 1759 law, for by that date they were successfully integrating into society. In 1753, Isaac DaCosta became the first of many Jewish members of the Charleston Masonic Lodge. Jews formed business partnerships with gentiles, and the two groups granted each other power of attorney and executed each other's wills. Four years later, Joseph Levy was appointed a lieutenant in the provincial forces. Jews served as interpreters in dealings with the Spanish and Portuguese, and Moses Lindo was the chief inspector of indigo and appraiser of all dyes and drugs produced in North America, of which South Carolina indigo was by far the most important export. In 1770 Lindo contributed five pounds (New) York currency to the new college being built in Rhode Island because it had "no objection to admitting the youth of our Nation without Interfering in Principles of Religion." (Jews at Brown were not required to attend chapel, but none attended that college during the few remaining years of the colonial period.) He hoped it would flourish as did a school he attended in London with his brother, where a number of Jews studied along with some three hundred gentiles, including two future lord mayors and seven aldermen. A businessman rather than a scholar, Lindo recalled that his education and the connections he made in school were "no small service to me when I was a broker on the royal exchange."[13]

Charleston Jews were only able to form the requisite minyan for the congregation Kahal Kadosh Beth Elohim (Holy Congregation and House of the Lord) in 1749. In 1753, the DaCosta family built the cemetery that still survives on Comyng Street, and transferred ownership to the congregation in 1762. Along with Francis Salvador, the DaCosta family of London were the principal Jewish merchants who hoped to settle poor Jews and surplus members of their own families in the New World. They first tried Savannah, sending over forty-two Jews with the original settlers of Georgia in 1733. However, when war broke out with Spain in 1740, all the Jews except the Minis and Sheftall families, fearing conquest and the possibility of an Inquisition, left the fledgling province, mostly for Charleston. The DaCostas and Salvador next tried to establish a Jewish colony on the South Carolina frontier. These hopes came to naught, but Jews from London, including several DaCostas, began arriving in Charleston in the 1730s: only one Jew was naturalized in South Carolina between 1715 and 1733, but nine between 1734 and 1743. From 1749 to 1775, at least twenty-one Jews arrived in Charleston: ten from England, eight from Germany, two from the Netherlands, and one from St. Eustatia, although immigrants from the West Indies in general and Barbardos in particular were not recorded.[14]

None of the Jews settled on the frontier, with the exception of Francis Salvador. In the hopes of attracting gentiles, the DaCosta and Salvador families bought some two hundred thousand acres in the new district of Ninety-Six (known as the "Jews' Lands") and successfully began to populate it. On the eve of the Revolution, Joseph Salvador sold seven thousand acres of frontier land to his orphaned nephew Francis. (The elder Salvador was a London merchant who had lost much of his fortune in the failure of the Dutch East India Company and the Lisbon earthquake, the latter a sign that despite the Inquisition, Jews remained silent and significant partners in the Portuguese economy.) Leaving behind a wife and four young children, the twenty-seven-year-old Francis moved in 1773 to South Carolina and set up a plantation. As the district's largest landowner, he was the natural choice for one of its two representatives in the provincial congress along with his friend and fellow planter Richard Rapley. Although Jews technically could neither hold office nor vote, no one objected to the presence of the cosmopolitan and wealthy Salvador, who served in the two provincial congresses and the state's first general assembly. That no one paid attention to the 1759 law limiting the franchise to Christians was probably the reason Salvador did not object when it was retained in the new state constitution. He was chosen for important committee assignments: drawing up the declaration explaining the purpose of the provincial congress to the people, obtaining ammunition, assessing "the state of the interior parts of the country," and making sure the state constitution was accurately engrossed.[15]

In July 1776, Salvador returned to Ninety-Six to combat attacks by Indians and loyalists on the frontier. On the thirty-first, Major Andrew Williamson captured two white loyalists, who led his 330 men into an ambush prepared by their fellow whites and the Seneca Indians on the Keowee River. The rebels won, but Salvador was one of three men killed. According to his commander, he met his death like a hero:

> He died, about half after two o'clock in the morning; forty-five minutes
> after he received the wounds, sensible to the last. When I came up to
> him, after dislodging the enemy, and speaking to him, he asked,
> whether I had beat the enemy? I told him yes. He said he was glad of it,
> and shook me by the hand—and bade me farewell—and said, he would
> die in a few minutes.[16]

In 1950, to celebrate the two hundredth anniversary of Charleston's Jewish congregation, the city erected a memorial to Salvador, the first Jew known to die in the Revolution. Although the inscriptions on such markers are usually predictable, the poem honoring Salvador could just as easily be a tribute to the patriotism of South Carolina's Jewish community as a whole.

> Born an aristocrat, he became a democrat;
> An Englishman, he cast his lot with the Americans;
> True to his ancient faith, he gave his life
> For new hopes of human liberty and understanding.[17]

South Carolina Jews overwhelmingly supported the Revolution. Of fifty-six identifiable Jewish men in the city, thirty-six served in the patriot forces, twenty-six enlisting in Continental army units. Fourteen of those joined Captain Richard Lushington's Charleston command known as the "Jews' Company," although a majority of its members were gentiles. Two Jews, Benjamin Nones and Isaac DaCosta Sr., were sufficiently obnoxious to be banished by the British, and eight others joined them in Philadelphia. Three Jews, Jacob Cohen, Philip Myers, and Jacob Henry, were among the 130 Charlestonians imprisoned in May 1781 on the British ship *Torbay*. There they joined with their gentile compatriots in forwarding a letter to

General Nathanael Greene from the British officer commanding the city that they would suffer death in retaliation if British prisoners of war were harmed. They did not urge Greene to free the prisoners, but reasserted their willingness to die for the cause. The petition concluded "that sho'd it fall to the lot of all, or any of us to be made Victims, agreeable to the menaces therein contained, we have only to regret that our Blood cannot be disposed of more to the advancement of the glorious cause to which we have answered."[18]

Even where South Carolina Jews were less heroic, their revolutionary credentials were sterling. Only ten of the thirty-six Jews who enlisted for the cause served in the state militia, generally a less onerous task than the Continental army, for it allowed men to stay at home most of the time and just turn out when the British were in the area. Only fourteen of the fifty-six Jewish men who lived in Charleston remained during the British occupation, and although nine signed a loyalty oath to the Crown—as did many patriots under duress—only two were charged after the war with loyalism.[19]

Still, despite their revolutionary ardor, Jewish merchants were singled out for exceptional criticism during the war. In October 1776, a patriot grand jury put "Jews" first before citing "others" who were undermining law and order by "allowing their Negroes to sell goods in shops, as such a practice may induce other negroes to steal and barter with them." That the citizens considered such behavior "a profanation of the Lord's Day" as well implies that Jews, who were forbidden by their religion from conducting business from Friday until Saturday night, were hoping to compensate for this disadvantage by engaging in trade on Sundays. The British also had complaints about the Jews. The commander of the royal troops found that "the retailers of goods . . . are mostly Jews [who] never pay their accounts until they are compelled because the cost of a suit is not near equal to the benefit they receive by retaining a considerable sum of money in their hands." Ironically, this selfishness was "productive of public benefit" because "money was so extremely scarce," and the Jews would always pay their debts and add to the amount in circulation, albeit at the last minute.[20]

It is hard to say whether the nine Jews who remained in Charleston under the British and signed a loyalty oath to Crown were in fact responsible for the bulk of the city's trade, although it seems doubtful given the large number of gentile inhabitants who also remained behind. Of the nine, none signed the oath before August 1780, whereas 110 of the "principal and most respectable inhabitants of Charleston" had done so as early as June 3. Two of the nine subsequently joined seven other Charlestonians in moving to Philadelphia, indicating they had signed, as did many gentiles, only to protect themselves and their families as they remained in town to do their business. Five of them had previously enlisted in Lushington's company, Sumter's brigade, the Savannah grenadiers, or James Bentham's company, suggesting their first loyalty was to the new United States.[21]

South Carolina punished only two Jews after the Revolution for supporting the Crown. Isaac DeLyon was fined 12 percent of his property despite his protestations of innocence, which are plausible since he fled from Savannah to Charleston after the British occupied the former city. DeLyon was the only one of ten Jewish immigrants to Charleston during the Revolution who displeased the patriots: three of the others were deserters from the Hessian army and British navy. One of them, Levi Moses, told his life story when he successfully petitioned for citizenship and ownership of 528 acres of land in 1785. He was born in New York in 1763, but his father sent him into the Royal Navy. After his discharge in Jamaica, he sailed for New York when the Revolution broke out, but as it was under British occupation took advantage of his ship's putting in at Wilmington, North Carolina, to go to South Carolina. Barnard Moses, on the other hand, who had previously served in Lushington's company, had joined DeLyon by the end of the Revolution in becoming "a loyal subject of His Majesty." In June 1783, the state forbade him "ever more being inhabitant or subject" of South Carolina and gave him permission to go to Nova Scotia. Moses, who signed his name with a mark, was thus a poorly educated and probably poor man. With these two exceptions, given the Jews' overwhelming support for the Revolution, it is no surprise that the state constitution of 1778 gave the franchise to all free white adult men who believed in God and owned fifty acres of land or a town lot. A second constitution, adopted in 1790, gave Jews the right to hold elective office fourteen years after Francis Salvador had already done so.[22]

Yet despite the Jews' overwhelming loyalty, during the Revolution explicitly anti-semitic remarks entered the South Carolina political debate for the first time since early in the century. In December 1778, someone published a notice in the town's newspaper, the *Charleston Gazette*. He

observed furniture and other goods loaded on wagons and horses belonging to newcomers to town, and "upon inspection of their faces and enquiry
I found them to be of the Tribe of Israel." The writer immediately jumped
to the conclusion that they had first taken "every advantage in trade the
times admitted of in the State of Georgia, [but] as soon as it was attacked by
an enemy, fled here for an asylum, with their ill-got wealth—dastardly
turning their backs upon the country when in danger." He predicted that
all the South Carolina Jews would do the same when the British came
northward.

"A real AMERICAN, and True-hearted Israelite" countered by explaining
the goods in question belonged to the women of the Minis family, female
refugees from Savannah, "who had happily arrived at an asylum, where a
tyrannical enemy was not at their or their dear offsprings heels." The Minis
men, for their part, were deeply involved in the Revolution in Georgia. Far
from fleeing to Savannah, a number of Jewish merchants in Georgia, "being
informed of the enemy landing [there], they instantly left this [city], as
many a worthy Gentile knows, and proceeded post haste to South Carolina,
leaving all their concerns unsettled, and are now with their brother citizens
in the field, doing that which every honest American should do." The writer
concluded with the accurate observation that "The Charleston Israelites, I
bless Heaven, have behaved as staunch as any other citizens of the state."[23]

Occasional expressions of anti-semitism surfaced after the war ended.
The remarks of one "WELLWISHER TO THE STATE" implied he was refuting
anti-semitism, for he began his newspaper notice by stating that "he who
hates another man for not being a Christian, is himself not a Christian.—
Christianity breathes love, peace, and good-will to man." Calling attention
to the Jews' "considerable share in our late Revolution," he urged the South
Carolina government to "invite the Jews to our state . . . a wise and politic
stroke—and give a place of rest at last to the tribe of Israel." While no formal invitation came, South Carolina Jews, attracted by the tolerant atmosphere, outnumbered those of any state besides New York in the first federal
census of 1790. It was entirely appropriate that at the United States Constitutional Convention, it was South Carolinian Charles Cotesworth Pinckney
who expressed the thought, "Our true situation is a new extensive country
containing within itself the materials for forming a Government capable of
extending to its citizens all the blessings of civil and religious liberty."[24]

Two incidents in late 1780s Charleston suggest that the populist anti-semitism found in other states was present in South Carolina as well. The first is problematic: in 1786, two Jewish newcomers brought on themselves the sort of legitimate although extralegal chastisement upper-class south-erners routinely inflicted on their impertinent social inferiors. Two men "dressed in the Moorish habit" proved to be Algerian Jews who had arrived in Charleston from Virginia. "The singularity of their dress" prompted a young lawyer to question them, but they answered "with so much impertinence and vulgarity that the gentleman proceeded to give one of the fellows a little manual correction, by way of reforming his man-ners." A mob formed and took them to the house of "a lady on the Bay" who was able to understand their language and identify them as belonging to "the Jewish nation." The second incident, the desecration on September 18, 1787, of the synagogue, the Tuesday after Rosh Hashanah, suggests more than sheer greed was at work. In addition to attempting to steal the silver, "the five books of Moses, which contain the law and command-ments of Almighty God, were wantonly thrown about the floor." With the exception of a silver spice box, all the loot was recovered from the one "vil-lain" who was captured, although two of the "sacrilegious robbers" made their escape.[25]

In general, however, Jews and Christians in Charleston got along in a lowland society where black slaves outnumbered free whites, and white people of all faiths were needed to uphold a precarious social order. The fifth of the private homes and small wooden buildings that had served the congregation as meeting places since 1749 proved inadequate. To give the Jews an appropriate presence in an economically booming society, on Sep-tember 20, 1794, one year after Eli Whitney invented the cotton gin, the synagogue on Hasell Street opened during the High Holy Days. Built in the Georgian style, it could hold its own with St. Michael's and St. Philip's, the city's elite Episcopal churches. "A numerous concourse of ladies and gen-tlemen," both Jewish and gentile, attended, including Governor William Moultrie. The *South Carolina Gazette*, after commenting on the beauty and "splendor" of the building that cost four thousand pounds raised "entirely by subscriptions of members of their [Jewish] churches [in Charleston and elsewhere]" noted, "The shackles of religious distinction are now no more; the oppressive and cramping capitation tax, that has for ages scattered them [the Jews] upon the face of the earth, is here unknown; they are here admitted to the full privileges of citizenship and bid fair to flourish and be happy." Costing twice as much as Newport's Touro synagogue, the synagogue reflected both Charleston's wealth and the Jews' participation in its creation.[26]

So close were the relations between the Jewish and Christian communities that Charlestonian Gershom Cohen felt obliged to write to Harmon Hendricks in New York that the Jews willingly participated in a Sunday service with the town's Christian congregations—"the day being most convenient for Jews and Christians" to raise money for the town's orphan asylum. "A great number of Gentlemen of character and liberality" of all faiths joined together to collect forty-eight pounds. Both the money and the precedent of Jews and Christians cooperating for various purposes promised great "service to future generations." (The Jews formed their own asylum in 1801, aware that the orphans were being given a Christian education.) In 1804, the *Massachusetts Spy* reported that the manager of the theater in Charleston, "at the special request of the gentlemen of the Jewish nation in that city," declined performing Shakespeare's play *The Merchant of Venice,* in which the Jewish merchant Shylock is depicted as ugly, dishonest, and materialistic, in short, a composite of anti-semitic stereotypes. The play had regularly been performed in New York and Philadelphia.[27]

One family history, that of the Charleston Levys, gives a somewhat different picture. In the 1790s, Fanny Yates, the bride of Jacob Levy, was the leader of "the best Jewish society" and "the admiration of the whole city. . . . [A]t her first appearance in the dress circle of the old Charleston Theatre in Broad St., the whole house rose in tribute to her matchless beauty." Jacob Levy, for his part, belonged to the Charleston Library Society, "the resort of the 'illuminati' of Charleston." Yet the family historian commented that whereas in Savannah the Levys were accepted into "social rank with the best people in that eminently refined society," in Charleston, thanks to the "narrow minded bigotry" of the elite, "the higher circles were closed to Jews."[28]

However, unlike in Savannah, Charleston Jews simply did not have the wealth and prestige to enter this elite. Charleston's richest citizens were planters who kept mansions in town: the slaves they owned numbered dozens, and sometimes into the hundreds. Only one Jew, Isaac de la Motta, was among the top fifty men who loaned money to the South Carolina revolutionary government between 1776 and 1780, and his contribution of £129,000 in inflated money ranked twenty-fourth behind those who lent up to £500,000. That de la Motta did not belong to the highest echelons of the elite appears in that he is listed on the rolls merely as "Isaac Motte," suggesting he was not universally known. The state census of 1790 lists only one Jew who owned more than six slaves, Philip Hart, who owned fifteen on a small plantation, the only plantation apparently owned by a South Carolina Jew before 1800 besides the Salvadors. Three Jews owned six slaves, two five, five four, two three, eight two, and eight one, typical numbers for city shopkeepers who also kept house slaves.[29]

Jews were also involved in the slave trade. Abraham Seixas, member of the distinguished intercolonial Jewish family, was notable for his poetic advertisements, egregious examples of verse and of South Carolinians' casual acceptance of their peculiar institution. In 1784, "ABRAHAM SEIXAS [pronounced Say-shas], All so gracious," offered for sale men, women, youths, and boatmen:

> For planting, too,
> He has a few
> To sell, all for the cash,
> Of various price
> To work the rice
> Or bring them to the lash.

Seixas was not the only successful South Carolina Jew who had wide acquaintances and was well connected. For instance, the congregation's hazan, Jacob Raphael Cohen (1738–1811), had previously lived in London, Montreal, and Philadelphia.[30]

South Carolina Jews were reluctant to venture into the backcountry, for reasons Joseph Salvador (1716–1786), Francis's uncle, made clear after attempting to take over the land grant belonging to his late nephew. Although the "soil is excellent and would produce anything," he detested the "naked, famished, and immensely lazy" inhabitants, whom he compared to "a set of Tartars." "As poor as rats and proud as dons [Spanish aristocrats]," they "hate society," "prize [their horses] more than their wives and families," and are "always happy when they can do any ill natured thing and molest their neighbors." Instead of God ("they have no belief in Christ, little in Judaism or a future state"), "Rum is their Deity." The aged Salvador died after spending less than two years in the "wild country" of Ninety-Six.[31]

South Carolina Jews became involved in the political struggles between Federalists and Republicans in the 1790s. As with many of their contemporaries, they disdained in theory the partisanship in which they engaged. Charleston's Jews, like the inhabitants of the low country in general, apparently voted for at least one Federalist of "sterling integrity and liberal sentiments" to serve as a delegate to the 1790 state Constitutional Convention that granted the Jews full political rights. The man, Christopher Knight, offered the congregation Beth Elohim $350 to help the Jewish poor in gratitude for Jews' support during the election, but parnas Jacob Cohen refused, "as it might be suggested at some future period that members of our community were to be bought." Charleston's Jewish community, being well-off, could easily afford such sentiments.[32]

Support for Knight and the Federalist-sponsored 1790 constitution, which made sure that the elite of the low country would continue to dominate the state despite some mild reapportionment, confirms that Charleston Jews, like most of the city's voters, were initially Federalists. By 1793, however, they had joined Jews throughout the nation in supporting the French Revolution and the Jeffersonian Republicans who looked upon it sympathetically. Jews belonged to the Republican Society of Charleston, and Abraham Sasportas served as agent for American privateers who returned with British, Dutch, or Spanish cargoes. Sasportas had a mixed record in arguing before federal courts that his clients were in fact entitled to the prizes they seized. In 1794, United States judge Thomas Bee declared Sasportas incompetent and obliged him to pay court costs when he maintained that American vessels could be officially turned into French ones by the French consul, and thus were legally entitled to the prizes. But the following year, Sasportas successfully defended the capture of a British merchant ship by a Charleston vessel of which he was half owner and whose arming he had personally supervised. This time, Bee seconded Sasportas's argument that American ships were entitled to arm in preparation for war with Britain, and ruled that they had every right to take British prizes. Americans could thereby obtain "redress for depredations committed by

the British on their trade," and justifiably so, because of "the general unanimity then prevailing"—with which British consul Benjamin Moodie as
well as the United States government itself emphatically disagreed—that
naval hostilities between the powers were de facto under way. In another
incident, Sasportas arranged to send fifty-six slaves from Santo Domingo
seized on a captured prize ship to Georgia, where they could be sold since
South Carolina had banned the importation of slaves in 1787.[33]

In 1800, twenty-two-year-old Thomas Sheppard left Philadelphia to
establish the Federalist *Charleston Times*. In its very first issues of October
1800, at the height of the Adams-Jefferson election struggle in which
Charleston's Charles Cotesworth Pinckney was Adams's running mate, one
of Sheppard's columnists employed the same anti-semitic tactics as the
Philadelphia Federalists were currently using in an effort to defeat Jefferson. "A.B." and "C.D." criticized "a federal or state officer [who] affected to
join in worship with the Jews" and sought to help his cause by distributing
election tickets after the service. Sheppard, however, kept his columns open
to both sides: "E.F." identified himself as a Jew and attacked his alphabeti-
cal predecessors for the way that this charge "most wantonly asperses the
Hebrew nation." Denying that the official in question had attended the synagogue, E. F. responded that the writers were applying the traditional anti-
semitic stereotype of greed to the members of Beth Elohim, whom C. D.
had accused of selling their votes. The Jews had not "prostituted the temple
of the most High, for electioneering purposes," E. F. insisted.[34]

Eighteen years later the Federalist *Times* had no trouble taking the anti-
semitic side without offering the Jews a chance to reply. A writer attributed
the Jews' sufferings throughout history to their behavior in the Old Testament: "Outlawed and detested by the world, even their very name is the
brand of reproach, disgrace, and dishonesty." The same year, a Charleston
businessman remarked: "The only thing worse than a Jew is a Yankee. A
yankee can Jew a Jew directly." Anti-semitism appears to have increased in
Charleston in the early Republic as at least some aristocratic Charlestonians
distanced themselves from the Jeffersonian triumph and sought to maintain their Federalist credentials.[35]

Although politically united behind Jefferson, for religious purposes
Charleston Jews were divided among themselves along class and ethnic
lines. Unlike in New York and Philadelphia, where Ashkenazi and

Sephardic families had jointly constituted the prerevolutionary elite, in Savannah, where the elite was Ashkenazi, and in Newport, where there were few Ashkenazi immigrants, in Charleston the divisions corresponded more exactly to the newcomer Ashkenazi/old settler Sephardic paradigm. Seventy-seven Jewish men came to Charleston between 1776 and 1800 alone: that there were only fifty-three families in 1791, including those who predated the Revolution, indicates many newcomers were transients who never established themselves in the city. The first signs of division appeared as early as 1764. Two years after he succeeded Beth Elohim's first hazan, Moses Cohen, Abraham DaCosta, who had been educated in Portugal and belonged to one of Charleston's most numerous and prestigious Jewish families, resigned his office in a dispute with other members of the congregation. In 1775, five men belonging or related to the DaCosta family complained that Emanuel Abrahams and Myer Moses—whose names mark them as Ashkenazi newcomers—had somehow illegally seized power within the congregation, ousting one of the congregation's founders, a DaCosta, as parnas, four years earlier. Employing the language of the American Revolution then in progress, the DaCostas complained that the rival faction had "arrogate[d] to themselves rights of their own creation of an arbitrary nature," including changing the laws of the congregation, serving illegally on its junta, and admitting members without the general congregation's consent. It is hard to understand why the DaCostas, as they claimed, "tamely submitted" to this behavior "for a long time past in the hopes that cool reason [would prevail] after they had their vanity satisfied" unless they had become a minority faction. But in any case the Sephardim led by the DaCostas asked the opposition to sit down and work out their differences.[36]

The rapprochement did not occur. As South Carolinians were dividing into loyalists and patriots, the Sephardic, more elite and theologically liberal members of the congregation, seceded from the more recently arrived Ashkenazi majority whose legitimacy they refused to recognize. The precise date when Kahal Kadosh Beth Elohim Unveh Shalom split from Kahal Kadosh Beth Elohim is uncertain, but by 1785 Charleston newspapers were speaking of two burial grounds, and in their wills Jews were bequeathing funds to the "Portuguese [Sephardic] synagogue" instead of "the synagogue." (The additional words *Unveh Shalom* adopted by the newcomers for the name of their synagogue means "Mansion of Peace," an implicit comment that the original congregation had ceased to fit that description.) In 1786 Joseph Salvador—significantly, a recently arrived foreigner who lived on the frontier and probably had no brief for either party—left money to both congregations in his will.[37]

The two merged in 1791, when the united synagogue was incorporated under the original Sephardic name of Kahal Kadosh Beth Elohim, but the disputes continued. In 1795, Sephardic Jew Emmanuel de la Motta felt sufficiently insulted by Beth Elohim's ruling Ashkenazi junta that he wrote a lengthy, unpublished account of his suspension from the synagogue. On December 12, 1794, de la Motta's father, Isaac, formerly a merchant of St. Croix in the West Indies, died after "puking blood." De la Motta claimed that his father wished to be laid to rest in the smaller of the two Jewish burial grounds beside his sister. Other members of the congregation claimed that Isaac desired to be interred in the larger. A friend of the old man offered the opinion that he had only expressed the latter wish once, and that was "in a pet fit talking about the DaCostas," who were fellow Sephardic Jews.

A committee of two from the synagogue next visited de la Motta, who claimed that under South Carolina, if not Jewish, law, he had the legal right to bury his father where he wished. They tried to appeal to the solidarity of the Jewish community by telling him that his conduct "would cause a Scism in the Congregation, and revive the distinction of portuguse & Todeska [German]." The men who called on de la Motta were Israel Joseph and Andrew Harris, clearly showing that the Ashkenazim had come to dominate the congregation. De la Motta for his part was in no mood to be conciliatory. He defended his and his father's piety—his father had been a *yahid*, or elder, of the congregation—and wondered how they could suppose him "so damned a Scoundrel as to wish to act contrary to the wishes of my deceased parent." The argument escalated to the point where de la Motta used the words "rascally, infamous, unjust, arbitrary, Despotic, unprecedented, unlawful and Tyranick" (although he denied using "Villain," as the men charged) to describe the conduct of the synagogue's ruling junta, before he "sent [told] them [to go] to hell." He also promised to bury his father himself if the congregation prevented the town's other Jews from assisting him.

De la Motta was able to recruit three fellow Sephardim, whose names were Cardozo, Abendanone and Senore, to help bury his father. In turn, the synagogue summoned him for having "ill-treated their committee . . . in a very opprobrious manner." De la Motta responded that they had failed to present charges against him in advance, as their rules required, so he could prepare his defense (which they refused), and proceeded to explain in great detail how the junta's conduct toward him suited the known English definitions of each of the opprobrious terms he had used to describe them. De la Motta was suspended from the synagogue for six months, and then required to apologize and pay thirty-nine shillings before he could be readmitted.[38]

Class as well as ethnic divisions began to plague late-eighteenth-century Charleston Jewry at the same time the Charleston crowd became active against the ruling elite in addition to joining with it in opposing the British. The Jewish community included obscure immigrants who are otherwise difficult to trace. One was a woman. On September 21, 1765, the *Charleston Gazette* ran an advertisement from New Yorker George Vissels, who reported that his wife, a Jew who had converted, had moved to South Carolina and resumed her maiden name of Catherine Solomons after she had persuaded various New York merchants to give her £105 of goods on her husband's account. Having briefly suffered imprisonment for his wife's debts, Vissels warned the Charlestonians that "lest she should persevere in the like enormous proceedings, I hereby declare that I will not answer or pay any debt or debts for her, and hope this will be sufficient caution for any person to evade the infatuations of so implacable a mortal."[39]

At least eight Jews became involved in criminal activity in South Carolina between 1773 and 1806, a number that seems high in proportion to the Jewish population of about fifty families. At least one case is notable for anti-semitism in that the word of a black slave was used to convict a Jew, since testimony by slaves was generally not accepted against whites. On November 1, 1773, the *Charleston Gazette* reported that "Jacob Ramos (a Jew)" was convicted of receiving stolen money from a slave who had been convicted and hanged for robbery. Before his execution, the slave had claimed that Ramos had enticed him to commit the crime. Ramos had to pay a fine of £350 (suggesting he was reasonably wealthy in this period before revolutionary inflation), receive thirty-nine lashes, and stand in the pillory for an hour. The *Gazette* noted that "he was most severely & incessantly pelted by an enraged populace," but to their credit they "were so orderly, as not to use any other Materials than rotten eggs, Apples, and Onions." The punishment for Ramos, too, was of the physically humiliating sort inflicted on a slave or lower-class person rather than someone who could come up with £350.[40]

Other Jews committed crimes. In an instance of swift justice, on June 21, 1786, Levi Cohen and James Morris were sentenced to hang for a burglary they committed on June 6. Two days later, they were reprieved before being pardoned on July 13. On January 23, 1792, Levi Pollock was pardoned for larceny on condition of leaving the state. In September 1796, Samuel Jacobs was sentenced to six months in jail, a half-hour in the pillory, and a fine of £180 sterling for forgery. His prison term was commuted to banishment after nearly five months when some citizens petitioned for his release. On June 9, 1802, Moses Solomon was pardoned for an assault, and on May 30, 1806, Abraham O. Valentine, perhaps a descendant of the Simon who may have been the colony's first Jew, was pardoned after being convicted and sentenced to hanging for stealing a slave. Such pardons were by no means limited to Jews: juries frequently imposed stiff sentences, leaving it to friends of the convicted to approach the governor, who would be open to appeals for both political reasons and personal sympathy.[41]

In addition to appearing in criminal records, Charleston Jews, who undertook innumerable business ventures both with each other and with gentile merchants, were frequently involved in litigation. They also fought physically with both each other and with Christians. Fourteen Jews were prosecuted for assaulting other Jews between 1806 and 1835, although only two resulted in guilty verdicts. For instance, in 1806, Moses Rodrigues claimed that Philip Moses struck him in the chest with an umbrella and called him a brigand. Four years later, Alexander Marks allegedly "took down a sword" and threatened to chop Solomon Cohen in pieces after he had called Cohen "a damned rascal & thief . . . undeserving of the appellation of an officer" in the synagogue. In the same period, nine Christians were accused of assaulting Jews, two of stealing from them, and one of trading with a Jew's slaves.[42]

Charleston Jews, like Christians, also resorted to dueling when they believed their honor was attacked. At least two Jews fought their coreligionists: Manuel Mordecai Noah with John Cantu (who was wounded in the leg) and a Moses and a Cohen in 1834, which resulted in the latter's death. Duels Noah and Gershom Cohen almost fought with gentiles were, as occurred in most such cases, mediated by third parties and apologies made. The implication, however, was that Jews and gentiles of equal social status could confront each other on the field of honor.[43]

The personal, political, ethnic, and class divisions within Charleston's Jewish community mirrored those of the new state. Hitherto excluded elements in both Charleston and the backcountry sought not so much to displace the elite as to join it. Historians Clarence Ver Steeg and Robert Weir have argued that the nouveau riche of South Carolinians, most of whom made their fortunes during the indigo and cotton booms of the late eighteenth century, exhibited many of the nasty stereotypes of those who acquire wealth without breeding. Much like film and sports stars in the late twentieth century, their exaggerated defense of their personal honor and independence—and collective insistence on liberty during the war for independence—was inversely proportional to the role of their own efforts in acquiring their wealth. They were in fact the least independent people imaginable. Their high style of life represented the contributions of a variety of communities: slaves who worked the plantations, merchants who took away their product, manufacturers who processed it, and consumers who bought it. Because they clustered in Charleston rather than spending most of their time on their individual plantations, as did Virginia planters, South Carolina's rich were in greater contact with people who shared the same mentality. Charleston was a hothouse of huge egos and fortunes that could easily come to blows. Although they were not planters, Charleston's Jews exhibited the same characteristics as their gentile counterparts, clustering together on King Street, where 55 percent of them lived in 1809.[44]

It is no wonder that American Reformed Judaism began in Charleston in 1824. In 1820, Kahal Kadosh Beth Elohim abandoned the democratic constitution it had established when incorporated in 1791, replacing it with the traditional, European method in which elders chose their successors and other synagogue officials. This led Charlestonians who considered themselves Jewish, but refused to belong to a synagogue they considered overly authoritarian and concerned with observance of archaic rules, to form their own congregation. Twenty-eight of its first thirty-eight members had not been members of Beth Elohim, and had shown little interest in Judaism previously. They were either middle class or wealthy, highly literate, wealthy, and young, aged thirty-two on average. The action of these men mirrors a wave of Protestant Christian proselytizing following the War of 1812, as well as what they conceived as the un-American and "dead" religion of their fathers: the average age of the Kahal Kadosh Beth Elohim junta that year was sixty-two.

Isaac Harby, a thirty-six-year-old former lawyer, playwright, journalist, publisher, and founder of the well-regarded Harby's Academy who had belligerently supported Napoleon (for emancipating European Jews), slavery, and westward expansionism, was the key figure in founding the congregation. It was an instant success, and Harby explained why in an oration on its first anniversary. Determined to "take away everything that might excite the disgust of the well-informed Israelite," he stressed that religion should appeal to "reason" and prayer proceed from "understanding" as well as piety. He compared the rabbis, "who converted into mystery and absurdity what God intended his people should plainly read and rationally understand," to the monks of the Middle Ages and to Catholicism before the Reformation. Such a comparison appealed to American Protestants who celebrated their own liberation from Catholicism and feared its contemporary incarnation would poison the Republic. Judaism posed no such threat, Harby argued. He urged Jews "to throw away rabbinical interpolations; to avoid useless recitations; to read or chant with solemnity," to follow Hebrew readings with English translation, and not simply to read the law, but to follow it with commentary "edifying to the young, gratifying to the old, and instructive to every age and class of society."

Reformed Judaism was the call of American Jews to Jews throughout the world to emancipate themselves, the equivalent of the American Republic itself, which implicitly invited the world's people to free themselves from political despotism. Outside of America, Harby noted, Jews "bow[ed] beneath the sway of bigotry." It was Reformed Judaism's mission to "divest [Judaism] of rubbish" and "beautify that simple Doric column which raises its plain but massy head amid the ruins of time and the desolation of empires." It was an interesting choice of words, linking Greeks and Hebrews as fellow founders of human freedom at the very moment the Greeks were fighting the Turks for independence.

Although the product of a proud, aristocratic city, rational and democratic Reformed Judaism was the logical product of contentious, individualistic, well-to-do, and highly educated South Carolina Jews. Like the elite Christian community in whose midst they flourished with only occasional anti-semitic discomfort, they were obliged to maintain equality, honor, and solidarity within the ruling class. South Carolina Jews joined their gentile counterparts as staunch defenders of a social order whose fear that it would be overthrown by a coalition of slaves and Yankees played a major role in bringing about the Civil War.[45]

CHAPTER 5

SAVANNAH, GEORGIA

COLONIAL GEORGIA WAS DESIGNED as a utopian experiment. A board of trustees carefully selected settlers from among prisoners, persecuted foreign Protestants, and the London poor, many of whom were refused transportation because it was believed they could find work in London. The trustees included several Protestant clergy, both Anglicans and Dissenters, and their minutes show continuous cooperation with leading missionary societies, such as the Society for the Propagation of the Gospel and the Society for the Propagation of Christian Knowledge. Moral order rather than personal profit was to be the colony's goal. Settlers received fifty-acre farms, which they could not sell without special permission from the trustees, and were forbidden the use of hard liquor, lawyers, and slaves. Funds for the new colony were raised primarily through parish collections.[1]

Even before King George II signed the charter, people were thinking of sending settlers over. England's largest and wealthiest Jewish congregation, Bevis Marks in London, authorized three of its members (not those who later approached Georgia's trustees, although two were related to them) to "interest themselves with those who have permission to arrange settlement in the English colony north [sic!] of Carolina," which is where they assumed Georgia to be located. At a meeting of the trustees on September 21, 1732, less than three months after Georgia received its charter, three of the richest Jews in England, Alvarez Lopez Suasso, a merchant, Francis Salvador, whose family was the largest stockholder in the Dutch East India Company, and Anthony DaCosta, a director of the Bank of England, were authorized to join the numerous Christians who raised funds to promote settlement. All money collected was to be given to the trustees.[2]

By December, however, the Jews had turned over no money. This cre-

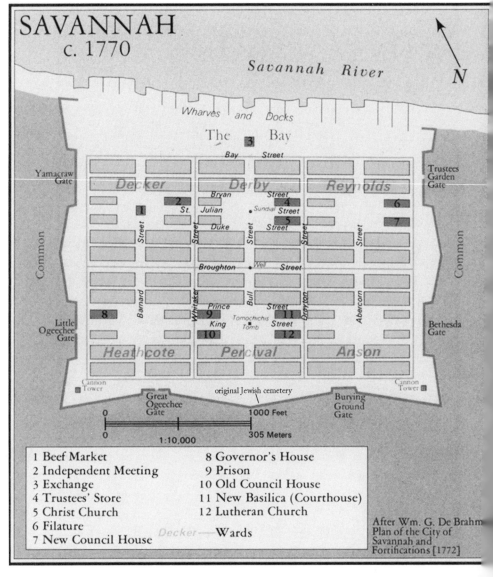

SAVANNAH
c. 1770

Savannah River

N

Wharves and Docks

The Bay

Bay Street

Yamacraw Gate

Decker   Derby   Reynolds

Trustees Garden Gate

Bryan Street

1 **2** St. Julian • Sundial Street **4** **6**

Duke Street **5** **7**

Common

Broughton • Well Street

Bamard Street | Whitaker Street | Bull Street | Drayton Street | Abercorn Street

Prince Street **11**

Little Ogeechee Gate

8 **9** King Tomochichis Street Tomb Bethesda Gate

10 **12**

Heathcote   Percival   Anson

Common

Cannon Tower

original Jewish cemetery

Burying Ground Gate

Cannon Tower

Great Ogeechee Gate

| 0 | | 1000 Feet |
| 0 | 305 Meters |

1:10,000

1 Beef Market	8 Governor's House
2 Independent Meeting	9 Prison
3 Exchange	10 Old Council House
4 Trustees' Store	11 New Basilica (Courthouse)
5 Christ Church	12 Lutheran Church
6 Filature	
7 New Council House	*Decker*—Wards

After Wm. G. De Brahm
Plan of the City of
Savannah and
Fortifications [1772]

Savannah, Georgia. Savannah had no synagogue in the eighteenth century. The first Jewish burial ground was located at the southernmost foot of Bull Street between the Great Ogeechee and the Burying Ground Gate. The cemeteries built by the Sheftall family and congregation were located outside the town limits, several blocks southwest of the Little Ogeechee Gate.

(After William G. De Brahm, "Plan of the City of Savannah and Fortifications" [1772]. Map adapted from Lester J. Cappon, *Atlas of Early American History: The Revolutionary Era, 1760–1790.* © 1976 Princeton University Press, renewed 2004. Reprinted by permission of Princeton University Press.)

ated both alarm and suspicion among the trustees, since the total collections had amounted to only twenty-one hundred pounds, a meager sum considering numerous appeals and a fraction of the ten thousand pounds annual subsidy voted by Parliament. Correctly suspecting the Jewish collectors were obtaining money for the purpose of sending their coreligionists to the colony without official sanction, four trustees, at a thinly attended meeting on December 7, split two to two on whether Jews "if they went of their own expense" should be allowed in Georgia. The wording of this motion implies that Jews, unlike the other settlers, had to be people of some means rather than the former prisoners and other poor individuals who constituted the bulk of the colonists. At a fuller meeting on January 17, 1733, the trustees voted to exclude Jews altogether. Two weeks later, being informed that some Jews had already been sent to Georgia, the trustees predicted the Jews' presence "will be of prejudice to the Trade and Welfare of the Colony," voted to recall the Jewish fund-raisers' commissions, and insisted they render an account of sums collected. The trustees claimed that the three Jewish fund-raisers had "designed their collections for their own use," which some historians of Georgia have misinterpreted to mean they were embezzling the money. But the more probable explanation is contained in the next clause of the dismissal: "the report of our sending Jews has prevented several [wealthy gentiles] from subscribing to us." "Their own use" suggests that the Jewish fund-raisers, like people of other denominations, were specifically raising money among and for the benefit of their own kind.[3]

To render the exclusion policy under debate moot, in early January 1733 the London Jews dispatched the *William and Sarah,* which contained forty-two Jews, for Savannah. It arrived only six months later on July 11 after a "disagreeable and boisterous voyage" in which "gale succeeded gale, and the ship came near being wrecked off the coast of North Carolina." So Benjamin Sheftall informed his son Levi. Amazingly, only one infant died. Fortunately for themselves and the colonists already in Georgia, the Jews arrived in the middle of an epidemic in which over twenty of the original settlers, including the single physician, had died. Of the 120 survivors, at least half were sick with and "many lives despaired of" from a fever brought about, Governor James Oglethorpe believed, from drinking rum. Among the Jews was the noted physician Samuel Nunes Ribiero, "who immediately undertook [to cure] our people and refused to take any pay for it. He proceeded by cold baths, cooling drinks, and other cooling applications. Since which the sick have wonderfully recovered, and we have not lost one who would follow his prescription." Later, after he lost his initial affection for the Jews, German Salzburger Rev. Johann Boltzius expressed the opinion that while the "old Jew" spoke Latin well, "he may, however, have understood his ars medicam badly."[4] But at the time no one questioned Nunes's abilities. A Sephardic refugee from the Portuguese Inquisition, Nunes practiced homeopathic medicine—as did his coreligionists, who were equally popular in Germany—rather than the bleedings and purges favored by Christian doctors. Among his patients in Portugal had been the Grand Inquisitor himself. Proof of Sephardic Jewish medical skill is suggested by the surprising number of early American Jews who lived into their eighties and nineties, including three of Nunes's children, Daniel (eighty-five), Zipporah (eighty-five), and Moses (eighty-two), and Georgia's Abigail Minis (ninety-three).[5]

Two versions have been put forward as to why Oglethorpe, who as the only trustee present had near dictatorial power, allowed the Jews to remain in Georgia. One, based on Nunes family tradition, is that the doctor refused to treat the settlers unless the Jews were allowed to settle. The other is that Oglethorpe's colony was in danger of failing, and the addition of forty-two healthy people would significantly increase a population of 120, many of whom appeared to be at death's door. Each reason could easily have reinforced each other, although Oglethorpe did not hint in his report that Nunes needed to make any threat of withholding services. In any case, for a brief period, about one-fourth of Georgia's colonists were Jews, a greater percentage than in any other colony or state in the United States at any time to this date.[6]

But there are other explanations for Oglethorpe's openness. He was one of five trustees present at their meeting in September 1732, and one of the three who voted in favor of authorizing the Jews to collect money for the new colony. With at least two others, George Heathcote and Thomas Tower, he belonged to the faction on the board that was more concerned with international affairs and economics than religious purity. He primarily saw Georgia as a base of operations against Spanish Florida and, secondarily, as a source of wine and silk, which England had to spend hard currency to import. A representative of the more pious faction that hoped to make Georgia a Christian utopia, James Vernon, complained that Heathcote and Tower had "too little regard for the religious part of our design, leaning to the new opinions that are unorthodox." They were also the men who provided the votes in December that postponed the question of the Jews' presence. At the head of this faction was Viscount Percival, later the Earl of Egmont, who wrote that he would have prevented the Jews' involvement had he been present at the meeting.[7]

Like Heathcote and Tower, Oglethorpe exhibited tolerance toward the Jews. In an anonymous *Appeal for the Georgia Colony,* which appeared on July 29, 1732, between the granting of the charter and the appointment of the Jewish collectors, Oglethorpe reprinted Sir Josiah Child's *A Discourse Concerning Plantations* from 1692. England's Jews must have paid special attention to the passage where Child noted that Spanish and Portuguese intolerance had redounded to the benefit of their enemies: they "hath and doth daily expel such vast numbers of rich Jews and their families and Estates into Germany, Italy, Turky, Holland, and England." Indeed, since some of Georgia's first Jewish immigrants, such as Nunes, were far from poor, the trustees' objection that the presence of "certain" Jews—not wealthy and self-supporting ones—threatened their colony should be read stressing "certain" rather than "Jews."[8]

Oglethorpe did not limit his efforts to diversify Georgia's population to Jews. He attempted to settle the Savoyard Amatis brothers, who were skilled in the cultivation of silk, and a group of French Protestants who would have immigrated if the colony's inheritance system was not based on primogeniture. The son of leading Jacobite parents who became a firm Hanoverian in the 1720s, Oglethorpe's lifetime interest in the toleration James II practiced, whether hypocritically or not, appears in the fact that his major interest during his thirty-odd years in Parliament was the naturalization of foreigners. Yet Oglethorpe himself was not above playing the anti-semitic card. In 1755 he singled out Jews, stockjobbers, brokers, and usurers as the only people likely to benefit from the war England began that year with Braddock's expedition to America. Given the failure of the "Jew bill" two years before, Oglethorpe may have been uncharacteristically appealing to this sudden spurt of populist anti-semitism in an effort to preserve peace.[9]

Yet what Oglethorpe thought about the surprise arrival of these particular Jews is impossible to figure out definitively. While he allowed the Jews to land and granted house and farm lots to all fourteen Jewish heads of household, he was nevertheless "displeased at their coming," according to Egmont. Because lawyers were not permitted in Georgia, Oglethorpe sought a legal opinion from the lawyers in Charleston, South Carolina, a city with several Jewish residents, in the hopes they would state that Jewish exclusion was legal, or at least so Egmont said. But had Oglethorpe acted with this motive, he would have completely changed his stance from the previous year. It is at least equally plausible Oglethorpe told Egmont what the majority of trustees wanted to hear, and pretended to do his best to keep the Jews out, all the while arranging to admit them. The Charleston lawyers' opinion could itself have been challenged had Oglethorpe wished to do so: they ruled that that he could not exclude the Jews because Georgia's charter provided that, with the exception of Roman Catholics, "forever, hereafter, there shall be a liberty of conscience allowed in the worship of God, to all persons." Still, the charter did not require that all comers be admitted to Georgia—the trustees were carefully screening immigrants—only that those who were admitted enjoyed freedom of conscience.[10]

The nature of Oglethorpe's land grants are also difficult to interpret. To judge by the later complaints of the Nunes, Henriques, and Minis families, their soil was swampy, and could not be adequately drained despite several years' efforts. Yet Jewish plots were not segregated from those of gentiles, but were dispersed among them in the four tithings of Decker's Ward in the western part of Savannah. The distribution suggests newcomers were simply being given the first available land rather than any displaying anti-semitism on Oglethorpe's part.[11]

Egmont and his faction, which dominated the board following Oglethorpe's departure, did not accept the Jews so easily. When in November 1733 they learned of Nunes's medical services, they were "very much pleased" and wrote Oglethorpe that "they have no doubt you have given him some Gratuity," before adding, "they hope you have taken any other Method of rewarding him than in granting of Lands." Their hostility was confirmed that December, when Captain Hanson of the *William and Sally* appeared before them. Perhaps to defend himself, Hanson claimed that the Jews cheated him out of three or four hundred pounds they agreed to pay for the passage, in addition to the cost of their provisions. At this inquiry, Egmont again revealed his objection to a Jewish presence: some of them "ran away from their Christian creditors," and, being accustomed to trade and business, "none of them would work when they came" to the new colony. Into early 1734, the trustees continued to argue with Suasso, Salvador, and DaCosta about the revocation of their commission, complaining of the "ill consequences" to the colony and "indignity" to its legitimate settlers if the "said Jews [not] be removed from the Colony." They commanded the Jews to remove themselves.[12]

But then the complaints ceased. Most of the trustees accepted the fait accompli that the Jews had received their land grants. One exception was Thomas Coram, most noted as the founder of London's Foundling Hospital, a refuge for babies that would otherwise be abandoned in the streets. But he was a bigoted Christian—he had lived in Massachusetts, and the intolerant Bay Colony was his principal philanthropic interest—who considered it "shocking" that "contrary to the will and without the consent of the Trustees," so many Jews came over that Georgia would "soon become a Jewish colony." The Christian refugees for whom it was intended would "fall off and desert it, as leaves from a tree in autumn" except for those "few carpenters, sawyers, and smiths &c. whom the Jews will find most necessary and useful." Coram predicted that not only would Christians cease to support the colony, but it would become "the reproach and scandal of the trustees." The trustees, who had agreed with Coram as late as January 1734, refused to expel the Jews after he presented these arguments in a letter of March 27. Egmont was relieved when in 1738 Coram "left our Board in disgust," although he continued to "prate against us."[13]

Far from being a reproach and a scandal, Georgia's Jews constituted a singular bright spot in a colony settler Elizabeth Bland called without too much exaggeration "a very hell upon earth." Oglethorpe complained of the "pride, ignorance, malice and rapaciousness" of a "diabolical people," while the settlers, without slaves, freehold tenure, or an elected government, considered themselves "restrained from the just freedom that all adjacent provinces possess" and "ill-used, harassed and abused" by the authorities.[14] Upon receipt of *A True and Historical Narrative of the Colony of Georgia* published in 1741 by the colony's malcontents, Egmont commented that the Jews had "behaved so well as to their morals, peaceableness and charity, that they were a reproach to the Christian inhabitants." Egmont had turned from the Jews' nemesis into their greatest defender. By 1740 Pastor Johann Boltzius, who had come to Georgia to administer the needs of an initial congregation of seventy-eight Lutherans escaping persecution in Salzburg, Austria, reported that the English "treat the Jews as their equal. They drink, gamble, and walk together with them; in fact let them take part in all their fun." Only three Jews were disciplined for antisocial behavior in the 1730s, all within two days, which suggests they may have been reacting or overreacting to some insults real or alleged. Hyam and Simon Abendanone were respectively fined thirteen pounds and four shillings for scandal, and three pounds and three shillings for defamation on September 27, 1734. The next day Abraham DeLyon was fined five pounds and six pence for assault and battery. Given that the authorities did not hesitate to whip or imprison culprits, the relatively light penalties suffered by the Jews suggest their crimes were either inconsequential or provoked. In any case, the entire Jewish community behaved itself until their mass exodus in 1740 and 1741.[15]

Still, many settlers were anti-semitic. The contemporary *True and Historical Narrative* puts the Jews first among the groups who came to Georgia, and states that "they were attracted by the temptation of inheritances." The Germans, on the contrary, were "oppressed and dissatisfied at home," whereas the English were "gentlemen of some stock and fortune" who "willingly expended part of the same." Where Christians sought religious and political freedom and were willing to sacrifice to expand the British Empire, Jews supposedly only cared about wealth. One hundred seventeen settlers petitioned the trustees, predicting Georgia's ruin if land and Negro slaves could not be bought and sold freely. They sought to ingratiate themselves with trustees they erroneously supposed were anti-semitic by noting that "the Jews applied for liberty to sign with us; but we did not think it proper to join them in any of our measures." Egmont was not impressed: "This I do not believe, for why should they be refused, being Freeholders? In a subsequent application they gladly admitted them to sign."[16]

How the Jews came to be respected appears in the diary of Johann Martin Boltzius. Observing the colony's large number of Jews upon his arrival, in January 1734 Boltzius expressed sadness that it is "a grave sin to have and to hear the gospel, but like the Jews, to lack its fruit." But the Jews soon

showed more Christian charity than many Christians. That March, Boltzius singled out Benjamin Sheftall, "who took the Salzburgers in and treated
them to breakfast with a good rice soup." His wife Perla also "seeme[d] to
be quite attached to us," and the couple frequently visited the Salzburgers
in their settlement in Ebenezer. Sheftall was the man who most came to
mind when the pious minister concluded that "God has awakened some
people here so they are very friendly toward us and show great kindness."
In return for numerous acts of charity for which the Sheftalls would take no
pay, the Lutherans cleared the Sheftalls' land and worked their soil.[17]

In their travel diary, Boltzius and his colleague Israel Christian Gronau
were even more lavish in their praise. Their language suggests that the Sheftalls were forcing them to abandon their prejudices in spite of themselves,
for the couple exhibited "an honesty and righteousness the like of which he
might seek in vain on others of his race and even in many Christians." In a
story reminiscent of one of Abraham Lincoln's virtuous deeds, Benjamin
Sheftall returned a half crown to a woman who had inadvertently, in the
darkness, given his wife twice that sum in payment. He added that "God
should keep him from having unjust property in his house since it could
not bring any blessing." This and other proof that "these two Jews love us
very much" made "a deep impression on the Salzburgers."[18]

John Wesley, too, the future founder of Methodism who served as a missionary in Georgia in 1736 and 1737, also worked with the Jews. He began
studying Spanish and German on his voyage over to be able to speak to both
the Sephardic and Ashkenazi Jews, and was pleased that some of the colony's
Jews attended his English sermons as well. While he was happy that "some
of them seem[ed] nearer the mind that was in Christ than many of those
who call him Lord," his efforts to convert them bore no fruit. Nevertheless,
he became a special friend of Dr. Nunes, who continued to teach Wesley
Spanish. During the summer of 1737, they visited each other nearly every
other day before they had an argument on August 31 that terminated their
friendship. Perhaps Wesley, who had purchased a book by Richard Kidder,
*The Demonstration of the Messias' Coming in which the Truth of the Christian
Religion is Defended Especially Against the Jews,* was pushing too hard.[19]

Wesley was not the only cleric who mistook the Jews' desire for acceptance and friendship with their willingness to embrace Christianity. Boltzius noted that in services of worship "Jews . . . attend and listen attentively.

They understand some German." Given that work was forbidden on the Christian Sabbath, one could well imagine the Jews showing up simply to have something to do. But the optimistic Boltzius sent away for some books in German to instruct the Jews in Christianity, commenting "there are some Jews here who do not follow the Jewish customs in eating, in celebrating the Sabbath, etc. There are some very fine persons among them." A visitor, Baron Von Reck, considered it "remarkable" that the "Jews in Savannah enjoy all the freedoms enjoyed by the other inhabitants." "They work hard," he added, and "they do their military exercises as well as the English."

The British Society for the Propagation of Christian Knowledge heard of Boltzius's hopes and, remarking on both the Jews' "civilities" and "some of them now and then looking into your assemblies," urged that he distribute New Testaments to them in German in the "hopes that the Time is not too far off when it may please God to bring those ancient people of God into the Christian World." Egmont was pleased when Oglethorpe reported one prospective convert, but this was all wishful thinking. The Reverend Mr. Samuel Quincy of the Society for the Propagation of the Gospel provided a realistic assessment of what was really going on:

> We have two sorts of Jews, Portuguese and Germans. The first having professed Christianity in Portugal or the Brazils, are more lax in their way, and dispense with a great many of their Jewish Rites, and two young men, the Sons of a Jew Doctor [Daniel and Moses Nunes], sometimes come to Church, and for these reasons are thought by some people to be Christians but I cannot find at that they are really so, only that their education in these Countries where they were oblig'd to appear Christians makes them less rigid and stiff in their way. The German Jews, who are thought the better sort of them [practicing Jews], are a great deal more strict in their way and rigid observers of their Law. Their kindness shewd to Mr. Boltzius and the Saltzburgers was owing to the Good temper and humanity of the people, and not any inclination to Change their Religion, as I can understand. They all in general behave themselves very well, and are industrious in their business.[20]

Benjamin Sheftall spoke fluent German as well as English, enabling the English and the large contingent of Salzburger Germans to communicate

through him. When a Mrs. Rhinelander, whom Pastor Boltzius condemned for using "gossip, lies, and slander, to set people against each
other" required an interpreter, she too employed Sheftall in the hopes of
having her sentence commuted from jail to mere removal from the
Salzburgers' settlement.[21]

The overall behavior of the Jews pleased the most important people in
the colony. Almost alone, they had arrived with resources of their own. As
early as January 22, 1734, Thomas Causton, the bailiff of Georgia, was asking the trustees if the freeholders could lease their land to Jews who
promised to improve it, and whether Jews—who were already freeholders—in turn could lease their land to new Jewish immigrants. In 1737, a Jew
married a widow and sought permission to sell her fifty-acre lot to fund
improvements on his own, which the trustees were willing to grant provided there were no children and they could approve the purchaser.
Although each settler was granted a fifty-acre farm, the Jews soon accumu-
lated far larger holdings than average. By the end of the 1730s, Doctor
Nunes owned six plots, Abraham Henriques seven, Jacob D'Olivera seven,
Moses de Ledesma ten, and David Cohen Delmonte thirty![22]

The Jews were especially forward in trying to fulfill another of the
trustees' goals for the colony, the production of wine. Having been given
swampy lots in the distribution of land, the Henriques and Nunes families
were able to switch to dryer plots because of their diligence in obtaining
vines ready to be planted. William Stephens, sent by the trustees to investigate Georgia's myriad troubles, singled out Isaac Nunes Henriques for having "expended more" than any one else in attempting to drain his lot. Abraham DeLyon, however, was the most successful in this regard. "Indeed,
nothing had given me so much pleasure since my arrival," Stephens
remarked in December 1737, than DeLyon's vineyard. Stephens's extravagant praise of DeLyon suggests he was partaking as well as looking at the
grapes. Thanks to DeLyon's "skill and management in pruning and caring," all his vines bore fruit "plentifully, a most beautiful, a large grape, as
big as a man's thumb, almost pellucid and bunches exceeding big." DeLyon
predicted that his crop of one hundred vines would increase to five thousand within two years if only he could obtain more help, for he currently
employed only four servants. Stephens concluded: "I could not but reflect
on the small Progress that has been made hitherto in propagating Vines in

the Publick Gardens, where the Soil being the same, it must be owing to the Unskillfulness and negligence of those who had undertaken the charge." The same sad fate had befallen the mulberry trees intended to foster silk-worms.[23]

The trustees responded to Stephens's report and DeLyon's efforts with a loan of two hundred pounds sterling repayable in six years, with no interest for the first three, to aid DeLyon's cultivation. When Oglethorpe refused to pay DeLyon more than twenty or thirty pounds, it was Egmont, the trustees' head, who insisted he pay DeLyon one hundred immediately "to see how faithfully the Jew" would "perform his covenants." And when DeLyon's production faltered, it was Egmont who defended him on the grounds that he "ran away for fear of the Spaniards" and that thanks to "others, who by his example took to planting vines, the design goes on with great alacrity and success."[24]

But Egmont's confidence was misplaced; when Stephens returned, he found a sorry decline. "Whilst others are advancing, Abraham Lyon, I fear, is falling back." Stephens attributed this "neglect" to the fact that he was a "near relation" to the Nunes family, which had already departed, and he was planning to leave as well. DeLyon tried to send some of his goods ahead of him, but Stephens had them "stopped on account of his engagement with the trustees," which had another three years to run. "I cannot any longer look upon him as a Person to be confided in," Stephens concluded. Still, DeLyon left in 1741, never to return. Stephens also accused a Jewish trader, Abraham Levi, of selling flour at an "exceeding dear" price to the frontier settlement of Frederica as hostilities with Span were under way in 1741.[25]

Stephens, however, judged individual Jews on their merits. He consistently supported and defended Abraham Minis, who performed essential services for the colony. Minis was the colony's first, and thus for a while, only merchant, and handled commercial transactions as the trustees controlled trade. Among other tasks, he imported food from Jacob Franks, the leading Jewish merchant in New York, supplied the settlement at Frederica and Oglethorpe's troops in the war against Spain, and owned a small sloop. In common with contemporary mercantile practice, he extended credit to the province when it was short of cash. In January 1736, for example, the trustees owed him £215. Yet Minis had to overcome the prejudice of some of the inhabitants to achieve his success in partnership with Colman Solomons. In March 1738, Stephens observed that "Mr. Minis, a Jew Freeholder . . . had been employing himself in the best manner" and "has a fair character of being an honest, industrious man." But Minis "had little encouragement to undertake anything" and "was unkindly used." His house lot was "frequently under water," and his commerce was undermined by local anti-semitism. A merchant, "an Importer of diverse kinds of useful and necessary provisions, consigned to him from New York," a cargo on equal terms with those he granted to Christians. But Minis "was obliged to sell them at a lower price . . . or else they would not be taken at all." In a second case, Bailiff Thomas Causton, keeper of the colony's stores, refused to accept Minis's goods at all. At first Stephens refused to take sides between the men, stating that Causton had "a reason for all he did," but Minis's troubles bolstered the case Stephens was preparing against this corrupt official. Seven months later, Stephens dismissed Causton for "great mismanagement" of the trustees' funds.

In 1744, Stephens again came to Minis's defense. Samuel Clee, who had been taken into the Minis family and business as a partner, absconded with three or four hundred pounds. Minis lost his court case, but was allowed to appeal; Stephens defended Minis hoping that the "Scoundrel" Clee would "be paid his Deserts." Despite these setbacks, Minis, and following his death in 1757 his wife Abigail, were among Georgia's leading merchants. Abigail's success, if anything, was greater when she was left on her own: her wealth steadily increased until her death in 1794.[26]

Not all the Jews were so successful. Boltzius noted that those who had capital did well in trade, while "others . . . who do not have the riches for it are really badly off."[27] Stephens reported that in June 1740, four Jews, two of them members of the Abendanone family who had earlier been in trouble, one with a wife and two children, left for New York: according to Stephens, they had "no visible livelihood" and were not "advantageous to the colony." Stephens and the trustees also found fault with three Jews as "idle fellows," another as "a wanderer," two others as "neglecting" their land, and one as a barber who restricted his activities to shaving people rather than farming his land. Thus, two classes of Jews were forming in Savannah in the 1730s. While both families of German Jews were doing well, perhaps half of the Sephardim—including several new immigrants after 1734—were having serious difficulties.[28]

Class tensions thus aggravated the ethnic divisions between the Sephardic and Ashkenazi Jews. Mordecai Sheftall and his son Benjamin passed over the local Sephardim and respectively chose their brides from the London and Charleston Jewish communities. Such were the tensions between the Jews that the Sephardim and Ashkenazim held separate meetings. The more numerous Sephardim rented a house on Market Square in 1733, while Sheftall notes that the German Jews had their minyan by 1735. Boltzius described this makeshift synagogue as "an old and miserable hut" in which the Ashkenazi ceremonies he had seen in Berlin were used. A boy who could speak several languages and was especially fluent in Hebrew was paid to read. Boltzius doubted the trustees would grant the Jews permission to build a real synagogue, for some Jews were complaining to him "that the Spanish and Portuguese Jews [in Georgia] persecute the German Jews in a way no Christian would persecute another Christian."[29]

By the early 1740, however, Boltzius's favorable attitude toward the German Jews changed. They had failed either to convert to Christianity or prove themselves able defenders of the colony once war with Spain broke out. This change began because the Jews remained unmoved by his efforts to convert them. Needless to say, Boltzius blamed the Jews rather than himself. In a detailed description of Savannah's Jewish community as of 1738, he began by noting that the Jews "ridiculed" his missionary literature, and "their attitude toward us has even deteriorated." Referring to divisions between the Sephardic majority, who would eat what the Christians did, and the Ashkenazi Minis and Sheftall families, who "would rather starve than eat meat they do not slaughter themselves," he described the Jews as "malicious": "there is hate and persecution among themselves."

Boltzius tried to make the most of this quarrel in a last-ditch although unsuccessful effort to secure converts: "If it is sinful to judge the Christian teachings by the way most Christians are living . . . how much more should he admit, that, according to the conduct among the Jews in Savannah and their displeasing attitudes." Indeed, one "might assume that the Old Testament is wrong and malicious." In contrast with the praise he showered on Sheftall and other Jews in 1734, Boltzius concluded his 1738 description by

Mill Street Synagogue, Shearith Israel Congregation, New York, as it might have appeared during services. From a filmstrip produced by the American Jewish Archive on American Jewish history. Note that the plain building resembles a small house and has no outward sign of Jewish affiliation. Mikveh Israel in Philadelphia had a similar appearance. Reproduced courtesy of Jacob Rader Marcus Center of the American Jewish Archives, Cincinnati Campus, Hebrew Union College, Jewish Institute of Religion.

"Little Synagogue," still preserved at the present synagogue of Shearith Israel, shows a far more elaborate interior for the Mill Street Synagogue. Photograph by Joanne Savio, from *Remnant of Israel: A Portrait of America's First Jewish Congregation*, by Rabbi Marc D. Angel (New York: Riverside, 2004). Courtesy of Congregation Shearith Israel.

Chatham Street Cemetery. It still survives in New York City. Unlike Christian cemeteries, usually found in churchyards, colonial Jewish burial grounds were on the outskirts of cities. Photograph courtesy of Jacob Rader Marcus Center of the American Jewish Archives, Cincinnati Campus, Hebrew Union College, Jewish Institute of Religion.

Jacob Franks (1688–1769), attributed to Gerardus Duyckinck, ca. 1735. Franks was New York's leading Jewish merchant. His portrait, and those of other wealthy Jews, was indistinguishable from those of gentiles. Leo Hershkowitz has questioned whether the portraits of the Franks family (figures 4 through 6) are genuine; they have been considered so whenever they have been published. Reproduced courtesy of the American Jewish Historical Society, Waltham, Mass., and Jacob Rader Marcus Center of the American Jewish Archives, Cincinnati Campus, Hebrew Union College, Jewish Institute of Religion.

Abigaill Levy Franks (1696–1756), attributed to Gerardus Duyckinck, ca. 1735. Wife of Jacob Franks, source of much contention in Shearith Israel. Reproduced courtesy of Jacob Rader Marcus Center of the American Jewish Archives, Cincinnati Campus, Hebrew Union College, Jewish Institute of Religion.

David Franks (1720–1794) and Phila Franks Delancey (1722–1811),
attributed to Gerardus Duyckinck, ca. 1735. Children of Abigaill
and Jacob Franks; both married Christians. Phila converted to her
husband's Anglican faith; although David remained Jewish, he was
denied burial in Philadelphia's Mikveh Israel's cemetery. Reproduced
courtesy of the American Jewish Historical Society, Waltham, Mass., and Jacob
Rader Marcus Center of the American Jewish Archives, Cincinnati Campus,
Hebrew Union College, Jewish Institute of Religion.

Naim Js: Carigal

Rabbi Chaim (or Haym) Carigal (or Karigal), a friend of Newport's Rev. Dr. Ezra Stiles, who had his portrait painted to hang at Yale when Stiles became that college's president. Unlike portraits of American Jews, Carigal's beard, hat, and robe were typical of European Jews, and some of the Jews who came to America after 1760. Reproduced courtesy of Jacob Rader Marcus Center of the American Jewish Archives, Cincinnati Campus, Hebrew Union College, Jewish Institute of Religion.

Torah Scroll, desecrated by two British soldiers during the American Revolution, still survives at Shearith Israel. Photograph by Joanne Savio, from *Remnant of Israel: A Portrait of America's First Jewish Congregation* by Rabbi Marc D. Angel (2004). Courtesy of Congregation Shearith Israel.

Elegant yet simple exterior of Newport, Rhode Island's Touro Synagogue, designed by Peter Harrison and completed in 1763. The school building is on the left. The building has no exterior symbol of the Jewish faith. Photograph courtesy of the Society of Friends of Touro Synagogue and the Jacob Rader Marcus Center of the American Jewish Archives, Cincinnati Campus, Hebrew Union College, Jewish Institute of Religion.

The beautiful interior of the Touro Synagogue, modeled on those of Amsterdam and London. Photograph courtesy of Kerstines, Newport, R.I., and the Jacob Rader Marcus Center of the American Jewish Archives, Cincinnati Campus, Hebrew Union College, Jewish Institute of Religion.

Beth Elohim Synagogue, Charleston, South Carolina. Opened in 1794, destroyed by fire in 1838, it resembles a Georgian English church. Reproduced courtesy of Jacob Rader Marcus Center of the American Jewish Archives, Cincinnati Campus, Hebrew Union College, Jewish Institute of Religion.

Beth Elohim Synagogue, interior. As with Newport, the synagogue's interior is considerably more elaborate than its facade. Reproduced courtesy of Purchgott Studios, Charleston, S.C., and the Jacob Rader Marcus Center of the American Jewish Archives, Cincinnati Campus, Hebrew Union College, Jewish Institute of Religion.

Portrait of Israel Israel (1744–1822). In his earliest portrait, Israel flashes the Masonic sign that saved his life in the Revolution. Reproduced courtesy of Abby Aldrich Rockefeller Folk Art Museum, Colonial Williamsburg Foundation, Williamsburg, Virginia.

Portrait of Hannah Erwin Israel (1757–1813), wife of Israel Israel. She wears the cap and dress typical of Quaker women. Reproduced courtesy of Abby Aldrich Rockefeller Folk Art Museum, Colonial Williamsburg Foundation, Williamsburg, Virginia.

Portrait of Israel Israel (1744–1822). He holds the proclamation dated 1793 from Governor Thomas Mifflin commending him for helping the sick in the yellow fever epidemic of that year in Philadelphia. Reproduced courtesy of Jacob Rader Marcus Center of the American Jewish Archives, Cincinnati Campus, Hebrew Union College, Jewish Institute of Religion.

Portrait of Hannah Erwin Israel (1757–1813), wife of Israel Israel. Reproduced courtesy of Jacob Rader Marcus Center of the American Jewish Archives, Cincinnati Campus, Hebrew Union College, Jewish Institute of Religion.

Sheftall ("Cocked Hat") Sheftall as he appeared in Savannah, Georgia, in old age, when he recounted stories of Jewish history and revolutionary era. Reproduced courtesy of Jacob Rader Marcus Center of the American Jewish Archives, Cincinnati Campus, Hebrew Union College, Jewish Institute of Religion.

Portrait of Israel Israel (1744–1822). In old age, he wears spectacles suggesting the nature of his work as a public notary. Reproduced courtesy of Jacob Rader Marcus Center of the American Jewish Archives, Cincinnati Campus, Hebrew Union College, Jewish Institute of Religion.

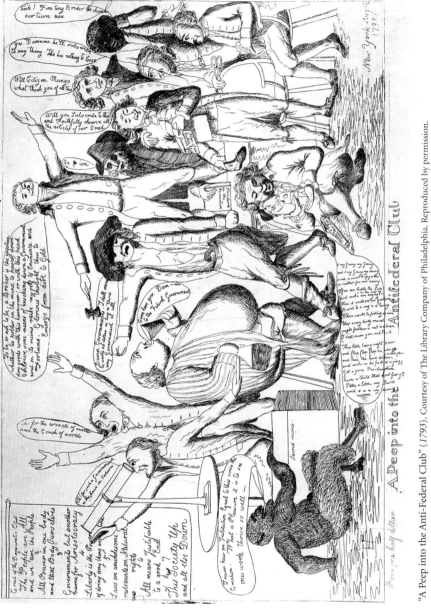

"A Peep into the Anti-Federal Club" (1793). Courtesy of The Library Company of Philadelphia. Reproduced by permission.

(facing page) "Das ewige Leben und die ewige Verdammni." Lancaster, Pa., 1820. The Ammon Stapleton Collection. Gift of Georgianna Hartzel in honor of Charles W. Mann, 1982. "Life Eternal and Eternal Damnation." In this Pennsylvania German fraktur (colored drawing) dating from about 1820, a Jewish peddler *(above detail)* is in the middle of the procession on the road to hell guarded by the "Whore of Babylon" along with a musician, dancer, and soldier (suggesting a pacifist executed the painting). He is short, has a large nose, and carries a sack of goods. Reproduced with the permission of Rare Books and Manuscripts, the Pennsylvania State University Libraries.

Rebecca Gratz (1780–1869), noted Philadelphia Jewish philanthropist and probable model for Rebecca in Sir Walter Scott's *Ivanhoe*. Reproduced courtesy of the Frick Art Reference Library and the Jacob Rader Marcus Center of the American Jewish Archives, Cincinnati Campus, Hebrew Union College, Jewish Institute of Religion.

dismissing the favors that the German Jews had done for his congregation "time and again" as "small": "as far as their religion is concerned, they have been obstinate and there is very little that we could do about it."[30]

Precisely because the Sheftalls were so involved with the Salzburgers, not only out of kindness but because their language skills made them the logical go-betweens, Boltzius and his colleagues took special pains to proselytize them. The two German ministers held "good discussions" with the elder Sheftall on the nature of Judaism and Christianity, and were pleased that he and his wife "are greatly in awe of God and long very much to be saved." The couple agreed with the ministers that the Jews' persecution was punishment for their sins, and also that both Jews and Christians were awaiting the coming of the Messiah. But when the missionary efforts failed, Boltzius's affection waned. As early as 1738, he was referring coldly to "one Sheftall, A Jew that had been appointed interpreter betwixt him and the Germans." In 1741, the Anglican priest Rev. Norris of Frederica tried to blame a German indentured servant, whom he had made pregnant, for seducing him. Boltzius was angry that Norris's friends did "their utmost to maintain his reputation," including persuading Sheftall to interpret the maid's words "maliciously and superficially in favor of the said preacher's followers." (Apparently no other qualified interpreter was available.)

The same year, Boltzius specifically blamed Sheftall for the increasingly bad feelings Georgia's government displayed toward the Salzburgers. At first, the authorities in Savannah gave Boltzius and other German notables a free hand in disciplining their followers. In case of complaints, he noted, "they shoved the matter back to me as if they did not wish to be entangled in our affairs." Then the officials began to listen to "obstinate people who are against us," because, "what is worse, they use a Jew [Sheftall] as an interpreter, and this causes annoyance." Rather than blaming the rambunctious settlers and the trustees' increasingly troubled representatives for the colony's problems, Boltzius's anti-semitism came to the fore. It was easiest to blame the Jew, the messenger, rather than focus on the extent to which his own pious community was becoming marginalized.[31]

Boltzius retained his anti-semitism over the next two decades. As late as 1756, he was castigating the "two German Jewish families in Savannah, who hold their divine service on the Sabbath in a house." The head of one (the Sheftalls) he called a "storekeeper and blasphemer of the Christian religion." The other, the Minises, he identified as a "large" family—Abigail and had nine children living at the time—whose daughters dressed "elegantly . . . despite their poverty." Boltzius must have been referring to their outward rather than real wealth, for the Minises were successful merchants and innkeepers, operating one of three taverns in Savannah.[32]

Yet even Boltzius's most negative remarks on the Jews display a positive tinge. Reading between the lines, it is easy to realize he considered them morally superior to the ethnically English majority of the colony. To be sure, they were a "wretched people" who refused to acknowledge their Lord and Savior, and supposedly practiced "abominable horrors . . . with impunity" such as committing "adultery and fornication," actions "patently against the Torah and the Sixth commandment." Yet they nevertheless "recognize and reward honesty in their economic activity": they "would rather deal with us [the Salzburgers] than anybody else because we keep our promises and pay in cash." When it came to socializing, however, the Jews were both assimilated and accepted by the English, but unlike them, did not pollute their own Sabbath, although they would "desecrate Sunday" with the English, "a thing that no Jew would do on their Sabbath just to please a Christian." When Boltzius criticized the "drinking, gluttony, gambling, [and] dancing (I will not mention other horrors) in which "people of all races, nations and religions" partook at the Minis tavern, he only incidentally mentioned that such activities were also found "in the other two taverns." Such was the nature of taverns, not necessarily of Jews, although Boltzius's rhetoric rather than his conclusion suggests he believed otherwise.[33]

The very fact that Georgia's Jews were displeasing to the pious Salzburgers reflects, in turn, their integration into the more general ethnically English community. This involved more than joining in the "debauchery" of which the authorities and clergy perennially complained. As early as 1733, Benjamin Sheftall and Samuel Nunes's sons Daniel and Moses belonged to King Solomon's Lodge No. 1 of Masons. Mordecai Sheftall served as master of the lodge in 1758. Like Benjamin Sheftall, Daniel Nunes was working as a government interpreter, in this case with the Spaniards and Spanish-speaking Indians, as early as 1736. And in 1740, in a remarkable display of ecumenicalism, Sheftall joined with Roman Catholic Peter Tondee and Episcopalian Richard Milledge to found the Union Society, whose first project was to build Bethesda, the first orphanage in British North America. (Tondee had somehow entered the colony and made his religion known despite the charter prohibition, another proof of Oglethorpe's toleration.) Their efforts inspired the great evangelist George Whitefield to make the first of his several voyages to America to raise funds for their endeavor, and indirectly brought Whitefield and Benjamin Franklin together when the preacher's eloquence moved Franklin to empty his pockets for the orphans' benefit. On a purely social level, Abigail Minis's tavern was the scene of more than one "elegant entertainment" attended by Georgia's leading government officials and inhabitants. The Sheftalls and Minises also formed business partnerships with gentile merchants and mariners in New York.[34]

But despite these promising beginnings, all of Savannah's Sephardic Jews left by March 1741, leaving only the Ashkenazi Sheftall and Minis families. Among the successful families, the Nuneses left for Charleston in August 1740: "fear of the Spaniards drove [them] to Charleston," as the War of Jenkins' Ear between Spain and England had spread to Florida and Georgia. As former conversos in Portugal whose Christian beliefs masked their Judaism, they feared they would be special targets of the Inquisition. Members of the Henriques and DeLyon families sailed north to New York and Pennsylvania, often moving between the two colonies. The Abendanones joined the Nuneses in Charleston. The family of Benjamin Sheftall, singled out by Rev. Boltzius for its piety, went to Charleston for worship after the Congregation Beth Elohim was founded in 1749, and thereafter traveled frequently between the two cities, enabling Oglethorpe to remark early in the 1740s that "all the Jews except one [Minis] had left the colony." But the Sheftalls returned, as did Daniel and Moses Nunes, and by 1750, they had joined Abigail and Abraham Minis and their nine children to give Georgia a population of sixteen Jews, out of a total population of fewer than two thousand whites.[35]

From the beginning, as in none of the other four mainland cities, Georgia's Jews were not only numbered among the elite, they constituted a substantial part of it, given the composition of settlement. Anglican Rev. Samuel Quincy referred to the two families of German Jews as belonging to the "better sort" as early as 1735. Although some Jews engaged in commerce, they also practiced agriculture as they generally did not elsewhere. Thus, when the trustees vacated Georgia's charter in 1754 and people could own land and slaves without restrictions, Georgia's Jews possessed the capital and reputation that gave them higher social standing than in South Carolina, where they almost exclusively concentrated on trade. Of the Sheftalls, at various times in the 1760s Benjamin owned 500 acres of land and had 5 slaves, his son Levi 750 acres and 9 slaves, and son Mordecai 1,000 acres and 9 slaves. In 1757, Abraham Minis left his horses to his three sons, his cattle to his five daughters, and other property to his wife Abigail. At her wealthiest, she owned 1,000 acres and had 17 slaves. In 1771, Moses Nunes was one of seven traders who brought 1 slave (one man brought 2) into Creek country "contrary to the law" despite the "considerable penalty" involved in doing so. On the eve of the Revolution, Savannah's six Jewish families had 22 slaves in the town itself, an average of 3.75 per family, a ratio that exceeded members of the Church of England (2.85), Lutherans (1.70), and Presbyterians (1.9). This did not include holdings elsewhere, such as most of Abigail Minis's slaves, and Levi Sheftall's 44 slaves, which, along with a plantation and other property worth ten thousand pounds, he claimed to have been "cheated" out of during the Revolution.[36]

Although few in number, the Jews not only rose to the highest levels of Georgia society, but became leaders in the province's political life. Samuel Nunes's sons did especially well. David served as a government interpreter with the Spanish as early as 1736, and in 1765 was appointed a waiter, a customs house job, for the port of Savannah. Moses Nunes was an Indian trader: as early as 1750 he was living in Creek country at Tuckabatchee on the frontier. He acquired considerable wealth, informed the government about hostile activities in the backcountry on the eve of the French and Indian War, served as an official interpreter and diplomatic negotiator, and was appointed Searcher of the Port of Savannah (for illegal cargo) in 1768 in reward for his services. In 1774, a year short of his seventieth birthday, he was still arranging meetings with the Creeks for the royal government and continued to do so until at least 1780 for the revolutionaries.[37]

Another prominent ethnic Jew was Joseph Ottolenghe. Born in Italy, he converted to Christianity in 1734 when he went to work for his uncle in the tobacco business. He came to Georgia in 1751 as a missionary for the Anglican Society for the Propagation of the Gospel in 1751. His special task was proselytizing and teaching black slaves. He also became the superintendent of silk culture for Georgia and a justice of the peace. Yet Ottolenghe was also popular with the voters: he served in the colonial House of Representatives from 1755 until his death in 1775 with the exception of one year.[38]

Georgia's Jews were poised to support the war for independence almost unanimously thanks to the belligerence of the Reverend Mr. Samuel Frink (1735–1770), Savannah's Anglican priest. Frink was a native of Rutland, Massachusetts, whose father had been driven out of several pulpits by New Lights during the Great Awakening. His father's financial straits prevented Frink from attending Harvard College until his twentieth year. Upon graduation he studied with the Anglican rector of Boston's King's Chapel, Henry Caner, before going to England for Episcopal ordination. He was assigned in 1765 to Augusta as the second Anglican clergyman in Georgia, but moved to Savannah in 1767 when the incumbent died. In a colony where the Anglican Church had only been established in 1758 and was fast becoming a minority as Dissenters flocked southward, Frink was an intolerant zealot. He condemned the Jews along with the "Methodistic Enthusiasts" and the "many Ignorant Baptist exhorters that stroll about the Country who are infamous rascals yet lead many astray." Unlike his more accommodating predecessors, Frink insisted on the letter of his privileges. He wanted Dissenters to pay him the required fees for funerals even if their own clergy presided, and sued one of the most prominent men in Georgia, Joseph Gibbons Jr., for the paltry sum of seven shillings when he buried a poor man without Frink's presence. (Ottolenghe, the presiding judge in the case, ruled in Frink's favor with the support of two Anglican vestrymen over the opposition of a tavern owner.) Nor would Frink walk beside the distinguished Presbyterian minister Dr. Johan Joachim Zubly in processions or allow the child of Baptists to be buried in Savannah's only cemetery.[39]

Frink's activities threatened the traditional right of non-Anglicans to be buried as they had since Georgia was founded. In March 1770, within three weeks of each other, the Jews and Presbyterians each petitioned the Georgia legislature to incorporate their existing plots in the town's common cemetery. This would guarantee possession in perpetuity and permit their own clergy to preside at funerals without payment to the Anglican Church. Zubly's plea that "every Freeholder had a legal and undeniable property in the common of Savannah" and that "it was the indefeasible right of all mankind, unmolested to bury their dead, after their religious profession" applied to Jews and well as Christians. Although the assembly approved

both petitions, which would have granted other burial grounds equal privileges with the Anglican graveyard, the upper house refused to approve the
measure and let it die as the session came to an end.[40]

Frink's offensive brought to Georgia the militant Anglicanism he had
observed in New England, where East Apthorp had built his church in
Cambridge, Massachusetts, across the street from Harvard College. As in
Philadelphia and New York, an insecure outsider employed anti-semitism
in an effort to deflect attention from his own precarious status. Interpreting
the efforts to incorporate Jewish and Presbyterian cemeteries as "an attack
on the privileges of the established church," Frink warned the provincial
councilors that they should not make a rule of the "extraordinary indulgence" shown to non-Anglicans in the past, predicting "precedents of that
nature would be attended with manifest inconveniences as every different
sect and denomination of Christians as well as those who totally differ from
the Christian Church in Discipline and Principle," an obvious reference to
Jews, "might think themselves entitled to that indulgence."[41]

That Jews had made the same request as Presbyterians led Frink to use
anti-semitic arguments in his successful campaign to have the council
reject both petitions. His attack on the Jews was backed up by a group of
Savannah property owners, who combined economic arguments with religious prejudice. Answering "several inhabitants" who supported the Jews
and could see "no objections" to the "reasonable request" that their plot be
preserved and extended to accommodate new burials, "sundry freeholders
and inhabitants" retorted that the Jews' graveyard was

> so contiguous to many of the houses on the South part of the town that
> it would become a nuisance and in some measure prevent the extend-
> ing of the town that way, and would also be a means of lessening the
> value of many of the lots, as they apprehended no person would chose
> to buy or rent an house whose windows looked into a burial ground of
> any kind, particularly one belonging to a people who might be pre-
> sumed, from prejudice of education to have imbibed principles entirely
> repugnant to those of our holy religion.

Besides, as a separate petition to the assembly had argued, some Jewish
corpses "for several years past, had been buried a considerable distance
from town [in the Sheftall family cemetery] which at this time can make

but little difference to them to continue there." As with the location of the Jewish synagogue in Philadelphia in the 1780s, many Christians wanted the Jews' visible presence to be removed from their own churches, cemeteries, and the center of town.[42]

The cemetery issue even reached the desk of Benjamin Franklin, Georgia's colonial agent in London at the time, via letters from Zubly and Noble Wymberly Jones, the speaker of Georgia's assembly. Zubly raised the interesting possibility that instead of the Presbyterians being harmed by association with the Jews, "it is not impossible that a bill in favor of the Jews for the same purpose met with the same fate for being in bad company." The elite Nunes, Minis, and Sheftall families, who comprised much of Georgia tiny Jewish population of six families and twenty-seven people as of 1771, were no threat to the Anglican establishment compared with the province's large number of Presbyterians. Significantly, the Jews, who could easily have remained out of the controversy, offered what weight they had in the political scales on the side of the Presbyterians, and Zubly was more than happy to accept their support.[43]

Frink thus turned what ought to have been an innocuous request into a major political issue. In Georgia, the general militant Anglicanism of the late colonial period took the form of a quarrel over cemeteries. Frink's behavior threatened the traditional religious liberties of both Jews and Dissenters, not to mention the assembly's competence. He was also a leading and vociferous advocate of an Anglican bishop, complaining that the Dissenters denied to the established church what they sought for themselves, "liberty for conscience," and "with consummate impudence" sought "to be in the saddle, that they may ride over us." Frink thus implicitly linked his assault on traditional burial rights with a proposal even most colonial Anglicans south of New England considered the doorway to tyranny. Frink elevated his desire to collect funeral fees onto the highest level of imperial and ecclesiastical politics, equating the assembly's approval of the Jewish and Presbyterian petitions with both the rising protest movement against Britain and an imaginary effort to end the establishment of the Church of England: "the late Commons House of Assembly were so far intoxicated with liberty principles as to endeavor to put Jews and Dissenters of all Denominations upon a footing with the church here." Of course, the Jews and Presbyterians were not asking for public financial support of their churches and ministers, which such equality would have implied, but merely for the right to continue to bury their dead in common ground set aside by Oglethorpe for that purpose.[44]

Frink's extremism even upset reasonable Georgia Anglicans. The provincial council attempted a compromise by allowing non-Anglican burials in the common cemetery, but still with a payment to the Anglican priest of two shillings, six pence instead of three shillings, six pence even if he did not preside. The assembly responded by imitating the council's previous action by tabling the bill, with one Anglican member suggesting it "be thrown under the table" rather than laid on it. Prominent Savannah merchant and devout Anglican Joseph Clay commented sarcastically on Britain's Anglican establishment for sending clergy such as Frink to Georgia: "their only care was to see that they were not religious men."[45]

Frink's death in October 1770, did not solve what had become a major point of contention between the council, which generally supported royal policy and Governor James Wright, and an assembly that increasingly favored resistance.[46] Nor did the Anglican Church become more pliable. In 1774, following the death of a young man who held the office for slightly more than a year, the Reverend Mr. Haddon Smith assumed this post that previously had been a deathtrap. Smith defended British policy in print, refused to pray for America when directed by Georgia's provincial congress, and fled to exile in England in 1775. Meanwhile, with the burial ground controversy still hanging fire, Mordecai Sheftall, the leader of the Jewish community, responded by donating part of the private burial ground he had been granted in 1762 as a cemetery for all Jews. He also hoped "a synagogue or building for the worship of those of the said profession" would be built alongside it. But it would take a while. In 1774, Savannah's six Jewish families mustered a minyan for the first time since 1740, and resumed services in Sheftall's house. But they were soon discontinued. During the Revolution that followed, as Sheftall's brother Levi wrote in a diary entry whose very syntax reflects the confusion that occurred: "the American Revolution at this time throughout America did occasion many Jews to be continually coming and going that there was no possibility to keep any register to there names as there was nothing but war talked of & every body had there hands & hearts full."[47]

It is thus no wonder that several of Georgia's Jews not only supported the Revolution, Mordecai Sheftall held a more important position in the revolutionary hierarchy than any Jew in North America. A year after the cemetery controversy, he emerged as the head of the Savannah Parochial Committee of Public Safety, Georgia's most important protest organization before the provincial congress was established in 1775. British governor Joseph Wright singled out Sheftall, "a person professing the Jewish religion," and "one *or more* members of the same persuasion, particularly Philip Minis," for their roles on this "particularly disagreeable" committee. Wright fingered Sheftall as the revolutionaries' ringleader on two further occasions. He hoped to impress his superiors with the heartlessness of the patriots by noting that "one Sheftall a Jew" turned away a cargo of slaves that he predicted would die of malnutrition, although the Parochial Committee refreshed them before sending them back to slavery in the West Indies. In an analysis of the committee, Wright branded it as "a parcel of the lowest people, chiefly carpenters, shoemakers, blacksmiths, etc. with a Jew at their Head." If internal revolution in Georgia was propelled by the lower classes, it was led by a Jew.[48]

Sheftall was joined in the cause by Dr. Zubly, his fellow petitioner from the burial ground controversy. The most important clergyman in Georgia, Zubly initially supported the Revolution, but he later became a loyalist. When he addressed Georgia's provincial congress, which supplanted the Parochial Committee in July 1775, Zubly was undoubtedly referring to the role of Jews in the current revolt along with their biblical forebears when he stressed the Jewish contribution to the history of liberty. "As to the Jewish religion . . . it is so replete with laws against injustice and oppression; and by one of its express rites proclaimed liberty throughout the land to all the inhabitants thereof."[49]

Georgia's Jews overwhelmingly favored the Revolution, no mean accomplishment in a state whose historians note, "Georgia did not join the Revolution; His Majesty's youngest settlement on the American continent had to be dragged into it." Mordecai Sheftall served as the state's commissary general and his son Sheftall Sheftall, after a stint as a private, as his deputy. In 1776, David Nunes Cardozo helped Mordecai Sheftall seize a British ship loaded with gunpowder that found its way to the Continental army. Cardozo was a sergeant-major in the Savannah volunteers when he was wounded, pensioned, and retired to Charleston. Abraham Seixas, brother of New York's hazan, and David Sarzedas held lieutenant's commissions. Merchants Cushman Polock and Philip Minis advanced large sums for the cause. Minis loaned over ten thousand dollars to the Continental army (in 1777, when that amount meant something), became commissary and paymaster for the Georgia troops in the Continental army, and guided American troops in the swampy terrain around Savannah.[50]

However, some Georgia Jews, like their gentile neighbors, remained loyal to George III or alternatively offered their allegiance to whichever side was in power. With a population of only some twenty thousand whites when the American Revolution began and the only province that used the hated stamps in 1765, Georgia was the most reluctant province to rebel. It came to life in August 1774, when Georgia patriots held a meeting at Tondee's Tavern to protest the blockade of Boston Harbor. Peter Tondee himself would not allow anyone other than twenty-six "official" delegates to enter, causing eighty Georgians to object to the fact that they lacked the liberty to disagree. Moses Nunes and Joseph Ottolenghe were among them.[51]

Ottolenghe supported the Crown, but he died the following year. The case of Nunes and his family is more complicated. A longtime business partner of Governor Wright and a provincial official himself, Moses Nunes nevertheless was paid by the patriots to continue his services as interpreter with the Creeks in 1777; in 1780, his old friend Governor Wright and the British were paying him to do the same job. Samuel, Moses's son, supplied the British forces with provisions: in 1779 he was acquitted by Wright and his royal council of stealing cattle from one Rebecca Gibbons since the acquisition was made for the imperial service and "his general Conduct" was approved of, although Nunes was rebuked for allowing his Negroes to kill Gibbons's geese. Samuel Nunes and his brother Jonas, who was also a frontier trader, were good friends of George Galphin Jr., the principal patriot leader working with the Creeks, and his brother John, who like them probably had an Indian mother. The two families were possibly related on their mothers' side. In 1785, the eighty-year-old Moses Nunes named his own two sons and George Galphin Jr. to execute his estate.[52]

Levi Sheftall also appears to have straddled the fence. He served on the Parochial Committee in 1774; the next year he signed a resolution with thirty-four other inhabitants of the city for a peaceful resolution of the imperial crisis. During the war, he served as a guide for the French troops near Savannah in 1779 and provided the patriots with provisions. The next year, however, he accepted a British amnesty and British general Cornwallis listed him as one of his spies. Indeed, his diary notes that he spent much of the war in North Carolina and Virginia. Sheftall remained in Savannah after the British seized it, only to move to Charleston in 1780 before they took that city. His name appeared on a British list of patriot sympathizers and a revolutionary list of Tory sympathizers. In 1782, he and Isaac DeLyon were the only two Jews in Georgia punished for disloyalty. Three years later, along with DeLyon, his rights were restored and the fine remitted through the efforts of his brother Mordecai. Sheftall had argued with his brother that DeLyon was no Tory either, but had become an enemy of Abraham Seixas, who spread the rumor that DeLyon had attempted to shoot Seixas's father. Seixas refused to fight a duel when DeLyon asked to defend his honor, and in retaliation insisted that "this young man was a spy, was a very bad man, and did all in his power to get him confined."[53]

Georgia was the least vindictive state in punishing Tories and opened its doors wide to British merchants immediately after the Revolution. In fact, like the state's leading gentile families, including the Houstouns, Joneses, Habershams, and Telfairs, the Sheftalls appear, perhaps deliberately, to have made sure members appeared to take opposite sides to protect the family as a whole and its property no matter who won the war. The puzzling behavior of the Nunes family could also be explained this way.[54]

The loyalty of the Minis family to the patriot cause, however, was unquestioned. It was headed by Abigail, born in 1701, widow of Abraham Minis, who had died in 1757. Despite supplying the American forces around Savannah, and the fact that her son Philip was paymaster for Georgia's troops in the Continental army, in January 1780 Governor Wright gave her permission with her five daughters—none of whom married until their mother died at the age of ninety-three in 1794—to leave for Charleston, where she and her family waited out the war. Although it is necessary to speculate, her exile was probably made possible by close ties among many loyalist and patriot leaders, and the fact that a woman and five daughters could easily claim to have been compelled to have supported the rebel forces. The petition was signed individually by Minis and all of her daughters to emphasize this point. But Minis's bold handwriting in her letter to

Wright does not reflect a victimized female. It reflects instead the strong personality and sense of business acumen she exhibited in her almost simultaneous request to Mordecai Sheftall: she not only asked him, while he was in Philadelphia, to try to get back the money she advanced for the rebel cause, but to reinvest it in a profitable venture. In the years after the Revolution, she rebuilt her business, and left her five daughters—"who with great affection have always treated me as their fond Mother, and by their industry to have helped not only to Gain what I possess, but by their frugality to keep together my estate"—eleven slaves, thirty-six head of sheep, nineteen cattle, and nearly £700 in household items along with cash and real estate. Abigail never retired: in 1793, the year before her death, she won a judgment in South Carolina for £1,000 sterling from the prominent Georgia merchants John and Joshua Gibbons.[55]

Jewish participation in the Revolution remained controversial into the 1780s. In late 1784 or early 1785, as the Georgia legislature was debating which foreigners could be naturalized, a "Citizen" circulated in Savannah a pamphlet entitled "Cursory Remarks on Men and Measures in Georgia." The immediate motive was a lawsuit between "a half-breed man, descended of a white father (who is also supposed to be of the race of Jacob) and a free Indian mother, [who] had brought suit against a full-blooded Jew," patriot leader Mordecai Sheftall. Each denied the other's right to legal standing, positions that the "Citizen" found "peculiarly droll" in what he claimed was "a Christian country." The court ruled, with Chief Justice George Walton speaking for two out of the three judges, that the Jew had the right to sue, the Indian did not.

Walton's ruling was understandable. His friendship with Sheftall went back at least until the founding of the Parochial Committee in 1774, and both men had suffered for their patriotism; Walton was badly wounded, and Sheftall spent two years in a British prison. Most backcountry Indians, on the other hand, had supported the Crown. The "Citizen" disagreed with Walton, arguing that Jews had never been granted citizenship either in England or Georgia, thereby ignoring the fact that they had made use of courts in both nevertheless. "Having said so much against the Jews," the "Citizen" amazingly claimed to be "as far removed from being a votary or friend to persecution as any man upon earth," insisting the Jews had brought their sufferings on themselves. "Had the Jews in this state but conducted themselves with common modesty and decorum," he would have been willing to permit them "to enjoy by *courtesy* some which it would be impossible to concede of *right* in a Christian country." But Georgia's Jews were "eternally obtruding themselves as volunteers upon every public occasion, one day assuming the lead at an election, the next asking upon them to direct the police of the town, and the third daring to pass as jurors upon the life and death of the freeman."

No Georgia Jews were more politically active than Benjamin and Sheftall Sheftall. If such practices were permitted, the "Citizen" predicted that soon they would have "Christianity enacted into a capital heresy, the synagogue [would] become the established church, and the mildness of the New Testament compelled to give place to the ferocity and severity of the Old." He concluded by arguing that the Jews were placing too much trust in Walton's ruling, and that most Georgians would turn out the chief justice, whose term was due to expire shortly.

To support his claim that he did not wish "to stir up the spirit of intolerance against that despised and unhappy people," the "Citizen" singled out "one whole family (and perhaps to these might be added two or three other individuals) whose long residence, upright demeanor, and inoffensive behavior have always claimed, and now procure for them the countenance and esteem of every honest Christian." He was speaking of the Minises, for he noted that "the females . . . are by far the largest part" of the family in question. He perhaps hoped to drive a wedge between Georgia's two most important Jewish families by identifying the good Jews as women, who had adopted an apolitical and passive stance. The Minis women, of course, could not be candidates for the vote or political office, so by praising them the "Citizen" hoped to lessen his own bigotry by showing he was not prejudiced against all Jews, but only against those who exercised their political rights. The "Citizen" tried to use the Jews' patriotism against them, perhaps hoping that most Georgians would forget the Jews' services to the Revolution in their zeal to establish a Christian republic and turn on the Jews for having intruded in "their" Revolution.

Sheftall's brother Levi responded by claiming the status of "A Real Citizen" in a notice in the *Georgia Gazette* of January 13, 1785.[56] He sarcastically noted the "hatred" manifested in "nine pages of this masterly piece of learning and wit," before asking "what the Jew particularly alluded to . . . has done that he should not also be entitled to the rights of citizenship." Sheftall pointed out his brother's imprisonment, refusal to beg for a British pardon—as opposed to many leading citizens—removal of his property so the enemy could not use it, and "discharge [of] the several trusts reposed in him." Levi Sheftall left it "to the Whigs to judge" whether they would reduce such a man to the legal status of "an African that deserts his master's service."

Sheftall's public reply, from a "Real Citizen," was based on a much less restrained, unpublished draft that he penned while in the heat of anger. Using the word "base" several times, Sheftall called the "Citizen" a "destroyer of the rights and privileges of a whole set of people" to mask the fact that he himself was a "base deserter of his country's cause." Sheftall originally sought to conclude his notice with,

> He [the "Citizen"] says he has traveled with the Jews through a wilderness of History [to prove they never enjoyed civil rights outside of ancient Israel]. It had been much better for him, had he traveled as far to the Northward, as some of them has done, and partook his share of the suffering, which they and many other good Whigs suffered, rather than basely submit themselves to become tools of the enemies and traitors to their country.

Sheftall noted that the "Citizen" had also begged pardon of Sir Henry Clinton and was ordered imprisoned by the American authorities. He thereby branded his brother's critic as a loyalist who attacked the Jews both to defeat Walton and to redirect attention from his own lack of patriotism. Yet, Levi Sheftall, too, may have been trying to expunge some guilt at his own waffling by identifying with his unequivocally heroic brother.

Sheftall's reply was effective. He noted that "the little Countenance" the "Citizen's" charges "met with from the public, in General, must long ere this have convinced him, that he might have imployed his time to some better purpose." That the letter was originally circulated "under cover of night" suggests that that the "Citizen" realized his ideas would not be popular. On February 13, the legislature authorized the naturalization of "all free white persons being Aliens nor subjects of any foreign state or kingdom at peace with the United States." Two Jews were among the first to register.

The Jews of Georgia, like the state itself in general and Jews throughout the new nation, undoubtedly supported the creation of a federal government. To all purposes, there was no antifederalism in an underpopulated state threatened with an Indian war. By the early 1790s, Jews had attained full civil rights in Georgia with the new state constitution, as they did in South Carolina. Like their coreligionists to the North, after 1793 they too declared their loyalty to the Republican party, which sympathized with the French Revolution that had emancipated the Jews. Both of Savannah's most prestigious Jewish families, the Sheftalls and the Minises, actively supported the French. Mordecai Sheftall served as agent for the prizes French privateers brought into Charleston and Savannah, and aided in smuggling slaves seized from the British, as the trade was then illegal. Sheftall's twenty-six-year-old son, Benjamin, served on the French privateer *Industry* and died at sea. Sixteen-year-old Abraham Minis wrote to his sister from Charleston in March 1794 that "war is all the theme here, four effigies were hung here on Saturday." "In the evening he went by the Republican Society" and despite his youth, expressed the "hope that I will not show myself a coward when my country calls." (Minis died in a carriage accident while visiting relatives in Rhode Island in 1801).[57]

Political and religious concerns merged in the turbulent late-eighteenth-century history of Savannah's Mikveh Israel, which was constituted for the third time in 1786. As with the congregations further north, newer members found the strictness of the synagogue's elders, who had struggled long and hard to maintain a Jewish presence, confining. In 1795, Samuel Benedix—who four years earlier had been temporarily suspended for doing business on Rosh Hashanah and the Sabbath—and Moses Simons blew a nonkosher shofar (ram's horn) on Rosh Hashanah and then ate their morning meal. Both men were recalcitrant when confronted by the elders: Simons spoke for both of them when he told the investigating committee that he "would do it again and that this Adjuncta had no jurisdiction over him—that he was no congregator." In 1799, the small congregation, in need of every member, repealed Benedix's second suspension.[58]

Publicly expressed anti-semitism was rare in Savannah, but as in Charleston became more, rather than less, prevalent with the new century. In 1800, Sheftall Sheftall placed a notice in the *Columbian Museum and Savannah Advertiser* offering a fifty-dollar reward for revealing the "evil minded person or persons [who] have destroyed the gate belonging to the burial ground of the Hebrew congregation of Savannah, and have injured the walls of said burying ground, in a shameful manner." Twelve years later, it was Moses Sheftall who offered a ten-dollar reward for identifying "those person who make a practice of setting up TARGETS against the gates of the burial ground . . . to shoot at."[59]

Who these culprits were is unknown, but we do know the names of the members of the Savannah Dancing Assembly who in 1807 refused to admit Moses Sheftall. Sheftall published them in the *Republican and Savannah Evening Ledger,* where he "bid defiance to your malignity." He asked his opponents "what has a religion to do with a ballroom. If this is a crime, take a look amongst yourselves and see whether there's none of you whose moral conduct has been more liable to censure than mine." Yet religion may have had less to do with Sheftall's exclusion than politics: he himself had asked, "can you . . . say that my political sentiments had no influence in your decision[?]" At the head of the list of his opponents was John Macpherson Berriam, a leading Federalist; Joseph Habersham, a relative of Robert Habersham, another signatory, had been appointed postmaster general of the United States by President Adams. As southern Federalists lost their political power, it seems they sought to retain whatever exclusivity they possessed by limiting their social circle.[60]

Sheftall's exclusion was ironic, for his brother Levi was one of the city's most prominent patrons of the theater, which the Federalists in general supported. He proposed performances on Saturday nights—after the Jewish Sabbath ended and before the Christian started—so that practitioners of both religions might attend. The town's Baptist minister, Henry Holcombe, an opponent of theater, blamed the choice of time on "a Jew . . . two deists, and . . . a Blockhead," showing that the city's cosmopolitan elite shared the contempt of a predominantly lower-class, evangelical church.[61]

Whether such anti-semitic conduct was exceptional or the expression of more general attitudes is hard to say. Perhaps it was not coincidental that

Georgia's Republican Jews began to hold political office as the Jeffersonians became the dominant party. In Savannah, Abraham Minis was clerk of the mayor's court (1798–1801), and Levi Sheftall served as commissioner of the market (1801–2). The post of fire chief and the three commissioners of the market almost seem to have been reserved for Jews. Levi Sheftall (1801–2, 1805–6), Isaac Minis (1804–5, 1809–10), and Moses Sheftall (1808–9) held the former position; Levi Sheftall (1800–1801), Levy Abraham (1802–3, 1804, 1807–9), and Moses Sheftall (1802–4, 1810–11, and 1818–19) the latter. Two other Georgia Jews, Abraham Simons and David Emanuel, unlike some of the Dancing Assembly's members, had been war heroes and frontier traders. Simons lived in Augusta and was considered Jewish by his fellow townsmen when they elected him to the Georgia legislature in 1804. Emanuel lived in Waynesboro, and although whether he remained a practicing Jew is in doubt, his ancestry was Jewish. He served repeatedly in Georgia's legislature and became governor of the state in 1801.[62]

Perhaps the best indication that Jews were treated as social equals by Georgians of all social strata was the outcome of the Stark-Minis duel in 1832. Sometime in the spring of 1832, James Stark, a member of the Georgia legislature, had been drinking at Luddington's bar in downtown Savannah and "without any provocation, cursed [Dr. Philip] Minis for a 'damned jew,' a 'damned Israelite,' [saying] 'he ought to be pissed upon' and 'he was not worth the powder and lead it would take to kill him,' and abuse of a similar character." When Minis asked for an apology, Stark demanded satisfaction. A duel was arranged for August 9, but various misunderstandings occurred. A letter from the town's standing committee that attempted to arbitrate these quarrels and reduce the alarming number of duels was misplaced; Minis failed to show up for an arranged encounter by mistake—he was only given five hours' notice, apparently—yet he was "openly laughed at as a coward" for his failure to appear. The following day Minis ran into Stark in the bar of the City Hotel and in turn called him a coward. When Stark "put his hand in his pocket, as if to draw something, and advance[d] upon Minis, Minis shot him dead with his pistol." Although a coroner's inquest returned a verdict of "deliberate murder," a jury acquitted Minis several months later on the grounds he had properly defended his honor. As with almost all the numerous Christian duelists in antebellum Savannah

and the South, Minis was permitted to defend his honor despite laws prohibiting duels. That Stark would agree to fight him, that prominent people
would defend him, and that a jury presumably composed of people of various classes would acquit him indicate that an upper-class Jew was considered the social equal of anyone in Savannah.[63]

When young Benjamin Sheftall died at sea, his uncle Levi copied into his
diary the poem a friend wrote to honor Benjamin that was published in the
Savannah Gazette on October 30, 1794. The most emotional utterance in
the Sheftall diaries, which span three-quarters of a century, from the
founding of Georgia in 1733 until Levi's death in 1809, it reflects the extent
to which the Sheftalls held together a community whose members departed
in the face of a threatened war with Spain in 1740 and again during the
American Revolution.

> Far—far from home, his cruel fate he met
> No father near, his drooping soul to cheer
> No mother from his brow to wipe the sweat
> No tender friend his languid head to rear—
> His memory will ever be dear to his friends, as he possessed
> A heart, alive to the calls of honor and Humanity.

Like Abigail Minis, Levi Sheftall's first loyalty was to the preservation of
his family and Judaism in its precarious situation in Georgia. The Sheftall
diary, which contains the birth, death, marriage, and arrival of every Jew in
Savannah, details Jewish history as does no other source in early America. It
remained unpublished until 1965, but Savannah and its thriving nineteenth-
century Jewish community possessed a living memorial in the form of Levi
Sheftall's nephew and Mordecai's son Sheftall Sheftall, who welcomed
Lafayette on his return in 1825 and lived until the age of eighty-five in 1847.
As historian Joseph Wearing wrote, "He was the only man in town who continued to wear the fashions of his youth—knee breeches and cocked hat of
the Continental line. As a boy he had been captured when the British seized
the town in 1778, and he had many a stirring tale to tell of those days, but-
tonholing his friends on Bay Street or pacing up and down on the long front
porch of his house on West Broughton Street." When in 1841 he was unable
to pay his taxes, the city gave him, "one of the oldest citizens of Savannah
and a relic of the revolution," a privilege it never awarded anyone else before

or since: an exemption from city taxes. Until his death, "Cocked Hat" Sheftall was one of the town's great attractions, always willing to entertain visitors with tales of Savannah's past and the role of the Jews and his family in shaping it. To this day, Minises and Sheftalls may be found holding prestigious jobs and living in good Savannah neighborhoods. And the Sheftalls still enjoy legal possession of the tombs of their ancestors.[64]

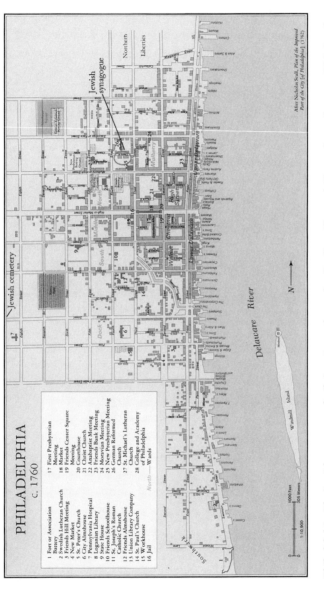

PHILADELPHIA
c. 1760

Jewish cemetery

Jewish synagogue

1   Fort or Association
    Battery
2   Swedish Lutheran Church
3   Friends Hill Meeting
4   New Market
5   St. Peter's Church
6   City Almshouse
7   Pennsylvania Hospital
8   Loganian Library
9   State House
10 Friends Schoolhouse
11 St. Joseph's Roman
    Catholic Church
12 Friends Almshouse
13 Union Library Company
14 St. Paul's Church
15 Workhouse
16 Jail

17 First Presbyterian
    Meeting
18 Market
19 Friends Center Square
    Meeting
20 Courthouse
21 Christ Church
22 Anabaptist Meeting
23 Friends Bank Meeting
24 Moravian Meeting
25 New Presbyterian Meeting
26 German Reformed
    Church
27 St. Michael's Lutheran
    Church
28 College and Academy
    of Philadelphia

North — Wards

Delaware River

Windmill Island

N

Southwark

Northern
Liberties

Mulberry

North
Front

South
Front

North Water

South Water

North

1000 Feet
305 Meters

1:10,900

After Nicholas Scull, *Plan of the Improved*
Part of the City [of Philadelphia] (1762)

Philadelphia. The Jewish synagogue built in 1782 was located at Sterling Alley and Cherry Street (between Third and Fourth Streets and Arch and Race Streets). The cemetery, not shown on the map, was on Spruce Street between Eight and Ninth Streets, opposite the Pennsylvania Hospital.
(After Nicholas Scully, "Plan of the Improved Part of the City" [1762]. Map adapted from Lester J. Cappon, *Atlas of Early American History: The Revolutionary Era, 1760–1790.* © 1976 Princeton University Press, renewed 2004. Reprinted by permission of Princeton University Press.)

CHAPTER 6

PHILADELPHIA, PENNSYLVANIA

THE PROVINCIAL COMMUNITY, 1737–1776

W E HAVE LITTLE INFORMATION ABOUT Isaac Miranda, the first known Jew who lived in Pennsylvania. The best guess is that he came from Italy and arrived sometime between 1710 and 1715. But the little we do know encapsulates much of the early Pennsylvania Jewish experience. He lived in Philadelphia before moving to Lancaster, thus dwelling in Pennsylvania's two centers of eighteenth-century Jewish settlement. Miranda made his fortune in the west, trading with the Indians, a major source of Pennsylvania Jews' wealth and the focus of much of their political activity before the Revolution. He rose to become deputy-judge of the court of vice-admiralty for Pennsylvania, the only major civic post held by any Jew in Pennsylvania until the election of Thomas Jefferson in 1800, signifying the close links between leading Jews and the philo-semitic, Anglicized elite.

Yet Miranda's experience points to the difficulty Jews would have assimilating into a society many of them warmly embraced, especially later on in the revolutionary era. Miranda encountered this problem all by himself even after he converted to Christianity. Provincial Secretary James Logan called him "the apostate Jew or fashionable Christian," a statement that conveys a hint of anti-semitism by stating that Miranda only became a Christian because it helped him achieve wealth and status. And that he did: he left his heirs two houses in Philadelphia and a farm in Lancaster in addition to silver plate, books, and furniture.[1]

Miranda felt sufficiently confident of his social position that he offered a handsome sum of money in his will to James Hamilton if he would marry Miranda's daughter, to whom he gave the unmistakably Christian name of

Mary (Rebecca, Rachel, Abigail, and Sara were the most frequent early American Jewish female names). Hamilton, a member of the elite, whose father Andrew was the original "Philadelphia lawyer" who successfully defended John Peter Zenger in New York during his libel trial of 1735, did not accept the offer. For despite Miranda's conversion and stipulation in his will of 1732, probated in Lancaster, that he receive a "Christian-like and decent burial," contemporaries continued to regard him as Jewish. Could this have been the reason for Hamilton's refusal?

Judaism functioned in early Pennsylvania both as a religion, which could be repudiated, and an ethnicity, which could not. Colonials frequently used the terms *race* and *nation* to describe the Jewish people. For example, Midrach, or Michael, Israel married Mary Paxton, an Anglican: their son Israel, born in 1744 and baptized a Christian in Pennsylvania two years later, became the principal target of Federalist anti-semitism in the 1790s for his Republican activism. David Franks, who had moved to Philadelphia from New York to tend to his wealthy family's business interests in Pennsylvania, married Margaret, daughter of Peter Evans, Philadelphia's registrar of wills. Their children were baptized at Anglican Christ Church, while Franks continued to be active in Jewish affairs, sometimes attending synagogue in New York before Philadelphia Jews began to hold their own services in the 1760s. The Franks family's faith did not preclude its rise in high society, as a poem written by Joseph Shippen to honor the belles at the 1774 Assembly Ball attests:

> With just such elegance and ease
> Fair charming [Miss] Swift appears;
> Thus [Miss] Willing, whilst she awes, can please;
> Thus Polly Franks endears.

David Franks's marriage to a gentile, however, prevented his burial in Philadelphia's Jewish cemetery despite his generous contributions to the synagogue. Gentiles, too, discriminated against ethnic Jews who crossed accepted boundaries. At the turn of the nineteenth century, Christian republican politicians Israel and John Israel, father and son, were the frequent targets of Federalist anti-semitism.[2]

Judaism was the only ethnic characteristic that united Pennsylvania

Jews. Otherwise, their origins of were as diverse as the general population's. Although the majority were of central European or Ashkenazi origin, Sephardic Jews tended to be wealthier and better connected with England. Philadelphia's first permanent Jewish settlers, brothers Nathan and Isaac Levy, arrived in the late 1730s. Born in New York, the Levys were of German descent like the Franks brothers, David and Moses, who followed them in 1740 from New York to Philadelphia.[3] Nevertheless, all had been raised in New York's Sephardic synagogue.[4] The Reverend Mr. Jacob Raphael Cohen, hazan or minister at the first Philadelphia synagogue from 1784 until his death in 1811, was of uncertain origin, but was commonly believed to hail from the Barbary Coast. He had arrived by way of London, then Canada—where he presided at the Spanish and Portuguese Jewish congregation of Montreal—and finally New York. Haym Salomon, the great financial supporter of the Revolution, was born in Poland of Portuguese stock and then fled to Philadelphia from New York during the Revolution. Benjamin Nones, heroic major in the Revolutionary War, interpreter for the French and Spanish to the United States government, ardent Jeffersonian Republican, and powerful apologist for Jewish citizenship, came from Bordeaux in France. His family then moved to Savannah, before he came to Philadelphia during the American Revolution following the fall of that city to the British. Merchant Jonas Phillips, of Spanish descent, was born near Aix-la-Chapelle in the Prussian Rhineland and came to Philadelphia by way of London, New York, and Charleston, South Carolina.[5]

Despite this diversity, a few interrelated families comprised the core of Pennsylvania's Jewish elite. Moses Raphael Levy (1665–1728), a wealthy New York merchant, had seven surviving sons—clearly too many to manage the family business in one city—and four daughters from two marriages. He sent the sons Nathan (1704–53) and Isaac (1706–77) to Philadelphia in the late 1730s. Despite the quarrel between his second wife, Grace Mears Levy, and her stepdaughter, Abigaill Levy Franks (see New York chapter), two sons, Samson (1722–1801) and Joseph (1728–1752), and one daughter, Hettie, joined their stepbrothers in Philadelphia when their mother Grace died in 1740, although Joseph later returned to New York. Arriving at the same time as the younger Levys were the Franks brothers Moses (1719–1789) and David (1720–1794), sons of New York's wealthiest and best-connected Jewish merchant Jacob Franks (1688–1769) and Abigaill Levy Franks. The Franks were thus the nephews of the two Levy brothers. Moses returned to England, where he became one of the wealthiest and most important Jews in the country, but David stayed in Philadelphia. The Franks family supplied British troops in Jamaica during the War of Jenkins' Ear and King George's War (1739–48), while also, through their agents in Charleston, assisting James Oglethorpe of Georgia in his attacks on the Spanish in Florida. Levy and Franks was also the first Jewish merchant partnership in Philadelphia: their ship *Myrtilla* brought the Liberty Bell to America in August 1752.[6]

Two other families comprised the core of Pennsylvania's elite Jewish community. Joseph Simon (1712–1804) arrived in Lancaster sometime around 1740: he soon became the leader of a group of Jewish merchants and traders who specialized in supplying frontier settlers and, when war came, the British army. Although his own two sons were described as "weak minded" and never married, his four daughters all wed capable men. With their father-in-law's help they launched prominent merchant families whose careers transcended colonial boundaries. Levi Phillips and Solomon Myers Cohen lived mostly in New York and Philadelphia, but Solomon Etting's heirs became the first important Jewish family of Baltimore after doing business in Pennsylvania and New York. Most impressive of all were the achievements of son-in-law Michael Gratz (1740–1811) and his brother Barnard (1738–1801), who arrived in Pennsylvania from Silesia about 1760. To complete the family circle, Barnard Gratz married Solomon Myers Cohen's sister Richea. Solomon Etting, upon the death of his wife, Rachel Simon, married the Gratzes' sister Richea. Michael Gratz's daughter, Rebecca (1761–1849), was famed as one of the most beautiful and intelligent women in America: choosing not to marry her beloved Samuel Ewing rather than renounce her faith, she may have been the model for another Rebecca, the Jewish heroine of Sir Walter Scott's *Ivanhoe*. The Gratz family's subsequent concern for Pennsylvania's history and their own role in shaping it led to their donation of one of the most important collections of papers at the Historical Society of Pennsylvania, an organization whose early success owed much to their endeavors.[7]

As can be learned from those papers, the Gratz story is the prototype of the American dream. Originally the brothers hailed from Langendorf in Silesia, a "wretched place, for the Jews are sorely oppressed with taxes by government," a relative reported in 1756 as the Seven Years' War began. Thanks to their cousin Solomon Henry, a London merchant whose trading connections stretched from the East Indies to the Western Hemisphere, Barnard was able to move to Kraków, then Prague, then London, then the East and West Indies (where he had no success), while Michael tried his luck in Berlin, Amsterdam, London, and India. Finally—thanks to the Henry family's connections with David Franks—they struck it rich in Philadelphia. The New York-Philadelphia axis of prominent Jews was extended when the two daughters of merchant Samuel Myers Cohen of New York married, respectively, Barnard Gratz and Mathias Bush; one of Cohen's sons wed Joseph Simon's daughter.

Barnard Gratz arrived in Philadelphia in 1753 or 1754, his brother Michael in 1760. It speaks much both for strong transnational family ties among the Jews, and for the influence of wealthy Jews with the British government, that Barnard and Michael were able to move to London in the midst of a war thanks to their cousin, whose son Jacob ran a branch of the family business in New York.

Along the way they developed a sibling rivalry. In 1758, twenty-year-old Barnard complained about his newly arrived brother to "Cousin Solomon" in a letter that also explained why Pennsylvania would be their final destination. Here at last, thanks to family capital, they could simply work hard and get ahead.

> This place requires honesty, industry, and good nature, and no pride, for he [Michael] must do everything pertaining to business, . . . [but] he has a mind to be stubborn. I would assist him as far as is in my power as a brother. That is not a great deal, as I am poor myself. But if he thinks himself wise enough and refuses to take advice of cousin Jacob and myself, then let him do what he pleases. I would not advise him to come here, as it would give me much pain and uneasiness.[8]

Michael would not let his character be challenged without an answer. Remarking that Barnard himself had been "very miserable" in India, he proceeded to vow by my very soul that everything I do is for the good of our family, even if it is not pleasant for me. I must learn the ways of the world and learn something of how things are done in the world. With what I have now I cannot support a family in our country, and not in this country. But there, I hope to get standing.

But within short order, perhaps realizing that a family that could send twenty-five hundred pounds in gold to impoverished Silesian relatives could bankroll more than one young man, the brothers were working harmoniously with each other, Joseph Simon, Solomon Etting, and numerous other Pennsylvania merchants both Jew and gentile.[9]

A good number of Pennsylvania's early Jews were thus wealthy, cosmopolitan people, easily accepted as members of an anglicized Philadelphia elite to which Quakers, Anglicans, and Presbyterians all belonged. Merchant Cosmus Alexander, in a 1769 letter he had delivered to a London wine merchant by "a sensible Jew," explained how religious differences were surmounted through business connections and personal friendship. He told his correspondent that "though you may have the same aversion to them that most of your country has, as you intend to follow business of some kind still [with America], he [the "sensible Jew"] can probably (over a glass) give you very good information of . . . most branches of business in America." Alexander then went on to relate how he had pleasantly lodged with a Philadelphia Jewess, and how the Jewish man bearing the letter had been "particularly generous" in freeing a debtor from prison by covering his debts to other parties as well renouncing his own. Benjamin Franklin set the pattern for colonial Pennsylvania's strain of philo-semitism when on September 15, 1737, about the time the Levys first settled in Philadelphia, he wrote in the *Pennsylvania Packet*: "The Jews were acquainted with the several Arts and Sciences long e're the Romans became a People, or the Greeks were known among the Nations."[10]

In the year 1744, three visitors to Pennsylvania were especially observant of the province's new Jewish community. That three travelers in one year should take notice of Pennsylvania's Jews and their cultural accomplishments is especially remarkable considering there were probably under fifty Jews in the province. Traveler Alexander Hamilton singled out Nathan Levy, who played "a good violin," as the only distinguished musician of a group he heard playing a "tolerable concerto." Witham Marshe, who visited Lancaster while on his way to representing Virginia at Indian negotiations in Philadelphia the same year, also commented on the Jews' gentility: "The only young ladies fit for a gentleman to dance with were the Jewish ladies." Another negotiator at the same conference, William Black, visited Samson Levy in Philadelphia. He not only praised the family's culture but was definitely attracted to Samson's sister Hettie.

> I went to Mr. Levy's a Jew and very Considerable Merch't, he was a Widdower and his Sister Miss Hettie Levy kept his House. We Staid Tea and was very agreeably Entertain'd by the Young Lady; She was of the middle Stature, and very well Made, her Complection Black but very comely she had two Charming eyes and well turn'd, with a Beautiful Head of Hair, Coal Black. . . . She was a Lady of a Great Deal of Wit, Join'd to a Good Understanding, full of Spirits, and humour Exceeding Jocose and Agreeable.[11]

Given such an attractive sister, it is no wonder that in 1748 Samson Levy was listed as a member of Philadelphia's Dancing Assembly, as was David Franks, who had married Mary Evans, the daughter of Philadelphia's city clerk, against his parents' wishes, although he himself remained a practicing Jew. Founded in 1738, the assembly charged the high annual fee of three pounds, fifteen shillings. Members included the proprietor, the governor, legislators, and leading merchants. Even today, the assembly marks the society debut of elite Philadelphia women. As Levy's admission shows, religion did not matter, class did: the assembly "had high vogue, partaking before the Revolution, of the aristocratic feelings of a monarchical government—excluding the families of mechanics, however wealthy," wrote annalist John Watson.[12]

Benjamin Franklin could not stomach the Dancing Assembly, which he could not have joined even had he wanted, but he and his fellow Pennsylvanians continued to welcome Jews both personally and in the various associations with which the town teemed.[13] These included the Philadelphia Academy (later the College of Philadelphia and University of Pennsylvania), where "the greatest liberality prevailed" of any college in America. When the Franklin Academy (later Franklin and Marshall College) was founded in Lancaster in 1787, four of the students to enroll in its first class were Jews, two of them women. In 1754, David Franks became a member of Franklin's Library Company. Levy Andrew Levy, Lancaster merchant (1734–1829), subscribed to that town's public library and belonged to its fire company. A significant proportion of Philadelphia's Jewish men belonged to the city's Masonic lodges: at the height of the influx of refugees during the American Revolution, thirteen of the fifty-six members of the Sublime Lodge of Perfection were Jews, including the deputy grand master, Solomon Bush. Four of the original subscribers to the Chestnut Street Theatre were Jews.[14] On the other side of the coin, gentiles Benjamin Franklin, Thomas McKean, Charles Biddle, and David Rittenhouse were among the donors when in 1788 the congregation Mikveh ("the hope of") Israel desperately needed money to finish and furnish its synagogue.[15] Portraits of eighteenth-century Pennsylvania Jews are indistinguishable from those of contemporary Christians.[16]

During the "Great War for Empire" (1754–63), well-to-do Pennsylvania Jews assumed a role their European brethren had filled for over a century. Service to one's country, although not without profit, was expected of the mercantile as well as of the military elite. Like the "court Jews" of various nations who had occasionally received titles of nobility—although less exalted titles than those given to gentiles for comparable services—their provincial counterparts were responsible for a good deal of wartime supply and finance. In 1760, Moses Franks was the only Jew belonging to a consortium of four merchants charged with keeping all the British troops in North America fed, clothed, and properly armed. The contractors relied heavily on Franks's connections and relatives to do their work in the New World: four of the five contractors in Canada were Jews; David Franks's brother-in-law Oliver Delancey and his partner John Watts handled New York matters; Pennsylvania was placed in charge of William Plumsted, merchant and former mayor of Philadelphia, and David Franks. David, in turn, went into partnership with three of his subcontractors, Joseph Simon of Lancaster, Levy Andrew Levy, and gentile merchant William Trent, to build the largest store in Pittsburgh, which remained opened from 1760 to 1769. Like Jews throughout Europe who had been able to play a critical role in supplying the armies of Marlborough and Prinz Eugen in the War of the Spanish Succession (1701–13), the Franks brothers and their connections were effective not because they were richer than Christian merchants and bankers, but because their international network permitted an especially rapid transfer of funds from one end of Europe to another, and then from Europe to America. The Jewish merchant community anchored by the Franks family of London, New York, and Philadelphia handled over three-quarters of a million pounds worth of provisions and munitions in the final years of the war.[17]

That Plumsted and Franks received this lucrative appointment because of wealth, reputation, and connections rather than experience appears in a letter Plumsted wrote to Colonel Henry Bouquet, who directed the royal forces on the Pennsylvania frontier, when he learned of his selection: "as we are in a great degree strangers to the methods used in supplying the Army," Plumsted requested "if your time will permit you may give us some instructions for our government in the conducting it." But Franks and his subcontractors did a good job: within a month of beginning their work, subordinates were informing Bouquet that the soldiers "are now pretty well supplied at every garrison." Much like Benjamin Franklin, Franks and his associates served as mediators between British officers who demanded that the provincials provide the sinews of war and Americans who did not want to part with their lives, wagons, or draft animals. They made numerous deals with reluctant colonials, cajoling or threatening them to do their duty, all the while trying to placate the British, as the following two examples illustrate. On June 8, 1760, David Franks wrote from Carlisle to Barnard Gratz in Philadelphia: "Give the Waggoners a strict Charge not to Stop by the Way, or they'l Loose their pay and be hang'd." During Pontiac's Rebellion, in June 1763, Slough and Simon, Franks's subcontractors at Lancaster, explained to Bouquet why he had to pay wagon drivers more than expected. Apologizing for their direct language, Slough and Simon added a postscript: "You will please excuse our dictating to you in this Manner, as it is our best for the Good of the Cause." Bouquet did more than excuse his correspondents, but considered himself "much obliged to you for the Pains you have taken."[18]

Wartime supply contracts led to Jewish trading with the Indians and speculation in western lands. Philadelphia's Jewish community entered this arena through the connection of Barnard and Michael Gratz, who at first assisted David Franks, with George Croghan, Sir William Johnson's deputy superintendent of Indian affairs for the Northern Department from 1756 to

1772. Croghan had immigrated from northern Ireland, gone bankrupt at least once before, sired at least two children, a daughter by a wife in Europe (who married the son of future British general Augustine Prevost, hence Prevost's friendly correspondence with the Gratzes) and another by a Mohawk woman. Somehow Croghan worked closely with Franks, Simon, Levy, and Trent, and to a lesser degree with their principal competitors, the predominantly Quaker firm of Baynton, Wharton, and Morgan. Because of his position, Croghan could decide who could—legally, at least—sell liquor to the Indians at Pittsburgh, and since he himself operated a series of trading posts stretching from the Susquehanna to that town, he or anyone who worked with him had a decided advantage.[19]

Croghan's official position, his connections with Jewish merchants, and his friendly relations with the Indians, who in 1755 launched a series of bloody attacks on the Pennsylvania frontier, provoked a good deal of hostility from frontier whites and fellow traders. James Kenny, the Quaker charged by the province of Pennsylvania with managing its own store and interests at Pittsburgh, complained that everything "Subtility [sic] can Invent" was used at the "Store kept by Trent and Levy here (Franks being concerned)," along with "Croghan's Pollyticks," to get the Indians to buy goods on credit and "draw all the custom to that store." Kenny charged that "Levy the Jew" was making Indians pay more for goods such as blankets and leggings than the white people, but the Indians did not seem to mind. Unlike the Quakers, some of whom were trying to convert and civilize the Indians, Croghan and his associates joyfully befriended them on their own terms. Kenny reported how "Levy the Jew and Crawford the Trader" invited him to a "Barbecue of Turtle," but he "had no appetite for the feast, being held on the Island and they come over about Dusk like so many Drunken Indians." With some satisfaction, Kenny reported that the Indian way of life appealed even more to Levy's slave, who ran away to join them.[20]

Croghan's wheeling and dealing was such that it even inspired mistrust among his business associates. In 1774, Levy Andrew Levy wrote confidentially to Michael Gratz that "he is such an artful person, I make no doubt he will take some person in," although Levy added the words "in Virginia," implying the ability of Pennsylvania Jews to keep up with the wily Croghan. Whether or not they themselves were taken in, Pennsylvania's Jews stuck by Croghan though thick and thin until his death in 1782. In 1765, Joseph

Simon loaned him over two thousand pounds of goods to restock his inventory when the "Black Boys," a vigilante group of Indian-hating western Pennsylvanians, destroyed a caravan on its way to Pittsburgh. The Gratz brothers held mortgages on Croghan's land and assisted him in selling off millions of acres when he needed to pay his debts. In 1777, western Pennsylvanians accused Croghan of loyalism because he was a friend of the Indians attacking the frontier and several other traders were Tories. Although acquitted at his trial, Croghan was compelled to flee east to escape popular wrath. The Gratzes' partner William Trent vouched for Croghan's revolutionary loyalty and told of his "ill" use. The brothers also supported him, first in Lancaster, and then in Passyunk, for the last four years of his life even though he owed them about four thousand pounds. Although perpetually in debt, Croghan felt guilty about owing money and made herculean efforts to acquire the wealth needed to pay off his creditors. Referring to his distresses, he told Michael Gratz that he was only enduring a poor old age because "it was of my own free will I promised to pay all those old Debts which was not commonly done by the people that failed in Trade." Croghan chose the Gratzes to be two of the five executors of his estate, stipulating that none of the executors could act without Barnard Gratz's consent. He also gave them gifts of land and his historically valuable papers, which wound up at the Historical Society of Pennsylvania thanks to the Gratz family's bequest.[21]

Besides assisting with much of their lucrative frontier trade, Croghan lobbied for the Pennsylvania Jews' interests with the British government. He had been the prime mover behind a meeting at the Indian Queen Tavern in Philadelphia, on December 7, 1763, where he was authorized to go to London and join David Franks's by then enormously wealthy and influential brother Moses. There they would present "A Memorial of the Merchants and Traders, relative to the losses sustained in the late and Former Indian Trade, occasioned by the Depredations and war of the said Indians." David Franks joined three others in preparing the memorial. Of eighty-six thousand pounds requested by twenty-three merchants, Simon, Franks, Trent, Levy, and Company claimed the largest amount, some twenty-five thousand pounds. What they hoped for was not cash, but compensation in the form of extensive land grants in the Old Northwest.[22]

Intense political maneuvering in England over the next decade led to the creation of the Indiana, Illinois, Ohio, and Vandalia Land Companies, all of which had prominent British investors. Through the Treaty of Fort Stanwix in 1768 several Indian nations made a massive territorial concession that paved the way for these companies' success. But only in 1773 did the Board of Trade recommend that the "Suffering Traders of 1763"—who had at various times joined with and been opposed to the "Suffering Traders of 1754"—be allowed to start a new colony west of the Appalachians. (Benjamin Franklin, another interested speculator, had named it Vandalia in honor of England's queen, a German woman descended from the Vandals.) Croghan was ecstatic, predicting profits from the new colony would make him a "[debt-]free man," while the Gratzes "flattered" themselves that Croghan would "not forget us among your old friends if anything should offer" in the way of public office or business opportunities. Before they could reap the fruits of years of lobbying, however, the Quebec Act of 1774 quashed all provincial claims to the west by placing the region north of the Ohio and east of the Mississippi under the jurisdiction of Quebec. Levy Andrew Levy broke the bad news to the Gratzes: "Lord Dartmouth has sent orders to Lord Dunmore not to grant a foot of lands to any person on the Ohio and for him to make null and void the patents he has already granted." Levy, the Gratzes, Joseph Simon, and every Jewish male in Pennsylvania with the possible exception of David Franks (see the subsequent discussion) joined the Revolution.[23]

George Croghan was not the only frontier agent who worked for the Gratz brothers and maintained a strong friendship with them. The Jew Meyer Josephson was another. He would send the Gratzes venison from deer he had hunted, although he begged them "not to tell the other Jews in Philadelphia that I killed a deer, otherwise they will be against me." Although Meyer slaughtered the deer in the kosher manner by cutting their throats and draining the blood, he did not possess the formal qualifications of a shochet (butcher) and feared this would displease the community.[24] A third Gratz agent was the gentile William Murray. He was on sufficiently good terms with them that he was able to joke with "Michael," as he addressed him, playing easily with stereotypes that branded both Jews and the Scots-Irish as greedy. After selling some horses for the Gratzes, which the buyer promptly resold and made a profit of eleven pounds "in a few minutes," Murray wrote: "You see, Michael, that a Scotch Irishman can get the better in the bargain of a Jew." He added a humorous reference to the Gratzes' strict observance of their dietary laws, pointing out that he was their true representative on the frontier: "I cannot have it in my power to transgress the Mosaic Law by eating swine flesh here. Not one ounce of it is to be had in this beggarly place, nor indeed of anything else." Murray could even use some Jewish humor to chide Barnard Gratz for not recalling him right away to Philadelphia when he needed to return for financial reasons, playing upon the fact that the brothers had become very important men and inventing a mock-Talmudic parable: "As the devil will have it, you must be informed forsooth. That Moses was on the top of a mountain upon a sacred expedition"—Murray's and the Gratzes' ventures, of course, were anything but—"in the month of May, consequently, his followers must for a certain number of days cease to provide for their familys, though perhaps he may be promoted to such high rank above, that he may think it beneath his dignity to associate with his countrymen."[25]

Unlike the Pennsylvania merchants, who accepted and worked with the Gratzes, the Virginians were their competitors. The Gratzes' enterprises in Virginia, unlike those in the Ohio Valley, were unfortunate. In 1776, they bought a captured British vessel at Fredericksburg, unaware that Virginian Robert Johnstone of Port Royal was half owner. Johnstone "blustered" against the commissioners who made the sale and said it was "illegal . . . that the commissioners prefer Turks and Jews." The commissioners hastened to inform Gratz that he, as well as they, was under attack, and defended their legal position: "we were under no greater obligation to give warning to Mr. Johnstone than to you or the Grand Seigneur," they wrote concerning the ship's capture, meanwhile recommending that the Gratzes accept Johnstone's offer to buy out the other half of the ship and be done with it. Of course, no Turks were involved in the sale.[26]

The captured ship was but a prelude to the Gratzes' more serious problems with the state of Virginia itself. In the late 1770s it looked like they would lose their frontier lands in the "Illinois and Wabache" companies. The state of Virginia claimed the region south of the Ohio River to the Mississippi (including present southeastern Pennsylvania) and had enacted a law forbidding "foreigners" from owning land within its jurisdiction. The Gratzes, aided by the aging Croghan, hoped to interpret the act to exclude only people living outside the new United States, for its main purpose was to prevent the many British people who had speculated in western lands from owning a good chunk of the state. Barnard Gratz himself traveled to Williamsburg to secure his titles, and pointed out that his firm had advanced a good deal of the expenses for the George Rogers Clark expedition that enhanced Virginia's claim to the very territory from which he was being excluded. But a committee of the house of burgesses, largely influenced by Patrick Henry, a populist and extreme advocate of states' rights who appealed to average voters with his oratory, turned him down. Gratz received most of his support from Virginia's "first families," several of whom were his business connections. Whether anti-semitic remarks were made against him is unknown, but several Philadelphians, angered by Virginia's decision, arranged in 1781 to publish the pamphlet *Plain Facts*, expressing their outrage at the "mockery of justice" and "shameful distinction, made between Mr. Simms, a Virginian, and Mr. Gratz, a Pennsylvania, both holding under precisely the same right deduced from Mr. Croghan." Gratz and Lord Fairfax (Washington's aged patron, who had long lived in America and did not become a loyalist) were deemed "foreigners in Virginia."[27]

In 1783, after the war had ended, Barnard made another trip to Williamsburg to persuade Virginia to at least reimburse the money the Gratzes had advanced to Clark. Despite the support of Richard Henry Lee and a personal appeal by Clark to the burgesses, Governor Henry again opposed the plan on the grounds the state had no money. In June 1783, the house agreed to a new tax that would pay off the loan in the fall of 1784, if the state could afford it, which Gratz was sure it could have done at once even without the tax. "I am distressed to think of the disappointments of our Da[mne]d people here, after my staying here so long, and at last to be deceived by them" was all he could report to brother Michael. In 1785, Gratz was still trying to get his land or compensation for it from Virginia, although even his friends told him the state had no money. In 1788, he approached the national government, to which the disputed land reverted following the passage of the Northwest Ordinance. Gratz hoped James Madison would use his influence on his behalf, but the territory was absorbed into the federal domain for the Northwest Territories and the Gratzes were never compensated.[28]

In Pennsylvania as in Virginia, Jews who were supported by the cosmopolitan elite were the victim of populist anti-semitism. The first public, institutional presence of Philadelphia's fledgling Jewish community was a grave: one of Nathan Levy's children died in 1738 and was buried on the north side of Walnut Street between Eight and Ninth Streets. Two years later, the cemetery was relocated to its present site, at Spruce Street between Eighth and Ninth. These locations are significant: whereas Protestant graveyards were adjacent to churches and in the center of the city, Eighth and Ninth Streets were several blocks west of the built-up city until after the American Revolution. Since no synagogue existed until 1771, the Jews had carefully placed the only visible sign of their community's existence where it ought not have invited the sort of vandalism to which Jewish graveyards in Europe were subjected. Yet in 1751, Levy was forced to run the following advertisement in the *Pennsylvania Gazette* to bring to a halt a spate of graveyard desecration not experienced by any comparable Christian ceme-tery in the colonial era:

> Whereas, many unthinking people have been in the habit of setting up marks, and fired several shots against the fence of the Jews' burying ground, which not only destroyed said fence, but also a tombstone in it; there being a brick wall now erected, I must desire the sportsmen to forbear (for the future) firing against said wall. If they do, whoever will inform, so that the offender be convicted thereof before a Magistrate, shall have twenty shillings reward paid by NATHAN LEVY.[29]

It is hard not to read the words "unthinking" and "sportsmen" ironically. "Unthinking" may even have a double meaning: that the people who shot at the cemetery not only did so without premeditation, but were not gifted with intelligence. The brick wall must have done its job, however, for such problems did not occur again for thirty-five years. Perhaps out of sympathy for Levy, the city of Philadelphia permitted him to expand the graveyard in 1752, although he had been petitioning without success for several years. The first stone or stones in the cemetery indeed were destroyed, for the old-est surviving grave in the Mikveh Israel burial ground is that of Nathan Levy himself, who died in December 1753. Benjamin Franklin—who was no longer publishing the *Pennsylvania Gazette* but whose philo-semitic atti-tude was carried on by his partner and successor David Hall—honored him with an obituary that seemed to go out of its way to refute the stereotype that Jews were underhanded and antisocial: "the fair character he maintained in all his transactions, the cheerful and friendly disposition that constantly appeared in him, make his death much lamented." Levy's probated will demonstrates the cosmopolitanism of the Jewish elite, for his books included the laws of Massachusetts, dictionaries in several languages, works by Voltaire, Plutarch's *Lives*, John Locke's *Essay Concerning Human Understanding*, twenty-five music books, numerous items in Hebrew, and the violin he played so well—a good one worth fifty pounds.[30]

Levy died shortly after news of England's hostility towards the "Jew Bill" reached America. Once again, the *Pennsylvania Gazette* took up the Jews' cause. It ran a long article arguing that every advantage ought to be given to encourage the Jews to settle and flourish economically in the mother country: they held a "very considerable" share of the national debt, and it was better it was held and spent or invested at home. They also "supported their own poor," and since they were persecuted in other countries, the better England treated them, the more likely they were to move there. The *Gazette* added that "the petitions in favor of the bill are signed by the greatest number of the most eminent and extensive merchants, traders, and manufacturers, that hath been known on any former occasion," in the hope that it would "encourage rich Jews, who live in foreign countries, to remove, with their substance, and settle here, instead of France or Holland." Opposition to the "Jew Bill," the article implied by its silence, came from ignorant people who placed prejudice over the true interest of the realm.[31]

The diary of Hannah Callandar Sansom (1737–1801), daughter and wife of prominent Quaker merchants, also shows that anti-semitic prejudices required little prodding to be expressed. Sansom visited New York in 1756, attended that city's synagogue, and commented: "Their mode of worship has nothing solemn in it, nor their behavior neither." Bound by the "Slavery of Tradition, this people once the chosen people, [had become] the scum of the earth!"[32] Like other Christian observers, Sansom did not understand that a Jewish worship service was not comparable to a Christian: it relied on reading and explanation of texts rather than sermons and hymns, lasted several hours, people came in and out, and private conversations were the rule rather than the exception. Sansom's strong language shows that not all members of the elite shared the generous attitude toward Jews exhibited by Benjamin Franklin, the Masons, and the College of

Philadelphia. One of the reasons little anti-semitism was visible in prerevolutionary Pennsylvania was that the Jews were not much of a collective presence. They did not worship in a (tiny) synagogue until 1771, whereas in New York they had maintained one since the 1690s.

Yet beginning in the 1750s, attacks on Pennsylvania's handful of Jews, while not routine, were definitely disproportional to their numbers and influence. Pennsylvania's midcentury wars and their aftermath brought to the surface a latent anti-semitism that previously had little opportunity to manifest itself. Like their gentile counterparts who used the metropolis as a point of departure for inland settlement, Jewish tradesmen settled at Chestnut Hill, New Hanover, York, Reading, Pittsburgh, Easton—where one of eleven town founders was Jewish—and present-day Allentown and Harrisburg. (The supposed Jewish settlement at Schaefferstown, about twenty miles north of Reading, dating from around 1720, however, is mythical.) Most of these Jews were men, merchants, and peddlers, whose commercial occupations exposed them to the stereotype that Jews were greedy and nefarious. But after brutal warfare engulfed the Pennsylvania frontier from 1754 to 1765, Jewish merchants could also be blamed for their close connections with the pacifist Quakers and the Indians with whom they traded. Pennsylvania became an early site of a new form of a more virulent, political anti-semitism in North America in which Jews were blamed for the ruin of the country rather than simply being considered greedy and unpleasant people. At the same time Indians were being defined as "red" and a separate "race" that possessed unchangeable negative characteristics, Jews were also being recast in an increasingly, unflattering racist mold.[33]

Since the brunt of the war fell on the west, the brunt of much anti-semitism was borne by the Jews of Lancaster, Pennsylvania's largest Jewish community outside Philadelphia and the jumping-off point for frontier settlement and trade. Joseph Simon, the town's wealthiest merchant, presided over the several Jewish families in the area, where as early as 1747, perhaps even before Philadelphia, a minyan of ten men permitted religious services to be held at his house Aside from Simon's own extended kinship network and other merchants, the Jewish community included the physician Isaac Cohen of Hamburg, Germany, who advertised that he would treat poor people for free if they could present a certificate from a clergyman stating that they were really poor. (This appears to have been common practice—physician Andrew Judah, who came to New York in 1761, made the same offer.) In 1747, Richard Locke, an Anglican missionary belonging to the Society for the Propagation of the Gospel, expressed his surprise at Lancaster's ethnic composition: "here are less Quakers than in many other counties, and but few Indians appear," he noted, but "here are ten families of Jews."[34]

In 1766, the Lancaster Jews became the target of anti-semitism. In *Der Wochentlichte Philadelphische Staatsbote,* Pennsylvania's German-language newspaper published by Christopher Saur, Ludwig Weisz referred to Simon and his kinship network when he attacked "the Jew landlords" as "terrible people [who] make false claims and purchase land for a small sum of pocket money, then set upon German plantations" to the "ruin" of the families who lived there. Weisz implicitly compared Jewish financial practice to Indian warfare as a source of devastation for peaceful Christian families.[35] Simon, who had prospered as frontier refugees flocked to the town during the war, was a conspicuous target. Even David Brener, the sympathetic historian of Lancaster's Jews, termed Simon a "wheeler dealer of the first degree," although he qualified this remark with the phrase "he did it with class and honesty."[36]

The very people who testified to Simon's good character in response to Weisz illustrate why ordinary German farmers would dislike him. His support came from prominent inhabitants such as gunsmith William Henry, who called him "a Wealthy Jew of High Character," and Lancaster's Anglican minister Thomas Barton, who termed him "worthy [and] honest." On the other hand, Presbyterian minister David McClure condemned the town's Jews for their punctilious observance of the Sabbath on the one hand, while they "hesitate not to defraud," and "neglect the weightier matters of the Law, as Judgment, mercy, and faith," on the other: "They swallow a camel but strain at a gnat."[37]

That community leaders thought so highly of Simon may explain why spokesmen for the area's disgruntled German and Scots-Irish settlers may have criticized him, for provincial Lancaster was a conflict-ridden town and county, and the Scots-Irish and Germans bore the brunt of frontier warfare.[38] Even before warfare had broken out, the local Lutheran minister Johann Friedrich Handschuh revealed the nature of these prejudices. He was surprised when five Jewish women "behaved very decently and outwardly devout, so that I would not have recognized them for Jewesses if I had not been told so after." Over the next two years, he turned down repeated efforts by a former Jewess who wished to leave the Dunker community at Ephrata and convert to Lutheranism: "this woman appears to me to have a Jewish heart and earthly intentions." Even among the elite, there may have been latent anti-semitism. Brener notes: "It is interesting that most Gentiles found it necessary to describe Jews as being of high character or honest as if this were the exception rather than the rule."[39]

Another series of anti-semitic incidents in Lancaster County involved Barnard (sometimes Bernard) Jacob (or Jacobs) of Heidelberg, Schaefferstown, and Lancaster, a merchant who from 1757 to 1790 doubled as the itinerant circumciser for Pennsylvania. (That he only performed thirty-three ceremonies over an equal number of years illustrates the trouble the Jewish community had reproducing itself.) Jacob had a good reputation with local Christians: he was sufficiently respected that in 1760 he believed a letter from him published in the *Staatsbote* would effectively defend from criticism "the late and old Justice of Berks County," none other than the famous Conrad Weiser (1696–1760), and a neighbor of Jacob. The recently deceased mediator between Pennsylvania and the Indians had been attacked in some unspecified way by one Friedrich Robel, who was circulating his rumors in writing. Nevertheless, Jacob seems to have also offended Andreas Kreuzer and Alexander Schaffer, who were traveling with him. Dubbed "the so called Jew Rabbi at the Mill Creek," Jacob suddenly ran away from them yelling "murder, murder, murder," claiming they sought to kill him.[40]

If these men were either playfully or seriously threatening Jacob, they were clearly exceptional. Shortly thereafter, Pennsylvania Germans in the town of Mühlbachen trusted him with the management of a five-hundred-pound lottery for the building of a church (it was customary to hold lotteries to finance public buildings in colonial times). However, a dispute soon developed that dragged on for over three years because when the accounts were checked, forty pounds were missing. Joost Hoffman, whom Jacob entrusted with some of the sales, "decried me to the people . . . [and] this is what many foolish people say: He is a Jew, and has no qualms to keep the church money of the Christians, or, as one might say, steal it from them." Jacob published his side of the story, complete with the accounts, in the

Staatsbote for four weeks in a row beginning in August 1765. The only conclusion to be drawn, he argued, was "that the Jew does not have the Christian money in his hands, but Joost Hoffman wants to keep it, I believe,
because he had a Jew next to him, and wants to hang on to his honest
name"—"that is, as a good Christian," Jacob added sarcastically. Jacob further warned that he had given Hoffman, as the church's representative, a
bond for the five hundred pounds, which Hoffman refused to return. He
announced in the newspaper that he would under no circumstances pay
any debts Hoffman would charge against his bond. As with his sarcastic reference to Hoffman's good Christian name, Jacob turned the stereotype of
the dishonest Jew against his antagonist. He went even further—or perhaps
was trying to mock the very notion of stereotyping—with the ethnic slur
that Hoffman's behavior could be traced to the fact that "he has red hair."
Since red hair was far more common among the Scots-Irish than the Germans, Jacob could have been calling Hoffman's own ethnicity into question
by associating him with a group the Germans generally did not like.[41]

Jacob did not have the last word. One Jacob Schaub stated he had an
unfair reputation as "a great liar" thanks to Bernard Jacob, but that "a Jew
named Bernard Jacob . . . far surpasses me; indeed I believe he is the King
of Liars in all North, South, and West-America." Apparently Schaub was a
nobody, for Jacob did not respond, and later the city of Lancaster erected a
plaque to honor Jacob as the Jew who had helped the Christians build their
church. The Jewish merchant's last publication in the German paper,
which appeared three times in November and December 1766, was a reward
of ten pistoles for his runaway servant, a German named David Berger and
a potter by trade, who was identifiable by his "porpelgruebicht [pimply]
face and fine clothes." He was about twenty-five years old, five foot seven,
and spoke English well, although he "spoke little," mostly lies. Jacob added
that it was possible that Berger's wife—her name was Hanna Weberin, but
she was known as "proud lazy Anna"—and child had accompanied him,
and that he too had changed his name. Why Jacob waited until Berger, who
ran away on July 1, had been absent for nearly five months before posting
the reward remains a mystery. Jacob lived in Lancaster until the 1780s,
when he moved to Philadelphia and subsequently Baltimore, where he
probably died in the early 1790s.[42]

Besides demonstrating anti-semitism pure and simple, the attacks on

Simon and Jacob show how condemnations of biblical Jews served as a storehouse of popular anti-semitic stereotypes to be trotted out by Christians when the occasion was ripe. To be sure, most of the time when Christians mentioned biblical Jews negatively, they did so to criticize each other. As Natalie Z. Davis has noted, such colonial references to Jews "are so standard that they don't necessarily refer to literal Jews in the eighteenth century. That is, sometimes Christians used Biblical discussion of the Jews to talk about themselves."[43] For instance, in a colony committed to pacifism until the Seven Years' War, David Dove, one supporter of the war, used a tribe of Old Testament Jews who were unprepared for battle and thereby perished to signify the Pennsylvania Quakers. His *Fragment of the Chronicles of Nathan Ben Saddi* also compared the advocates of peace to false prophets who misled the ancient Hebrews. On the other hand, in the aftermath of the war, a Quaker termed the "Presbyterians" who justified the massacre of Conestoga Indians "Pharisees," a group of Jews biblically associated with sanctimonious hypocrisy and the death of Jesus. But in other instances, biblical and present-day Jews were linked via negative, innate characteristics of their "race." When Rev. Mr. McClure explicitly pointed to Lancaster's Jews as punctilious observers of the law who lacked human decency, he was clearly linking them to the biblical Pharisees, and implying that Jews were ethnically, that is innately, more prone to hypocrisy than Christians. This characteristic, he was arguing, had persisted over nearly two thousand years.[44]

While Jacob and Simon were fending off anti-semitic attacks, Jews in Philadelphia were welcomed into the ranks of those protesting British policy toward the colonies. In 1765, the Stamp Act, which required payment of a tax on all legal documents, imposed a heavy burden on Pennsylvania's Jews. Of some fifty Jewish families who lived in the colony, most were headed by merchants, peddlers, and storekeepers whose businesses depended on the transfer and authentication of letters of credit and customs documents such as invoices for goods that stated their value and place from which they were imported. On October 25, 1765, nine or ten (one person's religion is uncertain) Jews joined Philadelphia's merchant community in adopting a Non-Importation Agreement, pledging not to import goods from Britain until the Stamp Act was repealed. They included the Gratzes, David Franks, three members of the Levy family, and Mathias Bush.[45]

Even as Pennsylvania Jews were experiencing threats to their well-being from imperial rule, they also became aware of a threat from below: the increasing gap between rich and poor that historians Gary Nash and Billy Smith have found in the postwar city. Nowhere did this dual threat appear more vividly than in a 1769 letter from Mathias Bush to Barnard Gratz, who was in London at the time. While complaining of "dull" trade, Bush approvingly noted that when the local sailors found out who had informed the Philadelphia customs collector that "forty odd pipes of wine belonging to John Ross, Merchant" had been imported illegally, "they rolled the informer in tar and feathers and paraded through the streets with him." But at the same time Bush was declaring his solidarity with a fellow merchant and observing how people of different classes united in the struggle against British tyranny, he expressed concern that class divisions threatened the social order. "We are plagued with a parcel of New Jews," Bush complained. "They have wrote a foolish, ill-natured paper against the few old Jews settlers," who proceeded to retaliate: Bush, along with Moses Mordecai and Michael Gratz forbade one "R," the leader of the troublemakers, from coming to their houses "owing to his abusing Joseph Simon," Michael Gratz's father-in-law. Since synagogue services were held at the houses of prominent Jews before Mikveh Israel was built in 1771, this was more than a social prohibition. Bush only identified the man "who keeps all these Jews together" as "H." "Pray prevent, what is in your power to hinder, any more of that sort to come," Bush asked his correspondent.[46]

Contention within the Jewish community seems to have begun early on. Philadelphia Jews had begun worshiping at a house in Sterling Alley as early as 1747. Although the requisite ten men required for services could be mustered within a decade of the Levys' arrival, internal divisions prevented the construction of a synagogue until 1771. In 1761, in a letter to his cousin Barnard Gratz, New York merchant Jacob Henry rejoiced at "the great and mighty news with you in Philadelphia, that the building of a synagogue is actually resolved on, and, according to my intelligence, is to be put into execution with the utmost vigor." Since he had previously doubted "that the same could be talked of . . . for years to come," Philadelphia Jews must have been forming two factions by the late 1750s. Henry's misgivings proved more accurate than his hopes. During the High Holy Days of 1768, two rival minyans were meeting in people's houses. Since ten men were required for worship and there were only about Jewish twenty-five families in the city, this fact indicates a fairly equal division within the community.

Henry had offered a clue to the nature of the split when he inquired whether Philadelphia's anticipated synagogue would be modeled on the "Hambro [Hamburg], Pragg, or Poland style." Of the possible models, the Hamburg synagogue was noted in Europe as the center of Enlightened Judaism, whereas Prague and Poland were strongholds of the more conservative Ashkenazim. When meeting in unison, Pennsylvania Jews, although primarily of Ashkenazi descent, worshiped in the Sephardic manner of New York, from whence many of them had emigrated. Not only was the Sephardic service considered more socially respectable, the Sephardim were more liberal in their customs and assimilationist in their attitudes than the frequently poor eastern European and German-speaking Ashkenazim. The latter clung more tenaciously to observance of dietary and marriage regulations, sometimes wore beards and robes that distinguished them from other inhabitants, and observed the Sabbath more strictly.[47]

Henry expressed a wish that Philadelphia's Jews could unite in "the old mode of Pennsylvania," which "Seemingly Suites every Body." But it was not to be. The Jewish immigrants making their way to Pennsylvania in the 1760s and 1770s were generally either people of some wealth and education who had fallen on hard times, or else scoundrels or servants, several of whom ran away from their masters. Respectable Jews were worried that the presence of such newcomers would compromise the favorable reputation they had carefully cultivated among the gentile population.

Guilt by association with several Jews who had stolen goods and money in the Pennsylvania hinterland was probably at least partly responsible for the anti-semitism directed at Joseph Simon and Barnard Jacob in the 1760s. On December 4, 1760, the *Pennsylvania Gazette* reported that a trader named Meyer Levy, who had made his way to Pennsylvania from Surinam after living in New York and New Jersey, absconded with his trade goods, owing his creditors some £2,300. Fellow Jews Barnard Gratz and David Franks joined with five other merchant houses in offering the sizable sum of eight hundred dollars for his capture. Another two Jews ran into trouble in 1764 during the postwar depression. That August, Michael Isaac was reported as a fugitive. He was "supposed to be a Jew" who pretended to be a captain in the army, and had defrauded a weaver of fifty-six dozen pairs of stockings worth £133 16s. that he had promised to sell on his behalf. That December, Meyer Josephson, the Jewish shopkeeper in Reading, informed Barnard Gratz that someone claiming to be a Reb (rabbi) Mordecai had fallen into "serious financial difficulties" and was about to be jailed for debt. Josephson paid the money to "Bit [Biddle] the lawyer" and gave two reasons for this act of charity. First, Mordecai was "an honest man, but he has an erring head." Perhaps more importantly, Josephson was concerned that the imprisonment of a man purporting to be a rabbi not compromise the reputation of Jewish merchants such as himself or provide an excuse for anti-semitism: "Since the children of Israel have been in Reading, not one of them has ever been in jail, and Mr. Josephson does not want to start with the Reb Mordecai."[48]

The Jews' willingness to help their own inspired several postwar Jewish immigrants to Pennsylvania to play confidence games, pretending to be professional rabbis or scholars—neither of which the Philadelphia Jews had at the time—or merchants and gentlemen. (The situation was complicated by the fact that Jews with real wealth, such as Eleazar and Abraham Levy, were also arriving.) Emmanuel Lyon, a German who had lived in London, and "pretended to be a great scholar and well versed in the Hebrew tongue," was "abusive" and used "threatening language" when his benefactress Rachel Moses asked him to repay money she had advanced to set him up in trade. Isaac Jacob, another German who arrived by way of Ireland, was an "atrocious villain" who absconded with merchandise he had promised to sell on commission. Joseph Simon warned the Gratzes that someone was traveling around the province claiming to be the son of prominent London Jew Haym Galt, a relation of Levy Andrew Levy, and a friend to other prominent Jews. Although riding a horse, wearing a "cape, boots, wig, spurs, and otherwise appearing as a gentleman" in the company of another man "also dressed genteely," he reminded Simon of a vagrant who had previously appeared in Lancaster. The suspect began to cry when trying to convince Simon that David Franks had "loaned" him the horse and outfit. Although Simon was sure the man was an imposter and a convict, Simon's partner Matthias Slough let him stay overnight at his house "and was repaid for his goodness with counterfeit bills."[49]

Another associate of Simon, Benjamin Nathan, also ran afoul of the powerful Lancaster merchant. By 1759, he was the first Jewish shopkeeper in

Schaefferstown, although he had moved to Heidelberg by 1763. Simon and Andrew Levy worked with him until 1773, when they accused Nathan of both dishonesty and intemperance. They took him to court, seized his property, and left him with only his prayer book and shawl to attend synagogue, and a grindstone and knife to enable him to observe kosher dietary rules.[50]

Impoverished and importunate newcomers were sufficiently notorious that in 1783, Haym Salomon told his own uncle, who was living in England, to stay there. Stating that he had enough trouble providing for a father, mother, wife and three children, Salomon wrote: "your bias of my riches are too extensive. . . . It is not in my power to give you or any relations yearly allowances. . . . Don't fill your mind with vain and idle expectations and golden dreams."[51]

In addition to Jews who could fool others that they were reasonably well-to-do and educated, Jews who were genuinely poor came to Pennsylvania. The *Pennsylvania Packet* quoted a London newspaper: "Jews are brought into this kingdom, who beg their passage, and are set on shore without sixpence in their pocket," before setting out on their way to America. These included at least three Dutch Jewish indentured servants who arrived in 1772 in Philadelphia, along with poor Jews from Germany, France, Ireland, and the West Indies in the early 1770s. Between 1771 and 1776, six advertisements for runaway Jewish servants appeared in the *Pennsylvania Gazette*, the first ones recorded for Jews with the exception of a German Jew in his thirties who absconded in 1763 and could be recognized by his constant talk about setting up as a peddler. All were distinguished by their dark (in one case yellow) complexion. Their heights (from four feet, five inches to five feet, nine inches) and ages (sixteen to twenty-eight) were typical of young indentured servants. Several of them spoke bad English but good "Dutch" according to the advertisements. "Dutch" referred to Pennsylvania German, and although these men probably spoke a different dialect of German, perhaps Yiddish, it was as Dutch speakers that they would be recognized. Those who could converse in English were termed "artful" and "addicted to lying and swearing," respectively. Two of the men ran away twice: Abraham Peters, who absconded in 1771 with the gentile John Brown, along with two horses and clothes from Baltimore County, Maryland, joined Brown and five others who tried to escape from a Maryland plantation in Harford County in 1775. The diminutive Reuben Leapeman, four feet, five inches tall, who went by the alias of John Miller, escaped from Chester as a sixteen- or seventeen-year-old in 1773 and then from Lancaster in 1776, having grown to four feet, ten inches. Having proven intractable, it seems these two men were sold to people who lived further from the coast in the expectation they would be less likely to escape. Leapeman talked about moving to the city, and Peters and his gentile companions (all white) stole a boat and put out to sea.[52]

Considering that at best twenty-five Jewish families lived in Philadelphia with perhaps an equal number scattered elsewhere, Jews provided their share of the unprecedented immigration to North America that occurred after the Seven Years' War. Like the majority of voyagers traced by Bernard Bailyn, the Jewish servants were poor, single men in search of the main chance. Joseph Cohen's adventures were typical. Born in 1745 in Westphalia, Cohen's father died when he was four, and he did not get on with his stepfather. "He traveled from town to town and from village to village until . . . after much traveling and hardships, he arrived in London at the age of nineteen, alone and friendless." There, a merchant named Solomons gave him a job, and he acquired a good education and command of English. His next employer, a Jewish widow, fell in love with him, and when he quit his job to avoid her advances, she followed him to Portsmouth in an ineffectual effort to persuade him not to go to America. But his mind was made up, he arrived in Philadelphia about 1768 and was employed by the Gratzes, who had business dealings with Solomons. Cohen's "savings became considerable." When he visited his mother in Germany and his friends in England, they called him "the rich American." He then returned to Pennsylvania. Although he was a single young man, Cohen could rely on his Jewish faith and connections to obtain employment that would have been closed to gentiles.[53]

A few exceptions like Cohen aside, elite Philadelphia Jews had no use for their impoverished coreligionists. Not only did they impose financial burdens—religious denominations were expected to care for their own poor—but they were likely to bring out an anti-semitism that had previously appeared only rarely. Rebecca Samuel, who later moved to Petersburg, Virginia, put her finger on how even a handful of disreputable Jews boded ill for Christian-Jewish relations. Hostility toward Jews in Philadelphia came from two sources, she believed: "German Gentiles and [German] Jews. The German Gentiles cannot forsake their anti-Jewish prejudice; and the German Jews cannot forsake their disgraceful conduct." Discounting her prejudice, Samuel correctly recognized that as the city's poor and middle-class German Christians became politically active, their anti-semitism would be reinforced by the presence of poor German Jews who fit the stereotype of rootless and unscrupulous people.[54]

Elite Jews, on the other hand, had their defenders, at least among their gentile counterparts. In the midst of the proliferation of poor Jews and confidence men, octogenarian Jacob Franks, the continent's most prominent Jewish merchant, died. The Pennsylvania Gazette's obituary, reprinted from a New York newspaper, showed how Franks's sterling character contradicted all the stereotypes his coreligionists' bad behavior was reinforcing in the minds of gentiles:

> Last Monday Morning died in an advanced age, MR. JACOB FRANKS, . . . A Gentlemen of a most amiable Character; in his Family, a tender and kind Master; as a Merchant, upright and punctual in all his Dealings; as a Citizen, humane and benevolent; a Friend to the Poor of all Denominations, affable and friendly in his behavior to all.[55]

Franks's magnanimity could also serve as a lesson to New York's and Philadelphia's own severely divided Jewish communities.

For the mechanics and artisans of Philadelphia, the city's Jews, at least half of whom belonged to the same social class as the elite proprietary and Quaker factions, were implicitly linked with the gentile upper class for not favoring a vigorous resistance to Britain. Even though nearly all the town's Jewish merchants protested the Stamp Act, Jews became the collective scapegoat for those whose avarice led them to defy the protestors. In April 1766, the Pennsylvania Gazette reported that in an unspecified "neighboring government," a man who refused to pay a debt because a writ was not stamped was hauled up before an assembled crowd. They voted that a stamp user could not be a Christian, but because he "ought to be of some religion," it was decided "that he be a Jew" and "that he be circumscribed." This threat to his manhood caused "the poor creature . . . to beg forgiveness for his impudence" and "make a confession of his faith." The Gazette did not censure either this slur on the Jews as the most likely people to abandon the communal good in search of ill-gotten gain, but treated it as a comic yet just punishment for a crime against society.

Just before the provincial 1770 elections, a number of tradesmen complained that the assembly had always "been chiefly composed of merchants, lawyers and millers (or farmers)" nominated by "a certain company of leading men . . . without ever permitting the affirmative or negative voice of a mechanic to interfere." Urging the lower orders to vote for their own, "Brother Chip" noted that "a Jew or a Turk" had previously had as much of a chance of election as a working man. The writers were thus appealing to the perceived prejudice of ordinary voters, who would have never thought of voting for a Jew (there were no Turks in Philadelphia). Three years later, taking issue with the theater supported by the elite, "Philo-Virtutis" argued that such an institution "might appear better from a Jew or a Pagan," but he was angry that Christians "should seem to build again those things which the coming of Christ hath destroyed."[56]

Thus, the Philadelphia Jewish community was dividing along class lines precisely when lower-class city folk were organizing a political alternative to both the Quaker and proprietary factions and attacking Jews in general as lacking in patriotism. Ethnic tensions, too, split the Jews as the German Lutheran and Reformed Churches and Scots-Irish Presbyterians were challenging the longtime rule of the ethnically English Quakers and Anglicans. This division among the Jews was institutionalized in 1801, when an Ashkenazi group, which had first formed a permanent minyan in 1795, incorporated as the Hebrew German Society Rodeph Shalom and purchased its own cemetery. In 1812, they began to worship "according to the German and Dutch rules," conducting services in Yiddish and expelling any members who attended the rival Sephardic synagogue.[57]

THE REVOLUTIONARY STRUGGLE FOR POLITICAL RIGHTS, 1776–1790

Unlike with their Christian neighbors, social divisions among Pennsylvania's Jews were not reflected in divided revolutionary allegiances. With one problematic although prominent exception, David Franks, they supported the Revolution. One example of Jewish patriotism included twelve-year-old Jacob Mordecai, who belonged to a boys' military group that escorted the Continental Congress into Philadelphia when it first met in September 1774. Another was provided by merchant Jonas Phillips, who in July 1776 sent a copy of the Declaration of Independence to Amsterdam merchant Gumpel Samson, predicting victory: "The war will make all England bankrupt. The Americans have an army of 100,000 fellows and the English only 25,000 and some ships. The Americans have already made themselves like the states of Holland." Militarily, Philadelphia's Solomon Bush was the most distinguished Jew in the Revolution, retiring as a lieutenant colonel after serving as deputy adjutant general of the state militia. Bush was wounded in the thigh at the Battle of Brandywine; the surgeons were sure he would die. He survived, however; within two months his limb was "perfectly Strait" and he could not wait to get into action again "and revenge the wrongs of my injured Country." Bush also took some satisfaction in that British soldiers who raided the area around his country house in Chestnut Hill "did not take the least trifle from us, though our neighbors, the poor Tories, lost everything." Pennsylvania Jews lived up to the expectations of a British correspondent of Barnard Gratz, who hoped that "the colonies will not give up their freedom and be like the Irish." British soldiers, during the occupation of Philadelphia, returned the Jews' animosity by shooting their deserters at the gates of the Jewish cemetery, a gesture that also may have added insult to the soldiers' punishment by implying they were not worthy of a Heaven limited to Christians.[58]

In Lancaster, the Levy family did their part for the home front. In 1778, Levy Andrew Levy was put in charge of some prisoners, whom he described as having "neither shoes, stockings nor even a shirt to cover their naked skins." Out of "humanity," he advanced the money to clothe them. On June 16, 1779, Levy was one of twenty-one men who met as the town's Committee of Inspection and Observation. They sought to ease inflation by fixing prices and the value of continental money, resolving at the same time "that no person inimical to the interest and independence of the United States be suffered to remain amongst us." As in Philadelphia, these restrictions on what some considered profiteering, others legitimate private enterprise, met with opposition. On the Fourth of July, after the committee met again, a crowd took to the streets, "behaved themselves like drunken madmen, cursed the committee, [and] called them Rebels and all the

Whigs that took their part." At the courthouse, fighting broke out, and committee chairman Christopher Marshall singled out Levy's son Simon for his prominent role in repulsing the attack. When one Barton refused to apologize for his "ill behavior [even] to the best man in the county," Levy knocked him down and "gave what he thought sufficient, with promise to serve him so whenever he met him till he asks his pardon." At the very least the incident must have relieved Michael Gratz's boredom, for three months earlier he had claimed to be "almost tired of such a dull life" in Lancaster.[59]

Only one family of Jewish loyalists from Pennsylvania, that headed by David Franks, can be identified, and even Franks's loyalism was a belated decision stemming from the consequences of the impossible job he was given by Congress. In eighteenth-century warfare, each side would make arrangements with the other to take care of its captives behind enemy lines. Once large numbers of British soldiers became American prisoners of war, "and it became very expensive to the country (no British commissary residing here to supply them with necessaries), Mr. David Franks was by a resolve of Congress authorized to continue in his former capacity of agent to his brother" Moses, who with his Christian partners had supported the British troops in the latter half of the Seven Years' War. As was customary in commercial dealings, the Franks brothers advanced their own funds to do their job, in the amount of "about seven thousand pounds sterling" to pay for five hundred thousand daily rations, and then applied for reimbursement. But in 1778 they became involved in a jurisdictional struggle between the Lords of the Treasury, who insisted that payment had to come from Sir Henry Clinton, commander of the British army, and Clinton, who refused to pay. As a result, David Franks was told by his brother's London company that "it cannot be expected that we, as individuals, should maintain the King's army." After a long description of their "tedious" efforts to get their money, they "entirely disengaged from any further connection in this business," adding as a postscript to David, "If you proceed in it, we wish you prosperity." Franks's London relatives and partners were telling him he would be a fool for continuing to rely on the promises of the British government.

Even before his employers cut him off, Franks himself was refusing to proceed without further funds. A 1778 letter from John Beatty, the American commissary general for prisoners, to George Washington suggests that Franks was "neither furnished with money or authority" from Britain, leading to the "impropriety" of the Americans "maintaining their prisoners and at the same time furnishing those of ours in their possession with cash and provisions." Franks apparently grew testy and refused to supply the prisoners with wood on his own account. "Informed of the naked situation of the Prisoners as to Clothing," Franks claimed "he had nothing to do with it." Concerned that the British might retaliate, the Congressional Board of War sought both to put the blame on Franks—"we are at a loss to account for the conduct of this Gentleman"—while at the same time suggesting that the British straighten out their affairs: "Mr. Franks does not seem competent to the Business, we presume from want of authority."[60]

While dealing with these headaches, Franks was charged with treason. A federal jury acquitted him in December 1778, but he was rearrested by the Commonwealth of Pennsylvania shortly thereafter, to be acquitted again in April 1779. The anti-semitic, anti-elite supporters of the state's 1776 constitution were furious at his release. To arouse popular sentiment against Franks and his defenders (their political opponents the Republicans), Constitutionalist Timothy Matlack published two documents that he thought made the case against Franks open-and-shut. One letter from Franks to his brother Moses reported the high cost of provisions because the French had arrived in America and were offering premium prices; the other rejoiced that "Billy Hamilton," friend of David's son Moses and brother of his own son-in-law, was acquitted of treason, after a trial of twelve hours, by a jury that only took two minutes to reach a verdict. "People are taken and confined at the pleasure of every scoundrel," Franks commented. "Oh, what a situation Britain has left its friends!" Furthermore, Franks had sent the letters through New York to ensure they would reach Britain, guaranteeing that they would be opened and read as evidence that the Americans were short of provisions and that disaffection with the patriot cause was both rampant and justified. "Had this letter been wrote from General Washington's camp, the writer would have been hanged as a spy," Matlack argued. He then went on to attack the jury that acquitted Franks for "disregarding all those rules of justice and necessity which prevail among other nations," by allowing someone such as Franks to "hold office and grow rich

by their connections with their and our avowed enemies [and] to communicate to those enemies our situation, circumstances, and abilities to carry
on a war."[61]

Franks and the jury both had their defenders. Assuming the persona of
Sir Philip Sidney, British martyr to seventeenth-century Stuart absolutism,
someone condemned Matlack's "attack upon juries, the first that was ever
made in a free country," and goaded him to admit outright that he "wishes
that juries should be abolished as troublesome restraints upon our rulers,
and that a few *Tory-hunters* should hang, burn, or gibbet all who do not
think with themselves, without law, judge, or jury." Another writer argued
that a full disclosure of the evidence at the trial would reveal David's correspondence with Moses Franks was a necessary and innocuous means of trying to obtain funds to supply the prisoners, and that sending the letters
through New York was the only way they could reach Britain. As for
Franks's remark that people were being imprisoned without due process of
law, his defender noted that "history, the key of knowledge and experience,
the touchstone of truth, tells us" that "bad men . . . have at all revolutions
taken advantage of the times to gratify their vengeful passions upon their
private enemies." This author cited Billy Hamilton's acquittal "the moment
his case was inquired into" as an example, to set beside Franks's own persecution, of popular tyranny masquerading as revolutionary patriotism. And
when Franks complained that Britain had left its friends in the lurch, he was
simply "charging our enemies with ingratitude and want of humanity,"
thereby providing a good argument for the Revolution.

At the base of the Franks case was a conflict between two visions of society and government, one the emerging democratic creed of the more
extreme revolutionaries, the other the genteel code elite Jews shared with
upper-class gentiles. Matlack made much of the fact that even though
Franks had sent the two sealed letters in question by way of New York in
care of a close friend and his own brother-in-law Oliver Delancey, respectively, "did the jury think a seal so sacred a thing in time of war and ground
their verdict thereupon? The supposition would affront them, unless they
resign all pretentions to common sense." Subordinating the freedom of
juries to decide according to the law and the civil rights of defendants to the
demands of "carrying on a war with a bitter and implacable nation," Matlack argued that "a juryman, as such, is a public character; and as it is the

privilege of the people to scrutinize public measures and characters, they must expect to submit . . . to the public eye." Matlack's anti-elitism was especially pronounced because he himself was an apostate member of a prominent Quaker family who went out of his way to prove his worthiness to be one of the common folk. His is the only portrait at National Independence Park Gallery of a man in a working-class cap. One of his birds in 1770 had fought a cockfight with one belonging to Oliver Delancey's brother James, symbolically enacting the class conflict that accompanied the Revolution.

On the other side, as historian Judith van Buskirk has pointed out in her study of relations among members of the elite across British and American lines, an aristocratic code of conduct that permitted the very exchanges with the enemy the populist champion Matlack found "illegal and unjustifiable" was an everyday fact of life. A gentleman's word was his bond; officers were released upon their word not to fight again until formally exchanged, and people crossed the lines frequently to visit and assist family members. For instance, the "infirm" Jewish refugee Daniel Gomez of New York convinced the Supreme Executive Council of Pennsylvania to let him send his grandson to that city "to try to secure some rents." His justification was that because of "his real affection and zeal for the welfare of this Country" he "has left his property among the enemies of these states." The prosecution of David Franks not only reflected the radical Constitutionalists' anti-semitism, it exhibited their impatience with individual rights and the elitist ethos of their political opponents.[62]

Two successive not guilty verdicts failed to satisfy Franks's enemies. He tried to remain in Philadelphia, holding a meeting of the Indiana Company's land claimants at his house in January 1780. But that November popular pressure forced Franks to leave the city—he was obliged to sell all his books—and he became a loyalist in spite of himself. Franks ultimately received an annual pension of one hundred pounds from the British government as partial compensation for losses totaling twenty thousand pounds. It is hard to believe that in 1785 he returned to Philadelphia to resume his business because he could not live on this relatively paltry sum, since he could have worked in England with his immensely wealthy brother or other Jews had he chosen unless, perhaps, his love of America stood in the way. His return suggests strongly that the accusations against him were false, that he loved Philadelphia, and was an American at heart. Yet despite his contributions to Mikveh Israel and having served as parnas or president of the congregation, he was denied burial in the cemetery when he died in 1794 for having married a Christian and raised his children in that faith.[63]

The loyalty of Franks's daughter Rebecca was also complicated. Known to all as "Becky" and "the beautiful Jewess," she had nevertheless been raised in the Christian faith by her mother and, unlike her father, took no interest in Jewish affairs. For Becky, life under British occupation of the city was "continued amusement," she once wrote during the little time she "stole" before dressing to go out to tea. She urged a friend from Baltimore to come to town, where she would "have an opportunity of rakeing [having a good time] . . . at plays, balls, concerts, or assemblies." A belle of the Meschianza, the huge farewell pageant the British enacted before they left Philadelphia in 1778, Becky would have up to seven dance partners per evening and confessed herself "almost tired" of the social whirl. Becky's concern with social life in the midst of a war exemplifies those members of the loyalist elite whose lack of public spirit so enraged lower-class revolutionaries. Yet she could laugh at the absurdity of her own position: she mocked one of her outfits as "more ridiculous and pretty than anything I ever saw," and qualified her allegiance to the Crown with at least one sarcastic jibe. When the commander of the British army, General Sir Henry Clinton, ordered a band to play the tune "Britons, Strike Home!" she quipped, "he meant to say: 'Britons, go home!'" But Becky's wit was nonpartisan. On another occasion, after the British had left Philadelphia and Lieutenant Colonel Jack Steward of Maryland dressed in scarlet to ape their appearance, she remarked: "How the ass glories in the lion's skin." Rebecca Franks was one of many astute women on both sides of the fence during the revolutionary era in the middle colonies who acquired political consciousness. In her case, she used her wit and family connections to express her complex feelings in a humorous manner that did not endanger her safety.[64]

Yet as with many loyalists Becky felt homesick abroad. Writing to her friend Willy (Williamina) Bond Cadwalader from Ireland in 1784, she not only mourned "dear Philadelphia, which in spite of everything I shall always prefer to every other place," but appears to have regretted her marriage to a British army officer: "where *he* can he will *stay*, either in Ireland or England, and his wife must obey," she sighed, concluding her letter with a plea that if Willy saw Benjamin Tilghman, "tell him his *old Flirt* sends her love to him." Opening and closing her letter expressing her love for Philadelphia, literally underlining her discontent with her husband and his posting in Killarney at the start and finishing with an expression of love for her old beau, a patriot officer, Becky expressed the disillusionment of many exiles with the nation to which they remained loyal. She still had those feelings when in 1810, she remarked to a friend: "Would to Heaven, I too had been a patriot," and made the same point to General Winfield Scott when he visited England following the War of 1812.[65]

Another David Franks—a major in the revolutionary army whose middle name of Salisbury was always used to distinguish him from his relative—was also accused of disloyalty. Anti-semitism as well as the Franks name were probably at work. He also had the misfortune to be the friend and aide-de-camp to General Benedict Arnold, the military commander of Philadelphia in 1778–79. The sustained barrage of trivial and seemingly trumped-up accusations against him, while not unique, was certainly unusual against a revolutionary officer. Franks first got into trouble in 1779, when Arnold was accused of showing favoritism to loyalists and profiteering during an embargo he himself had ordered. Franks successfully defended himself by claiming that a document in which it seemed he and Arnold were planning to purchase large quantities of goods was only a prospectus for when Franks would return to his prewar employment as a merchant, this time in partnership with Arnold. Angered at the accusation, Franks noted in his defense that he had been "injured in his private affairs very considerably" by joining the army and was planning to resign. But since he decided to remain in service, nothing came of these transactions. Soon thereafter, however, Franks was also accused of exempting one "Miss Levy" from the general policy that civilians could not cross into enemy lines, since by going to New York she could collect money that was owed to her that she needed to support her elderly, blind mother. Franks argued that "a serious refutation would be as ridiculous as the charge itself." Such exemptions were routinely granted in these instances, especially among officers and gentlefolk who trusted the honor of their social equals on the other side. Perhaps the most amusing and trivial yet telling charge against Franks was that he had forced a sergeant to perform "the office of a menial servant . . . an indignity to a free citizen" by fetching the major's barber. The sergeant in question was none other William Matlack, son of revolutionary leader Timothy Matlack, who had imparted to his son his extreme democratic principles. Franks was easily able to show that officers routinely had soldiers perform such tasks.[66]

After Arnold defected, rumors abounded that both Franks and Colonel Varick, Arnold's other aide, were involved in his treason. To clear their honor, they insisted on a military court of inquiry to investigate the charge that "there is just reason to suspect [they] are enemies of the American cause," and to have held an unlawful and dangerous correspondence and intercourse with the enemy in New York." General Henry Knox testified on their behalf, but perhaps the court martial did not assuage all doubt because most of the testimony consisted of Varick and Franks questioning and exonerating each other. Varick revealed that Franks showed his true colors when he had offended Arnold by insulting British intermediary Joshua Smith, whom he thought a "Rascall and a Lyar," at Arnold's dinner table. Arnold rebuked him, stating that "if he asked the Devil to dine with him, the Gentlemen of his Family should be Civil to him," to which Franks responded that if he had run into Smith anywhere else, he "would have sent the Bottle at his Head." (High-ranking officers sometimes referred to their usual associates as "family.") Franks had also told Varick that when Arnold was suspiciously absent from West Point at the time of his flight, he "believed Arnold was a villain or a rascal" based on the report that "one Anderson" (John André) had been seized as a spy. Why didn't Franks tell anyone? Varick testified that he talked Franks out of jumping to conclusions based on slender evidence and enjoined him to be silent until there was proof.[67]

The military court concluded, after only a single day's testimony on October 2, 1780, that the two men's "Language and Conduct on all Occasions betrayed a very strong attachment to the Rights of our country." But "malicious" people still spread rumors that although Franks may not have supported Arnold's treason, he had still committed "the abominable" crime of perjury by testifying on his superior's behalf the previous "winter to save Arnold from merited punishment" that would have forestalled his treason. Franks insisted and obtained yet another inquiry clearing him on this score, following Washington's suggestion that a civil inquiry conducted on the spot in Philadelphia rather than a military tribunal could more effectively establish his innocence and preempt the charge that the army might be protecting its own. Thereafter, Franks proved his loyalty through his commercial ventures with Superintendent of Public Finance Robert Morris and his partner Thomas Willing, and with diplomatic assistance to John Jay, Thomas Jefferson, and John Adams, who worked extensively with Franks and his European connections to obtain funds and arrange financial transactions. Franks's abilities led Congress to choose him to negotiate the new nation's commercial treaty with Morocco in 1785. In the meanwhile he served as American consul at Marseilles. Franks's repeated defense of his honor, and insistence that a court clear his name when Washington and other generals were willing to drop the matter, typifies the behavior of colonial Jews in general. Realizing the existence of anti-semitism, they struck back verbally whenever criticized to make sure popular rumors and insinuations were at least formally refuted.[68]

But we can only wonder if the rumors of disloyalty persisted. In 1789, Franks wrote a letter to the newly elected President Washington asking for public office, pointing out his "short and rigorous imprisonment," "expenditure of his own funds in the public cause when there was not a farthing in the military chest," meritorious service in the "families" of General Benjamin Lincoln, Benedict Arnold, and (in Paris) Minister Thomas Jefferson, and his diplomatic work. He enclosed letters from Jefferson, Benjamin Franklin, Arthur Lee, and Robert Morris attesting to the fact that he had "devoted eleven years of the best part of my life to the service of my country, in all which time, I am bold to say that, I have ever been activated by a disinterested Zeal for her Honor and Prosperity." Yet nothing came of his request, perhaps because the president had few offices to dispose of compared to the number of those who sought them.[69]

Following the end of the British occupation in 1778, Philadelphia Jews took in numbers of their coreligionists from the four other major Jewish communities in the new nation. Savannah, Charleston, Newport, and especially New York, were all occupied at the time by the British. As a result, Philadelphia became for patriotic Jews what New York was for loyalists—a magnet for political refugees. (At least one New York Jew, Joseph Nathan, went to Easton, Pennsylvania, for when he returned to New York in 1783, his wife Jane had "eloped . . . and is said to cohabit with a Barnard Levi" of that town. If she returned to New York, Levi promised to have "all animosities buried in oblivion.") In 1782, when Philadelphia Jews sought to construct a new synagogue for the congregation Mikveh Israel, 103 men subscribed. Yet by 1790, Philadelphia had no more than twenty-five Jewish families; most of the synagogue's subscribers went home. So did the community's hazan and de facto rabbi Gershom Mendes Seixas, a Portuguese Jew who returned to New York City in 1784. Philadelphia's Jewish community then reverted approximately to its prerevolutionary size.[70]

Besides the attacks on both David Franks, anti-semitism became an explicit political issue in Pennsylvania during the Revolution. If the triumph of Jeffersonian Republicanism in 1800 ended threats of persecution and foreshadowed the general acceptance of Jews in the United States, the partisan smears of the preceding quarter century anticipated an undercurrent of intolerance that has frequently surfaced. It is arguable that the debate in revolutionary and Federalist Philadelphia over the role of Jews in the Republic fused for the first time in the United States two strains of anti-semitism—a preexisting, largely latent popular one, and an emerging elite political one—that served to scapegoat Jews in the political life of the new nation.

Linked attacks on both Jews and Pennsylvania's cosmopolitan elite explains why, despite their patriotic exertions in both the Great War for Empire and the War of Independence, Jews failed at first to win the equal rights they had sought by participating in the Revolution. Unable to vote or hold public office before 1776, Jews were doubly victimized, by provincial as well as imperial laws in which they had no voice. Like the underrepresented people of Berks, York, Northampton, and Cumberland counties and the unrepresented lower orders of Philadelphia, Pennsylvania's Jews fought not only for home rule, but to earn the right to be among those who ruled at home. However, the grassroots "radicals" from western Pennsylvania and Philadelphia did not extend to the Jews the same rights they seized for themselves. Popular anti-semitism was made explicit in the new constitution of 1776 that required a Christian oath for voting and officeholding. As historian Owen Ireland has so tellingly argued, there was nothing "democratic" about this internal revolution. Rather, it marked the ascendance of previously disfranchised elements who sought to replace those in power: paradoxically, although Jews were among those groups, they were closely linked to the elite that the radicals were hoping to supplant. The oath of allegiance disfranchised nearly half the state's voters: not only Jews, but also Quakers and all those who in conscience would not swear an oath of loyalty on a Christian Bible to a controversial new constitution.[71]

On September 26, 1776, as this new constitution was being debated, the *Philadelphia Evening Post* brought the radicals' anti-semitism into the open. An anonymous correspondent urged that an early draft that had omitted the Christian oath be changed. The author predicted that otherwise Jews and Turks might "become in time not only our greatest landholders [Jews already owned extensive property], but principal officers in the legislative or executive parts of our government, so as to render it not only uncomfortable but unsafe for Christians, which I hope every American would wish to prevent as much as any other national slavery."

> An Episcopal church, a Presbyterian meeting-house, a Roman Catholic church, a mosque, a synagogue, a heathen temple have now in Pennsylvania all equal privileges! Will it not be an asylum for all fugitive Jesuits and outcasts of Europe. . . . If blasphemers of Christ and the Holy Blessed Trinity, despisers of the revelation and the holy bible may hold public office, . . . Wo unto the city! Wo unto the land![72]

The biblical language with which the pamphlet concluded argued that for a person to be a practicing Christian required striving to make Pennsylvania, and by extension, the United States, a Christian country, excluding nonbelievers from citizenship and political participation. In whatever other sense the new Pennsylvania constitution was "radical," it marked perhaps the first significant triumph for anti-semitism in the new nation, less than three months after the Declaration of Independence proclaimed that "all men are created equal."

That less than fifty Jewish voters in Pennsylvania could enslave some three hundred thousand Christians seems to be an extreme case of paranoia. But exclusion of Jews from political rights reflected several popular prejudices. In Anglo-American political rhetoric Jews were frequently linked with Turks, infidels, and occasionally atheists as diabolic conspirators who threatened liberty throughout the world. Hostility to Turks can be explained readily enough, for colonial writers regularly cited the "Great Turk" (the Ottoman sultan) and "bashaws" or "pashas," as symbols of a severe form of despotism toward which the British Empire might be heading.[73]

But why were Jews mentioned in the same breath? The driving force behind the Christian oath was Henry Melchior Mühlenberg, most prestigious leader and senior minister of the United Lutheran Church in America, who ten days before the letter was published had tried to persuade his fellow Philadelphia clergymen that granting political rights to non-Christians might lead to their taking over the country. Mühlenberg's scapegoating of the Jews makes sense as an effort to redirect similar suspicion away from both the Pennsylvania Germans and himself, whose loyalty was being questioned for the second time in a quarter century in a Pennsylvania at war. While the vast majority of German-speakers in Pennsylvania were Lutheran and Reformed, small groups of pacifists such as the Moravians— who had built the impressive stone buildings at Bethlehem that still survive—were highly visible and suggested that Germans in general might be remaining aloof from the struggle. Furthermore, before 1776, the Germans' political participation was almost invariably limited to support for the Quakers, who were themselves pacifists and neutrals (who frequently did business with the British) during the Revolution. The Germans also had a past to live down: during the French and Indian War, Mühlenberg wrote that they were "represented as a nation so roguish and mischievous . . . that in times of war they would probably join the French and villainously espouse their cause. . . . The Irish, the Swedes and the Welsh keep their languages, yet for all that are not looked upon as a disloyal people."[74]

Returning to Philadelphia in March 1776 after spending seven months in Georgia, Mühlenberg was startled by the rumors flying about. His enemies had insinuated that he had turned Catholic, persuaded the king of England—whom he supposedly had visited—to do likewise, and conspired to institute tithes. One German asked him: "How is it that the German Lutheran preachers have brought about such a great tragedy, have betrayed the liberty of our country, and have caused this great war?" Mühlenberg must have been especially sensitive to such remarks, for his German correspondence establishes his loyalist sympathies beyond a shadow of a doubt. Nevertheless, he had to retain the support of a flock that either favored the Revolution or preferred neutrality.[75]

Mühlenberg had been trained at the German missionary institute in Halle, which devoted special attention to the conversion of the Jews as a prerequisite for the millennium. Mühlenberg had known Jews in Germany, where they either conformed to the stereotype of the Jew by maintaining their distinctive dress and appearance, or else were cosmopolitan city folk who held Enlightenment ideals and hardly seemed Jewish at all. Philadelphia's leading Jews, whom Mühlenberg termed "the representative men in the city, with whom I associate," fit the latter model. He took great, although futile pains, to convert them, claiming that they were atheists and "admit[ted] their Messiah was an imposter." A Judaic influence in the new Republic, therefore, would take the form of spreading atheism, a subject very much on Mühlenberg's mind at precisely the time the Pennsylvania constitution was under debate. On August 29, he wrote in his journal of "bad news" that a revolutionary Colonel von Zedwitz of the New York line—"a favorite with the governors and other gentry in this country because he spoke well and was a virtuoso on the violin"—was executed for treasonous correspondence with loyalist Governor William Tryon. Mühlenberg blamed Zedwitz's fate on creeping atheism among the revolutionaries:

> Where the Christian religion and its morality is not employed as the criterion of knowledge and practice, there mere natural, pretended honor, uprightness, parole, and similar vaporing are not in the least to be trusted. . . . Our pretended, refined naturalists may conceal themselves ever so clearly behind natural religion and their own righteousness, and still the fallen old Adam with his rotten morality peeps out.[76]

Yet while hostile to the new Republic, Mühlenberg was perfectly willing to use it to further his religious aims, thereby deflecting attention from his own problematic allegiance and that of the Pennsylvania Germans. He found an opportunity to do so on September 16, 1776, when he heard a complaint that under the proposed state constitution, "the Christian religion is paid scant or no respect, but is rather considered an indifferent, arbitrary matter." Moreover, "every religious party and persuasion shall, without distinction have equal freedom to believe and teach what it pleases." Mühlenberg agreed "that the condition of the Christian religion seemed in danger after independence had been declared." The "honorable, loyal, citizens and mechanics" who "appear to be favorably inclined toward the Christian religion" comprised the majority of the convention. Although they "had a good understanding of farming and trade," they had been misled by "powerful orators" who had omitted a Christian oath from the constitution's first draft. Mühlenberg asked himself: "What could I, a poor, cast-off old fogey, do about it?"

He could do plenty. Several clergymen from Philadelphia met on September 16, and Mühlenberg warned them that they "were supposed to be the pillars of the Christian religion . . . and if they were to remain silent now and not defend this good cause they would surely be held accountable." Despite his plea, a franchise restricted to believers was opposed by Philadelphia's Rev. Dr. Francis Alison, conservative "Old Light" Presbyterian minister, and Rector Jacob Duché of the Anglican Church, leaders of the two most elite and pro-Enlightenment congregations in the city, whose members socialized freely with Jewish merchants and their families. To Mühlenberg's plea that without the religious test it would seem "as if a Christian people were ruled by Jews, Turks, Spinozists, Deists, [and] perverted naturalists," Alison spoke for himself and Duché by remarking "that the form of government had nothing to do with the matter of religion and expressed the opinion that it was sufficient if members of the new government merely confessed faith in a Supreme Being as creator and upholder of all things." Mühlenberg had not only placed Jews first on the list of threats to the Republic, he included the apostate Dutch Jew Spinoza as the logical prelude to deism and atheism. Looking at the spread of Enlightenment tendencies in Europe, Mühlenberg used Spinoza—generally considered an atheist philosopher who was a forerunner of the Enlightenment—and tolerant Holland as examples to argue implicitly that toleration of the Jews, even where numerically minuscule, could be the first step toward rejection of the Deity altogether. Duché for his part made light of Mühlenberg's fears, commenting that an oath not limited to Christians was "well-suited to the present time and conditions, for, after all, in God's forbearance there must be one corner in the world where practical atheists, so-called deists, perverted naturalists, and similar genteel rabble could have their place of abode," that is, in Pennsylvania. Ironically, Duché himself would turn loyalist by 1778.[77]

Getting nowhere with Philadelphia's elite ministers, Mühlenberg went and spoke to the Swedish and Reformed clergy that afternoon, who approved their request. Mühlenberg may even have written or inspired the September 26 plea to the convention's delegates, for the letter in the *Penn-*

sylvania Packet of that day cited the respective worship of Turks, Jews, and infidels in that order. This motion was then passed on to the constitutional convention by none other than Benjamin Franklin. Franklin, whose *Pennsylvania Gazette* had praised the Jews when most useful for countering prejudice or increasing public awareness of their achievements, who had praised and done business with Jews before and would later contribute to Philadelphia's first synagogue, sacrificed the state's tiny Jewish minority to what he considered the more urgent need of Christians to tolerate each other. He wrote to scientist Joseph Priestley that he was "overpowered by Numbers" and effected a compromise that "no further or more Extended Profession of Faith" than mere Christianity "should ever be exacted." It was critical that Franklin go along with the radical revolutionaries, whose titular head he had become, to erase the stigma placed on him as the leading supporter of a royal government for Pennsylvania in the 1760s. A model for Pennsylvania's elite anti-semitism thus appeared for the first time: immigrants such as Mühlenberg and Reformed minister Caspar Weyberg (who, Mühlenberg admitted, was "not thoroughly conversant in the English language" although he had lived in Pennsylvania for thirteen years), uncertain of their own place in America, and members of the elite whose own loyalty may have been suspect, such as Franklin, capitalized on or compromised with populist anti-semitism to further their own interests and reputations.[78]

Attacks on Jews were pretty much "free shots" that could be taken by any of the political, ethnic, or religious groups in Pennsylvania when they were trying to show that they themselves were not outsiders, but "real" Pennsylvanians or Americans.[79] Jews could muster at best a handful of voters before the mid-nineteenth century and were no threat to anyone. Anti-semitism thus passed from one group to another as suited the various political climates of 1775–1800, for Pennsylvania was such a diverse society that depending on who was in political power, anyone from Quakers and Anglicans to Germans and Scots-Irish, from westerners to easterners, could either be, or perceive themselves to be, outside a shifting political consensus. But such attacks on a tiny group would have made no sense unless anti-Jewish feelings were widely held among Christians. For instance, despite the fact that with the exception of the Franks family Philadelphia's Jews supported the Revolution, Philadelphia poet, musician, noted revolutionary, and signer of the Declaration of Independence Francis Hopkinson had no trouble linking loyalists and Jews in his 1780 broadside "A Tory Medley." Calling attention to the fact that seven of Philadelphia's Jews (about one-third of all heads of household) were "brokers"—people who exchanged currency, lent money, accepted goods on pawn, and auctioned off the items of delinquents—Hopkinson wrote about a Tory "broker" in cahoots with a "cock ey'd Jew": "His designs with mine Tally," claimed the fictional Tory. Much like Philadelphia militiamen who attacked James Wilson's house in 1779 for his alleged friendliness toward loyalists, Hopkinson sought to stigmatize Jews as false patriots who, like the loyalists, were financially victimizing their countrymen at this economic low point of the Revolution.[80]

Other revolutionary Americans, however, held up Jews as models of virtue. Also in 1780, at the time Esther DeBert Reed was urging fellow Philadelphia elite women to raise money for the patriot cause, someone claiming to be "An American Woman" called "to mind with enthusiasm and admiration, all those acts of courage, of constancy, and patriotism, which history has transmitted to us." She singled out the Jews, "the people favored by Heaven, preserved from destruction by the virtues, the zeal, and resolution of Deborah, of Judith, of Esther! The fortitude of the mother of the Maccabees in giving up her sons to die before her eyes."[81] Perhaps the author chose "Esther" to refer to both the biblical and contemporary Esthers. Four years later a Protestant minister urged his fellow Christians to at least refrain from doing business on Good Friday: "the Jews set us the example; who, at the time of their Passover, refrain from the tempting lucre of gain during the course of almost a week."[82]

Jewish leaders themselves did not share this vision of their community's superior virtue. In common with the heads of other denominations whose members pushed for more democracy in accordance with revolutionary principles—such as Roman Catholics, Anglicans, Lutherans, and Methodists—Philadelphia's Jewish elite complained that increasing numbers of their congregation were "completely irreligious people," and that unlike in Europe "the congregation here has no power to discipline anyone." Jews marrying gentiles was an especially sore spot, since there were so few Jews in America, especially outside of the handful of urban communities, that congregations were in real danger of going out of existence. But like the second-generation Massachusetts Puritans of the 1660s whose condemnations of "declension" proved how religious many of them were, postrevolutionary Jewish leaders were determined "to make an impression on the public" in those matters "where the congregation has jurisdiction," such as expelling deviant members even though bodies were sorely needed. In one case, Mordecai Mordecai's niece Judith had married a Christian army lieutenant in a civil ceremony. Mordecai, at his sister's urging, reconciled his brother-in-law, who had ostracized the young woman, and married them in a Jewish ceremony. When the Jewish community of Philadelphia ruled the marriage illegal and accused Mordecai of violating Jewish law, he responded that his critics "have resorted to the laws of Spain and Portugal, the laws of the inquisition," by judging him guilty without allowing him to testify on his own behalf. He could have shown them, he was certain, that their amateur knowledge of Judaic law was wrong. It is not surprising that Mordecai went out of his way to defy the congregation in yet another instance by reburying Moses Clava, a Jewish merchant who had also married a gentile. The congregation ruled that Clava "shall be buried in a corner of the cemetery, without ritual washing, without shrouds, and without a ceremony." Mordecai reburied Clava with the proper ritual and wearing a shroud; when the president of the congregation protested, Mordecai "quoted rabbinic laws against him." The president was prepared and cut the shroud to pieces, but Clava technically had had his Jewish burial. Such was the congregation's concern with these matters that it requested the opinion of a leading European rabbis as to where justice resided (the response, if any, does not survive). Mordecai, for his part, moved to Richmond, Virginia, where he was in 1789 among the founders of that city's first synagogue, Beth Shalom, before relocating to Baltimore, where he died in 1809.[83]

Ethnic as well as class divisions compounded the troubles of Pennsylvania's small Jewish community. In 1782, the city's newspaper readers were treated to a bitter series of mutual recriminations in Eleazer Oswald's newspaper, the *Independent Gazetteer and Chronicle of Freedom*. The adversaries were Benjamin Nones (Nunes), a Sephardic Jewish merchant who had arrived from Savannah in 1779 after fighting against the British, and Abraham and Eleazar Levy, Ashkenazi merchants who had been doing business in Philadelphia for fourteen years. On October 10, a brief notice suddenly appeared in the paper, in which Nones "begged . . . pardon" for his "truly inconsistent, and even Rude," behavior to Abraham Levy, expressing his sorrow "for treating so very ill an elderly gentleman who I have every reason to think is an honest man." But twelve days later, Nones took back his words and presented a complicated story as to why he had made an insincere apology. The trouble, he claimed, began in August or September of that year, when Abraham Levy met Nones in Front Street and assured him of "the most generous commission" if he could obtain £500 of goods on three months credit to satisfy "advantageous contracts" he could make in Baltimore. Nones promptly went to the French merchants Le Maigre and Mercier, who sent him the goods and told him they would be glad to enter into this transaction. When informed of the Frenchmen's cooperation, however, Abraham and his son Eleazar "started to speak Polish, then after handling the goods" claimed the price was too high and refused to take them. (Nones served directly under Casimir Pulaski at the siege of Savannah, and thus probably could have recognized the Polish language even if he was unaware of the Levys' country of origin.) However, no sooner had they left Nones's company than they went to Le Maigre and Mercier, made a deal for the goods, and "hugged themselves, no doubt reflecting the custom of their own country, by which they had bilked me of the commission they promised." When confronted with this duplicity by Nones, the older Levy "assumed by turns all the colors of the rainbow" before assuring Nones he would pay up. Nones gave him five weeks, but the Levys kept postponing the reckoning to "next morning, then next afternoon" for nine additional days. When the son finally offered to pay him at a 2.5 percent discount, Nones lost his temper, seeing "at a glance the base scheme that was attempted to be practiced on me." Proceeding to ask the elder Levy "civilly" for the money, Nones was told by Levy that "he had no money, he would get no money, he would not pay me, I might do my worst." Only after Nones agreed to publish his apology would the Levys give him the money.

Nones's effort to brand the Levys as foreigners who spoke Polish and engaged in secret and underhanded deals that were incomprehensible to American Jews as well as gentiles went even further. He threatened to shave the elder Levy's beard, "which induces many people falsely to imagine him a distinguished member of our congregation in which his ignorance disqualifies him from holding the humblest office," and would show to the world that he is a "very Jacob, altho' he has the heavy hands of Esau." A Sephardic Jew who, like most of his fellows, appeared largely indistinguishable from gentile Americans, Nones was angry that Ashkenazi newcomers to America would use their exotic appearances and pretended ignorance of mercantile custom to fool their unknowing business associates. Nones himself, an immigrant from France and a more recent arrival in Philadelphia than the Levys, whose own English was insufficiently fluent for Nones to write his own articles for the newspaper, in effect assumed the role of the anti-semite in this controversy. He tried to show he was more American than the Levys, much as people prejudiced against Jews in general were usually those whose own patriotic credentials left something to be desired. Nones even descended to sanctioning wretched poetry that attributed the Levys' moral vices to an ineradicable heredity, much as Christian anti-semites considered the Jews' very blood corrupted on account of their backsliding and punishment for it in biblical times:

Go, if your ancient, but ignoble blood,
Has crept thru *Scoundrels,* ever since the flood;
Go, say yourself are new, your family young,
Nor as your father have been fools so long.

For his part, on October 30, Eleazar Levy's spokesman referred the *Independent Gazetteer's* readers to Nones's published apology, commenting on his "ridiculous charges" and turning the accusation of being a stranger against Nones: "I am exceedingly surprised, that a man, who so lately commenced trade, should so easily addict himself to such dire calumnies and palpable falsehoods." He then reduced his adversary one step down from an alien: "I suspect that Mr. Nones malignantly means to strike at my reputation and credit, agreeable to the custom of the savages, who, if they cannot strike their antagonist, will aim their tomahawks at their next of kin." Levy concluded by reaffirming his own ethical superiority to Nones—"I flatter myself my punctuality and steadiness to my course of business, will effectively defeat his wicked purpose"—and his father's intellectual preeminence as "superior," in that he was "educated in the Hebrew language," of which Nones, like most American Jews, was ignorant.

The last laugh, however, was had by an anonymous gentile who mocked both Levy and Nones for "a quarrel which is equally disadvantageous." To begin with, he charged, "neither of you is sufficiently familiar with the English language, to understand the essays published in your name." He warned both parties that while only "mercenary" interpreters would put their talents at the disposal of participants in such a ludicrous dispute, "you must respectively abide the consequences of their . . . malignity." Instead of arguing over each other's fidelity to the teachings of Judaism in the gentile press, the commentator suggested, they should turn their dispute over to "your church discipline," for "you may rest assured that no Christian, for the sake of settling your dispute, will be at the trouble of studying the Talmud, the commentaries upon it, together with the books of controversy which relate to your religious ceremonies and customs." As to the two parties' mercantile reputations, the writer suggested they submit their differences to the private arbitration of four reputable merchants, each appointing two. These arbiters would be honest because both the Levys and Nones's reputations were known to the commercial community, and no merchant would benefit from supporting a trader known to be dishonest. The men had apparently also threatened to take each other to court, for the third party's final effort was to "dissuade you from engaging in a paper war with your antagonist, as from prosecuting him at law," for in either case "you must both give yourself up to men who will either pick your pockets or gratify their resentment at your expense." Needless to say, as the commentator noted, this dispute harmed the Jewish community as a whole in the eyes of the Christians, for at that very moment they were attempting to build a synagogue near the German Reformed congregation.[84]

The decision to erect this building also brought out anti-semitism. The site chosen was next to the German Reformed Church in Sterling Alley. The German congregation, which at that moment was supporting a revolution against royal authority, found no inconsistency in confronting the Jews with the universal practice of monarchical Christian Europe that synagogues be located "in such a place where the neighbors and the public in general will not be inconvenienced by too much clamor." (Given the internal contention of Philadelphia's Jewish community in the 1780s the Germans may have had a point. Some Jewish services, as during High Holy Days, and business meetings could be held on Sundays.) Their citation, in fact, came from Frederick the Great, from whose military despotism at least some Pennsylvania Germans had fled. In an effort to be accommodating, the Jews offered the Reformed church the chance to purchase the property they had selected at the same price paid, but the church refused. Rather than keep the controversy alive, the Jews auctioned off the property and relocated to Cherry Alley, where they began to hold services in September 1782. Of £2,200 required for a new building £1,200 was raised by 1783: Haym Salomon contributed £341, Isaac Nones £96, Hayman Levy £73, and Jonas Phillips £144. As if to show up the German Reformed as narrow-minded, the synagogue was located close to Episcopal and Presbyterian churches whose clergy had defended their rights in the past.[85]

Since the Pennsylvania Constitutionalists, of whom Reformed Germans were an important element, refused to grant Jews political rights, the Jews overwhelmingly supported their Republican, soon to be Federalist, opponents. The support was mutual. In May 1783, the *Pennsylvania Gazette* published a long article addressed to the people of New Jersey, who were in the process of forming a constitution, arguing that like the ancient Jews, they should mix "aristocracy and democracy." Citing the special privileges granted to the Levites or priests who acted as a counterweight to the other eleven tribes, the author inveighed against most of the state constitutions of the day—especially, by implication, that of Pennsylvania, where the article was published—on the grounds that "the rulers of the Jews well knew, that an attempt to make a rope of sand was not more vain, than an attempt to erect a government that partook largely of democracy over an ignorant vile people." He concluded: "as our government is built on the same foundation as that of the Jews, so its continuance will depend on the same causes." A month earlier, the *Gazette* approvingly noted that the Spanish had abolished the Inquisition, thereby allowing the Jews "to live in Spain on the same footing as in France," where they were tolerated. Expressing pleasure that Spain seems to be "at last emerging from that Gothic mist, which has darkened our horizon for so many ages," the author cited a positive change of attitude toward the Jews as proof that "the light of reason and true philosophy" was finally descending even on that backward nation.[86]

In late December 1783, with the war successfully concluded, the British troops hardly a month out of New York City, and the anticonstitutionalist Republicans gaining political ground in the state, the Jews made an effort to repeal the Pennsylvania Test Oath. Led by Gershom Seixas, members of the congregation of Mikveh Israel, including Barnard Gratz and Haym Salomon, pointed out the unjust "stigma" placed upon them.

> The Jews of Pennsylvania in proportion to the number of their members, can count with any religious society whatsoever, the whigs among either of them; they have served some of them in the continental army; some went out in the militia to fight the common enemy; all of them have cheerfully contributed to the support of the militia, and of the government of this state;[87] they have no inconsiderable property in lands and tenements, but particularly in the way of trade, some more, some less, for which they pay taxes;[88] they have upon every plan formed for public utility, been forward to contribute as much as their circumstances would admit of; and as a nation or religious society, they stand unimpeached of any matter whatsoever, against the safety and happiness of the people.

Seixas made a careful study of every state constitution (his notes on them survive) in an effort to convince Pennsylvania of its error. He used three sorts of arguments. First, he offered an escape clause that would permit the council of censors to note contradictions within the constitution that needed to be clarified. Section 40 did not prevent Jews from holding military, executive, or judicial office; elsewhere it noted "that no man . . . can be justly deprived or abridged of any civil right on account of his religious sentiment." But section 10 required "an acknowledgement of scripture for voting or holding office," thus depriving "the Jew of [the] most eminent right of freeman." Seixas hoped the group charged with suggesting reforms to the state constitution would recognize this inconsistency and recommend in favor of the Jews. Second, assuming the censors would recognize Jews as valuable members of the community, he offered the practical argument that the disabilities in Pennsylvania would discourage Jewish immigration and redirect it to New York, "where there is no such restraint laid upon the nation of the Jews." Finally, Seixas hoped to shame the censors by showing Pennsylvania trailed behind most other states in acknowledging the rights of Jews, grouping the state with only North Carolina, Maryland, and Delaware. He had to fudge this point, since New Jersey, South Carolina, and Georgia only permitted Protestants to participate in civic life, by making the ingenious argument that Jews were really Protestants since they were not Catholics. (He also omitted Rhode Island, where

Jews could not vote under the still functioning charter of 1664 but which had no constitution at the moment.) In any event, the council of censors tabled the petition.[89]

On the national front, Jews were more successful. Pennsylvania Jews were Federalists—at first. In the 1780s, not only had the Constitutionalists or Anti-Federalists spurned their plea for equality, but the Jewish revolutionary experience fit the Federalist profile. They had spent the war at the seat of power, experiencing America's problems from a national rather than from a local perspective. They had extensive interstate connections and had firsthand experience of the war as refugees or those who cared for them. They were involved in the military, national government, and international commerce. They too suffered during the "Critical Period": four of Philadelphia's twenty-odd Jewish heads of household declared bankruptcy in the mid-1780s.[90] Furthermore, the most prominent of the Founding Fathers had personal relationships with Pennsylvania's Jews and were well aware of their patriotism. Haym Salomon had made his escape from New York in 1778, where he had been arrested as a spy but freed after the commanding Hessian general realized his knowledge of "French, Polish, Russian, Italian, etc." made him invaluable. His mercantile skills were valuable too, and he was entrusted with supplying the French and American prisoners; he did more, however, and "assisted them with money and helped them off to make their escape." Such exploits imperiled his own freedom, and he was forced to leave his wife and an infant child in New York along with "all his effects and credits to the amount of five or six thousand pounds sterling." Forced to start afresh, he petitioned Congress for "any employ in the way of his business whereby he may be enabled to support himself and his family." Congress took him at his word, and Salomon was essential in ensuring lack of funds did not undo the new Republic. As Superintendent of Finance Robert Morris's papers show, Salomon was responsible for negotiating many of the European cash transfers that gave the new government what fiscal backing it had.[91] Along with Thomas Jefferson, Arthur Lee, and others, Morris benefited from Salomon's hospitality in Philadelphia. Another Jew friendly to Morris, Benjamin Levy of Baltimore, offered Morris the use of his home in case Congress was compelled to evacuate Philadelphia. Salomon, for his part, helped James Madison out with emergency personal loans.[92]

As a result, when Philadelphia Jewish leader Jonas Phillips petitioned the members of the 1787 Constitutional Convention to attach no religious qualification to officeholding, he was too late: the convention that so hotly debated the powers of the president and the representation of slave owners had already agreed upon that point without a murmur.[93] Jews are conspicuous by their absence in the debates of the Federal Convention: it is as though the Founders did not even conceive of excluding them. But the praise heaped upon immigrants, to whom the new Republic would be open, by Pennsylvania's James Wilson, would explain the convention's attitude toward Jews as well: "Almost all the general officers of the Pennsylvania line (of the late army) were foreigners. And no complaint had ever been made against their fidelity or merit. Three of her deputies to this convention (Mr. [Robert] Morris, Mr. [James] Fitzsimons, and himself), were also not natives."[94]

When Pennsylvanians met in convention in 1789 to revise their state constitution, the question of enfranchising non-Christians was much more controversial than it had been for the framers of the federal charter. Article 7 of the proposed revision, although not mentioning Jews specifically, stipulated "that all men have a natural and indefeasible right to worship almighty God according to the dictates of their own consciences, and no person who acknowledges the being of a God and a future state of rewards and punishments shall on account of his religious sentiments be disqualified to hold any office or place of trust." But a liberalization of the franchise to include all freeholders and their sons over the age of twenty-one was only narrowly approved when a motion to table it failed by five votes, thirty-four to twenty-nine. With the exception of three yes votes in Chester County, two in Berks, and one from Philadelphia County, all those who opposed an unrestricted franchise came from the West: Westmoreland, Washington, Fayette, Dauphin, Northumberland, Cumberland, and Bedford Counties voted yes eighteen to zero, Philadelphia City and County, Lancaster, York, Northampton, Delaware, and Bucks Counties voted no twenty-seven to two. Once again, the more cosmopolitan and established counties proved more tolerant than those in the west. On the other hand, an even more tolerant proposal, which would open public office to anyone regardless of whether they believed in God at all—it specifically omitted the words "who acknowledges the being of a God and a future state of rewards and punishments"—only received thirteen votes out of sixty, among them Timothy Pickering (who voted no on the previous proposal) and Albert Gallatin (who voted yes).[95]

The convention's impending meeting coincided with a new outburst of populist anti-semitism. On July 19, 1789, Philadelphia's Mikveh Israel held a special meeting to respond to the first recorded desecration of the Jewish cemetery since Nathan Levy posted his reward in 1753. "Whereas the burying place had been opened several times, and wishing to remedy the evil," the congregation's elders advertised for "a person willing to build a habitation near it at his own expense." Their desire to achieve security without cost reflected the recent unsuccessful campaign to finance the synagogue building. Although planned back in 1782 when the community teemed with revolutionary exiles, it had run into trouble when they had left the city followed by "delicate and distressing circumstances"—the economic hard times of the Critical Period. Of the leading contributors in 1783, only Jonas Phillips was alive and residing in Philadelphia, and he refused to contribute further after the synagogue's creditors had begun dunning him (he was parnas in 1783–84) for payment of the congregation's debts for construction of the edifice. In 1788, Mikveh Israel begged "their worthy fellow citizens of every religious denomination" to contribute toward the eight hundred pounds required if the synagogue was not to be "converted to profanation" and sold to pay the debts incurred in building it. Those "worthy" reads like a who's who of gentile Philadelphia and included octogenarian Benjamin Franklin, who contributed five pounds, General Peter Mühlenberg nine pounds (he did not share his father's prejudices or loyalism), Charles Biddle and future governor Thomas McKean three pounds each, Thomas Fitzsimons one pound, fifteen shillings, David Reddick, future leader of the Whiskey Rebellion, one pound, ten shillings, and an anonymous "worthy Friend" who adopted the modesty associated with the Quakers, three pounds. The total fell far short, but in 1790 the congregation's problems were solved when the state of Pennsylvania, at the same time its new constitution permitted the Jews to engage in political life, authorized a lottery that raised the money.[96]

But even in an early 1790s Pennsylvania dominated by the Federalists, practical equality for Jews beyond the franchise was another matter. Although Jews as individuals finally received the vote in Pennsylvania and the right to hold state public office under the Federalist-sponsored Constitution of 1790, respect for the Jewish religion as equal to Christianity was another matter. Solomon Bush, a wounded war hero, petitioned four times in vain for various posts in both the Pennsylvania and federal government between 1780 and 1795.[97] In 1793, prominent merchant Jonas Phillips was fined ten pounds for refusing to be sworn as a witness in a court of law on a Saturday. The following year, the Pennsylvania legislature passed a law forbidding work on Sunday, which meant in effect that Jews who could only work five days a week had to compete with Christians who could work six. In 1816, Abraham Wolff was convicted for violating this law despite his contention that he kept his own Sabbath.[98]

Doubts about the Jews' suitability for citizenship and the question of who was a Jew or exhibited Jewish behavioral characteristics led Pennsylvania political leaders in the new Republic to exploit and give focus to popular anti-semitism. As with the German-born Mühlenberg and the Pennsylvania Constitutionalist and the German Reformed opposition to the Philadelphia synagogue, people of dubious allegiance and outsiders to Pennsylvania's political world scapegoated the Jews to demonstrate their own loyalty. In 1784, Miers Fisher, a Quaker lawyer who during the Revolution had been sent to a detention camp in Winchester, Virginia, for his loyalist sympathies, tried to persuade the state legislature to abolish the Bank of North America headed by Republican-Federalist Robert Morris and replace it with a rival scheme. Although the loyalist lawyer Fisher was everything the Pennsylvania Constitutionalists abhorred, he was not above appealing to their prejudices in an unsuccessful effort to promote a bank that would supplant the one set up by their opponents. In a speech that does not survive, Fisher hoped to discredit the bank by pointing to the purchase of its stock by Jewish merchants in Holland and by Haym Salomon, who had just returned to New York from Philadelphia. Fisher's point was clear: the new government was threatened because its primary financial institution depended for support on (foreign) Jewish investments.

Salomon was probably the "Jew Broker" who published, or arranged to have published, the long refutation addressed to Fisher in the March 13, 1784, issue of Philadelphia's *Independent Gazetteer*. Since Salomon italicized the words indicated, it is conceivable that in these cases he turned Fisher's language and arguments back at him. Salomon was filled with outrage that such an *"odious"* character, *"fetid* and *infamous,"* known for "Toryism and disaffection," would launch a *"wanton"* attack on an entire "religious persuasion." Salomon took pride in being both a Jew and a broker, since "we have in general been early uniform, decisive whigs, and were second to none in our patriotism and attachment to our country!" To Fisher's charges that "the Jews were the authors of high and unusual interest," Salomon retorted: "It was neither the Jews or Christians that founded the practice, but Quakers—Quakers worse than *heathens, pagans, or idolators*" who were "unwilling to venture money in trade during the war." In his anger, Salomon seized on the public stereotype of all Quakers as Tories. We can only speculate whether he did so to show the absurdity of Fisher's accusation, because he was adopting the tactics of his enemy, or like many of his countrymen he may have disliked Quakers for their refusal to fight in the war.[99]

Salomon did not have the last word: a "Spectator" condemned the vehemence of Salomon's riposte, claiming to be "at first amazed at the still persecuting spirit of those crucifiers subsisting among us," those "despisers of Christianity" possessed of "worse than a Shylock's temperament."[100] Salomon had the disadvantage that his vitriolic comments were published for all to see, whereas Fisher's remarks only circulated by hearsay. But then the "Spectator" claimed that the "Jew Broker" was but a stalking horse for the owner of the *Independent Gazetteer,* Continental army veteran Colonel Eleazar Oswald, who probably helped write, or in fact wrote, Salomon's powerful essay. Originally an Englishman who had worked for printers in New York and Baltimore, Oswald, newly arrived in Philadelphia, was a close friend to many in the Jewish community. The town's Jewish brokers paid for much of his advertising space. Furthermore, Oswald was cantankerous: he had been involved in a protracted libel suit in 1783 and would find himself in and out of the courts until he died aged forty-five in 1795 during the third of eight yellow fever epidemics that swept the city between 1793 and 1805.[101]

Calling attention to Oswald's wooden leg, the "Spectator" identified him as "fathering" the "Jew Broker's" article by relating an anecdote that also relied on a stereotype used to demean Jews: that they made money through trickery and cunning rather than honest labor. The author, the "Spectator" claimed, "was a person who not long since, when a subject of philosophy was debated, offered to lay a bet, that he could find a man who would keep his leg in any fluid scalding hot." He was supposedly exposed, however, by "a knowing E[nglish]man, well used to all the various finesse at New Market, the Exchange, etc.," the last of these an implicit swipe at the "Jew brokers" who were prominent there. While denying that a Jew had written the attack on Fisher, the "Spectator" nevertheless appealed to traditional antisemitic stereotypes by speculating that only a person of comparable avarice and cunning would take their part.[102]

The "Spectator" also was the first Pennsylvanian, and probably the first American, to express in print the desire to be completely rid of the Jews: referring to a recent hot air balloon experiment, he wished the device would convey "all the Jew-Brokers to New-Scotland, where they will be more abundantly thought of, than in Pennsylvania." New Scotland was "Nova Scotia," which in 1784 was filling up rapidly with loyalist refugees.[103] The "Spectator" thus tried to link the town's Jewish merchants with the loyalists: although the Jews of Philadelphia were almost unanimously revolutionaries, they could be distorted to resemble British partisans during the immediate postwar era, when the overimportation of British goods by American merchants plunged the country into a postwar depression.

We can only wonder why Oswald printed the "Spectator's" reply: he could have either felt obliged to give both sides their due, or else perhaps he thought the "Spectator's" extreme anti-semitism would appear sufficiently ludicrous to his audience that he could safely print it and hope for a backlash. Or, more simply, purple prose sold papers. But Salomon/Oswald's analysis had zeroed in on the main reason for elite anti-semitism in the late eighteenth century. Individuals who themselves were marginalized—former loyalists and recent immigrants—would try to show they belonged in the United States by redefining the new nation as a Christian republic and deflecting and incorporating attacks against themselves onto a group they hoped to stigmatize instead. Since Jews were few and not a major political constituency, although several were prominent for their business activities, they were highly visible targets and yet incapable of harming their persecutors.

TWO CHRISTIAN ISRAELS AND THE DEFEAT
OF FEDERALIST ANTI-SEMITISM, 1790–1800

Until 1793, when the Federalists turned against the French Revolution—which granted Jews full political and civil equality—and the Jews turned against the Federalists, political anti-semitism remained the tool of the Federalists' opponents. The only two remarks disparaging to Jews in the state debates over the Constitution I have discovered were made by Anti-Federalists, neither from Pennsylvania.[104] One Pennsylvania Federalist writing in the *Pennsylvania Gazette* went so far as to make fun of anti-semitism along with anti-Catholicism. Claiming to have surveyed the farmers of Montgomery County after the Bill of Rights had been attached to the Constitution, he mocked people who feared that without a constitutional amendment to the contrary "a Roman Catholic and a Jew stood as good a chance of being President of the United States as a Christian or a Protestant." Such rural folk also wanted amendments that guaranteed fishing and hunting, the building of better roads, and the abolition of the theater written into the Constitution.[105]

When Alexander Hamilton proposed his financial program in 1790, the *Pennsylvania Gazette* and the *New York Journal*, the latter an antifederal organ, printed items linking Federalists, financiers, and Jews as traitors to their country who profited from the high taxes required to pay off the government's outstanding debts:

> Tax on tax young Belcour cries
> More imposts, and a new excise.
> A public debt's a public blessing
> Which tis of course a crime to lessen.
> Each day a fresh report he broaches
> That Spies and Jews may ride in coaches.
> Soldiers and Farmers don't dispair
> Untax'd as yet are Earth and Air.[106]

An anonymous "Farmer," writing to the *Pennsylvania Gazette*, maintained that by paying the current owners of public securities rather than the soldiers, farmers, and artisans who had sold off their notes, Hamilton's plan would benefit unpatriotic men "who bore no part in the late war," considered it a "rebellion," and refused to loan the new nation money. The "Farmer" argued against Hamilton's contention that such payments were necessary for establishing the nation's credit overseas by identifying those creditors as Jews. "If you don't pay us," the creditors were supposedly arguing, "there is not a Jew nor a broker [a profession linked with Jews] in London or Amsterdam [both cities noted for Jewish financial activity] that will ever trust you again." The next year, "Square Toes," in an article in the *Philadelphia Advertiser,* also reprinted in New Hampshire and Connecticut, again invoked the specter of anti-semitism by including "Amsterdam Jews" along with "British riders, . . . American tories, and speculating Lawyers, Doctors, and Parsons," as the people who really benefited from the American Revolution through profiteering and speculation, whereas ordinary people had "ruined themselves by their honesty and industry." The term "Square Toes" refers to someone wearing wooden or home-made shoes; whether or not the author was of poor or middling condition, he clearly was appealing to the belief that ordinary folk regarded Jews as members of a greedy elite. Ironically, as historian Richard B. Morris has noted, "every conspicuous Jewish figure who was involved in financing or supplying the Continental forces," including Haym Salomon, "ended up broke."[107]

During the political crisis of the 1790s, the elite anti-semitism of the 1770s and 1780s became rampant. Mindful of the disabilities placed upon Jews in ancien régime Europe, Pennsylvania's Jews cheered the equal rights granted to their coreligionists during the French Revolution. For the sake of that equality, Jews began supporting the Pennsylvania Democratic-Republicans and actively campaigned for Jefferson's supporters in national and local elections. As contests between Federalists and Republicans became hotter, Federalist printers and propagandists appealed to an anti-semitism their leaders had previously repudiated. The elections in Pennsylvania were especially critical in the 1790s. At a time when the two parties were divided almost equally, a handful of votes in Philadelphia could determine the way the state's electoral vote or congressional delegation would swing. Despite their small numbers, Jews were considered by Federalist polemicists to be among the greedy, power-hungry leaders of a motley crew of Irishmen, "Jacobins," Frenchmen, African Americans, and the poor striving to wrest the government from a virtuous elite. A reversal had occurred: the Anti-Federalists and their successors among the Jeffersonian Democrats welcomed the Jews into their ranks and defended them. The Federalists, on the other hand, now grouped Jews with the "wild" Irish and French Jacobins who were trying to destroy their newfound vision of America as a Christian, native-born nation.[108]

As almanac humor and popular literature reveal, stereotypes of Jews, unlike most groups signified negatively in early America, at least gave them backhanded credit for having the intelligence and guile to (mis)lead their gullible followers. The first widely publicized expression of Federalist anti-semitic propaganda, the 1793 cartoon "A Peep into the Antifederal Club," distinguished which undesirable traits characterized each group (see illustrations). Although published in New York, the cartoon attacked the newly formed Democratic Society of Philadelphia, demeaning it as both "anti-Federal" rather than supporting a positive ideal, and a "club" rather than a society. The tall, thin man towering over, and thus directing, the others is probably Israel Israel, and not either Thomas Jefferson or Aaron Burr, as previous scholars have maintained. Unlike those out-of-town notables, Israel actually was a member (the treasurer and later vice president) of the Democratic Society of Philadelphia and a subscriber to its constitution, published on July 4, 1793, in the *Pennsylvania Gazette*. In addition, the "tall, rawboned" figure in the cartoon fits Israel's description by John Fenno (see quotation at n. 125). Moreover, neither Jefferson nor Burr had to raise themselves from "dirt to gold": both were already in the highest circles of government. Finally, the cartoonist applies to the figure anti-semitic stereotypes that would make no sense with respect to Jefferson or Burr. He is a greedy "broker," intelligent yet manipulative, and power hungry. He proclaims: "To be or not to be, a Broker is the question, whether tis nobler in the mind to knock down dry goods with this hammer; or with this head Contrive some means of knocking down a Government, and on its ruins raise myself to Eminence and Fortune; Glorious Thought thus to Emerge from dirt to Gold." The final phrase links Israel with the mysterious and heretical art of alchemy, recalling the sinister cabbalistic practices attributed to European Jews. Note that he is standing on a box: his rising above his fellow ne'-er-do-wells is not the result of his natural abilities, but of an easily decoded trick, although Israel in fact was over six feet tall.[109]

The cartoon is notable for other reasons. It mocks the Democratic Society's constitution, at which astronomer David Rittenhouse (the society's president) peers as he speculates about what sort of government exists on the moons of Saturn. Black figures—the devil and an ignorant African American—frame the others, who comprise a variety of ethnic groups. Thomas Paine, the fifth figure from the right, holds in his hand "A Plan for the Entire Subversion of Government." The large German at the center, Michael Leib, was also a leading figure in the society; he is associated with the slothful overconsumption of food and strong drink. The French are present, too; not only the ugly character who says "Ça ira," the title of a French revolutionary tune, but also Edmond Genet, the French minister to the United States. The small print reveals Genet to be the diminutive fellow pouring coins into the hands of one of the town's Republican printers (a scroll at his feet says, "Printing is a Better Trade than Law"). This Federalist cartoon is the first instance in American history I have seen in which Jews, blacks, head-in-the-sky intellectuals, and members of immigrant groups are depicted as un-American conspirators against the government and as tools of a foreign enemy.

Of this assortment of newly politicized people, Israel Israel took center stage. His father, Midrach (or Michael, d. 1754), had been Jewish. Israel's mother was an Anglican, and he was baptized two years after his birth in 1744 by none other than the Lutheran pastor Henry Melchior Mühlenberg. People frequently used whatever minister was handy in this era of high infant mortality, and while Mühlenberg was visiting the towns of New Hanover and Oley, he came upon "an edifying society" of the Anglican Church among whom Mary Paxton Israel (1724–1777) lived "in friendly fellowship." In 1784, Mühlenberg wrote to Israel to make sure he was fulfilling his baptismal covenant and told the story of how he had been baptized "upon the serious petitioning of your Tender loving Mother and on whose Breast you lay yet." The aged Mühlenberg, who lived four more years, wrote as a "dying friend" to add emotional weight to his plea that Israel attend to his Christian obligations if he had not. Israel had indeed been fulfilling his baptismal covenant, at first as an Anglican. Then, like many Philadelphia working- and middle-class people, he converted in the 1780s to Universalism and in 1790 was one of the founders of the church on Lombard Street. He kept this faith until his death, as the beginning of a codicil to his will written in 1820 testifies: "In the Name of the Everlasting God the

Savior of *All* Men through the Atonement of Jesus Christ the Lord, I ISRAEL ISRAEL." His own name appeared in huge letters as if to emphasize the irony that a man with such a name was a devout Christian, as his careful disposition of his religious books including an annotated version of the New Testament and life of Christ by John Wesley revealed. (He also bequeathed an unspecified number of guns.) Yet Israel's Jewish ethnicity could not be erased. As his vituperative critics demonstrate, Judaism was treated by eighteenth-century Pennsylvanians as a religion, which could be changed, and as an ethnic or national affiliation, which could not. This permitted racial stereotypes to cling to people who were no longer Jews.[110]

Israel left the Philadelphia area at the age of twenty-one, sailing to Barbados, where he lived for ten years. There he made, and lost, a fortune before moving in 1775 to a small farm in Delaware. During the Revolution, Israel had at least two close calls with the British. In 1777, he was arrested as a spy when the Tory neighbor who gave him the password so he could cross the British lines betrayed him to the commander of H.M.S. *Roebuck,* which was anchored in the Delaware in sight of Israel's farm. Israel claimed he was going to Philadelphia to visit his mother, quite plausibly, as she would die that December, but his story is told by his granddaughter Elizabeth Ellet, a renowned upper-class author who would probably not have admitted her ancestor was a spy. We will never know, although Israel served as a member of the local Committee of Safety in 1777 and named one of his sons James Hutchinson Israel after a leading Philadelphia radical. Earlier, Israel had said that he "would sooner drive his cattle as a present to General Washington than receive thousands of dollars in British gold for them," the remark that provoked his neighbor to betray him and so angered the commander of the *Roebuck* that he ordered his men to round up Israel's cattle and slaughter them. In her book *The Women of the American Revolution,* Ellet includes in the chapter on her mother—whose story she tells along with those of Betsy Ross, Martha Washington, and other well-known females—the story of how Israel's brave nineteen-year-old wife drove the animals away while the bullets whistled about her before escaping into the woods. Israel was tried for his life, and probably would have lost it if he had not flashed the secret Masonic distress sign to the judge, whom a sympathetic guard had informed him was a Mason. When Israel had his and his wife's portraits painted, he gave the hand signal that saved him.[111]

Two years later, a slave, Caesar, whom Israel had brought from the West Indies to serve and protect his mother, fingered him as a revolutionary. He saved himself this time by identifying his brother, Joseph, as the real rebel by fetching Joseph's uniform (which did not fit him) from upstairs in the house. Meanwhile he whispered to Caesar that he was a "damned rascal" and would kill him on the spot if he did not withdraw the accusation. Still, Israel nearly gave himself away while one of the Hessians who had come to arrest him bragged about his prowess at the Battle of Paoli, in which the British surprised General Anthony Wayne's army in their sleep and slaughtered many of them: "I stuck them myself like so many pigs, one after another, till the blood ran out of my musket." His daughter tells how Israel "started to his feet, with his face pale with rage, convulsed lips, and clenched hands," but his younger sister saved the day by fainting in his arms. Israel survived the Revolution and eight yellow fever epidemics in which he remained in town caring for the sick, dying in 1822 at the age of seventy-eight. His grave may be visited in South Laurel Hill Cemetery in Philadelphia.[112]

By the 1790s, Israel was a well-to-do stable-keeper and owner of the Cross-Keys Tavern at Third and Chestnut Streets. In the 1790 census he headed a household of five men, eight women, and three slaves over the age of sixteen. Israel's political rise began when he remained in Philadelphia, along with other leading members of the newly formed Democratic Society and many African Americans, to nurse the afflicted during the horrific yellow fever epidemic of 1793. Israel stayed behind while an elite, including President Washington, his cabinet, and most of Congress who founded their right to hold office on superior public virtue, fled en masse for healthier climes. Israel, like the blacks, used his life-threatening public service to dispel prejudice.[113] Such a claim to civic virtue gained him the respect the blacks failed to obtain, for they were accused of profiting by healing the victims. Israel was honored with a proclamation from Governor Mifflin, and when he had his portrait painted a second time, he made sure a scroll marked "1793" prominently appeared. Israel parlayed his emergency relief work into an important role in Republican politics, which led the Federalists to argue, when he ran in 1797 for the state senate, "Will anyone who values the privilege of an elector, choose a man to legislate merely because he risked his life in nursing the sick, or because he made a fortune by keeping a public house?"

About half the voters did, and Israel narrowly won that October election. Federalist printer William Cobbett, the acerbic "Peter Porcupine," bemoaned "the triumph of the Jews over the Gentiles" and sarcastically commented that Israel's public house was "a most excellent stand for collecting the sentiments of the *sovereign* people, who never speaks his mind freely except when he's half dun [drunk]." Israel ran repeatedly for public office in the 1790s, always losing—his 1797 election was disputed and reversed by a special ballot the following February—until the Jeffersonian triumph of 1800. (So did most other Philadelphia Jeffersonians, so it is impossible to say whether anti-semitism was a factor or not.) Cobbett, for his part, left Philadelphia for Britain and continued his anti-semitic publications (along with equally vehement pleas for Catholic emancipation) until his death in 1835.[114]

Israel and one of his leading opponents, the Federalist printer John Fenno, actually came to blows in 1795 during the annual campaign for the state legislature. Understanding why the fight occurred requires considerable background. As political parties were just forming, the two contending slates of candidates were known as the "Treaty" (Federalist) and "No Treaty" (Democrat) parties based on their stance on the Jay Treaty. On October 7, reflecting the fact that the modern idea of an organized opposition to the government had yet to achieve legitimacy, a supporter of the treaty calling himself "A Federalist" wondered whether the Democratic Society "represent[ed] the People of this district generally, or the particular, and perhaps clashing interest of their own Society." Arguing that only the elected government itself could represent the people as a whole, he suggested that the Democratic Society issue "a formal declaration of independence," and apply for "a regular admission into the Union as having an acknowledged interest separate from the rest of the union."[115]

At this point, the "Federalist" revealed himself to be an anti-semite as well as an early proponent of the "America, love it or leave it" school of thought. He urged that since the Democratic Society complained that the nation suffered "in a state of aristocratic vassalage" under the Federalists, its members should leave for the newly secured territories of the Old

Northwest. This, the "Federalist" sarcastically remarked, would "be a second going out of the Children of Israel, or rather of *Israel Israel;* and rather than they should not go, I will engage that the quiet citizens will be more willing than the Egyptians were of old to lend them, if not *jewels,* such other articles as may be more useful in a new country." The similarity of the words "Jews" and the italicized "Jewels," along with the linking of Jews and the lending of money, identified the Democratic Society members not only as un-American, but as dupes of a non-Christian, a Jew. Another ethnic Jew who was a practicing Christian, Moses Levy, had also joined Thomas McKean, Stephen Girard, and others on Philadelphia's official committee to protest the treaty to Congress.[116]

Five days later, the *Gazette of the United States* attacked Israel again. The previous year, while the Democratic Societies in Pennsylvania had formally joined with the Federalists in condemning the Whiskey Rebellion, evidence exists that many of the members privately supported what in retrospect seems less like a rebellion and more like a traditional case of the tax resistance endemic in Pennsylvania since the late 1770s.[117] The Federalists made Israel the special target of their charge that the societies had fomented the unrest. Someone claiming sarcastically to be "A Member of the Demoncritic Society" argued that Israel had "uttered a pious wish (for you must know he is accounted a pious man) that all those might be cut off and sent to heaven who had wickedly marched against our western brethren who had righteously taken up arms (but rather too soon for our society as matters were not thoroughly ripe for execution against the unjust measures of government)."[118]

In addition to accusing Israel of treason, the anonymous writer charged that he and his cohorts had concocted a scheme to manufacture accusations of prejudice against themselves in the hope of generating a backlash. They were plotting to "remind the people, that our [society's] Vice-President was once a Jew and that he is now an ugly Christian, and insert such other matters respecting his character as will enable me to say, in reply, a number of things in his favor." When one Democrat supposedly objected that this "artifice will be seen through," the consensus was that the ruse would fool "the ignorant, who are by far, the most numerous." Federalists who attacked Israel Israel on ethnic grounds to win the support of anti-semites thus also hoped to attract tolerationist voters by claiming that Israel himself was inventing the anti-semitic accusations. The Federalists played what they hoped would be the trump card of prejudice in two contradictory ways at the same time. Their satirist then went on to show that, to win votes, the Democratic Society ran along with Israel a "knight of the funding system," that is, someone involved in finance, a Quaker sugar-refiner, and a wealthy member of the German Reformed church—none of whom was fit for public office—to attract ethnic votes.[119]

This satire is significant in two ways. First, at this early stage of political organization, the Republicans were putting forward a "balanced" ticket representing Philadelphia's diverse population, though Federalists claimed that such a ticket aligned the Democratic Society with "particular" interests rather than with the welfare of "the People . . . generally." Yet the Federalists were clearly playing to ethnic prejudices themselves by implying that only a Jew and a traitor could have misled the society into adopting both treasonable politics and an unethical appeal to ethnicity to win votes.[120]

Second, by claiming the Democrats were manufacturing anti-semitic propaganda against themselves, the Federalists who attacked Israel were showing their awareness that a significant number of voters would not share their prejudice against Jews but might join in a backlash against what they perceived as illegitimate tactics. As Owen Ireland has shown, Pennsylvania Federalists—unlike those in the more ethnically homogeneous New England and parts of the southern tidewater where they predominated—had accommodated Pennsylvania's diverse population and traditional resistance to paying taxes, which they reduced almost to the vanishing point, to fare well politically in the state. They were undermined, however, by the zeal of Federalists associated with the national government from other countries (Britons Charles Nisbet and William Cobbett) or regions (John Fenno, the Boston-born editor of the *Gazette of the United States*) who were not familiar with Pennsylvania's politics of diversity.[121] For example, Joseph Dennie, a New Hampshire man who served as Secretary of State Timothy Pickering's personal secretary in 1799 and 1800, believed that his career as a writer had failed in Philadelphia because "this region, covered with the Jewish, and canting and cheating descendants" of the first Quakers, gave "polar icy" treatment to "men of liberality and letters" such as himself.[122]

Yet the year after making these remarks, Dennie reviewed a pro-Jewish play in his *Port Folio:* "we praise it for its evident tendency to obviate those unjust and illiberal prejudices which have too long been entertained in every country except this against that unfortunate race of men." In the interim, the Federalists and their intolerance of foreigners had been massively repudiated with the election of Jefferson and a Republican Congress and state governments, suggesting that if some Federalists, such as Alexander Hamilton (see New York chapter), tolerated anti-semitic rhetoric in which they did not believe because they thought it would further their cause, others, such as Dennie, hid his true feelings as an anti-semite in an effort to rebuild his party's fortunes after 1800.[123]

Why did the Federalists renounce the toleration they displayed during the Constitutional Convention and which their hero George Washington endorsed so strongly in his initial addresses? New England and southern Federalists, used to more stable polities and fewer contested local elections, were uncomfortable with the ethnic mixture and lively political life of the nation's temporary capital in Philadelphia. New Yorkers such as Hamilton also lived in a pluralistic state, but one where politics were sharply polarized rather than accommodationist, as were Pennsylvania's in the 1790s. For example, during that decade, Thomas Mifflin, a bipartisan candidate, was elected governor of Pennsylvania every three years, almost unanimously twice, and once by a nearly two-to-one margin. He distributed patronage to both parties and refused to call out the state militia against the Whiskey Rebels until President Washington federalized it. Furthermore, the Federalists did have a point that most immigrants were against them. Many "transatlantic radicals"—most notably Joseph Priestley, discoverer of oxygen and Jeffersonian pamphleteer, driven from the British Isles for supporting the French Revolution—arrived in Philadelphia in the 1780s and 1790s and opposed conciliatory Federalist policies toward Britain. They joined a large Catholic and Protestant Irish immigration of perhaps some twenty-six thousand people between 1780 and 1800, lending token plausibility to Federalist fears that it was not "the people" who were opposing them, but in the words of Fenno's *Gazette,* "the revolutionary vermin of foreign countries." Jews were an ideal scapegoat in this atmosphere, as non-Christians had been granted equal rights by the French revolutionary "atheist" government.[124]

To return to the fight between Israel and Fenno: any possibility that

Israel and his supporters concocted the anti-semitic article of October 7 to generate a backlash in their favor was disproven by another article Fenno published on October 14. He reported that the day after Israel and his "No Treaty Ticket" lost their election by about fifteen hundred to one thousand votes each:

> he met me in the market, and without ceremony told me that if I ever published anything about him, he would flog me (his exact words). I answered that I should continue to publish as I had heretofore done, a free & impartial paper. He repeated his threat, & walked off. I was buying some apples, he returned & attacked me very unexpectedly by giving me a violent blow on the mouth. It rained. I had an umbrella, with which I struck him twice. It was then taken from me and we exchanged five or six blows with our fists. The bystanders then rushed in & parted us.

Fenno, who was bested by Israel, "a rawboned man six feet high at least," commented that the assault proved to his satisfaction that Israel was "a very improper person to make a representative." Fenno thought that Israel's proper course would have been to take legal action after requiring Fenno to divulge the author of the libels. But Fenno did not take Israel to court for the assault either: he "suffered no pain nor confinement" from this "true-blooded Jacobin" and claimed, "I do not regret the attack since he & his coadjutors were defeated."[125] Nor did Israel "flog" Fenno for his opposition during his two state senate races in 1797 and 1798. After his first, narrow victory was overturned, Fenno printed a notice: "A Jewish Tavern Keeper, with a very Jewish name (viz. Israel Israel) is chosen one of the Senators of this commonwealth for the city of Philadelphia solely on account of his violent attachment to the French Interests." But this time, Fenno made certain that the author, Charles Nisbet, another non-Pennsylvanian, a Scots-born Presbyterian divine of extreme antidemocratic and anti-French prejudices and the first president of Dickinson College, took the credit.[126]

Interestingly, Nisbet was one of three faculty members at Dickinson who subscribed in 1797 to British Jew David Levy's critique of Thomas Paine's *The Age of Reason*, published both in New York (by Naphtali Judah, a staunch Jeffersonian) and in Philadelphia. Levy, who had previously refuted Joseph Priestley's anti-semitic remarks in print, branded Paine's castigation of traditional religion as "one of the most violent and systematic attacks on the word of God that ever was made." Levy hoped that as a "poor simple Levite" he could refute the world-renowned revolutionary's effort to "dazzle the eyes of the ignorant and unwary." That by the late 1790s immigrants Paine and Priestley had joined with America's Jews in supporting the party of Jefferson shows the diversity of the early Republican party.[127]

William Cobbett, the other major Federalist printer in Philadelphia, also engaged in anti-semitism and thereby provoked the wrath of another lapsed Jew, Moses Levy. When on June 30, 1798, Benjamin Franklin Bache, Franklin's grandson, heir, and a leading Jeffersonian printer, was arrested for violating the Sedition Act, Cobbett organized a mob that took justice into its own hands and attacked Bache's press, claiming he deserved the same treatment as "a Turk, Jew, a Jacobin, or a dog." Along with his best friend Alexander Dallas, a fellow attorney and founder of the Democratic Society, Levy defended Bache, who died in September while awaiting trial. Levy also appeared for the plaintiff, Dr. Benjamin Rush, in a libel suit against Cobbett, for which the irascible printer was convicted in December 1799, and fined four thousand dollars. Calling Rush "the killer doctor" whose remedy for everything was supposedly to "bleed them," Cobbett also criticized Levy's defense tactics, blaming them on his Jewish heritage. Levy apparently had tried to use Cobbett's loyalist past against him, and also supposedly accused him of trying to kill off Republicans by directing them away from Rush's essentially sound medical practice. Cobbett complained: "Such a diabolical thought never could have been engendered but in the mind of a Jew! . . . I cannot for my life, however, muster up anything like anger against a poor devil like Moses. He didn't believe a word that he said. He vash working for all monish dat vash all." Cobbett was not only linking Levy with a religion he had renounced, he was depicting one of the nation's finest lawyers, a graduate of the College of Philadelphia, as an ignorant foreigner. Cobbett, himself a native of Britain, soon proved that he in fact was the one working for "monish" who "didn't believe a word that he said." In 1800 he tried to smear Bache's successor, William Duane, as "once a Jew," which he never was. Cobbett or another anti-semitic Federalist that year also invented an imaginary Jew, "Moses S. Solomon of Second Street, Philadelphia," who endorsed Federalist attacks on presidential candidate

Thomas Jefferson's atheism as "a common cause" of "all religions." Duane exposed the fraud.[128]

Anti-semitism remained a political issue in Pennsylvania as long as the Federalists were viable contenders for political power. For instance, on August 5, 1800, the year of the Adams-Jefferson race and numerous state and federal campaigns, the *Gazette of the United States* attacked the Democratic Society of Philadelphia as "composed of the very refuse and filth of society." After designating a black man who was present as "Citizen Sambo," an "Observer" then noted the presence of "Citizen N—— the Jew," who supposedly stated in dialect: "I hopsh you will consider dat de monish is very scarch, and besides you know I'sh just come out by de Insholvent Law." Several others replied: "Oh yes let N—— pass." In other words, "N" could enter the Democrats' deliberations precisely because he was bankrupt.[129]

"N" was Benjamin Nones. At the siege of Savannah, Georgia, in 1779, he had come to the attention of General Pulaski. His immediate superior, French Captain Vernier, commended Nones: "his behavior under fire in all the bloody actions we fought has been marked by the bravery and courage which a military man is expected to show for the liberties of his country." Members of the Nones family had been among the earliest Jews in Savannah and then Lancaster, but Benjamin settled in Philadelphia after the British took Georgia and South Carolina. He was active in Mikveh Israel and in 1793 was one of twenty-four people of French ethnicity who founded the French Benevolent Society to assist French immigrants in distress. Although they aided refugees regardless of political creed—they helped both revolutionary exiles and slave owners fleeing the rebellion in Saint Domingue—their sympathy was definitely with the Revolution: their seal had a liberty cap mounted on a pike, and they were the first group to welcome Minister Edmond Genet to Philadelphia. Nones also traded with the French in the West Indies during the Quasi-War despite government prohibitions, leading to the seizure of one of his vessels and a lawsuit that his descendants pursued for much of the nineteenth century.[130]

Nones had already exhibited his feisty character in the dispute with the Levys in 1782 and a subsequent one with various elders of Mikveh Israel in 1793. That year, three leaders of the synagogue barred his entry after he had "subjected them to gross indignities unbefitting their status." The problem had something to do with Nones asking Manuel Josephson to return the congregation's shofar, the horn that summoned worshipers, in such a manner that Josephson responded, "the congregation might be damned." In his reply to the "Observer's" 1800 attack, which Fenno's paper refused to print but upon which William Duane of the Jeffersonian *Aurora* seized eagerly, Nones (either his English had dramatically improved or he still employed a ghost writer) showed that his mettle had not changed. In defiant terms reminiscent of Haym Salomon's reply to Miers Fisher of 1784, he rejoiced in the very epithets hurled against him. "I am accused of being a Jew, of being a Republican, and of being Poor," he began before explaining why he "gloried" in each of these accusations. Other Jews had included "Abraham, and Isaac, and Moses and the prophets, and . . . Christ and his apostles; I feel no disgrace in ranking with such society, however it may be subject to the illiberal buffoonery of such men as your correspondents." A Jew had to be a Republican, for "here, in France, and in the Batavian republic alone we are treated as men and as brethren. In republics we have rights, in monarchies we live but to experience wrongs." And Nones argued that his poverty was honest, his family "soberly and decently brought up. They have not been taught to revile a Christian because his religion is not so old as theirs." Only among a "purse-proud aristocracy" would poverty be considered a crime, and the French-born Nones offered to pay his creditors when the nations of the world stopped making war on republican France and permit him to trade with his fellow countrymen.[131]

The Federalists' criticism of Nones reflects their desperation in 1800. While other Jews were criticized as brokers who profited excessively in America, Nones proved his unfitness for democracy by failing to succeed. By grouping Jews with blacks, Federalists who were becoming more elitist in their ideology and relying more on their ethnically Anglo-Saxon base of support were indiscriminately lumping together groups they believed were signified negatively in the popular mind.

Another last gasp of eighteenth-century anti-semitism occurred in Pittsburgh. John Israel, Israel's son, whose only Jewish grandparent was his father's father, had begun the *Herald of Liberty,* the first newspaper in Washington, Pennsylvania, in 1798 when he was twenty-two years old. Cementing the alliance of western and eastern Pennsylvania Democrats, he married the daughter of David Reddick, who was ethnically Irish and, four years earlier, was a leader of the Whiskey Rebellion in Washington County. For the election of 1800, Israel moved to Pittsburgh and began the *Tree of Liberty* to challenge the only paper then printed there, John Scull's Federalist *Pittsburgh Gazette*. Hugh Henry Brackenridge, author of *Modern Chivalry* and the region's leading Jeffersonian, became his staunchest supporter.[132]

As Brackenridge explained to Thomas Jefferson, "the patronage of this paper has drawn upon me personally much abuse and ribaldry." No sooner had Israel's paper been launched than a circular with the following doggerel appeared.

Have you heard	of the New Press?
Echo:	*of the Jew Press?*
What, is it published	and by a Jew?
Echo:	*and by a Hugh [Henry Brackenridge]?*
Of the Aurora	another edition?
Echo:	*a mother of sedition?*
Jacobinism imaginary is	or Is real
Echo:	*Israel.*

Israel's counterarguments against these slurs included reasoned defenses of toleration and free speech in which the young newcomer adopted the mantle of mature wisdom. A letter in the *Tree of Liberty*—doubtless planted by Brackenridge or another friend—argued that Israel had a right to edit his paper without plunging into "the mire of scurrility and personal defamation of private characters which some of the western presses wallow in." Israel responded to Scull's Federalist nativism by arguing that "every man of good character coming into this country ought to be admitted." Israel was sufficiently confident of his audience that he even used the Federalists' anti-semitism against them. "Watchman" warned that if returned to power the Federalists would "amend that part of the Constitution which admits a Jew as President" as a prelude to installing "an established religion of some sort," the sort perhaps practiced in the three most Federalist states, New Hampshire, Massachusetts, and Connecticut. The alternative was Thomas Jefferson, who had introduced laws in Virginia "by which religious oppression is abolished . . . after the manner of William Penn." Philadelphia Democrats endorsed this line, sending Israel a toast to print that they had drunk in his honor: "May the *Israelites* lift up their voice, and their enemies fall before them like the walls of Jericho." Far from supporting tradition as they claimed, the Federalists were exposed by Israel as dangerous enemies of the true, tolerationist tradition of Pennsylvania.[133]

Yet Israel and his writers were not above having some fun at the expense of a rival with so inviting a name. They called him "John Numb Scull," a "silly, stupid boor," whose "Leaden Brains Assimilate so well with John Scull." Israel did not hesitate to stoop to anti-Hibernianism, either, to retaliate against Scull. Running unsuccessfully for Congress himself and supporting the ethnically Scots Thomas McKean in the 1805 race for governor, in which the Pennsylvania Republicans split, Israel commented negatively on the Irish proclivity for politics, which was apparently as great in turn-of-the-century Pittsburgh as it would be in New York, Boston, and Philadelphia later in the century. Scull's paper responded, "The apostate Israel can't refrain from abusing the Irish—he says: 'their shoes are not twice soled after landing before they meddle with state affairs.' . . . Who fed and clothed the apostate when he first came poor and naked to the western country? The Irish!" Scull next accused Israel of being on McKean's payroll and probed the depths of "the fallen Israelite's . . . numerous . . . acts of apostasy," mentioning "Your close association with the most violent Federalists. Your malignant abuse in private of the most upright Democrats and your mean and dishonorable act of having yourself nominated for Congress." Scull concluded: "Defend yourself, you apostate of apostates."

In the 1800 elections, the Federalists lost just as decisively in the west as in the east. Proof of Israel's success in defending the Jews came during the election of 1802. When the *Fayette Gazette* attacked "the Israelite" hoping to prove "the Jew a fool," Federalists in Pittsburgh held a political meeting to "take this public opportunity of declaiming our abhorrence of the vile calumnies, falsehoods and slanders" that associated the party with anti-semitism. They then published their manifesto in Scull's *Gazette*. Scull also held his tongue, but it did no good. As a writer in Israel's paper commented in 1805, the Federalists lost Pittsburgh and the surrounding area because their "extravagance and folly, with the insulting manners of some of their hangers-on, drive many moderate and thinking men from their party." The writer was indirectly calling attention to the fact that moderate Federalists were forced to rely on bloviating printers, who were in a precarious trade and relied on sensationalism to sell papers. Israel became captain of a republican militia company, was active in the civic life of Pittsburgh, and died at the age of twenty-nine in 1806, a year after selling the *Tree of Liberty* and moving to Washington County. In his will, Israel Israel left John's son Joseph, a Pittsburgh bricklayer, an inheritance equal to his surviving uncles and aunts. John had named Joseph after a heroic uncle, Joseph Israel (1783–1804), a midshipman on the U.S.S. *Constitution* who had sneaked onboard a small boat that was blown up in Tripoli harbor on a risky mission to do likewise to an Algerian vessel. Joseph is commemorated by a plaque in the Washington Navy Yard.[134]

Ethnically Jewish Jeffersonians reaped the fruits of their partisan labors. In 1800, Benjamin Nones was appointed notary public by Pennsylvania's new Jeffersonian governor Thomas McKean, a position that enabled him to pass on applications for citizenship by immigrants. The same year, Israel Israel received the satisfaction of becoming the elected sheriff of Philadelphia. His third and last portrait depicts him in early-nineteenth-century garb wearing spectacles and as an elder statesman. Thomas Jefferson even considered appointing Moses Levy, who had defended Rush against Cobbett's libels, attorney general of the United States, but backed down when Albert Gallatin, his secretary of the treasury and point man in Pennsylvania, noted that Levy was not well known in political circles. Instead, Levy served as recorder of the city of Philadelphia for twenty years (1802–22) and became a member of the Pennsylvania legislature in 1825, the year before he died.[135]

If we discount his partisan rhetoric, Israel Israel's congratulations to Thomas Jefferson on his election as president—his only extant writing besides his will I could discover—explained how their triumph had freed the nation from a Federalist party that had cast a shadow over both the traditional toleration and the revolutionary achievement of Pennsylvania's Jews. Anti-semitism, confined largely to folk culture in a colonial society dominated by a cosmopolitan Quaker/Anglican elite before 1776, paradoxically became a more visible and political issue as Jews worked vigorously to bring the new United States into being. Jews then heartily endorsed a French Revolution that permitted elite opponents of radicalism to use anti-semitism as a political weapon. But because Jews were such a minuscule percentage of the population, the worst of anti-semitism lay far in the future. For the moment, French "Jacobins" and "wild" Irishmen posed a far more potent threat to the Federalist party. Israel therefore noted that Jefferson's victory confirmed the original vision of 1787—that America offered the diverse people of the world either an example on which to model struggle for their own liberty or a place of refuge should they fail to attain it.

> Permit me to offer at this time my congratulations on the triumph of the principals [*sic*] of republicanism over the deep laid plans of monarchy and despotism; you Sir, under the will of Heaven is placed in a situation to be enabled to give new life and vigor to the drooping cause of Liberty and the rights of man in America, and to you the People look up to for the operation and true effects that is to be derived from the Constitution, for as yet we have had no fair trial of that Instrument. To you, Sir, do the groaning republicans over the World look up to for relief; now do we expect under your administration that this country will be an asylum for the oppressed of all nations.[136]

In his last line, Israel recalled the stirring words of Thomas Paine's *Common Sense,* who also predicted the United States would become "an asylum for mankind." Israel had no way of knowing that over a million Jews would act on his words, but had not he and his allies opposed the Federalist vision of a Christian, Anglo-American nation, they never would have.

THE ACCEPTANCE OF JEWS IN THE AMERICAN NOVEL: CHARLES BROCKDEN BROWN'S ARTHUR MERVYN AND HUGH HENRY BRACKENRIDGE'S MODERN CHIVALRY

As Louis Harap and Heather Nathans have shown in their work on the image of Jews in early America, the novels and plays of the early 1790s did little more than play to traditional stereotypes. By the end of the decade, however, Jews began to triumph in literature as they did in Jeffersonian politics. Nathans shows that the negatively signified Shylock, from Shakespeare's *The Merchant of Venice,* was giving ground to more favorable representations of stage Jews in the Philadelphia's theater.[137] Two of the first major novels published in the United States only brought up anti-semitism to expose its flaws. Both Charles Brockden Brown's *Arthur Mervyn* and Hugh Henry Brackenridge's *Modern Chivalry* deal with Jews. Both authors lived in Pennsylvania during the 1790s, and both admired and befriended Jews—or rather Israel Israel and John Israel, respectively, political figures who could change their religion but not their ethnicity.

Brown lived in Philadelphia during some of the yellow fever epidemics that attacked the city eight times from 1793 to 1805 and brought tavern-keeper Israel Israel to public attention for his dedicated efforts to relieve the sick and dying.[138] Biographies of Brown do not hint that he knew Israel personally, although everyone in town knew about him: the only evidence Brown had a Jewish acquaintance is that he and Solomon Simson were fellow members of the New York Mineralogical Society. Like Israel in Philadelphia, Simson was a leader of the Democratic Society in that city, and butt of a Federalist publisher's—in this case James Rivington's—anti-semitism.[139]

Published in two parts in 1799 and 1800, *Arthur Mervyn* is subtitled *Memoirs of the Year 1793*. Philadelphia's first yellow fever epidemic is one of the events observed by the protagonist, a country boy who comes to Philadelphia to make good, gaining in experience what he loses in innocence as he navigates a social world that is presented as "maze of perils and suspicions, of concealments and evasions" (187). Mervyn is in many ways an autobiographical character. Brown survived yellow fever in 1798 when the epidemic came to New York: his best friend, the young physician Elijah Hubbard Smith, who attended him, did not.[140]

In the novel, Mervyn returns to Philadelphia to persuade a man to return to the country and escape the epidemic he himself has risked. "Terror"—the word being used simultaneously to describe the French revolutionary government—is Mervyn's term for the yellow fever that had caused so many of the city's inhabitants to abandon it (98, 331). In the process, Mervyn's good intentions—to distribute money to the needy and run the hospital at Bush Hill more humanely—come to nothing. Calling attention to a dismal public reaction for which Israel's behavior was a sterling exception, Brown turned the hospital into a symbol of the city: "While the upper rooms of this building are filled with the sick and the dying, the lower apartments are the scenes of carousal and mirth. The wretches who are hired, at enormous wages, to tend the sick and convey away the dead, neglect their duty and consume the cordials which are provided for the patients in debauchery and riot" (131). Mervyn's "City of Brotherly Love" resembled the Athens of Pericles as described by Thucydides when the plague struck: all pretense of public virtue went out the window. Mervyn himself is assaulted, mistaken for a corpse, and almost buried alive. This episode can be read to suggest the heroism Brown wished he could have displayed while at the same time reflecting on how virtuous behavior can punish as well as reward the moral person, such as Dr. Smith.

Another personal element in *Arthur Mervyn* is that Brown had hoped to marry, but he took his mother's disapproval of his non-Quaker fiancée to heart and never wed. The story of Achsa Fielding, the Jewish convert Mervyn does marry as the novel ends, subverts conventional prejudices such as Brown's mother displayed.

Achsa does not appear until the twenty-third of the twenty-five chapters in *Mervyn*'s second part, at the very end of the novel. Like Israel Israel, she suddenly arrives on the scene to save a desperate situation, although her task is to sort out Mervyn's confused existence rather than to organize yellow fever relief. In what Harap has termed "perhaps the earliest breakaway from the stereotype [of the female Jew] in all literature in English," Achsa, a recent English immigrant, is neither the mysterious oriental beauty nor the pawn of a grasping father, as fictional Jewish females had been stereotyped in a tradition going back at least to Shakespeare's *Merchant of Venice.* As with many upper-class London Jews, her father had fled from the Inquisition in Portugal: he too had "few of the moral or external qualities of Jews," being "frugal without meanness, and cautious in his dealings, without extortion."

Achsa is far from beautiful physically, yet Brown leaves us with the overwhelming impression that she is a beautiful human being. Dr. Stevens, the surrogate for Brown's recently deceased friend Dr. Smith, remarks: "A brilliant skin is not hers, nor elegant proportions; nor majestic stature; yet no creature had ever more power to bewitch. Her manners have grace and dignity that flow from exquisite feeling, delicate taste, and the quickest and keenest penetration. She has the wisdom of men and books. Her sympathies are enforced by reason, and her character regulated by knowledge." In fact, when Mervyn tries to think of reasons not to marry her, he describes her as "unsightly as a night-hag, tawney as a moor, the eye of a gypsey, low in stature, contemptibly diminutive, scarcely bulk enough to cast a shadow as she walks, less luxuriance than a charred log, fewer elasticities than a sheet pebble." That Achsa is a composite of negative physical and racial stereotypes, at least as ugly as the stereotypical Jew, is irrelevant to Mervyn, as is her Jewish heritage. "Hush! Hush! Blasphemer," he tells his own inner voice that would equate appearance and reality, surface and substance. After following his heart irrationally for most of the novel, with disastrous results, Mervyn is saved through the use of reason. Achsa's enchantments are those of the Enlightenment, and he rejects an innocent farm lass for the charms of the urban and urbane Achsa.

Politically, Achsa has the same philosophy as Israel Israel and the Philadelphia Democratic Society of which he was vice president. Mervyn notes, "I have heard her reason with admirable eloquence, against the vain distinctions of property and nation and rank. . . . Her nation has suffered too much by the inhuman antipathies to religious and political faction." Like Israel Israel, Achsa possessed, lost, and regained a fortune. Her troubles came from her father's bankruptcy, a fate shared by several wealthy Jews during the American Revolution, not through his own fault but because leading continental houses had failed. Her husband, for whom she converted to the Church of England, ran away with another woman to France (he became prominent in the French Revolution and lost his head). Achsa's father committed suicide, her mother went mad, and her child died. Like the Jews themselves, in Europe, she suffered greatly both through misfortune and prejudice, her "wealth" providing the "chief security from the contempt of the proud and the bigoted."

But in America Achsa found a new and even richer life. A new, republican cultivation replaced the "pomp and luxury" she had unthinkingly enjoyed in England. "They were once of moment in her eyes; but the sufferings, humiliations, and reflections of years, have cured her of her folly." In Philadelphia, "she lived in great affluence and independence, but made use of her privileges of fortune chiefly to secure to herself the command of her own time." Her aim was the personal independence cherished by male revolutionary Americans—exercised increasingly as well by women who attended female academies that opened in the early Republic—not the luxury they disdained (at least in theory). "She had been long ago tired and disgusted with the dull and fulsome uniformity and parade of the play-house [opened in Philadelphia in 1793] and ballroom [the elite Dancing Assembly, target of Benjamin Franklin in 1740 and still functioning today]." "Formal visits were endured as mortifications and penances, by which the delights of privacy and friendly intercourse by contrast increased." Perhaps Brown was here attacking the formal society, the "Republican Court," presided over by Federalist hostesses Anne Willing Bingham and Martha Washington. "Music she loved, but never sought it in place of public resort, or from the skill of mercenary performers, and books were not the least of her pleasures," perhaps another reference to the recently opened theater.

If Achsa Fielding is a surrogate for Israel Israel and Philadelphia's Jewish community, which overwhelmingly supported the Republicans once France granted Jews complete equality during the French Revolution, Brown is arguing that these scapegoated people exhibit superior republican virtue, and are better Americans (A. Mer-vyn = "American"?) than the Federalists who claimed to exemplify such behavior. The latter indulged in quasi-aristocratic practices such as formal and closed public rituals and attending the theater and dances, not to mention leaving town to save themselves during epidemics. Even so, Brown offers a caveat: Achsa's husband joined the French Revolution itself and perished in its convulsions. Like many sympathizers, Brown realized the French went too far. Only in the United States can Achsa's culture and intelligence be synthesized with Mervyn's naïveté and goodwill, a land where despised peoples, such as those exemplified in Achsa's physical appearance, can amalgamate in a morally if not physically beautiful whole. Achsa embodies Brown's sympathy with the feminist philosophy of Mary Wollstonecraft, and the way in which, according to scholar Julia Stern, he exposes "the fragile underpinnings of a Founding based on the social death and live burial of those 'others' who do not count as citizens . . . women, blacks, Native Americans, and alien émigrés."[141]

Brackenridge, unlike Brown, does employ anti-semitic stereotypes. However, much as it is foolish to guess at Shakespeare's personal opinions from those of his unattractive characters, it is important when analyzing

Modern Chivalry to note who says what and in what context. Modeled on Cervantes' Don Quixote and his servant Sancho Panza, Captain Farrago and his servant Teague have various adventures that reveal that in republican America as in aristocratic Europe, ideological pretensions to the contrary, an unqualified upper class rules over the gullible lower orders. In Brackenridge's work, the person of Jewish heritage does not make a sudden, spectacular, and completely positive intervention in a corrupt milieu, as does Achsa Fielding. Jews, as in Brackenridge's own life, are an ongoing part of reality, and are dealt with differently depending on the people, place, and situation involved. Whereas Brown wrote *Arthur Mervyn* quickly, in response to yellow fever, personal misfortune, and, one can imagine, the heroics of Israel Israel, Brackenridge took over two decades to compose *Modern Chivalry* (1792–1815). Jews appear from time to time as they would in the course of life and discourse in a frontier society.

Jews are first mentioned several times in a mock-heroic poem that satirizes a member of the Society of the Cincinnati for the excessive pride he takes in belonging to that order. A hereditary society of Revolutionary War officers and their descendants, the Cincinnati were at first feared as a possible aristocracy that would destroy the Republic. When the uproar against them prompted fierce denials that they intended any such thing, the society became a source of amusement on account of the members' pretensions. Thus, a clergyman tells the "Cinncinat" that his much-esteemed badge is derived from 'the hist'ry of the Jews" rather than the Romans, to which the veteran replies that the "priest . . . should be reasoning with the Jews" rather than "meddling with our institutions." Real Jews are not mentioned, nor do they appear, in the poem. Instead, Brackenridge is suggesting that America's Jewish heritage is as noble as its Roman.[142]

A different character doesn't like Jews: a ballad singer. He juxtaposes the anti-semitic stereotype of the moneygrubbing Jew against the "bog trotter"—the Irishman—who is content to do as little work as he can to survive in the frontier's fertile environment:

Up to the mountains bog-trotters;
Our shamrocks are fresh, and are green.
Set traps for your beavers and otters
And musk-rats the best ever seen.

Though I am too lazy to rough it
And go to the waters with you
Because I have had just enough'f it;
Don't like to be rich as a Jew.
(570)

Besides attacking Jews as covetous, these stanzas also seem to be criticizing anti-semitism as the prejudice of lazy folk who lack the Jews' work ethic.

Most frequently, Brackenridge has "Captain"—later "Governor"—Farrago, the proto-aristocrat who has contempt for the crowd—use the morality of the Jewish prophets to attack popular follies. Brackenridge to some extent sees himself in Farrago, trying to guide an obstreperous people, yet he is also having fun at Farrago's expense, as his very name indicates. The captain muses:

> How do you distinguish the demagogue from the patriot? The demagogue flatters the clown, and finds fault with the sage. The patriot and the sage . . . mean the same thing. The Jewish prophets were all of them sages. They were seers or men that saw far into things. You will find they were no slouches at blaming the people. "My people Israel, is destroyed for lack of knowledge." I am wounded in the house of my friends. This may be said of liberty, when republicans give it a stab. The lamentations of Jeremiah are but the weepings of a patriot over the errors of a people. (415)

In another instance, unlike the Federalists who blamed the "people" for following the Republicans, Brackenridge uses his own voice to suggest that the Republicans could successfully use the example of the ancient Jews to reform the people of New England—who had betrayed their country by refusing to support the War of 1812.

> I have often thought, that if a president of the United States, in our time, had a Jewish prophet to denounce to the people their political transgressions; that is to say, the swerving from the true faith; in other words, his own part; how much securer his standing would be; how much less vexed by the calumny of editors and paragraphs in gazettes. (762)

Yet even here Brackenridge is being playful: instead of finding a genuine prophet, he suggests President Madison obtain fifty thousand dollars to pay

off the New England clergy to change their allegiance. Surely, too, Brackenridge had mixed feelings about gazettes and editors, having been a close
colleague of John Israel during the campaigns against western Pennsylvania
Federalists between 1798 and 1800. Their mutual use of the press was a
major reason the Republicans became dominant in the region. The nature
of the press, and of Israel's role in its development, appears in an episode
when a new paper is founded on the frontier. Brackenridge here implicitly
alludes to the trouble Israel had with the masthead for his paper, the *Tree of
Liberty:* "and the Leaves of the Tree were for the Healing of the Nations."
Israel's Federalist critics, seizing on his name to appeal to the popular but
false belief that he was Jewish, argued that "one of the circumcised" had "no
right to meddle" with (that is, quote from) the Christian New Testament.
Brackenridge makes fun of the whole idea of what symbols are appropriate
for a newspaper, for the founder of the fictional paper places on his masthead an owl, symbol of wisdom, a cat, standing for vigilance, and a bat, signifying "impartiality being of equivocal formation, and doubtful whether
bird or beast." Brackenridge is sufficiently comfortable with his own toleration that he has the fictional printer—perhaps a stand-in for Israel—
encourage his subscribers to be generous and not fit the stereotype of the
greedy Jew:

> We want a little money to begin with, dear honey,
> So bring it and take you the news.
> Have a little heart, nor be sorry to part,
> With a trifle like misers and jews.
>
> (547/8)[143]

In a humorous reversal, the paper is named the *Twilight* on the grounds
that since the (Republican) paper in the eastern part of Pennsylvania was
the *Aurora,* a later part of the day—and the night creatures who flourished
then—better fit the west.

At other times, Farrago compares the follies of contemporary frontiers-
men with those of the biblical Jews. He tries to talk them out of establishing
courts and their fondness for suing each other since only the lawyers will
profit, but met with "similar success, as Samuel dissuading the people of
Jewry, not from a jury [a wordplay on jury and Jewry] trial, but from
monarchy, in the days, when they wished the kings to succeed judges. And

the fact is, that tyranny gets her best foot-hold on the backs of the courts of law and judges" (540). Another popular obsession Farrago denounces is the camp meeting of the Second Great Awakening—a "burlesque on religion" and "symptoms of a diseased understanding . . . where multitudes, as Moses proposed to Pharaoh the Israelites should do, go out three days into the wilderness, with their wives, and their little ones, and remain congregated, bellowing with uncouth sounds, and gesticulations. This cannot be religion, but madness" (628).

Brackenridge also associates both contemporary Jews and Judaic tradition with intelligence. A Jew joins a German and an Irishman in denouncing a deceitful peddler who tries to get sympathy from people to buy his goods on the pretext they burden his back. " 'It is all de love of de monish,' said a Jew. 'His conscience is monish; I go anoder way to de exchange dish morning' " (442). Here a gentile peddler is exposed for his "Jewish" greed by a Jew who goes about getting his profits "anoder way." Brackenridge also joins the Jewish intellectual heritage with the Christian to argue that unlike human beings, animals do not have elaborate ideas of this life and none of the hereafter (687). He therefore concludes that "there seems to be more probability in the cosmogony of that Hebrew writer [Moses] than in the reveries of [Erasmus] Darwin in his *Temple of Nature,* or *Zoonomia*" (709).[144] Grandfather of Charles Darwin, Erasmus Darwin (1731–1802) had many of the same ideas. Brackenridge cites the titles of his two most famous works, respectively published in 1794–96 and 1802.

On the other hand, Brackenridge argues against misuse of the Jewish tradition by applying biblical examples uncritically. He has Farrago oppose capital punishment for most crimes and favor the rehabilitation of criminals. To cite the ancient Jews' use of the death penalty as a binding precedent was foolish. It was a sensible decision shaped by their circumstances, for their "unsettled life [in the wilderness] did not admit of places of confinement sufficiently safe to secure offenders" (731), as did modern cities.

Farrago only resorts to outright use of a contemporary anti-semitic stereotype once, at the end of the novel, when he is at his wits end. Driven to distraction by the people he governs, he abdicates because the legislature had rejected his plan to "establish the government and render it *vigorous;* taxation and no borrowing from Jew brokers, like minors that have their estates in expectancy" (782). A mature populace, he is arguing, needs to break out of its infantile dependence on others and stop living on borrowed money. He hopes, in vain, to shame the people out of their fiscal irresponsibility by asking if they would prefer to remain dependent on greedy Jews. Yet Farrago's resort to anti-semitism in a time of panic reflects the use it received from the Federalists in the 1790s. Politicians appeal to deep-seated popular prejudices in desperate times when arguments based on self-interest fail.

Brackenridge was both sympathetic to and critical of most of his characters. Like the respective virtues and vices of Don Quixote and Sancho Panza, like the complementary virtues and vices of democracy and aristocracy the Founding Fathers sought to balance to achieve republicanism, the virtues and vices found on the Pennsylvania frontier come up against each other. The struggle, however, is not one of life and death, but a comic scenario enacted in a stable and prosperous society where there is essential agreement on the ground rules. To the extent that he identified with Captain Farrago, Brackenridge recognized the Jews and their heritage as important and positive forces in shaping America.

Yet traditional anti-Jewish stereotypes remained in the new nation and in Pennsylvania, as expressed by the characters in Brackenridge's book as well as in the popular culture that it reflected and courted. If we contrast the novels with two poems and one painting produced in Pennsylvania in the early nineteenth century, the continued presence populist of anti-semitism is clear. In 1808, *The National Songster,* published by Thomas Desilver in Philadelphia, contained two anti-semitic poems, written in mock Jewish dialogue.[145] The first was "The Jew Volunteer" (sung to the tune of "In the Days of My Youth).

I'm a Jew you may tell py my peard and my progue,
And somehow de folks have found I'm a rogue,
And it vou'd pe a vonder if dat vasn't true,
Because I'm a lawyer as well as a Jew.

Of de lawyer and oyster you read in de pook,
He gave pack de shell, put de oyster he took,
But all other lawyers at dat I excel;
I first eat de oyster, and den shteal de shell.

Den I turn Volunteer, in de time of de vars,
Wid a long sword and gun all so fierce as Mars;
Dere caps all your warriors a feather vear in,
But I vear my feather a top of my chin.

But instead of go fighting de play I go see,
Vere all de musicianers are just like me;
Dat he take in de flats ev'ry viseacre harps,
But fiddlers and Jews take in both flats and sharps.

Den at courting de ladies I'm not much afeard;
Though they all say I've got such an ugly long peard;
But says I, "If you tink vat my peard be too pig,
My dear, shave it off—it will make you a vig."

Here, the Jew is presented as the most dishonest of a dishonest group
(lawyers), a pretended patriot in time of war, and an ugly man who still is a
formidable threat to the ladies. "The Jew Broker" is more ambivalent.

Ye chobbers, underwriters, ye drips of pen and ink,
Who on your alway parties, do dea and goffee drink,
Come rattling up de yellow poys, come hider at my call,
I be pyer unt I's seller, unt I can serve you all.

Ye captains unt ye Colnls, ye chointed widows all,
To Abetnick apply, von your stocks bekin to fall,
Or if your lifes you would insure, dats olt and cracky grown,
Te vays and means I'll let you know, to ket te pisness tone.

If marchants should want relief, ven all deir money's spent,
My heart relents, I draw de bont, and lends at 5 per shent,
Its I can give segurity, its I can raise de dusht,
Put den you must excuse me if I sarve myself de first.

I gives advice to every one, but physic und de law,
For dey outvits de Jews demshelves, for bills at sight dey draw,
It's ten I lents my monies, I runs some risk, do small,
But dey kits all de monies, and runs no risk at all.

Mankint is all my broders, vat if dere rich or boor,
Nor shall de shild of mishery, e'er pass my humple toor,

I like de gristians dearly, would die to pleasure you,
If dey but as sincerely, would try to love de Jew.

Here, a Jew is presented as the ultimate refuge when people are out of money. He at least runs financial risks, whereas doctors and lawyers are the ultimate scoundrels. On the one hand, the Jew is foreign, speaks terrible English, is acquisitive, and is the sharpest operator around. On the other hand, he is charitable, but insists it is up to the Christians to love him first. It is hard to say whether the song mocks the stereotypical Jew (who will never love a Christian) or is recognizing the humanity and potential for reciprocal treatment of Jews and Christians.

There is no ambiguity whatsoever in *Das ewige Liebe und die Ewige Verdamnis* (Eternal life and eternal damnation). A Pennsylvania Dutch fraktur (colored drawing) from about 1820, it clearly reflects the anti-semitism this group exhibited in colonial Pennsylvania. A Jewish peddler, with his distinctive nose, pack, and hat, stands squarely in the middle of people on their way to hell—the soldier (these Germans were probably pacifists), drunkard, musician, and others, all parading to encounter "die Babylonische Hüre."

Still, there is a difference between this anti-semitism and the ferocious political sort of the 1790s. The Jew may be greedy, but he is no longer a threat. He is no longer a distinctively immoral threat to the Republic, but merely one of many of sinners marching off to hell. Such stereotypes, however, remained, and were trotted out by the nation's best and brightest in the late nineteenth century, when Henry Adams, Brooks Adams, and Charles Francis Adams II, great-grandsons of John Adams, and John Jay II, historian and grandson of the man who wrote New York's tolerationist constitution, managed to convince a fair number of their countrymen that Jews both rich and poor threatened to rule and destroy the country "they" inherited. Ignoring the Jewish presence in the American Revolution and their own ancestors' practice, they only betrayed the history they were pretending to defend by asserting freedom and national greatness were peculiarly Anglo-Saxon. Their colleagues in Germany preferred the word *Aryan* as they cited America's "Manifest Destiny" in the nineteenth century as a precedent for their twentieth-century expansionism.[146]

CHAPTER 7

CONCLUSION

IN 2003, ROMAN CATHOLIC intellectual Michael Novak published *On Two Wings,* a book that challenged the accepted wisdom that the American love of liberty and struggle for independence were primarily motivated by either a Whig belief in the rights of Englishmen or Enlightenment devotion to the rights of man. Novak took a leaf from a fairly obscure article by Donald Lutz showing that references to the Bible, mostly the Old Testament, outnumbered those to any other source by over three to one in the writings of the founders of the American nation. Jewish ideals, Novak argued, were the principles on which the United States was constructed: "The language of Judaism came to be the central language of the American metaphysic, the unspoken background to a special American vision of the nature of history and the destiny of the human race." For example, in 1788, the Reverend Samuel Langdon, former president of Harvard College, explained to the New Hampshire legislature that shortly after the Israelites had crossed the Red Sea, God granted them a "permanent constitution," in which a "Senate" of seventy men shared power with Moses, the "chief commander," and "the government therefore was a proper republic." Only when they were "sunk into contempt" did God give them a king "in his anger," reducing them to the level of the rest of the world, a "sad experience of the effects of despotic power."[1]

Whether or not a historian wishes to acknowledge the biblical tradition as equal to others in the creation of the United States is probably a matter of temperament and training: I myself agree with my former professor Richard B. Morris, who noted the revolutionaries used whatever arguments they could that they thought would work after they had already decided what to do. In any case, revolutionary Americans interpreted the Puritan tradition, English constitutional history, classical republicanism, and the Old Testament as sufficiently coincidental with each other and their own colonial practices that the question of relative importance and influence is impossible to answer.

Similarly, American Jews of the revolutionary era shared in the belief that God had ensured that the chosen people of Israel were to be protected by, and flourish under, the aegis of the chosen people of the United States: "The wonders which the Lord of Hosts hath worked in the days of our fore-fathers, have taught us to observe the greatness of his wisdom and his might throughout the events of the late glorious revolution," the congregations of Philadelphia, New York, Charleston, and Richmond wrote to George Washington, who agreed that "the power and goodness of the Almighty were strongly manifested [both] in the events of our late glorious revolution and . . . in the establishment of our present government."[2]

Yet despite this apparent coincidence of missions, the place of the Jews, both in British North America, and then in the United States, has always been problematic. In exploring the relationship between Jews and Gentiles in the five leading Jewish communities of early British America, the question arose over and over, in various forms, as to whether Jews were to be separate but equal, separate but unequal, integrated and equal, or inte-grated and superior members of the body politic. In short, what was the relationship of Judaism and citizenship? Two further questions made answering this more complicated: first, who was a Jew? A practicing mem-ber of a synagogue in good standing? Anyone claiming to be a Jew whether recognized by a synagogue or not? Or even a person who had renounced Judaism but could not shed inherited ethnic or racial characteristics? Finally, a further problem, raised by contemporary scholars of Judaism such as historian Arthur Hertzberg and attorney Alan Dershowitz, as Der-showitz entitled his book, was *The Vanishing American Jew.* Fewer than 2 percent of Americans, 5.5 million people, were Jews in the year 2000, as opposed to 4 percent in 1937. Current demographic trends—low birth and high intermarriage rate—if continued suggest a decline to under one mil-lion by 2076. Given the absence of persecution and strong pressure to assimilate, will American Jews be seduced into renouncing their faith? This was no small problem in early America, where the Jewish communities of Newport and Lancaster vanished around 1800, and an extremely high proportion of Jews never married, or married outside the faith and converted. Until a sizable migration from Germany occurred, the Jewish population hovered around the thirteen hundred to three thousand mark from 1790 until 1820, remaining absolutely almost static and decreasing as a percentage of the nation's rapidly growing population.[3]

In their quest for citizenship, early American Jews, like African Americans following the Civil War or women in the late nineteenth century, almost invariably used the argument not that they were people (meaning, at the time, white, propertied males) like any other, and therefore entitled to equal rights, but had earned citizenship thanks to their special virtues. No one put all the arguments together as well as the Jews of Philadelphia's Mikveh Israel, when at the end of the Revolution they unsuccessfully tried to persuade the state of Pennsylvania to lift restrictions on Jewish voting and officeholding.[4] Appealing first to Pennsylvania's economic self-interest and a sense of rivalry with neighboring New York for the nation's commercial leadership, they pointed out that Jews had immeasurably enriched the countries, such as Holland and England, that had accepted them, and impoverished those that had expelled them, Spain and Portugal. Politely but firmly, the Jews gave Pennsylvania the choice of enhancing its wealth or watching immigrant Jews enhance the prosperity of New York, which had granted them equal rights.

Furthermore, pointing to the connection between Jewish Old Testament republicanism and an American Revolution modeled in part upon it, they pointed out that "in the religious books of the Jews, there are no such doctrines or principle established, as are inconsistent with the safety and happiness of the people of Pennsylvania." Since America's synagogues were completely autonomous, both from each other and from those of Europe (they sometimes asked advice from overseas rabbis and congregations but did not always follow it), they were far less connected to foreign authorities than the Presbyterian (Church of Scotland), Anglican (Church of England), Lutheran and Reformed (German), and Catholic (Roman) Churches.

Finally, Mikveh Israel stressed its patriotism: "the conduct and behavior of the Jews in this and the neighboring states, has always tallied with the great design of the revolution; that the Jews of Charlestown, New-York, New-Port and other posts, occupied by the British troops, have distinguishedly suffered for their attachment to revolution principles."

The problem with an appeal to citizenship based on special virtue is that the appeal falls flat if the virtue does. Anti-semitism in the twenty-first century is founded precisely on arguing with the very three points the Philadelphia Jews raised over two hundred years ago. Anti-semites link the Jews' economic success, their support of a foreign nation (Israel), and the liberal or radical politics of many Jews in order to brand them as unpatriotic. The remark of "Curtiopolis" in the *New York Daily Advertiser,* which opposed the United States Constitution because it did not exclude Jews from political participation, strikes a nerve even today: "given the command of the whole militia to the President—should he hereafter be a Jew our dear posterity may be ordered to rebuild Jerusalem." To be sure, such accusations, like outright racism, have been relegated to the margins of political debate. Or they are kept hidden, as the Nixon tapes revealed the president's anti-semitism. But the popularity of figures such as Pat Robertson and Pat Buchanan suggest these sentiments are still there, although overshadowed at the moment by other issues.[5]

Just as alarming, in the late eighteenth century as now, is that anti-semites pay little attention to the real characteristics of Jews they actually confront. Contradictory stereotypes are applied to Jews with little regard for the truth. For Quaker and loyalist Miers Fisher, Jews were wealthy and disloyal, the patriotic, philanthropic Haym Salomon to the contrary. Before 1793, Anti-Federalists and Republicans used against Jews exaggerated versions of the criticisms they directed against Hamilton and the Federalists: that they were wealthy speculators who undeservedly profited on the backs of their countrymen. After 1793, when Jews began to support the French Revolution, Federalists turned against them their usual attacks against Jefferson's followers: they were poor folk who sought to use politics to rise to unearned wealth and power, or, alternatively (as with Israel Israel) had already done so. They even accused Israel of manufacturing anti-semitic rhetoric against himself because he thought the public would be too enlightened to accept it!

Similarly, Jews could be blamed for not being religious at all or for being mired in archaic superstition. Henry Melchior Mühlenberg's charges in 1776 implied that Jews would lead their countrymen into atheism, as Dutch Jew Baruch Spinoza had supposedly attempted to do in Europe; criticism of Jews' underhanded dealings convinced their enemies that they had "no

God but Mammon." On the other hand, Thomas Jefferson and Benjamin Rush only valued Jews as individuals to the extent they repudiated Judaism as a religion, which they found repugnant.

And finally, Jews were urged to convert to Christianity, yet in the eyes of anti-semites they could not shed their innate, negative, racial characteristics, any more than the Cherokee nation could convince America that they, by learning to read, write, farm, form a representative government, dress as whites, take white names, and even own slaves, were considerably more civilized than the Georgia frontier folk who hungered after their land. Israel Israel had a Jewish father and Christian mother, his son was ethnically only a quarter Jewish, and yet their enemies trotted out all the usual canards, including the backhanded compliment that their very intelligence and wealth made them far more dangerous than the blacks, Germans, Irish, and others they misled.

American Jews themselves were worried about these concerns. In fact, it seems they went out of their way to refute the stereotypes of anti-semites. First, no major anti-semitic newspaper essay penned between 1776 and 1800 went unchallenged. Interestingly, no one, even Christians such as Israel or John Israel, ever merely answered by saying, "I'm no longer Jewish; get over it." By keeping their names (they could have changed them, as Boston's conservative Thomas Paine did to Robert Treat Paine to avoid confusion with the author of *Common Sense*) and taking pride in their ethnic heritage, they foreshadowed American Jews who define themselves in cultural rather than spiritual terms. As with practicing Jews who also combated bigotry in print, they turned their accusers' charges against them, showing, in many cases quite effectively, that the disloyalty, greed, and marginality attributed to Jews more appropriately belonged to the former loyalists, itinerant newspapermen, and recent immigrants who trumpeted them. (Federalist New England too was politically marginal by the time it became the last refuge of elite anti-semitism after 1800.)

Jews were especially concerned with proving they were neither greedy nor dishonest in their means of acquiring wealth. Haym Salomon and Aaron Lopez were major contributors to both Jewish and non-Jewish charities; in the early nineteenth century, Judah Touro and Rebecca Gratz became two of the best-known philanthropists in the United States. (Touro's lengthy will left money to hundreds of charitable societies, Jewish, gentile, and nonsectarian, throughout the world.) Rank-and-file Jews joined general charitable societies as well as caring for their own both at home and overseas. Hence the repeated appeals of traveling rabbis to aid Jews in the Holy Land.

Just as importantly, though, the new nation's tiny Jewish population rigorously examined themselves and their faith not only to refute their opponents, but to ensure a precarious survival in a country where their small numbers and the failure of anti-semites to cause serious harm left them susceptible to conversion. It is significant that whereas the Pennsylvania legislature did not respond positively to the Jews' plea for political equality in 1783, a newspaper writer did so on the amazing grounds that true Christians could convert the Jews by showing them that they were thus forgiven for the crime of killing Christ, which he assumed they acknowledged with his own matter-of-factness: "it would tend to the propagation of Christianity, by impressing the Jews, from this generous treatment, with sentiments in favor of the gospel," and show them that "the true disciples of Christ" were willing "to reflect what the Redeemer of Mankind uttered when he was extended on the cross, 'Father forgive them, for they know not what they do.'"[6]

Between 1782 and 1794, the four surviving Jewish congregations, in Philadelphia, New York, Savannah, and Charleston, along with Richmond's synagogue, built in 1789, all adopted new constitutions in which the majority of the male members in good standing (who paid dues and attended service on a regular basis) could vote for governing officials who had formerly elected their own successors. (Interestingly, in 1820, as the South was beginning to support slavery as a positive good rather than necessary evil and identify it with medieval feudalism, Charleston reverted to the former, more traditional aristocratic system of government; one result was the creation of the first Reformed Jewish congregation in 1824, with a democratic constitution.) The Jews, like the Anglicans, who became Episcopalians, were more successful implementing their reforms than the Roman Catholics, who despite the efforts of American clerics like Bishop John Carroll remained under the control of the worldwide church and retained the same governance as European Catholics.[7]

In addition to becoming more democratic, the synagogues hoped to become more respectable. All of the postrevolutionary constitutions and by-laws provided that people in the synagogue should comport themselves in good order: they were to pay attention to the service, not hold private conversations, not bring in noisy young children, sing in harmony with the group, come and leave quietly in the middle of services, and (in Savannah) not even appear in boots. Jews wanted their decorum, as well as their synagogue polities, to approximate the majority of American Protestant churches rather than retain the stigma of the archaic and superstitious they had previously borne.

Jewish concern with respectability was not exceptional in the early Republic, but it was perhaps greater than other groups who were more sure of their place in the mainstream. As Toby Ditz has shown, men in trade regarded their business failures as moral rather than market problems. Hence attacks on their reputation not only threatened their livelihood, but their self-image as respectable people. Jews, who were generally involved in trade, were especially anxious to vindicate their reputations: hence the newspaper exchange in Philadelphia and lawsuits in Newport and New York where Jews sued each other before gentile judges for huge, symbolic amounts to cover damages to their reputation by other Jews. All involved charges of theft and dishonest business dealings, traditional stereotypes of the Jew. And in New York and Philadelphia, assimilated Jews who in appearance resembled gentiles used anti-semitic stereotypes (that their opponents could not speak English, wore beards, or dressed in a European manner) to impugn their opponents, as did Jews who believed the arrival of poor Ashkenazim after the Seven Years' War compromised their carefully cultivated reputations. Furthermore, in the early nineteenth century, like Americans throughout the nation who conducted the affairs of honor of which Joanne Freeman has written, Jews were willing to fight to the death to keep their reputations intact, and Christians considered it legitimate for them to do so.[8]

Historian Jonathan Sarna has noted that throughout their history, American Jews have been resourceful, able to reinvigorate their faith at times when it seems threatened. This renewal, he also notes, has always taken a variety of forms: some Jews throw themselves into charitable work, others into supporting endangered foreign Jews, others into education, some into revivals of orthodoxy where the pious can retain traditional purity, others into reforms where people less concerned with formal regulations can feel welcome. These actions, which Dershowitz recommends to keep American Jews from vanishing, are in fact the courses they took two hundred years ago, when small Jewish congregations were able to survive in several cities to ensure that Jewish immigrants in the 1820s did not have to begin in a vacuum. That American Judaism has never had a central governing body—each synagogue formed and incorporated on its own—has facilitated this diversity. In the years following the American Revolution, Jews democratized to ensure their survival, and orthodox congregations relaxed discipline to retain members. In turn, their fellow Americans, to a large extent, repudiated political anti-semitism without renouncing entirely the popular anti-semitism that has prevailed over the centuries.

NOTES

PREFACE

1. Jonathan Sarna, *American Judaism: A History* (New Haven: Yale University Press, 2004), 45.

2. Jonathan Israel, *European Jewry in the Age of Mercantilism, 1550–1750*, rev. ed. (Oxford: Clarendon Press, 1989), esp. chaps. 1, 2, 4.

3. Jacob Katz, *Exclusiveness and Toleration: Studies in Jewish-Gentile Relations in Early Modern Times* (New York: Schocken, 1962), chap. 6; Israel, *European Jewry*, esp. 22, 47, 59, 161–63, 239–45.

4. Frank Manuel, "Israel and the Enlightenment," *Daedalus* 111 (1982): 33–51; Adam Sutcliffe, "Myth, Origins, Identity: Voltaire, the Jews, and the Enlightenment Notion of Toleration," *Eighteenth Century* 41 (1998): 107–26; Todd Endelman, *The Jews of Georgian England, 1714–1830*, rev. ed. (Ann Arbor: University of Michigan Press, 1999); Abram Vossen Goodman, "A German Mercenary Observes American Jews during the Revolution," *Publications of the American Jewish Historical Society* (hereafter *PAJHS*) 59 (1969): 227.

5. Jacob Rader Marcus, *The Colonial American Jew: 1492–1776*, 3 vols. (Detroit: Wayne State University Press, 1970), 2:712–13; Edwin Wolf II and Maxwell Whiteman, *The History of the Jews of Philadelphia from Colonial Times to the Age of Jackson* (Philadelphia: Jewish Publication Society of America, 1956), 40, 55–56.

6. Rosalind J. Beiler, "Distributing Aid to Believers in Need: The Religious Foundations of Transatlantic Migration," in Nicholas Canny, Joseph Illick, Gary Nash, and William Pencak, eds., "Empire, Society, and Labor: Essays in Honor of Richard S. Dunn," special supplemental issue, *Pennsylvania History* 64 (1997): 73–87; Frederick B. Tolles, *Quakers and the Atlantic Culture* (New York: Norton, 1960); Carl Bridenbaugh, *Mitre and Sceptre: Transatlantic Faiths, Ideas, Personalities, and Politics, 1689–1775* (New York: Oxford University Press, 1962).

7. See Nuala Zahedieh, "Making Mercantilism Work: London Merchants and Atlantic Trade in the Seventeenth Century," *Transactions of the Royal Historical Society*, 6th ser., 9 (1999): 143; Rowena Olegario, "'That Mysterious People': Jewish Merchants, Transparency, and Community in Mid-Nineteenth Century America," *Business History Review* 73 (1999): 161–89; and especially the introduction to Bernard Bailyn and Philip D. Morgan, eds., *Strangers in the Realm: Cultural Margins of the First British Empire* (Chapel Hill: University of North Carolina Press, 1991).

1. INTRODUCTION

1. Hector St.-John de Crèvecoeur, *Letters from an American Farmer* (New York: New American Library, 1957), 64, 62.

2. Ira Rosenwaike, "An Estimate and Analysis of the Jewish Population of the United States in 1790," in Abraham Karp, ed., *The Jewish Experience in America*, vol. 1, *The Colonial Period* (Waltham: American Jewish Publication Society, 1969), 393; Frederic Cople Jaher, *A Scapegoat in the New Wilderness: The Origins and Rise of Anti-Semitism in America* (Cambridge: Harvard University Press, 1994), 123–24; Sarna, *American Judaism*, 375.

3. Arthur Hertzberg, "The New England Puritans and the Jews," in Shalom Goldman, ed., *Hebrew and the Bible in America: The First Two Centuries* (Hanover, N.H.: University Press of New England, 1993), 105–20; Michael Novak, *On Two Wings: Humble Faith and Common Sense at the American Founding* (New York: Scribners, 2003).

4. *Pennsylvania Gazette*, September 27, 1739, February 10, 1743; Steven C. Bullock, "A Mumper among the Gentle: Tom Bell, Colonial Confidence Man," *William and Mary Quarterly*, 3d ser., 55 (1998): 246.

5. Frank Felsenstein, *Anti-semitic Stereotypes: A Paradigm of Otherness in English Popular Culture, 1660–1830* (Baltimore: Johns Hopkins University Press, 1995).

6. See Julian H. Preiser, *Pioneer American Synagogues: A State by State Guide*, rev. ed. (Bowie, Md.: Heritage Press, 1997); Lester Cappon, editor in chief, *Atlas of Early American History: The Revolutionary Era, 1760–1790* (Princeton: Princeton University Press, 1976), 8–12. Philadelphia's cemetery, between Eighth and Ninth and Spruce Streets, is located just above the uppermost limit of Cappon's map. Charleston's Comyng Street cemetery is near the top right of the map, beyond the settled area. Savannah had three Jewish cemeteries: the original one, at the present corner of Oglethorpe and Bull Streets, was separated from the gentile burying ground at Oglethorpe and Abercorn Streets; the Mordecai Sheftall and Sheftall family cemeteries were located well beyond the city limits, west of the present Boundary Street between Cohen and Spruce Streets. For architecture, see Rachel Wischnitzer, *Synagogue Architecture in the United States* (Philadelphia: Jewish Publication Society of America, 1955), 11–19.

7. *Pennsylvania Gazette*, March 31, 1753.

8. See, for example, Robert K. Dodge, *Early American Almanac Humor* (Bowling Green, Ohio: Bowling Green State University Popular Press, 1987), 53–84; Alison Gilbert Olson, "The Pamphlet War over the Paxton Boys," *Pennsylvania Magazine of History and Biography* 123 (1999): 31–56.

9. W. D. Rubinstein, *A History of the Jews in the English-Speaking World* (New York: St. Martin's, 1996), 46–56.

10. See, for example, Jacob Rader Marcus, *The American Jew: 1585–1990, A History* (Brooklyn: Carlson, 1995), 41–42.

11. Thomas Paine, *Works*, 10 vols. (New Rochelle: Thomas Paine Press, 1925), *The Age of Reason*, 8:116; *Reply to the Bishop of Llandaff*, 9:40, 62; Louis Harap, *The Image of the Jew in American Literature* (Philadelphia: American Jewish Publication Society, 1974), 30–34.

12. Jacob Rader Marcus, ed., *American Jewry: Documents, Eighteenth Century* (Cincinnati: Hebrew Union College Press, 1959), 131.

13. Benjamin Rush to Elias Boudinot, July 9, 1788, and Rush to Elkanah Winchester, May 11, 1791, in Lyman H. Butterfield, ed., *Letters of Benjamin Rush*, 2 vols. (Prince-

ton: Princeton University Press for the American Philosophical Society, 1951), 1:470, 581–82.

14. Thomas Jefferson to Benjamin Rush, "Syllabus of an Estimate of the Merit of the Doctrines of Jesus Christ, compared with Those of Others," April 21, 1803, in Paul Leicester Ford, ed., *Writings of Thomas Jefferson,* 9 vols. (New York: G. Putnam's Sons, 1892–99), 8:226.

15. See Peter Onuf, "'To Declare Them a Free and Independent People': Race, Slavery, and National Identity in Jefferson's Thought," *Journal of the Early Republic* 18 (1998): 1–46; Christian B. Keller, "Philanthropy Betrayed: Thomas Jefferson and the Origins of Indian Removal Policy," *Proceedings of the American Philosophical Society* 144 (2000): 39–66; Mark Häberlein and Michaela Schmolz-Häberlein, "Competition and Cooperation: The Ambivalent Relationship between Jews and Christians in Early Modern Germany and Pennsylvania," *Pennsylvania Magazine of History and Biography* 126 (2002): 409–36. Häberlein and Schmolz-Häberlein cite Aaron Levy, who founded Aaronsburg, Pennsylvania, and contributed generously to local Lutheran and Reformed churches; but note also Judah Touro and Aaron Lopez of Rhode Island, Benjamin Sheftall of Savannah, and the Jewish community of Charleston. Jefferson, of course, was familiar with Haym Salomon. All are discussed in the following chapters.

16. Jack D. Foner, "Jews and the American Military from the Colonial Era to the Eve of the Civil War," *American Jewish Archives* 52 (2000): 55–111.

17. Lewis Abraham, "Correspondence between Washington and Jewish Citizens," in Karp, *Jewish Experience in America,* 352–61, reprints several such messages by Washington to Jews. See also "Washington's Thanksgiving Proclamations," *American Jewish Archives* 20 (1968): 156–62.

18. John Adams, *Works,* 10 vols., ed. Charles F. Adams (Boston: Little, Brown, 1850–56), 9:609.

19. *Litchfield Monitor,* July 17, 1796, July 31, 1799. Many thanks to Doron Ben-Atar for sharing his research in this newspaper with me.

20. Jaher, *Scapegoat in New Wilderness,* 136.

21. Ibid., 135.

22. See chapters for each city. Eli Faber, *A Time for Planting: The First Fruits, 1654–1820* (Baltimore: Johns Hopkins University Press, 1992), 88, 120–21; Marcus, *American Jewry: Documents,* 118; Wolf and Whiteman, *Jews of Philadelphia,* 231; Manuel Josephson to Mikveh Israel, May 21, 1784, *American Jewish Archives* 27 (1975): 221–22; Frederic Cople Jaher, *The Jews and the Nation: Revolution, Emancipation, State Formation, and the Liberal Paradigm in America and France* (Princeton: Princeton University Press, 2002), 153.

23. Wolf and Whiteman, *Jews of Philadelphia,* 125–27.

24. Ibid., 195.

25. Malcolm H. Stern, "The Function of Genealogy in American Jewish History," in *Essays in American Jewish History* (Cincinnati: American Jewish Archives, 1958), 69–98, esp. 89, 90.

26. James William Hagy, *This Happy Land: The Jews of Colonial and Ante-bellum Charleston* (Tuscaloosa: University of Alabama Press, 1993), 69.

27. Jaher, *Scapegoat in New Wilderness,* 130–69; and Leonard Dinnerstein, *Antisemitism in America* (New York: Oxford University Press, 1994), 16–22, agree that the period between 1800–1840 marked an ebb tide for American anti-semitism. Part of the

reason was there were few Jews in the new nation; many of the early Jews converted to Christianity.

28. Jonathan D. Sarna, "The Cult of Synthesis in American Jewish Culture," *Jewish Social Studies* 5 (1998–99): 52.

29. Jaher, *Jews and the Nation.*

2. NEW YORK

1. Patricia U. Bonomi, *A Factious People: Politics and Society in Colonial New York* (New York: Columbia University Press, 1971). Many of the names in this chapter are spelled in different ways: for example, Barrak, Barak, Baruch Hays; Simpson or Simson, etc. I have standardized them according to the most common usage to prevent confusion.

2. Israel, *European Jewry,* 62–64; Frederick Zweirlein, *Religion in New Netherland* (Rochester: John Smith, 1910), 25–28.

3. Jonathan Israel, *Empires and Entrepots: The Dutch, the Spanish Monarchy, and the Jews: 1585–1713* (London: Hambledon Press, 1990), 425.

4. Ibid., 400–405; Israel, *European Jewry,* 64.

5. Herbert I. Bloom, *The Economic Activities of the Jews of Amsterdam in the Seventeenth and Eighteenth Centuries* (Williamsport, Pa.: Bayard Press, 1937), 125–26.

6. Israel, *Empires and Entrepots,* 388; Morris U. Schappes, ed., *A Documentary History of the Jews of the United States: 1654–1875,* 3rd ed. (New York: Schocken, 1971), 565; David de Sola Pool and Tamar de Sola Pool, *An Old Faith in the New World: Portrait of Shearith Israel, 1654–1954* (New York: Columbia University Press, 1955), 5; Sarna, *American Judaism,* 6.

7. Bloom, *Economic Activities,* 24, 6, 124–44.

8. Israel, *Empires and Entrepots,* 431, 422; Schappes, *Documentary History,* 1; Zweirlein, *Religion in New Netherland,* 70. For the economic goals of New Netherland, see Van Cleaf Bachman, *Peltries or Plantations: The Economic Policies of the Dutch West India Company in New Netherland, 1623–1639* (Baltimore: Johns Hopkins University Press, 1969).

9. Bloom, *Economic Activities,* 137–39.

10. Israel, *Empires and Entrepots,* 361.

11. Evan Haefeli, "The Pennsylvania Difference: Religious Diversity on the Delaware before 1683," *Early American Studies* 1 (2003): 28–60.

12. Schappes, *Documentary History,* 1.

13. Zweirlein, *Religion in New Netherland,* 70.

14. Ibid., 243; Charles R. Boxer, *The Dutch Seaborne Empire, 1600–1800* (London: Hutchinson, 1965), 144–46.

15. Zweirlein, *Religion in New Netherland,* 182–84; Joyce D. Goodfriend, *Before the Melting Pot: Society and Culture in Colonial New York City, 1664–1730* (Princeton: Princeton University Press, 1992), 13–14.

16. Zweirlein, *Religion in New Netherland,* chaps. 4 and 8.

17. See the biographical sketch by Paul Otto in John Garraty and Mark Carnes, eds., *American National Biography,* 24 vols. (New York: Oxford University Press, 1999), 21:99–100.

18. Zweirlein, *Religion in New Netherland,* 250–53; Bloom, *Economic Activities,*

144–50. Isaac S. Emmanuel and Suzanne Emmanuel, in *History of the Jews of the Nether-lands Antilles,* 2 vols. (Cincinnati: American Jewish Archives, 1970), 1:37–45, blame the first colony's failure on hostility from the predominantly gentile population and the refusal of the company to permit slavery. They argue as well that the second colony may never even have been planted.

19. Leo Hershkowitz, "New Amsterdam's Twenty-Three Jews—Myth or Reality," in Goldman, *Hebrew and the Bible,* 171–83; Max Kohler, "Civil Status of the Jews in Colonial New York, *PAJHS* 6 (1897): 84–85; Pool and Pool, *Old Faith,* 11–12; James Homer Williams, "'Abominable Religion' and Dutch (In)tolerance: The Jews and Petrus Stuyvesant," *Halve Maen* 71 (1998): 85–91.

20. Schappes, *Documentary History,* 1–2; Pool and Pool, *Old Faith,* 14–15.

21. Pool and Pool, *Old Faith,* 8–12; Schappes, *Documentary History,* 565.

22. Schappes, *Documentary History,* 1–2; Pool and Pool, *Old Faith,* 15.

23. Johnanes Megapolensis to the Classis of Amsterdam, March 18, 1655, in J. Franklin Jameson, ed., *Narratives of New Netherland, 1624–1664* (New York: Scribner's, 1909), 391–92.

24. Pool and Pool, *Old Faith,* 8; Berthold Fernow, ed., *Records of New Amsterdam,* 8 vols. (New York: Knickerbocker, 1897), 1:244; Samuel J. Oppenheim, "The Early History of the Jews of New York, 1654–1664," *PAJHS* 18 (1916): 1–91. The evidence in these sources only indicates that the goods sold could not pay for the journey, which could mean they were a glut on the market or simply not of sufficient value. John R. Brodhead and E. B. O'Callaghan, eds., *Documents Relative to the Colonial History of the State of New York,* 15 vols. (Albany: Weed, Parsons, 1853–87), 12:96.

25. Megapolensis to Classis, March 18, 1655, in Johnson, 391–92.

26. Zweirlein, *Religion in New Netherland,* 223, 169, 261.

27. Pool and Pool, *Old Faith,* 20.

28. For general discussion of poor laws, see Walter Trattner, *From Poor Law to Welfare State: A History of Social Welfare in America,* 6th ed. (New York: Free Press, 1999), 6, 19–22; "Minute Book of the Congregation Shearith Israel," *PAJHS* 21 (1913): 2–3, 73, 81, 89, 91, 99, 117.

29. Schappes, *Documentary History,* 2–4.

30. Ibid., 4–5.

31. Trattner, *Poor Law,* 21.

32. Zweirlein, *Religion in New Netherland,* 261.

33. Hershkowitz, "Twenty-Three Jews"; Schappes, *Documentary History,* 567; Cathy Matson, *Merchants and Empire: Trading in Colonial New York* (Baltimore: Johns Hopkins University Press, 1998), 28, 340.

34. Schappes, *Documentary History,* 5–13, 566–68; Pool and Pool, *Old Faith,* 16–34; Zweirlein, *Religion in New Netherland,* chap. 8.

35. Leon Hühner, "Asser Levy: A Noted Jewish Burgher of New Amsterdam," *PAJHS* 8 (1900), 9–23; Pool and Pool, *Old Faith,* 25, 336–37; Matson, *Merchants and Empire,* 98. Given the perennial shortage of hard currency in early America, people would express their wealth in, and use, a variety of currencies, hence the use of guilders even under British rule. Levy has been extensively studied; see Leo Hershkowitz, "Asser Levy and the Inventories of Early New York Jews," *American Jewish History* 80 (1990): 23–55, which lists in detail the elements of his considerable fortune, and Malcolm H. Stern, "Asser Levy—a New Look at Our Jewish Founding Father," *American Jewish*

Archives 26 (1974): 66–77, which shows how members of the Myers, Cohen, Bush, and Sheftall families had all intermarried with the Levys by 1800.

36. Kohler, "Civil Status of Jews," 86–88.

37. Schappes, *Documentary History,* 12.

38. Pool and Pool, *Old Faith,* 32–34; Kohler, "Civil Status of Jews," 88–96; Goodfriend, *Before the Melting Pot,* chap. 9.

39. Hühner, "Asser Levy," 17–23.

40. Jacob Rader Marcus, *Early American Jewry,* 2 vols. (Philadelphia: Jewish Publication Society of America, 1951, 1953), 1:35–38.

41. *Minutes of the Common Council of New York, 1675–1776,* 8 vols. (New York: Dodd, Mead, 1905), 1:34, 42, 50, 67, 68; Hühner, "Asser Levy," 89–96.

42. Morris Dyer, "Points in the First Chapter of New York Jewish History," *PAJHS* 3 (1895): 47; John M. Murrin, "English Rights as Ethnic Aggression: The English Conquest, the Charter of Liberties of 1683, and Leisler's Rebellion in New York," in William Pencak and Conrad E. Wright, eds., *Authority and Resistance in Early New York* (New York: New-York Historical Society, 1988), 56–94.

43. Schappes, *Documentary History,* 15–19, 568–69.

44. Kohler, "Civil Status of Jews," 91–95.

45. "Form of Association Proposed to the Inhabitants," Jacob Leisler Papers, Fales Library and Special Collections, New York University, available at http://pages.nyu.edu/~dwv1/jun—1689-.html; Jacob Melyan Letterbook, American Antiquarian Society. That Melyan's letterbook is written partly in Dutch and partly in English suggests the imperfect Anglicization and complex ethnic relationships in early New York. I thank Evan Haefeli for this reference.

46. Pool and Pool, *Old Faith,* 34–35; Israel, *European Jewry,* 127–31; "Mr. Atwood's Memorial concerning New York, his posts there & in neighboring provinces," Misc. Mss. Atwood, Ch. Justice Wm., New-York Historical Society. My thanks to Evan Haefeli for this reference.

47. See Robert C. Ritchie, *Captain Kidd and the War against the Pirates* (Cambridge: Harvard University Press, 1986), 65–66, 191–92, 132, 186; Bellomont to Lords of Trade, *Documents Relating to the Colonial History of New York,* 15 vols., ed. J. R. Brodhead (1853–83), 4:512.

48. Bellomont to Lords of Trade, October 17, 1700, 4:720.

49. Douglas Greenberg, *Crime and Law Enforcement in Colonial New York, 1664–1783* (Ithaca: Cornell University Press, 1976), 26–27, 112–13. For identification of the attorneys general as anti-Leislerians, see Robert C. Ritchie, *The Duke's Province: A Study of New York Politics* (Chapel Hill: University of North Carolina Press, 1977), 198, 225, and *Documentary History of New York,* 3:651, 662, 768.

50. "Hachan [Hazan] of Congregation in Curacao to Parnass of Congregation in New York," 1729, *PAJHS* 27 (1917): 3–4.

51. Leo Hershkowitz, "Some Aspects of the New York Jewish Merchant and Community, 1654–1820," *American Jewish Historical Society Quarterly* 87 (1977): 3, 10; Abraham de Lucena to Governor Hunter, September 13, 1710, de Lucena file, American Jewish Archives (hereafter AJA).

52. Leo Hershkowitz and Isidore S. Meyer, eds., *The Lee Max Friedman Collection of American Jewish Colonial Correspondence: Letters of the Franks Family, 1733–1748*

(Waltham: American Jewish Historical Society), xix (hereafter cited as *Franks Letters*); Rosenwaike, "Estimate and Analysis," 395–96; Pool, *Portraits Etched in Stone*, 284.

53. *Franks Letters*, xxii, 71–72, 79–82, 106–7; Marcus, *Early American Jewry*, 1:91–92.

54. *Franks Letters*, 57–58; Edith Gelles is working on a new, annotated edition of the Franks letters.

55. Ibid., 50, 62, 48, 58, 60.

56. Peter Kalm, *The America of 1750*, ed. Adolph Benson (New York: Wilson-Erickson, 1937), 130, 631; "Minute Book of Shearith Israel," 74–75.

57. *Franks Letters*, 8, 65, 66, 25.

58. Ibid., 4, 8, 37, 51, 60, 104; T. H. Breen, "An Empire of Goods; The Anglicization of Colonial America, 1690–1776," *Journal of British Studies* 24 (1986): 467–99; and Carla Mulford, introduction to *Only for the Eye of a Friend: The Poems of Annis Boudinot Stockton* (Charlottesville: University of Virginia Press, 1995).

59. *Franks Letters*, 13, 23–24, 41, 48, 55.

60. Kalm, *The America of 1750*, 129–30, 630; Naphtali Phillips, "Unwritten History," *American Jewish Archives* 6 (1954): 82; Marcus, *The Colonial American Jew*, 3:1027.

61. *Franks Letters*, 17–18, 23–27, 36–37, 40–41.

62. Pool and Pool, *Old Faith*, 447–48.

63. Kohler, "Civil Status of Jews," 98–99; William Smith Jr., *History of the Province of New York*, 2 vols. (Cambridge: Harvard University Press, 1972), 2:37–41; Marcus, *The Colonial American Jew*, 1:409–10.

64. *A Journal of the Votes and Proceedings of the General Assembly of His Majestye's Colony of New York, in America (1737–1738)*, esp. 13, 23, 25, 27, 31–33, Evans microprint. For a fine summary of the complicated questions of who could vote in this election, see *New York Colonial Documents*, 6:56n.

65. Smith, *History of Province*, 2:37–41.

66. Jack P. Greene, "The Role of the Lower Houses of Assembly in the Eighteenth Century," *Journal of Southern History* 27 (1961): 451–74.

67. Rodrigo Pacheco to James Alexander, January 14, 1738, box 6, Alexander Papers, New-York Historical Society; Hershkowitz, "New York Jewish Merchant," 14.

68. *Minutes of Common Council*, 2:164, 168, 169.

69. Ibid., 3:186, 210, 211, 4:153; 5:128, 231.

70. Ibid., 4:346–47, 351; 5:62, 66, 177, 200.

71. Ibid., 3:327, 374, 393; 7:84, 127, 189, 230, 317, 378, 383, 447, 8:57, 107, 111.

72. Kalm, *The America of 1750*, 129.

73. Samuel Johnson to Peter Jay, May 27, 1740, Jay Papers, Columbia University Special Collections.

74. Clinton to the Duke of Bedford, June 28, 1749, *New York Colonial Documents*, 6:513–16; Bonomi, *A Factious People*, 162–65; Mary Lou Lustig, *Privilege and Prerogative: New York's Provincial Elite* (Madison: Fairleigh Dickinson University Press, 1995), 57–69.

75. *Franks Letters*, 114, 116–19, 124–25, 129.

76. Ibid., 28.

77. Kalm, *The America of 1750*, 130.

78. Ibid., 129, 131, 108–10, xvi, xxii–xxiii; Richard Brilliant, *Facing the New World: Jewish Portraits in Colonial and Federal America* (New York: Prestel, 1997), 12–13, 103.

79. Leo Hershkowitz, ed., *Wills of Early New York Jews (1704–1799)* (New York: American Jewish Historical Society, 1967), 119–21; Robert Cohen, "Jewish Families in Eighteenth-Century New York: A Study in Historical Demography," seminar paper, Brandeis University, 1972, 31, copy at AJA.

80. *Franks Letters,* xvi, xviii, 28, 42, 47, 72, 81.

81. Ibid., 28.

82. *New York Weekly Journal,* May 16, 1745; Paul Gilje, *The Road to Mobocracy: Popular Disorder in New York City, 1763–1834* (Chapel Hill: University of North Carolina Press, 1987), 15–16.

83. *Pennsylvania Gazette,* January 18, 1743.

84. *New York Gazette or Weekly Post-Boy,* July 21, 1746, September 10, 1751; *New York Weekly Journal,* September 10, 1751, Evans microfilm.

85. George Clinton to Mr. Catherwood, February 17, 1749, in Edmund B. O'Callaghan, ed., *Documents Relative to the Colonial History of the State of New York,* 16 vols. (Albany: Weed, Parsons, 1853–87), 6:471; Gilje, *The Road to Mobocracy,* 15–16, 21.

86. *New York Weekly Journal,* May 8, 1749; Pool, *Portraits Etched in Stone,* 244–45.

87. For Jewish-Christian social relations, see Samuel Oppenheim, "The Jews and Masonry in the United States Before 1800," *PAJHS* 19 (1910): 42–49.

88. Letters from John Watts to Moses Franks, *Letter Book of John Watts, 1762–1765, Collections of the New-York Historical Society,* 61 (1917), esp. 59, 75–76, 91, 101, 191, 200–201, 240, 261, 357, 376–77, 392.

89. Cecil Roth, "Some Jewish Loyalists in the American War for Independence," in Karp, *Jewish Experience in America,* 298.

90. Phillips, "Unwritten History," 86, 87, 95.

91. "Minute Book of Shearith Israel," 50–51.

92. Ibid., 70–72.

93. Ibid., 82; Karla Goldman, *Beyond the Synagogue Gallery: Finding a Place for Women in American Judaism* (Cambridge: Harvard University Press, 2000), 41.

94. "Minute Book of Shearith Israel," 82–85; *Franks Letters,* 28; Naphtali Phillips, "Memoir of Shearith Israel," *PAJHS* 21 (1910): 217; Phillips, "Unwritten History," 82; *New York Gazette and Weekly Post-Boy,* September 6, 1756.

95. Robert Rogers, *A Concise Account of North America* (London: J. Millan, 1765), 66.

96. New York City file, copy of poll list for election of representatives, February 17–19, 1761, AJA; Bonomi, *A Factious People,* 305–11.

97. "Minute Book of Shearith Israel," 91; deleted minutes, keyed to p. 100, in published minutes, *PAJHS* 21 (1911), AJA.

98. Ibid., deleted minutes, keyed to pp. 73, 94.

99. Information on Joseph Simson may be found in Hershkowitz, *Wills,* 201.

100. Evidence for the complicated case of *Josephson v. Simpson,* finally heard on April 23, 1772, may be found in New York file, Lawsuits involving Jews from John Tabor Kempe Papers, New-York Historical Society, copy at AJA.

101. New York—Shearith Israel file, Opinion of Judge Whitehead Hicks, AJA.

102. "Minute Book of Shearith Israel," 103–5; deleted minutes, keyed to pp. 94 and 99.

103. J. Solis-Cohen Jr., "Barak Hays: Controversial Loyalist," *PAJHS* 45 (1955): 54–57.

104. Shearith Israel, deleted minutes, keyed to 114–15 in published minutes, *PAJHS* 21 (1911), AJA New York file, cases relating to Jews, 1769–72, from John Tabor Kempe Papers, New-York Historical Society, for cases *Hays v. Seixas* and *Simson v. Hays*. All at AJA.

105. Deleted minutes, "Shearith Israel," keyed to 117 in published minutes, *PAJHS* 21 (1911), AJA.

106. Schappes, *Documentary History*, 51–52.

107. *New York Gazette and Weekly Post-Boy*, July 23, 1770.

108. Arthur Lee, "The New York Jew," *American Jewish Archives* 6 (1954): 105–6.

109. Cecil Roth, "A Jewish Voice for Peace in the War of American Independence," *PAJHS* 31 (1928): 67, 70, 71.

110. Roth, "Some Jewish Loyalists," 307–9, 314–18; Schappes, *Documentary History*, 50–52, 577–80; Samuel Rezneck, *Unrecognized Patriots: The Jews in the American Revolution* (Westport, Conn.: Greenwood Press, 1975), 27–35, 115–16; Naphtali Phillips, "Sketch of Shearith Israel," *PAJHS* 21 (1911): 216; Phillips, "Unwritten History, 84, 86.

111. Greenberg, *Crime in New York*, 81; *Minutes of Common Council*, August 8, 1727, 3:414; "New York City Mayor's Court Minutes, 1679–1797," June 12–13, 1727, 344, copy at AJA.

112. Judith van Buskirk, *Generous Enemies: Civility and Conflict in Revolutionary New York* (Philadelphia: University of Pennsylvania Press, 2002); Rezneck, *Unrecognized Patriots*, 61, 141–43; Roth, "Some Jewish Loyalists," 316–17; "Minute Book of Shearith Israel," 145.

113. "Minute Book of Shearith Israel," 159; Schappes, *Documentary History*, 50–52, 577–80.

114. Schappes, *Documentary History*, 41, 579.

115. Charles Z. Lincoln, *The Constitutional History of New York from the Beginnings of the Colonial Period to the Year 1905*, vol. 1 (Rochester: Lawyers' Cooperative Publishing, 1905), 421; Richard B. Morris, ed., *John Jay: The Making of a Revolutionary* (New York: Harper and Row, 1975), 392, 395.

116. William Smith, *Historical Memoirs*, ed. William H. W. Sabine, 2 vols. (New York: New York Times, 1969), 1:169.

117. Lincoln, *Constitutional History*, 541–45.

118. Henry P. Johnstone, ed., *The Correspondence and Public Papers of John Jay*, 4 vols. (New York: Putnam's Sons, 1890–93), 1:102–20; Pierre Jay to Daniel Gomez, December 31, 1724, and four letters in 1725; Pierre Jay to James Harding, June 13, 1750, Pierre Jay Letter Books, Papers of John Jay, Butler Library, Columbia University.

119. Marcus, *American Jewry: Documents*, 28–31; Morris, *John Jay*, 113–15; Stephen Schechter, ed., *The Reluctant Pillar: New York and the Adoption of the Federal Constitution* (Albany: New York State Bicentennial Commission, 1987), 182–83, 198.

120. Poole, *Portraits Etched in Stone*, 284.

121. Manuel Josephson to Moses Seixas, February 4, 1790, *American Jewish Archives* 27 (1975): 253–54.

122. Shearith Israel, New York file, Constitution and By-Laws Signed by Isaac Moses and Solomon Simson, 1790, AJA.

123. Ronald W. Kaplan, "A Study of the Religious Life of the Sephardic Congregation Shearith Israel . . . 1776–1840," 16–17, typescript, 1976, AJA; Marcus, *Early American Jewry*, 1:102.

124. Jaher, *Jews and the Nation,* 157; Gad Nashon, "Jews in the Socio-Political Life of New York and Philadelphia, 1783–1801," 5, 23–24, typescript, n.d., AJA. Moses was a close friend of Robert Morris and had become a Mason in 1767. See *American Jewish Archives* 27 (1975): 166–68; Marcus, *American Jewry: Documents,* 95, 118, 121, 128, 150, 153, 157–58, 177–78.

125. Isaac Jerusalemi, "Cultural Practices and Ideals of a New York Sephardic Congregation as Reflected in the Minutes of Shearith Israel, 1784–1789," Hebrew Union College. Cincinnati, unpublished paper, 1956, 5, 6, AJA; Mary Beth Norton, *Liberty's Daughters: The Revolutionary Experience of American Women, 1750–1800* (Boston: Little, Brown, 1980); Pool and Pool, *Old Faith,* 287–88.

126. Frederic Hudson, *Journalism in the United States from 1690 to 1872* (New York: Harper Brothers, 1873), 144–45, 181.

127. *New York Journal,* April 26 and May 11, 1790; the *Journal* had various subtitles, see Alfred F. Young, *The Democratic-Republicans of New York: The Origins, 1763–1797* (Chapel Hill: University of North Carolina Press, 1967), 602, for this information.

128. *Poughkeepsie Journal,* January 8, 1793, cited in Young, *Democratic Republicans,* 335.

129. Nashon, "Jews in Socio-political Life." Nashon's paper profiles the leading New York Jews who were both Masons and Democrats.

130. Morris U. Schappes, "Anti-Semitism and Reaction, 1785–1800," in Karp, *Jewish Experience in America,* 366–71; Mordecai Myers file, "Reminiscences 1780–1814," copy at AJA, partially reprinted in Jacob Marcus, ed., *Memoirs of American Jews,* 3 vols. (Philadelphia: Jewish Publication Society of America, 1955–56), 1:50–75.

131. Schappes, "Anti-Semitism and Reaction, 1785–1800," 366–71; Schappes, *Documentary History,* 84–88, 588–89; "A Peep into the Anti-Federal Club" is reprinted in Randall M. Miller and William Pencak, eds., *Pennsylvania: A History of the Commonwealth* (University Park: Pennsylvania State University Press, 2002), 141.

132. Schappes, *Documentary History,* 84–88, 588–89.

133. Ibid., 89–92, 589–91; Schappes, "Anti-semitism and Reaction," 377–80.

134. Entry for Naphtali Judah, Bertram Korn Collection, AJA; Nashon, "Jews in Socio-political Life," 21; Schappes, *Documentary History,* 591, 595. At least one New York Jew supported the Federalists at this time, although the fact that he was living in England explains his sympathies. Writing from London on September 5, New Yorker Benjamin S. Judah offered to use his European contacts to supply arms for a war he considered inevitable, but just: France was "an insidious foe" that threatened the United States' "independent existence," and "every American must feel the ardour of aiding his country to justify her rights."

135. Quoted in Robert P. Franzin, "The Sermons of Gershom Mendes Seixas," Hebrew Union College Paper, 1963, copy at AJA.

136. Schappes, "Anti-semitism and Reaction," 382–83; Rezneck, *Unrecognized Patriots,* 56. Levy converted to the Episcopal faith and is buried at St. Peter's Church, Philadelphia.

137. It is interesting how anti-semitic printers such as John Fenno, William Cobbett, Thomas Greenleaf, and James Rivington were themselves unsettled, moving from place to place in search of the main chance, much like the stereotype of the wandering Jew. See their biographies in the *Dictionary of American Biography:* Cobbett, 4:248; Fenno, 6:325; Greenleaf, 7:584; Rivington, 15:637–38.

138. Schappes, *Documentary History*, 83.

139. Undated note, *Papers of Alexander Hamilton*, 26 vols., ed. Harold Syrett (New York: Columbia University Press, 1961–87) 26:774; Alexander Hamilton, "Law Practice Involving Jews, 1782–1800," copies of papers at AJA; Rebecca Gratz to Rachel Gratz, July 18, 1804, item 31 in "Index to American Judaica Collection of Mark Boartman," AJA; Marcus, *United States Jewry, 1776–1985*, 3 vols. (Detroit: Wayne State University Press, 1989–93), 1:538; *New York Journal*, November 1, 1799.

140. Leon Hühner, "Jews in Connection with the Colleges of the Thirteen Original States Prior to 1900," *PAJHS* 19 (1910): 118–19.

141. Gershom Seixas file, "Hebrew Address by Sampson Simson," 1800, AJA; Schappes, *Documentary History*, 92; Jacob Rader Marcus, *The Handsome Young Priest in the Black Gown: The Personal World of Gershom Seixas* (Cincinnati: Hebrew Union College, 1970), 33.

3. NEWPORT, RHODE ISLAND

1. Morris A. Gutstein, *The Story of the Jews of Newport: Two and a Half Centuries of Judaism, 1658–1908* (New York: Bloch, 1936), 35, 340–41; this work needs to be used with caution, but contains information not available elsewhere; Theodore Lewis, "History of Touro Synagogue," Touro Synagogue website, http://www.tourosynagogue.org; Jacob Rader Marcus, *Early America Jewry*, 2:117, notes that the first concrete evidence of Newport's Jewish congregation was the purchase of the burial ground. A community must have preexisted this date for this to have been possible.

2. Roger Williams, "The Bloudy Tenent of Prosecution for the Cause of Conscience," quoted in Maxwell H. Morris, "Roger Williams and the Jews," *American Jewish Archives* 3 (1951): 24–26; for Williams's political and religious thought, see Edmund S. Morgan, *Roger Williams: The Church and the State* (New York: Harcourt Brace, 1957); Perry Miller, *Roger Williams and His Contribution to the American Political Tradition* (New York: Atheneum, 1965); and Edwin S. Gaustad, *Liberty of Conscience: Roger Williams in America* (Grand Rapids: Eerdmans, 1991); Marcus, *Early American Jewry*, 1:117.

3. Jaher, *Scapegoat in New Wilderness*, 92–94.

4. Carl Bridenbaugh, *Fat Mutton and Liberty of Conscience: Society in Rhode Island, 1636–1690* (Providence: Brown University Press, 1974), 65, 198; Marcus, *Early American Jewry*, 1:116.

5. There is no study of Dyer, but scattered information may be found in Robert N. Toppan, *Edward Randolph*, 7 vols. (Boston: Prince Society, 1898–1909), 3:62, 317, 339–40; David S. Lovejoy, *The Glorious Revolution in America* (New York: Harper and Row, 1972), 24, 26, 31, 96, 110–11, 153, 159, 175–77; Bridenbaugh, *Fat Mutton*, 175; J. H. Trumbull and C. J. Hoadly, eds., *The Public Records of the Colony of Connecticut* (Hartford: Brown and Parsons, 1850–90), 3:344; Herbert Levi Osgood, *The American Colonies in the Seventeenth Century* (New York: Columbia University Press, 1904), 2:131, 162–64, 184, 369.

6. Marcus, *Early American Jewry*, 1:118; David Katz, *The Jews in the History of England* (Oxford: Clarendon Press, 1994), 145–54.

7. Katz, *Jews in History of England*, 145–50; Edward Randolph to Sir Robert Southwell, January 29, 1684, Toppan, *Edward Randolph*, 4:5, 3:339–40.

8. Gutstein, *Jews of Newport*, 40–44; Marcus, *Early American Jewry*, 1:117–18.

9. Sydney V. James, *Colonial Rhode Island: A History* (New York: Scribner's, 1975), 111, 208; Gutstein, *Jews of Newport*, 46, 53.

10. George A. Kohut, ed., *Ezra Stiles and the Jews: Selected Passages from His Literary Diary concerning Jews and Judaism* (New York: Philip Cowen, 1902), 108–9; Arthur Chiel, "Ezra Stiles and the Jews: A Study in Ambivalence," in Goldman, *Hebrew and the Bible*, 156–67; I refer to Rodrigues Rivera as Rodrigues: it is standard Spanish, Portuguese, and Latin American practice to this day to include the mother's last name after the father's. Rodrigues was one of the few colonial Jews who did so.

11. Elaine Forman Crane, *A Dependent People: Newport, Rhode Island in the Revolutionary Era* (New York: Fordham University Press, 1985), 24–29.

12. For general biographical information on Lopez and his family see Stanley F. Chyet, *Lopez of Newport: Colonial American Merchant Prince* (Detroit: Wayne State University Press, 1970). For an excellent brief discussion of Lopez's mercantile activities and the reasons for his quick rise to wealth, see Holly Snyder, "A Sense of Place: Jews, Identity, and Social Status in Colonial British America, 1654–1831," Ph.D. diss., Brandeis University, 2000, 158–72. The information on the slave trade and the statistics (which are approximations and deductions) are based on Jay Coughtry, *The Notorious Triangle: Rhode Island and the African Slave Trade, 1700–1807* (Philadelphia: Temple University Press, 1981) 80, 84, 88, and tables from 248–60 for statistics on mortality; see also, for instance, Lopez Account Book, 1771–73, no. 768, box 3, Lopez Papers, copies at AJA. The originals of the Lopez Papers are found mostly at the Rhode Island Historical Society and the John Carter Brown Library. They are divided into a variety of boxes, folders, series, and microfilm reels that makes sorting them out extremely difficult. They are used most easily in the collected version at the American Jewish Archives.

13. See, for example, the web page of the Anti-Defamation League (http://www.adl.org) and Sara Deutsch, "The Elusive Guineaman: Newport Slavers, 1735–1774," *New England Quarterly* 55 (1982): 229–53; Virginia P. Blatt, "And Don't Forget the Guinea Voyage: The Slave Trade of Aaron Lopez of Newport," *William and Mary Quarterly* 32 (1975): 601–18.

14. Gutstein, *Jews of Newport*, 54, 55.

15. Chyet, *Lopez of Newport*, 42–51.

16. Records of Rhode Island Superior Court, 13:824, Naphtali and Isaac Hart to Abraham Solomons of St. Eustatia, August 4, 1763, Miscellaneous Correspondence, John Carter Brown Library; Obadiah Brown to Tench Francis, November 27, 1758, and January 10, 1759; Nicholas Brown to Aaron Lopez, January 16, 1769, Lopez to Brown, May 20, 1769, box 3, Lopez Papers, John Carter Brown Library. Copies of all material in this note at AJA.

17. Records of Rhode Island Superior Court, 13:922, May 30, 1763, copy at AJA.

18. Records of Rhode Island Superior Court, 13:711, 823, testimony from March 1766 relating to an incident of November 1765, copy at AJA.

19. Naphtali Hart Jr. to Aaron Lopez, March 2, 1773, box 1, General Correspondence, Lopez Papers, Rhode Island Historical Society, copy at AJA; Chyet, *Lopez of Newport*, 118.

20. Gutstein, *Jews of Newport*, 51, 52, 168–70; Will of Jacob Rodrigues Rivera, in folder of Documents Pertaining to Jacob Rodrigues Rivera, Rhode Island file, AJA.

21. Town Meeting Records, May 5, 1760, Newport, copy at AJA; ledger for 1767, p. 121, box 2, Lopez Papers, John Carter Brown Library, copy at AJA; Ruth Wallis Hern-

don, *Unwelcome Americans: Living on the Margin in Early New England* (Philadelphia: University of Pennsylvania Press, 2001); *Newport Mercury,* May 1, 8, 15, 22, 1769, copy in "References to Jews of Rhode Island" in the *Newport Mercury* file, AJA.

22. Will of Jacob Rodrigues Rivera, documents pertaining to Jacob Rodrigues Rivera, AJA; Lopez Account Book, 1770, no. 720, Lopez Papers, AJA.

23. Andrew Burnaby, *Travels through the Middle Settlement in North America in the Years 1759 and 1760,* 2nd ed. (Ithaca: Cornell University Press, 1963), 120–21; Carl Bridenbaugh, *Peter Harrison: First American Architect* (Chapel Hill: University of North Carolina Press, 1959), 9, 17, 53, 91, 101–2; Lewis, "History of Touro Synagogue."

24. Chyet, *Lopez of Newport,* 54–57; Gutstein, *Jews of Newport,* 91–98.

25. Ezra Stiles, *Literary Diary,* ed. Franklin Bowditch Dexter, 3 vols. (New York: Scribner's, 1901), 1:11; James, *Colonial Rhode Island,* 208; Goldman, *Beyond the Synagogue Gallery,* 42–43.

26. Gutstein, *Jews of Newport,* 170–72.

27. Kohut, *Stiles and the Jews,* 52, 132; Stiles, *Literary Diary,* 1:422–23, November 23, 1773.

28. Kohut, *Stiles and the Jews,* 79–81.

29. The Zohar is mentioned in ibid., on 20, 21, 52, 53, 81–83, 93, 100, 113–15, 131, 132, 188, an indication of how seriously Stiles took it.

30. Kayim Isaac Carigal, "A Sermon Preached at the Synagogue in Newport, Rhode Island, called 'The Salvation of Israel.' . . ," May 28, 1773, Rhode Island file, AJA, 11–16; Stiles, *Literary Diary,* August 10, 1769, 1:11; Ezra Stiles, *Extracts from the Itineraries and Other Miscellaneous Items* (New Haven: Yale University Press, 1904), June 29, 1768, 58; Kohut, *Stiles and the Jews,* 9.

31. Kohut, *Stiles and the Jews,* 66–67; Stiles *Literary Diary,* 1:226.

32. Stiles, *Literary Diary,* August 4, 1770, 1:61, February 16, 1771, 1:91.

33. Chyet, *Lopez of Newport,* 194.

34. See Redemption Doudle to Aaron Lopez, December 11, 1779, Lopez Papers, AJA, and Chyet, *Lopez of Newport,* 101–3, 110–17, 155–71, 180–82, 187.

35. Jacob Rodrigues Rivera to Moses Brown, March 21, 1779, John Carter Brown Library, copies of material relating to Rhode Island Jews at AJA; Petition to Rhode Island Assembly, Rhode Island State Archives, 11:37, August 23, 1762, copy at AJA; Kohut, *Stiles and the Jews,* 33; Records of Superior Court of Rhode Island, 13:286, copy at AJA; John Russell Bartlett, ed., *Records of the Colony of Rhode Island and Providence Plantations,* 10 vols. (Providence: The Legislature, 1856), 5:307, 375, 6:262, 272; Gutstein, *Jews of Newport,* 56.

36. For the freemanship and naturalization petitions, which are difficult to disentangle from each other, see David S. Lovejoy, *Rhode Island Politics and the American Revolution, 1760–1776* (Providence: Brown University Press, 1958), 76, 204; Chyet, *Lopez of Newport,* 34–41.

37. For Rhode Island's complicated political history from the 1750s to the Revolution see especially Mack E. Thompson, "The Ward-Hopkins Controversy and the American Revolution in Rhode Island: An Interpretation," *William and Mary Quarterly,* 3rd ser., 16 (1959): 363–75; Lovejoy, *Rhode Island Politics,* 5–47. Snyder, "A Sense of Place," 141–49, argues that religious bigotry, rather than politics, was the motive for the Superior Court's refusal to naturalize Elizer and Lopez. I believe the two worked hand in hand.

38. Lovejoy, *Rhode Island Politics,* 17, 26–28.

39. Bridenbaugh, *Peter Harrison,* i; Lopez to John Nazro, November 12, 1781, Aaron Lopez Letter Book, copy at AJA; also Chyet, *Lopez of Newport,* 19–20, 34–41.

40. Chyet, *Lopez of Newport,* 37–38.

41. Ibid., 39–40.

42. Lovejoy, *Rhode Island Politics,* 49–50; James, *Colonial Rhode Island,* 327.

43. Petition of Rhode Island Merchants, Rhode Island State Archives; Petition to the General Assembly, July 1764, Records of the General Assembly, copy at AJA; Lovejoy, *Rhode Island Politics,* chap. 4 for Stamp Act.

44. Lovejoy, *Rhode Island Politics,* 145; Crane, *A Dependent People,* 133; Chyet, *Lopez of Newport,* 137; letter to committee of Boston sent by committee of New York, June 11, 1770, Lopez Papers, copy at AJA.

45. Kohut, *Stiles and the Jews,* 33–34.

46. Chyet, *Lopez of Newport,* 125–26; *Pennsylvania Gazette,* June 7, 1770.

47. Crane, *A Dependent People,* 133–34; Chyet, *Lopez of Newport,* 164–72; Lopez Papers, John Carter Brown Library, entry for March 27, 1775, his accounts as the *sedakah* or treasurer of the synagogue, box 3, folder 5, copy AJA.

48. Kohut, *Stiles and the Jews,* 35; Chyet, *Lopez of Newport,* 149–53; Gutstein, *Jews of Newport,* 183, Crane, *A Dependent People,* 139.

49. Chyet, *Lopez of Newport,* 159–60.

50. Crane, *A Dependent People,* 5–29, 139; Gutstein, *Jews of Newport,* 181–84; Chyet, *Lopez of Newport,* 157–60; Kohut, *Stiles and the Jews,* 34–35.

51. Gutstein, *Jews of Newport,* 181–84; Kohut, *Stiles and the Jews,* 34–35; Crane, *A Dependent People,* 139; Petition of Isaac Touro to Sir Guy Carleton, British Headquarters Papers, College of William and Mary, copy at AJA under Rhode Island file.

52. Gutstein, *Jews of Newport,* 183–84.

53. Chyet, *Lopez of Newport,* 192–95.

54. Aaron Lopez Letter Book, 1781–82, November 2, 1781, to Caleb Bilel; Lopez inventory, register of deeds, Worcester, Mass., May 16, 1783, copy in Lopez Papers, AJA; Lopez to Captain John Wiley, September 21, 1781, copy in Lopez Papers AJA.

55. Josephine H. Pierce, "Secured from Sudden Alarms: The Portuguese Jews in Leicester," manuscript at AJA, 17–19.

56. Gutstein, *Jews of Newport,* 214–17, 228–35, 256–59; Snyder, "A Sense of Place," 432–35.

57. I am deeply indebted to Elizabeth Covart, "Live Free or Die: A Generation Remembers the Battle of Bunker Hill," senior honors thesis, Pennsylvania State University, 2003, for her research on Touro. See also Schappes, *Documentary History,* 333–41, 656–62.

58. Gutstein, *Jews of Newport,* 204–6.

59. The correspondence between Washington and the Jewish congregations is printed in Schappes, *Documentary History,* 77–84.

60. Crane, *A Dependent People,* epilogue; Gutstein, *Jews of Newport,* 241, 251–57.

4. CHARLESTON, SOUTH CAROLINA

1. Hagy, *This Happy Land,* 30–31, quoting articles 95 and 96 of the Fundamental Constitutions; Eugene M. Sirmans, *Colonial South Carolina: A Political History,*

1663–1763 (Chapel Hill: University of North Carolina Press, 1966), 3. Carolina was one province until 1719; I thus refer to Carolina before that date and South Carolina thereafter.

2. W. Noel Sainsbury, ed., *Calendar of State Papers, Colonial Series: American and West Indies, 1669–1674* (London, 1889), 178–87, prints the relevant documents.

3. Wilfred S. Samuel, *The Jewish Colonists in Barbados in the Year 1680* (London: Purnell and Sons, 1936), 51–52, 63–65, 91, 93–94.

4. Agnes L. Baldwin, *First Settlers of South Carolina* (Easley, S.C.: Private printing, 1935); Richard S, Dunn, "The English Sugar Islands and the Founding of South Carolina," *South Carolina Magazine of History* 72 (1971): 81–93; Kinloch Bull, "Barbadian Settlers in Early Carolina: Historiographical Notes," *South Carolina Magazine of History* 96 (1995): 329–39, notes that while the Barbadian settlement and influence on early Carolina were considerable, they have been overstated. Many immigrants who came from Barbados had been there briefly and used the island merely as a port of embarkation.

5. Samuel, *Jewish Colonists in Barbados*, 93–94, 113–25; Joseph Archdale, "A New Description of That Fertile and Pleasant Province of Carolina" (1707), in Alexander S. Salley Jr., *Narratives of Early Carolina, 1660–1708* (New York: Charles Scribner's Sons, 1911), 300; "Jews in a Place Called Charleston," chart 1, Early Settlers, 1695–1800, 22–26, Charleston, South Carolina file, AJA; Hagy, *This Happy Land*, 6–8.

6. *Journals of the [British] House of Commons, 1693–1697.* (London: For the House, 1803), 423–24; Richard B. Morris, "Civil Liberties and the Jewish Tradition in Early America," *PAJHS* 46 (1956): 30–31; Joyce Appleby, *Economic Thought and Identity in Seventeenth Century England* (Princeton: Princeton University Press, 1978).

7. *Journals of House of Commons*, 440, 491, 428; Hagy, *This Happy Land*, 24–25, 31–32, 54–55; Baldwin, *First Settlers*, 8.

8. Sirmans, *Colonial South Carolina*, chaps. 2–5, esp. 17–18, 76; Clarence L. Ver Steeg, *Origins of a Southern Mosaic: Studies of Early Carolina and Georgia* (Athens: University of Georgia Press, 1975), chaps. 1 and 2, esp. 34–36; Hagy, *This Happy Land*, 32–33; Arthur Hirsch, *The French Huguenots of Colonial South Carolina* (Durham: Duke University Press, 1928), 105–18.

9. Marcus, *The Colonial American Jew*, 1:345; Hagy, *This Happy Land*, 7, 10–11.

10. Hagy, *This Happy Land*, 7–8; Sirmans, *Colonial South Carolina*, chap. 6.

11. William L. McDowell Jr., ed., *South Carolina Indian Relations*, 3 vols. (Columbia: South Carolina Department of Archives and History, 1955–70), 1:69, 70, 79, 83, 91, 105, 115, 108, 124, 160, 162, 171n, 193n, 140, 157.

12. Hagy, *This Happy Land*, 31–34.

13. Ibid., 55 for Masons; 42–44, 47–50, 112; Moses Lindo to Sampson and Solomon Simpson, April 17, 1770, Lindo file, AJA. The number of naturalizations probably understates the number of Jews, since only a minority of Jews took out the necessary papers in New York and Rhode Island, where records exist.

14. Barnett A. Elzas, *The Jews of South Carolina from the Earliest Times to the Present Day* (Philadelphia: Lippincott, 1905), 33, 35; Hagy, *This Happy Land*, 9–13, 34; "Bicentennial Celebration of the Jews of Charleston, 1750–1950," Eleanor Halsey Papers, South Carolina Historical Society, Charleston.

15. Hagy, *This Happy Land*, 34–36, 11; Schappes, *Documentary History*, 45.

16. Schappes, *Documentary History*, 46–47.

17. Hagy, *This Happy Land*, 35; see also papers of the Commission to Celebrate the Bicentennial of the Jews of Charleston, South Carolina Historical Society.

18. Stephen More et al. to Nathanael Greene, May 18, 1781, South Carolina General file, AJA.

19. Hagy, *This Happy Land*, 113–19.

20. Ibid., 38; James Simpson to William Knox, December 31, 1780, K. G. Davies, ed., *Documents of the American Revolution*, 21 vols. (Shannon: Irish University Press, 1972–81), 18:269; I thank Stanley Weintraub for this reference.

21. Hagy, *This Happy Land*, 113–19, lists the Jews and their activity during the Revolution.

22. Elzas, *Jews of South Carolina*, 106; Hagy, *This Happy Land*, 36, 37; Levi Moses, Petition of March 28, 1785, to South Carolina legislature, South Carolina file, AJA, and Barnard Moses folder, South Carolina Refugees file, AJA.

23. Schappes, *Documentary History*, 53–54.

24. Hagy, *This Happy Land*, 119; *South Carolina Gazette*, August 30, 1783; Jaher, *Jews and the Nation*, 163.

25. John C. Meleney, *The Public Life of Aedanus Burke: Revolutionary Republican in Post-revolutionary South Carolina* (Columbia: University of South Carolina Press, 1981), 52, 104, 107, for riots; "An Early American Synagogue Desecration," from *New-Haven Gazette and the Connecticut Magazine*, November 23, 1787, reprinted in *American Jewish Archives* 58 (1968): 136. For the Algerines, see William L. King, *The Newspaper Press of Charleston, South Carolina* (Charleston: Edward Perry Press, 1872), 44.

26. Hagy, *This Happy Land*, 42, 43; Solomon Breibart, "The Synagogue of Kahal Kadosh Beth Elohim, Charleston," *South Carolina Historical Magazine* 80 (1979): 215–21; Solomon Breibart, "An Architectural History of Kahal Kadosh Beth Elohim, Charleston," *South Carolina Historical Magazine* 98 (1997): 6–55; *South Carolina Gazette*, September 20, 1794, South Carolina file, AJA.

27. Gershom Cohen to Harmon Hendricks, November 27, 1791, Hendricks Papers, AJA; Hagy, *This Happy Land*, 71; *Massachusetts Spy*, March 7, 1804, from "Items in the Massachusetts Spy Relating to Jews," AJA.

28. Hagy, *This Happy Land*, 54; "Family History," Yates, Samuel, and Lazarus Family file, AJA.

29. Hagy, *This Happy Land*, 92; W. Robert Higgins, "The South Carolina Revolutionary Debt and Its Holders, 1776–1790," *South Carolina Historical Magazine* 72 (1971): 15–29, esp. 22–23.

30. Bertram W. Korn, *Jews and Negro Slavery in the Old South, 1789–1865* (Elkins Park, Pa.: Reform Congregation Keneseth Israel, 1961), 44; *South Carolina State Gazette*, September 6, 1784; Hagy, *This Happy Land*, 96.

31. Joseph Salvador to Emanuel Mendes da Costa, January 22, 1785, in Cecil Roth, ed., "A Description of America, 1785," *American Jewish Archives* 17 (1965): 27–33.

32. Hagy, *This Happy Land*, 73; "A Bicentennial Anniversary in Charleston: The Story of Congregation Beth Elohim," South Carolina file, AJA.

33. Melvin H. Jackson, *Privateers in Charleston, 1793–1796* (Washington, D.C.: Smithsonian Press, 1969), 58, 69–73, 93.

34. Hagy, *This Happy Land*, 52; *Charleston Times*, issues October 6–16, 1800; King, *Newspaper Press of Charleston*, 72–73.

35. Gary Zola, *Isaac Harby of Charleston, 1788–1828: Jewish Reformer and Intellectual* (Tuscaloosa: University of Alabama Press, 1994), 117.

36. Hagy, *This Happy Land*, 14, 60, 61; Kahal Kadosh Beth Elohim, box 1, folder 54, memorial of January 27, 1775, AJA; unfortunately, early records of the congregation do not survive with this exception. Solomon Breibart, "Two Jewish Congregations in Charleston, South Carolina before 1791: A New Conclusion," *American Jewish History*, 69 (1980): 360–63.

37. Breibart, "Two Jewish Congregations"; Hagy, *This Happy Land*, 64–68.

38. Memorandum of Isaac De La Motta, 1795, AJA.

39. For Vissels, see *Charleston Gazette*, September 21, 1765, copy in South Carolina file, AJA.

40. Hagy, *This Happy Land*, 122–23.

41. File entitled "Material in South Carolina Archives," AJA.

42. Hagy, *This Happy Land*, 50–52, 120–26.

43. Jack Williams, *Dueling in the Old South: Vignettes of Social History* (College Station: Texas A&M University Press, 1980); Ver Steeg, *Origins of Southern Mosaic;* Robert M. Weir, *"The Last of American Freemen": Studies in the Political Culture of the Colonial and Revolutionary South* (Macon, Ga.: Mercer University Press, 1986); Hagy, *This Happy Land*, 120–21.

44. Hagy, *This Happy Land*, 46.

45. Steven A. Channing, *Crisis of Fear: Secession in South Carolina* (New York: Scribner's, 1970); Zola, *Isaac Harby of Charleston*, esp. 112–13, 119–25; "Constitution of Hebrew Congregation of Kahal Kadosh Beth Elohim or House of God, Charleston, S. C. [1820]," 113–21, and "Reformed Society of Israelites, Charleston, S.C., Constitution, 1825," 131–37, in Daniel J. Elazar, Jonathan D. Sarna, and Rela G. Monson, eds., *A Double Bond: Constitutional Documents of American Jewry* (Lanham, Md.: University Press of America, 1992).

5. SAVANNAH, GEORGIA

1. Milton Ready, "Philanthropy and the Origins of Georgia," and Phinizy Spalding, "James Edward Oglethorpe's Quest for an American Zion," both in Harvey H. Jackson and Phinizy Spalding, eds., *Forty Years of Diversity: Essays on Colonial Georgia* (Athens: University of Georgia Press, 1984), 46–79.

2. Malcolm H. Stern, "New Light on the Jewish Settlement of Savannah," *PAJHS* 52 (1963): 173.

3. Ibid., 174; B. H. Levy, *Mordecai Sheftall: Jewish Revolutionary Patriot* (Savannah: Georgia Historical Society, 1999), 12–13, B. H. Levy, "The Early History of Georgia Jews," in Jackson and Spalding, *Forty Years of Diversity*, 167.

4. Levy, "Early History of Georgia Jews," 166–67, 174–75; James Oglethorpe to Trustees, letter of August 12, 1733, in Mills Lane, ed., *General Oglethorpe's Georgia, Colonial Letters, 1733–1743* (Savannah: Beehive Press, 1975); 9–13; George Fenwick Jones, ed., *Henry Newman's Salzburger Letterbooks* (Athens: University of Georgia Press, 1966): 609; Avner Vossen Goodman, *American Overture: Jewish Rights in Colonial Times* (Philadelphia: Jewish Publication Society of America, 1947): 189.

5. Robert Jutte, "Contacts by the Bedside: Jewish Physicians and Their Christian Patients," in Ronnie Po-Chia Hsia and Hartmut Lehmann, eds., *In and Out of the Ghetto: Jewish-Gentile Relations in Late Medieval and Early Modern Germany* (Cambridge: Cambridge University Press, 1995), 137–50; Joseph R. Rosenbloom, *A Biographical Dictionary of Early American Jews* (Lexington: University of Kentucky Press, 1960), 136.

6. Levy, "Early History of Georgia Jews," 166; Mark I. Greenberg, "'A Haven of Benignity': Conflict and Cooperation between Eighteenth Century Savannah Jews," *Georgia Historical Quarterly* 86 (2002): 545, 547.

7. Betty Wood, "The Earl of Egmont and the Georgia Colony," in Jackson and Spalding, *Forty Years of Diversity*, 86–87; Allen D. Candler, Kenneth Coleman, and Milton Ready, eds., *The Colonial Records of the State of Georgia*, 32 vols. to date (Athens: University of Georgia Press, 1904–), 1:73.

8. Rodney M. Baine, ed., *The Publications of James Edward Oglethorpe* (Athens: University of Georgia Press, 1994), 197.

9. Amos A. Ettinger, *James Edward Oglethorpe: Imperial Idealist* (Oxford: Clarendon Press, 1936), esp. 88–89, 276; Baine, *Publications of Oglethorpe*, 281.

10. Compare lists in Rabbi Saul Jacob Rubin, *Third to None: The Saga of Savannah Jewry, 1733–1983* (Savannah: Congregation Mikveh Israel, 1983), 2–3, with the grantees in Charles C. Jones, *History of Georgia*, 2 vols. (Boston, 1883), 1:155–62; Levy, "Early History of Georgia Jews," 167; Clarence L. Ver Steeg, ed., *A True Historical Narrative of the Colony of Georgia by Patrick Telfair and Others, with Comments by the Earl of Egmont* (Athens: University of Georgia Press, 1960), 48.

11. For complaints, see Stern, "New Light," 187; William Stephens Diary, in Candler et al., *Colonial Records of Georgia*, 3:43–44, 105.

12. Levy, "Early History of Georgia Jews," 178–79.

13. Stern, "New Light," 190; *Egmont Manuscripts*, 3 vols. (London, 1920–23), 1:311; Thomas Coram to Trustees, March 27, 1734, in Candler et al., *Colonial Records of Georgia*, 2:96–98.

14. See Lane, *General Oglethorpe's Georgia*, for Bland letter, 516; also see 521, 541, and numerous other pages on troubles in early Georgia.

15. Ver Steeg, *True Historical Narrative*, 48; Stern, "New Light," 185–86, 196–97.

16. Ver Steeg, *True Historical Narrative*, 41, 88–96.

17. Ibid., 48; George Fenwick Jones, ed., *Detailed Reports on the Salzburger Immigrants Who Settled in America*, 18 vols. (Athens: University of Georgia Press, 1968–95), 1:43, 60, 70; Goodman, *American Overture*, 18; Stern, "New Light," 184.

18. Jones, *Salzburger Immigrants*, 1:65.

19. John C. English, "John Wesley and His 'Jewish Parishioners': Jewish-Christian Relationships in Savannah, Georgia, 1736–1737," *Methodist History* 36 (1998): 220–27.

20. Nehemiah Curnock, ed., *The Journal of John Wesley*, vol. 1 (London: Epworth, 1938), 1:60, 140; Jones, *Henry Newman's Salzburger Letterbooks*, 118; Stern, "New Light," 184.

21. Jones, *Salzburger Immigrants*, 5:123, 164, 226.

22. Candler et al., *Colonial Records of Georgia*, 2:375; Stern, "New Light," 180.

23. Candler et al., *Colonial Records of Georgia*, 3:43–44; Ver Steeg, *True Historical Narrative*, 62.

24. Stern, "New Light," 185–86, 192–93.

25. Candler et al., *Colonial Records of Georgia*, 2:195; 4 (supplement): 185, 273.

26. In an unfortunate exception to his superb scholarship, Stern, "New Light," 188–90, terms Stephens's justification of Causton "anti-semitic," ignoring his praise of Minis and the fact he was still early in his fact-finding against Causton; Candler et al., *Colonial Records of Georgia*, 3:105; Stephens Diary, in Candler et al., *Colonial Records of Georgia*, 3:105; Kaye Kole, *The Minis Family of Georgia, 1733–1992* (Savannah: Georgia Historical Society, 1992), 4–5, 8.

27. Goodman, *American Overture*, 187.

28. Stern, "New Light," 191, 192.

29. Stern, "New Light," 185–86; Goodman, *American Overture*, 192; George Fenwick Jones, "Sephardim and Ashkenazim Jewish Settlers in Colonial Georgia," *Georgia Historical Quarterly* 85 (2001): 531.

30. Stern, "New Light," 185–86.

31. Ibid., 184; Jones, *Salzburger Immigrants*, 1:70, 8:107, 114, 276.

32. George Fenwick Jones, "A Letter by Pastor Johann Martin Boltzius about Bethesda and Martial Irregularities in Savannah," *Georgia Historical Quarterly* 84 (2000): 292; Kole, *Minis Family*, 18.

33. Jones, "Letter by Boltzius," 292; Stern, "New Light," 186; Jones, *Salzburger Immigrants*, 8:130.

34. Rosenbloom, *Biographical Dictionary*, 136; Sheftall Papers, University of Georgia, descriptive materials, box 23; Kole, *Minis Family*, 9; Snyder, "A Sense of Place," 176–77.

35. Stern, "New Light," 192–93; Rubin, *Third to None*, 18.

36. For Rev. Samuel Frink's statistics that there were 1,996 inhabitants and 781 slaves in Savannah, see Frink's letter of 1771 to the Society for the Propagation of Christian Knowledge, *Georgia Historical Quarterly* 57 (1973): 138–39; Rubin, *Third to None*, 81; "Abigail Minis, Matriarch," typescript at Georgia Historical Society, Savannah; Daniel Pepper to Gov. Lyttleon, March 30, 1757, in McDowell, *South Carolina Indian Relations*, 3:357; Levi Sheftall, "Autobiography," Sheftall Papers, Special Collections, University of Georgia.

37. Jones, "Sephardic and Ashkenazim Settlers," 524; Rubin, *Third to None*, 18–21; "Minutes of the Executive Council of Georgia," ed. Lillian Hayes, 34:26, 42, 107, Georgia State Archives; Candler et al., *Colonial Records of Georgia*, 7:744–45, 923, 8:285, 417, 10:333, 11:114–15, 204, 226, 12:163–64, 28(2): 329–30. Many thanks to Joshua Piker of the University of Oklahoma for his discussion of the southeastern frontier and these references.

38. Rosenbloom, *Biographical Dictionary*, 137.

39. Clifford K. Shipton, *Biographical Sketches of Those Who Attended Harvard College* (Boston: Massachusetts Historical Society, 1966), 14:270–75; Frink arrived in Georgia in March 1765, took his post in Savannah in January 1767, and died in October 1770. Harold Davis, *The Fledgling Province: Social and Cultural Life in Georgia, 1733–1776* (Chapel Hill: University of North Carolina Press, 1976), 223–29.

40. B. H. Levy, "Savannah's Old Jewish Cemeteries," *Georgia Historical Society Quarterly* 66 (1982): 1–5; Candler et al., *Colonial Records of Georgia*, 15:145–46, 151–52, 17:568–69, 572–73.

41. Candler et al., *Colonial Records of Georgia*, 15:137, 140, 17:559–61.

42. Candler et al., *Colonial Records of Georgia* 17:572–73, 15:138, 151–52.

43. Benjamin W. Labaree et al., eds., *The Papers of Benjamin Franklin* (New Haven: Yale University Press, 1974), 18:54n; and Franklin to Noble Wymberly Jones, March 5, 1771, and Johan Joachim Zubly to Franklin, July 9, 1771. Frink statistics, *Georgia Historical Quarterly* 57 (1973): 138–39 show that as of 1771, there were six Jewish families comprising twenty-seven people who owned twenty-two slaves in Savannah. Candler et al., *Colonial Records of Georgia*, 15:138–39.

44. Samuel Frink to Society for the Propagation of Christian Knowledge, July 6, 1770, in *Georgia Historical Quarterly* 57 (1973): 140–41; Shipton, *Biographical Sketches*, 14:270–75.

45. Davis, *The Fledgling Province*, 198, 227; Clay became a strong revolutionary, delegate to the Continental Congress, and state treasurer of Georgia. See *Letters of Joseph Clay*, (Savannah: Collections of the Georgia Historical Society, 1913) 35–37.

46. On Georgia politics, see Kenneth Coleman, *The American Revolution in Georgia, 1763–1789* (Athens: University of Georgia Press, 1958).

47. Davis, *The Fledgling Province*, 229–30; Rubin, *Third to None*, 23–25; Malcolm Stern, ed., "The Sheftall Diaries: Vital Records of Savannah Jewry, 1733–1808," *PAJHS* 54 (1965): 251.

48. Levy, *Mordecai Sheftall*, 61–62; Rubin, *Third to None*, 27.

49. Rubin, *Third to None*, 27.

50. Ibid., 32–34.

51. Ibid., 27.

52. Michael Morris, "George Galphin: Portrait of an Early South Carolina Entrepreneur," *Proceedings of the South Carolina Historical Association* (2002): 29–44; Rosenbloom, *Biographical Dictionary*, 136; Lillian Hayes, ed., "Minutes of the Georgia Executive Council," 34:107, and "Proceedings and Minutes of the Governor and Council of Georgia," 35:31–60, 198, Georgia State Archives. I am indebted to Joshua Piker for sharing these sources with me.

53. Levi to Benjamin (or Mordecai) Sheftall, March 17, 1783, box 23, 13, Sheftall Papers, University of Georgia.

54. Forrest McDonald, *E Pluribus Unum: The Formation of the American Republic* (Baltimore: Penguin, 1965): 84–85; Levy, *Mordecai Sheftall*, 61–62; Rubin, *Third to None:* 34–35; Hagy, *This Happy Land*, 116.

55. "Abigail Minis, Matriarch," typescript at Georgia Historical Society, Savannah. Also at the Georgia Historical Society see the following: Minis to "Dear Sir" in Charleston, January 4, 1780, requesting reimbursement for advances to the Continental army, Minis Papers, Collection no. 1515; see also will of Abigail Minis and writ of attachment, March 28, 1793, both in Minis Papers, Collection no. 568, Georgia Historical Society. Holly Snyder suggests Abigail Minis may never have learned to write, and thus another would have penned her missive. "A Sense of Place," 335.

56. For the draft, see "A Real Citizen," box 23, 13, Sheftall Papers, University of Georgia, Special Collections. *Georgia Gazette*, January 13, 1785 reprinted in Max Kohler, "Phases of Religious Liberty in America with Particular Reference to the Jews," *PAJHS* 13 (1905): 29–31. Snyder, "A Sense of Place," 131–34, believes that Mordecai and Levi Sheftall each wrote one of these letters, which is possible. However, only one was published, and similarities between the two suggests to me that the manuscript is a draft of the published version. My trivial disagreements with Dr. Snyder in this and concerning

Abigail Minis's literacy mentioned in the previous note are among my few caveats concerning her superb work.

57. Jackson, *Privateers in Charleston,* 78, 93; Stern, "Sheftall Diary," 266; Abraham Minis to Abigail Minis, March 7, 1794, Minis Papers, Collection no. 568, Georgia Historical Society.

58. Rubin, *Third to None,* 54–56.

59. Ibid., 95–97.

60. James Broussard, *The Southern Federalists: 1800–1816* (Baton Rouge: Louisiana State University Press, 1978), 90, 104.

61. Snyder, "A Sense of Place," 185–86; J. Max Patrick, *Savannah's Pioneer Theater: From Its Origins to 1810* (Athens: University of Georgia Press, 1953), 51.

62. Rubin, *Third to None,* 32–34, 88–90; Leon Hühner, "The First Jew to Hold the Office of Governor of One of the United States," in Hühner, *Jews in America in Colonial and Revolutionary Times* (New York: Geertz Bros., 1959), 136–44.

63. Joseph L. Blau and Salo W. Baron, eds., *The Jews of the United States: A Documentary History, 1790–1840,* 3 vols. (New York: Columbia University Press, 1963), 1:176–81; Thomas Gamble, *Savannah Duels and Duelists: 1733–1877* (Savannah: Review Publishing and Printing Co., 1923).

64. B. H. Levy, *Savannah's Oldest Jewish Community Cemeteries* (Macon: Mercer University Press, 1983), 63–65.

6. PHILADELPHIA

1. Brilliant, *Facing the New World,* 37; Wolf and Whiteman, *Jews of Philadelphia,* 33, 63; Goodman, "German Mercenary," 227.

2. Wolf and Whiteman, *Jews of Philadelphia,* 18–20, 22, 386.

3. Wolf and Whiteman, *Jews of Philadelphia,* 26–29.

4. Sidney M. Fish, *Barnard and Michael Gratz: Their Lives and Times* (Lanham, Md.: University Press of America 1994), 1.

5. Fish, *Barnard and Michael Gratz,* 11–12, 16–30; for more international connections among Jews, see Miriam Bodian, *Hebrews of the Portuguese Nation: Conversos and Community in Early Modern Amsterdam* (Bloomington: Indiana University Press, 1997); and Alan F. Benjamin, *Jews of the Dutch Caribbean: Exploring Ethnic Identity on Curacao* (London: Routledge, 2002), esp. 54–59.

6. Hershkowitz, *Wills,* 36–40.

7. Samuel Evans, "Sketch of Joseph Simon," in Gratz Papers, ser. 1, vol. 1; Monroe B. Hirsh, "Joseph Simon and the Hebrews of Lancaster during the Colonial Period," Gratz Papers, ser. 1, vol. 7, Historical Society of Pennsylvania, copies also at AJA; Henry Necarsulmer, "The Early Jewish Settlement at Lancaster, Pennsylvania," *PAJHS* 9 (1901): 29–44; Dianne Ashton, *Rebecca Gratz: Women and Judaism in Antebellum America* (Detroit: Wayne State University Press, 1997), 24, 28–32, 67–69.

8. Jonathan Block to Barnard Gratz, March 24, 1756; Barnard Gratz to Solomon Henry, November 20, 1758; Michael Gratz to Haym Gratz (1759), Gratz Papers, ser. 1, vol. 1, 57, 79–85, AJA (originals at Historical Society of Pennsylvania).

9. Fish, *Barnard and Michael Gratz,* 11–15.

10. Cosmus Alexander to Peter Renon, January 6, 1769, Historical Society of Pennsylvania, copy in Anti-semitism file, AJA; *Pennsylvania Packet,* September 15, 1737.

11. *American Israelite*, September 4, 1958, copy at AJA; R. Alonzo Brock, "Journal of William Black, 1744," *Pennsylvania Magazine of History and Biography* 1 (1877): 415–16; Journal of Witham Marshe, quoted in Elizabeth Kieffer to Malcolm Stern, July 22, 1765, Levy family file, AJA.

12. John F. Watson, *Annals of Philadelphia and Pennsylvania in the Olden Time*, 3 vols. (Philadelphia: E. Stuart, 1857), 1:276, 283.

13. William Pencak, "Beginning of a Beautiful Friendship: Benjamin Franklin, George Whitefield, the 'Dancing School Blockheads,' and a Defense of the 'Meaner Sort,'" *Proteus* 19 (2002): 45–50.

14. Leon Hühner, "Jews in Connection with the Colleges of the Original Thirteen States prior to 1800," *PAJHS* 19 (1910): 120–24; Oppenheim, "Jews and Masonry"; Marcus, *American Jewry: Documents*, 7, 69; Wolf and Whiteman, *Jews of Philadelphia*, 184; R. William Weisberger, "Freemasonry as a Source of Jewish Civic Rights in Late Eighteenth-Century Vienna and Philadelphia: A Study in Atlantic History," *East European Quarterly* 34 (2001): 419–45; for Levy A. Levy, see David Brener, *The Jews of Lancaster, Pennsylvania* (Lancaster: Private publication, 1979), 4.

15. Herbert Samuel Morais, *The Jews of Philadelphia* (Philadelphia: Levy-Type Co., 1894), 19–20.

16. For portraits, see those following in Faber, *A Time for Planting*, following p. 68; and Brilliant, *Facing the New World*.

17. Israel, *European Jewry*, 123–45; William Plumsted to Col. Henry Bouquet, February 25, 1760, *Papers of Henry Bouquet*, 6 vols., Sylvester K. Stevens, Donald H. Kent, and Louis Waddell, eds., (Harrisburg, Pa., 1951—), 4:469, and editors' notes: 4:469, 5:101, 282, 428.

18. William Plumsted to Henry Bouquet, February 25, 1760; Adam Hoops to Bouquet, March 14, 1760, *Papers of Henry Bouquet*, 4:469, 496; Fish, *Barnard and Michael Gratz*, 50, 57–58, citing material from the Etting Collection, Historical Society of Pennsylvania, and *Papers of Henry Bouquet*, 1A:191, 240.

19. Michael Mullin, "George Croghan," in Garraty and Carnes, *American National Biography*, 5:752–54; Albert T. Volwiler, *George Croghan and the Westward Movement, 1740–1782* (Cleveland: Arthur H. Clark, 1926), 151, 280.

20. John Langdell to Henry Bouquet, *Papers of Henry Bouquet*, 5:439; James Kenny Journal, July 17–21, August 4, August 8, December 25, 1761, excerpts in Gratz Papers, ser. 1, vol. 4; Volwiler, *George Croghan*, 151, 190.

21. Volwiler, *George Croghan*, 111, 286–87, 312, 327, 328, 379.

22. Ibid., 91; Fish, *Barnard and Michael Gratz*, 81–132.

23. Volwiler, *George Croghan*, 273, 284; Fish, *Barnard and Michael Gratz*, 81–132.

24. Meyer Josephson to Michael and Barnard Gratz, November 10, 1764, Gratz Papers, ser. 1, vol. 5.

25. William Murray to Barnard and Michael Gratz, May 5, 1773, and Murray to Barnard Gratz, May 16, 1774, Gratz Papers, ser. 1, vols. 11, 12; Levy Andrew Levy to Michael Gratz, May 25, 1774, ser. 1, vol. 13.

26. [Mr.] Tennet to Michael Gratz, September 6, 1776, Gratz Papers, ser. 1, vol. 1.

27. Barnard to Michael Gratz, May 16, 1783, May 30, 1783, June 27, 1783, ser. 2, vol. 6, Gratz Papers.

28. Barnard to Michael Gratz, November 5, 12, 26, 1779, ser. 2, vol. 3; "Plain Facts," December 18, 1785, ser. 2, vol. 7; May 13, 1786, ser. 2, vol. 7; July 16, 1788, ser. 2, vol. 8, Gratz Papers.

29. *Pennsylvania Gazette,* August 29, 1751, cited in Morais, *Jews of Philadelphia,* 20; "Philadelphia Jewry, 1655–1901," Bertram Korn Collection, at AJA.

30. George Alexander Kohut, "The Oldest Tombstones in the Jewish Cemeteries of Philadelphia and Newport," *PAJHS* 6 (1897): 107–12; Marcus, *American Jewry: Documents,* 9–10; *Pennsylvania Gazette,* December 27, 1753; *American Israelite,* September 4, 1958, copy at AJA.

31. *Pennsylvania Gazette,* November 1, 1753.

32. Hannah Callandar Sansom Diary (1756), p. 55 (original), American Philosophical Society; transcription by Karin Wulf. Thanks to Susan Klepp for this reference.

33. Marcus, *United States Jewry, 1776–1985,* 1:326–31; Brener, *Jews of Lancaster,* 7–13; Gustavus N. Hart, "Notes on Myer Hart and Other Jews of Easton, Pennsylvania," *PAJHS* 8 (1900): 127–34; Marcus, *American Jewry: Documents,* 358–60, for Meyer Josephson of Reading.

34. Richard Locke to SPG, April 11, 1747, quoted in Hirsh, "Joseph Simon"; Häberlein and Schmolz-Häberlein, "Competition and Cooperation," 430–36; Erna Drucker, "Settlers in Early New Amsterdam and Early New York, 1654–1825: A Selected Annotated Guide to Source Materials," M.L.S. thesis, Queen's College, City University of New York, 1984, citing the *New York Gazette,* September 3, 1761, copy at AJA.

35. Wolf and Whiteman, *Jews of Philadelphia,* 45, who translate the quotation from the May 12, 1766 *Staatsbote* (supplement).

36. Brener, *Jews of Lancaster,* 8–11.

37. Ibid.; Marcus, *American Jewry: Documents,* 275.

38. For unrest in Lancaster, see Thomas P. Slaughter, "Interpersonal Violence in a Rural Setting: Lancaster County in the Eighteenth Century," *Pennsylvania History* 58 (1991): 98–123.

39. Brener, *Jews of Lancaster,* 8; Häberlein and Schmolz-Häberlein, "Competition and Cooperation," 434–35.

40. *Wochentliche Philadelphische Staatsbote,* December 1, 1760, February 13, 1761, November 14, 1766, *Philadelphische Staatsbote* file, AJA. Translation of first and third items by Karin Weaver, Department of History, Pennsylvania State University.

41. Ibid., August 19 and September 16, 1765; Diane E. Wenger, "Creating Networks: The Country Storekeeper and the Market Economy," Ph.D. diss., University of Delaware, 2001, 58.

42. Malcolm H. Stern, "Two Jewish Functionaries in Colonial Pennsylvania," *American Jewish Historical Quarterly* 24 (1957): 29–35.

43. Email, Natalie Z. Davis to author, October 23, 2000.

44. [David Dove], *A Fragment of the Chronicles of Nathan Ben Saddi, A Rabbi of the Jews* (Philadelphia, 1758); for more discussion, see Alison Gilbert Olson, "Pennsylvania Satire before the Stamp Act," *Pennsylvania History* 68 (2001): 507–32; [anon.], *The Quakers Assisting, to preserve the lives of the Indians in Barracks, vindicated . . .* (Philadelphia, 1764), reprinted in John R. Dunbar, ed., *The Paxton Papers* (The Hague: M. Nijhoff, 1957), 387–95, quotation on 395.

45. Wolf and Whiteman, *Jews of Philadelphia,* 47; Samuel Oppenheim, "Nine Colonial Worthies: Jewish Signers of the Non-importation Resolutions of 1765," *American Hebrew,* September 10, 1926, 395, 530, 532, 536. I estimate twenty-five families in Philadelphia, ten in Lancaster, and perhaps ten elsewhere. At least a dozen of the

Philadelphia Jews were merchants or shopkeepers, as were most of those in Lancaster, and probably half or more elsewhere.

46. Mathias Bush to Bernard Gratz, November 7, 1769, Gratz Papers, ser. 1, vol. 9, Historical Society of Pennsylvania, copy at AJA.

47. Gary B. Nash, *The Urban Crucible: Social Change, Political Consciousness, and the Origins of the American Revolution* (Cambridge: Harvard University Press, 1979); Billy G. Smith, *"The Lower Sort": The Laboring People of Philadelphia, 1750–1800* (Ithaca: Cornell University Press, 1990); Marcus, *The Colonial American Jew,* 2:880; Faber, *A Time for Planting,* 58–60; Wolf and Whiteman, *Jews of Philadelphia,* 54, quoting Jacob Henry to Barnard Gratz, January 7, 1771, McAlister Collection, Historical Society of Pennsylvania, also in Gratz Papers, ser. 1, vol. 1, at AJA.

48. *Pennsylvania Gazette,* December 4, 1760; May 5, 1763; August 9, 1764; Matthew Josephson to Barnard Gratz, second day of Purim, 1764, ser. 1, vol. 5, Gratz Papers, AJA.

49. Marcus, *American Jewry: Documents,* 399–401; *Pennsylvania Gazette,* July 19, 1772, for Lyon and Jacobs.

50. For Nathan's story, see Wenger, "Creating Networks," 55–56.

51. For information on Jews in this paragraph: Marcus, *American Jewry: Documents,* 399–401; Joseph Simon to Gratz Brothers, 1772, Gratz Papers, ser. 1, vol. 11, AJA; "Joseph Cohen," in Marcus, *Memoirs of American Jews,* 1:28–30. *Pennsylvania Gazette,* July 29, 1772; Haym Salomon to Uncle, July 10, 1783, *American Jewish Archives* 27 (1975): 212–13.

52. *Pennsylvania Gazette,* May 5, 1763, January 10, 1771, January 9, 1772, June 30, 1773, March 29, 1775, May 3, 1775, November 25, 1773, January 10, 1776, March 21, 1776, and August 21, 1776.

53. Bernard Bailyn, *Voyagers to the West: A Passage in the Peopling of America on the Eve of the Revolution* (New York: Knopf, 1996).

54. Wolf and Whiteman, *Jews of Philadelphia,* 54, quoting Mathias Bush to Barnard Gratz, November 7, 1769, Etting Collection, Historical Society of Pennsylvania; Samuel quoted in Jonathan D. Sarna, Benny Kraut, and Samuel K. Joseph, eds., *Jews and the Founding of the Republic* (New York: M. Wiener, 1985), 84.

55. *Pennsylvania Gazette,* January 26, 1769.

56. *Pennsylvania Gazette,* September 20, 1770, November 25, 1773.

57. Jeannette W. Rosenbaum, "Hebrew German Society Rodeph Shalom in the City and County of Philadelphia," *PAJHS* 61 (1951–52): 84–86; Edward Davis, *The History of Rodeph Shalom Congregation, Philadelphia* (Philadelphia, 1926), 11–32.

58. Fish, *Barnard and Michael Gratz,* 134, citing Andres H. Grob to Barnard Gratz, London, October 24, 1770, McAlister Collection, Historical Society of Pennsylvania; Marcus, *American Jewry: Documents,* 74, 278; Jonas Phillips to Gumpel Samson, July 28, 1776, *PAJHS* 25 (1917): 128–30; Solomon Bush to Henry Lazarus, November 15, 1777, *PAJHS* 23 (1915): 177; Hyman Polock Resenbach, *The Jews in Philadelphia Prior to 1800* (Philadelphia: E. Stern, 1883), 38.

59. *Pennsylvania Gazette,* July 7, 1779; Christopher Marshall Diary, July 5, 1779, quoted in Barnard Gratz to Michael Gratz, April 13, 1779, Gratz Papers, ser. 2, vol. 3.

60. John Beatty to George Washington, October 20 and November 1, 1778; Board of War to Beatty, October 12, 1778, Beatty file, AJA.

61. *Pennsylvania Gazette,* December 12, 1778. Other relevant documents are reprinted in Marcus, *American Jewry: Documents,* 241–60, on which the next several

paragraphs are based. I am indebted to my colleague Daniel Letwin for letting me look at a superb paper on Matlack that he wrote under Edmund S. Morgan's direction while a graduate student at Yale, for information on Matlack, which I summarize in my essay on "The Promise of Revolution, 1750–1800," in Pencak and Miller, *Pennsylvania,* 117.

62. Van Buskirk, *Generous Enemies;* Daniel Gomez to Supreme Executive Council of Pennsylvania, 1779, Gomez file, AJA.

63. *Pennsylvania Gazette,* January 12, 1780, November 1, 1780; Cecil Roth, "Some Jewish Loyalists," 307–8. For the Delanceys' complicated and extensive relationships with the Franks see *Letter Book of John Watts, 1762–1765,* in *Collections of the New-York Historical Society,* 61 (1917); and Hershkowitz and Meyer, *Franks Letters,* whose extensive notes and commentary extend far beyond the given dates. Also see the New York chapter of this book.

64. Rebecca Franks to Anne Harrison, February 26, 1778, *American Jewish Archives* 27 (1975): 142–44. See Judith van Buskirk, "They Didn't Join the Band: Disaffected Women in Revolutionary Philadelphia," *Pennsylvania History,* 62 (1995): 306–29, for loyalists and neutrals, and Mulford's introduction to *Only for the Eye* for more on women's networks.

65. Morais, *Jews of Philadelphia,* 37; Becky Johnson [Franks] to Williamina Bond Cadwalader, February 19, 1784, Cadwalader Papers (new catalog number based on 1999 reorganization of collection), ser. 5, box 71, Williamina Bond Cadwalader Correspondence folders, Historical Society of Pennsylvania.

66. Abraham S. Rosenbach, "Documents Relative to Major David S. Franks While Aide-de-Camp to General Arnold," *PAJHS* 6 (1898): 158–73.

67. Ibid., 173–87.

68. Saul Friedenwald, *Jews in the Journals of the Continental Congress,* in Karp, ed., *Jewish Experience in America,* 330–39; David S. Franks to George Washington, October 16, November 1, 1780; Washington to Franks, October 21, 1780, David S. Franks file, AJA; Marcus, *Memoirs of American Jews,* 1:46–49.

69. David Salisbury Franks to George Washington, May 12, 1789, David S. Franks file, AJA.

70. Ira Rosenwaike, "Jewish Population in the United States in 1790," in Karp, ed. *Jewish Experience in America,* 397; Morais, *Jews of Philadelphia,* 15–16, lists all the founders of Mikveh Israel; *Pennsylvania Gazette,* October 22, 1783.

71. Owen S. Ireland, *Religion, Ethnicity, and Politics: Ratifying the Constitution in Pennsylvania* (University Park: Pennsylvania State University Press, 1995).

72. Cited in Wolf and Whiteman, *Jews of Philadelphia,* 81; *Philadelphia Evening Post,* September 26, 1776.

73. For examples, see Bernard Bailyn, *The Origins of American Politics* (New York: Vintage, 1967), 41, 137, 149, 150.

74. Charles H. Glatfelter, "The Colonial Pennsylvania German Lutheran and Reformed Clergymen," Ph.D. diss., Johns Hopkins University, 1952, 146.

75. Ibid., 183–85.

76. *The Journals of Henry Melchior Mühlenberg,* trans. Theodore G. Tappert and Jon W. Doberstein, 3 vols. (Philadelphia: Mühlenberg Press, 1945), 2:737. I am deeply indebted to Prof. Hermann Wellenreuther for his discussion of Mühlenberg's loyalism, and for referring me to his correspondence. Kevin Delappe, "Jacob Duché—Whig Loyalist?" *Pennsylvania History* 62 (1995): 293–305.

77. Mühlenberg, *Journals*, 2:739–741; Marcus, *Early American Jewry*, 2:255; "Letter of Henry Melchior Mühlenberg, October 2, 1776," *Pennsylvania Magazine of History and Biography* 22 (1898): 129–31.

78. Mühlenberg, *Journals*, 2:742–43; "Letter of Mühlenberg," 129–31; Glatfelter, "Colonial Pennsylvania Clergymen," 134; Morton Borden, *Jews, Turks, and Infidels* (Chapel Hill: University of North Carolina Press, 1984), 11, quoting Albert H. Smyth, ed., *The Writings of Benjamin Franklin*, 10 vols. (New York, 1905–7), 9:266–67.

79. Michael Zuckerman provided this insight at the McNeil Center presentation of this paper.

80. Hopkinson, "A Tory Medley" (Philadelphia, 1780). I am grateful to Brendan McConville for this reference. See Marcus, *American Jewry: Documents*, 447, for brokers. For Fort Wilson, see Steven Rosswurm, *Arms, Country, and Class: The Philadelphia Militia and the "Lower Sort" during the American Revolution* (New Brunswick: Rutgers University Press 1987), chap. 7; and John K. Alexander, "The Fort Wilson Incident of 1779: A Case Study of the Revolutionary Crowd," *William and Mary Quarterly*, 3rd ser., 31 (1974): 589–612.

81. *Pennsylvania Gazette*, July 21, 1780.

82. "A Protestant," 1784, reprinted in *American Jewish Archives* 27 (1775): 227–28.

83. Manuel Josephson and J. W. Carpeles to Rabbi Saul Loewenstamm, March 20, 1785, reprinted, ibid., 228–30; Wolf and Whiteman, *Jews of Philadelphia*, 127–31; Stern, "Two Jewish Functionaries in Colonial Pennsylvania," 35–48.

84. Abraham Levy file, newspaper articles published in the *Independent Gazetteer* and *Chronicle of Freedom*, October 10, 22, 24, 30 and November 11, 1782, AJA.

85. Marcus, *Early American Jewry*, 2:124–31.

86. *Pennsylvania Gazette*, April 9, May 14, 1783.

87. A criticism of the many Quakers and Anglicans who could vote yet did not support the Revolution.

88. An allusion to the idea that taxation required representation.

89. J. Paul Selsam, *The Pennsylvania Constitution of 1776: A Study in Revolutionary Democracy* (Philadelphia: University of Pennsylvania Press, 1936), 216–18; Gad Nashon, "The Social and Political Life of the Jews of Philadelphia and New York," citing p. 26, Council of Censors Journal, December 23, 1783, unpublished manuscript at AJA; Comments on "The Constitutions of the Several Independent States of America," Gershom Seixas file, AJA.

90. Stanley Elkins and Eric McKitrick, "The Founding Fathers: Young Men of the Revolution," *Political Science Quarterly* 86 (1961): 181–216; Jack N. Rakove, *The Beginnings of National Politics: An Interpretive History of the Continental Congress* (New York: Knopf, 1979); Marcus, *American Jewry: Documents*, 477, for bankruptcies; the modern biography of Salomon is Charles Edward Russell, *Haym Salomon and the Revolution* (New York: Cosmopolitan, 1930).

91. See numerous entries in the *Papers of Robert Morris*, E. James Ferguson and Mary Gallagher, eds., 9 vols. to date (Pittsburgh: University of Pittsburgh Press, 1973–99); I thank Mary Gallagher, current editor of the Morris Papers for calling these to my attention; Wolf and Whiteman, *Jews of Philadelphia*, 148; Haym Salomon to Congress, August 25, 1778, in *American Jewish Archives* 27 (1975): 146–47.

92. Wolf and Whiteman, *Jews of Philadelphia*, 163, 148–49; Benjamin Levy to Robert Morris, December 13, 1776, *American Jewish Archives* 27 (1975): 135–36.

93. Quoted in Morais, *Jews of Philadelphia,* 23.

94. Max Farrand, ed., *The Records of the Federal Convention of 1787,* 3 vols. (New Haven: Yale University Press, 1911), 2:268–69.

95. "Minutes of the Convention of the Commonwealth of Pennsylvania," 1789–90, Evans microfilm no. 22764, 37, 66.

96. Resenbach, *Jews in Philadelphia,* 38–39; Philadelphia, Pennsylvania, Wills, Mikveh Israel, AJA; Jerome C. Rosenthal, "A Brief History of Congregation Mikveh Israel, Philadelphia, 1776–1820," 11, typescript, AJA; Samuel E. Karff, "Problems, Practices, and Ideals of an Early Nineteenth Century American Sephardic Jewish Congregation as Reflected in the Correspondence of Mikveh Israel, 1782–1805," typescript, AJA citing congregational minutes, March 14 and 15, 1784, AJA.

97. Marcus, *American Jewry: Documents,* 278–80.

98. John Samuel, "Some Cases in Pennsylvania Where Rights Claimed by Jews Are Affected," *PAJHS* 5 (1897): 35–37.

99. *Independent Gazetteer,* March 13, 1784.

100. Ibid., March 20, 1784.

101. Saul Cornell, *The Other Founders: Anti-Federalism and the Dissenting Tradition in America, 1788–1828* (Chapel Hill: Published for the Omohundro Institute of Early American History and Culture by the University of North Carolina Press, 1999), 128–35; Vernon O. Stumpf, "Colonel Eleazar Oswald, Politician and Editor," Ph.D. diss., Duke University, 1968; for the best discussion of Philadelphia's multiple yellow fever epidemics, see P. Sean Taylor, "'We Live in the Midst of Death': Yellow Fever, Moral Economy, and Public Health in Philadelphia, 1793–1805," Ph.D. diss., Northern Illinois University, 2001.

102. *Independent Gazetteer,* March 20, 1784.

103. Ibid.

104. I have checked Herbert Storing, ed., *The Complete Anti-Federalist,* 7 vols. (Chicago: University of Chicago Press, 1981); and Jonathan Elliott, ed., *The Debates of the Several State Conventions on the Adoption of the Federal Constitution,* 5 vols. (Philadelphia, 1863–91).

105. *Pennsylvania Gazette,* November 14, 1787.

106. *Pennsylvania Gazette,* February 17 and March 17, 1790; *New York Journal,* April 26 and May 1, 1790.

107. Donald H. Stewart, *The Opposition Press of the Federalist Period* (Albany: State University of New York Press, 1969), 58, 671, citing the *Philadelphia General Advertiser,* July 14, 1791, *Exeter* [New Hampshire] *Gazette,* August 5, 1791, and *Norwich* [Connecticut] *Packet,* August 18, 1791; Richard B. Morris, "The Role of the Jews in the American Revolution in Historical Perspective," in Sarna, Kraut, and Joseph, *Jews and the Founding,* 21.

108. For an excellent study of how Federalists and their opponents reversed attitudes toward immigrants and minorities between the 1780s and 1790s, see Marilyn Baseler, *"Asylum for Mankind," 1607–1808* (Ithaca: Cornell University Press, 1998), chaps. 4–8.

109. "A Peep into the Anti-Federal Club" is reprinted and described in detail in Paul Pascal Dupuy, "The French Revolution in American Satire," *Printing Quarterly* 15 (1998): 372–74, and in James C. Kelly and B. S. Lovell, "Thomas Jefferson: His Friends and Foes," *Virginia Magazine of History and Biography* 101 (1993): 144–45. In both arti-

cles, the authors identify the figure I think is Israel as Thomas Jefferson, while Kelly and Lovell note that historian Noble Cunningham Jr. considered him to be Aaron Burr. I have examined three portraits of Israel, one at the Historical Society of Pennsylvania, one from the Hannah London collection at the Jacob Rader Marcus Center of the American Jewish Archives in Cincinnati, and one in Brilliant, *Facing the New World,* 36 (in which he makes the Masonic sign). All differ significantly from each other and from the figure in the cartoon, but all suggest the "tall, rawboned" man described by John Fenno in the quotation at note 125 to this chapter. Information on Israel may be found in Brilliant, *Facing the New World,* 37–38; John Alexander, *Render Them Submissive: Responses to Poverty in Philadelphia, 1760–1800* (Amherst: University of Massachusetts Press, 1980), 37–42; and Kenneth Keller, "Diversity and Democracy: Ethnic Politics in Southeastern Pennsylvania, 1788–1799," Ph.D. diss., Yale University, 1971; also Israel Israel and Joseph Williams Israel file, AJA.

110. Kurt Aland, Hartmut Lehmann, Carola Wessell, and Hermann Wellenreuther, eds., *Die Korrespondenz Heinrich Melchior Mühlenbergs,* 5 vols. (Berlin: Walter de Gruyter, 2003), 5:748–49 (Hermann Wellenreuther kindly made it available to me before publication); Brilliant, *Facing the New World,* 36; Ronald Schultz, *The Republic of Labor: Philadelphia Artisans and the Politics of Class, 1720–1830* (New York: Oxford University Press, 1993), 145–51.

111. See in addition to sources in notes 109 and 110, Israel Israel file, AJA, which contains Barbara Luck to Mrs. W. Cabell Hopkins, February 22, 1974, and a copy of the chapter on Hannah Erwin Israel from Elizabeth F. Ellett's *Women of the American Revolution.*

112. Ellett, *Women of the American Revolution,* copy in Israel material at AJA.

113. See notes 109–12 for sources on Israel Israel. For an excellent treatment of the yellow fever epidemics, see Taylor, "Midst of Death," 188–209. Taylor links the rise of Republicanism more generally, as well as Israel's in particular, to the willingness of nonelite people who became active in the Jeffersonian movement to remain in the city. For black civic participation and ideology, see Thomas E. Will, "A Prescription for Black Civic Participation: Public Virtue, Acquisitive Individualism, and Christian Charity in African-American Thought in the Early Republic," *Pennsylvania History* 69 (2002): 558–76.

114. *Gazette of the United States,* October 9, 1797; *Porcupine's Gazette,* October 16, 1797; the story of Israel's election losses from 1793 to 1798 is concisely told in Richard G. Miller, *Philadelphia: The Federal City—a Study in Urban Politics, 1789–1801* (Port Washington, N.Y.: Kennikat Press, 1976), although Miller accepts the charges that Israel was Jewish; Frank Funkenstein, *Anti-semitic Stereotypes: A Paradigm of Otherness in English Political Culture, 1660–1830* (Baltimore: Johns Hopkins University Press, 1995), 232–37.

115. *Gazette of the United States,* October 7, 1795.

116. Ibid.; Worcester (Massachusetts) file, AJA, newspaper items relating to Jews, *Worcester Gazette,* August 5, 1795.

117. For Democratic Societies, see John W. Davis, "'Guarding the Republican Interest': The Western Pennsylvania Democratic Societies and the Excise Tax"; for tax resistance, see Terry Bouton, "'No Wonder the Times Were Troublesome': The Origins of Fries' Rebellion," both in the special issue of *Pennsylvania History* on Fries' Rebellion, 67 (2000): 21–62.

118. *Gazette of the United States,* October 12, 1795.

119. Ibid.

120. The most sophisticated study of public opinion in the Federalist era is Christopher Young, "Contests of Opinion: The Public Sphere in Post-revolutionary America," Ph.D. diss., University of Illinois, Chicago, 2001. Young shows that the Federalists were as active in courting public opinion as the Democrats but denied particular minorities or interest groups the right to develop permanent, extragovernmental organizations to affect public policy.

121. Owen Ireland, "The Invention of American Democracy: The Pennsylvania Federalists and the New Republic," special issue on Fries' Rebellion of *Pennsylvania History* 67 (2000): 161–70.

122. Schappes, "Anti-Semitism and Reaction," 383–85.

123. Marcus, *United States Jewry, 1776–1985*, 1:527.

124. For Pennsylvania politics in the 1790s, see Ireland, "Invention of American Democracy"; Miller, *Philadelphia;* Harry Tinckom, *Republicans and Federalists in Pennsylvania, 1790–1801* (Harrisburg: Pennsylvania Historical and Museum Commission, 1950); Michael Durey, *Trans-Atlantic Radicals and the Early Republic* (Lawrence: University of Kansas Press, 1997); quotation from *Gazette of the United States,* November 12, 1798. For other examples, see Keller, "Diversity and Democracy," 201–3.

125. Letter of John Fenno, October 26, 1795, Fenno Papers, Chicago Historical Society, copies at Paterno Library, Pennsylvania State University. I thank Sally A. Heffentreyer, author of an M.A. thesis on "John Fenno," Pennsylvania State University, 2004, for this reference.

126. *Gazette of the United States,* October 9, 1797; David W. Robson, "Anticipating the Brethren: The Reverend Charles Nisbet Critiques the French Revolution," *Pennsylvania Magazine of History and Biography* 121 (1997): 303–28.

127. David Levy, *A Defence of the Old Testament, in a series of letters, addressed to Thomas Paine . . .* (Philadelphia: Hogan and McElroy; New York: Naphtali Judah, 1797), 4–5.

128. *Porcupine's Gazette,* September 19, 1797; "Peter Porcupine" [William Cobbett], *The American Rush Light* (New York and London, 1800), 69; *Gazette of the United States,* July 16, 1800; *Philadelphia Gazette,* September 5, 1800; Nashon, "Philadelphia Jews," 29–33.

129. Morais, *Jews of Philadelphia,* 26; Schappes, "Anti-semitism and Reaction," 386–87.

130. "The Jewish Lafayette," *Jewish Post and Opinion,* December 6, 1981, address by James Dallette, "The French Benevolent Society of Philadelphia and the Bicentennial," November 15, 1776, clipping, both in Nones family file, AJA.

131. Mikveh Israel, Minutes February 7 and 23, 1793, AJA copy; *Philadelphia Aurora,* August 13, 1800, reprinted in *PAJHS* 1 (1892): 111–15, and in Wolf and Whiteman, *Jews of Philadelphia,* 210–11.

132. Carl E. Prince, "John Israel: Printer and Politician on the Pennsylvania Frontier," *Pennsylvania Magazine of History and Biography* 91 (1967), 46–55.

133. *Tree of Liberty,* July 25, August 16, August 23, August 30, October 25, 1800.

134. *Tree of Liberty,* August 28, September 18, 1802, May 25, 1805; Prince, "John Israel," 53–55; Will of Israel Israel, Ellet Papers, Historical Society of Pennsylvania; Phillipson Collection, nos. 1–7, ms. 35, AJA.

135. Faber, *A Time for Planting,* 130; Wolf and Whiteman, *Jews of Philadelphia,*

216–17, 280, 444; Schultz, *The Republic of Labor,* 151; Morais, *Jews of Philadelphia,* 23; Henry Adams, ed., *The Writings of Albert Gallatin,* 3 vols. (Philadelphia: Lippincott, 1879), 1:206.

136. Israel Israel to Thomas Jefferson, February 22, 1801, Bixby Collection, of Jeffersoniana, Missouri Historical Society, copy in Israel Israel file, AJA. See also Daniel Sisson, *The American Revolution of 1800* (New York: Knopf, 1974), who writes: "With its emphasis upon individual liberty, equality, and democracy, all arrayed against elitism and the increasing power of the state, Jefferson's rhetorical skill gave voice to the hopes of men everywhere" (452).

137. Harap, *Image of the Jew,* chap. 1; Heather Shaw Nathans, "A Much Maligned People: Jews On and Off the Stage in the Early American Republic," *Early American Studies* 2 (2004): 310–42.

138. For information on Israel, see notes 109–11.

139. Harap, *Image of the Jew,* 40–44; William L. Hedges, "Benjamin Rush, Charles Brockden Brown, and the American Plague Year," *Early American Literature* 7 (1973): 295–311; Robert A. Ferguson, "Yellow Fever and Charles Brockden Brown: The Context of the Emerging Novelist," *Early American Literature* 14 (1979–80): 293–305.

140. Charles Brockden Brown, *Arthur Mervyn: Or Memoirs of the Year 1793* (New York: Holt, Rinehart, and Winston, 1962), book 2, chaps. 23–25, the source of all Mervyn quotations except where noted in parentheses. I thank my graduate student Dan Hicks for deepening my understanding of Arthur Mervyn and for the references to the *National Songster* in the following discussion.

141. Julia Stern, *The Plight of Feeling: Sympathy and Dissent in the Early American Novel* (Chicago: University of Chicago Press, 1997), 153.

142. Hugh Henry Brackenridge, *Modern Chivalry* (New York: Hafner, 1968), 176, 178. All future references to this work are placed in parentheses in the text.

143. *Pittsburgh Gazette,* August 23, 29, 1800.

144. For Darwin, see http://www.ucmp.berkeley.edu/history/Edarwin.html.

145. *The National Songster* (Philadelphia: Thomas Desilver, 1808), 71, 148–49.

146. I have discussed their anti-semitism in "From 'Salt of the Earth' to 'Poison and Curse'? The Jay and Adams Families and the Construction of American Historical Memory," *Early American Studies,* 2 (2004), 258–68.

7. CONCLUSION

1. Novak, *On Two Wings,* 7; Donald S. Lutz, "From Covenant to Constitution in American Political Thought," *Publius* 10 (1980): 101–33; Samuel Langdon, "The Republic of the Israelites an Example to the United States," quoted in Schappes, *Documentary History,* 70–71.

2. Schappes, *Documentary History,* 77–84.

3. Arthur Hertzberg, *The Jews in America,* 2nd ed. (New York: Columbia University Press, 1997), preface; Alan M. Dershowitz, *The Vanishing American Jew* (Boston: Little, Brown, 1997), 1–19, 23.

4. Schappes, *Documentary History,* 64–66.

5. *New York Advertiser,* January 14, 1788, reprinted in the *Hartford Courant,* cited in Jaher, *Jews and the Nation,* 44; Dershowitz, *The Vanishing American Jew,* chaps. 3 and 4, esp. 93, 149–52, 156–58.

6. *The Independent Gazetteer, or the Chronicle of Freedom,* January 17, 1784, quoted in Schappes, *Documentary History,* 66.

7. Jaher, *Jews and the Nation,* 156; Marcus, *American Jewry: Documents,* 95, 118, 121, 128, 150, 153, 157–58, 177–78; Elazar, Sarna, and Monson, *A Double Bond,* 103–37.

8. Toby L. Ditz, "Shipwrecked; or, Masculinity Imperiled: Mercantile Representations of Self and Failure and the Gendered Self in Eighteenth-Century Philadelphia," *Journal of American History* 81 (1994): 51–81; Joanne B. Freeman, *Affairs of Honor: National Politics in the New Republic* (New Haven: Yale University Press, 2001); Hagy, *This Happy Land,* 120–21. See also discussion of Stark-Minis duel in Savannah, Georgia, chapter in this book.

BIBLIOGRAPHIC NOTE

Study of early American Jewish history begins at the American Jewish Archives at Hebrew Union College in Cincinnati. Here Jacob Rader Marcus and his successors have collected primary and secondary sources from all over the world, either originals or microfilms or photocopies. For instance, the AJA holds copies of many of the items in the American Jewish Historical Society in New York, the records of New York's Shearith Israel and Philadelphia's Mikveh Israel (records do not survive for the other congregations), papers of notable Jews such as Haym Salomon, the Gratz family of Philadelphia and their connections, Aaron Lopez (collected from several depositories in Rhode Island), and unpublished monographs on Jewish histories. I also found several key documents at the Georgia Historical Society and University of Georgia relating to the Minis and Sheftall families, at the South Carolina Historical Society concerning Francis Salvador, at the New-York Historical Society on the disputed election of 1736 (Alexander Papers), at Columbia University in the John Jay Papers on the Jay family and the Jews, and at the Historical Society of Pennsylvania on Rebecca Franks and Israel Israel.

Professor Marcus has also produced the largest body of scholarship on colonial American Jews. The similar titles of his various works need to be kept straight: the most important are *The Colonial American Jew, 1492–1776*, 3 vols. (Detroit, Wayne State University Press, 1970); *American Jewry: Documents, Eighteenth Century* (Cincinnati: Hebrew Union College Press, 1959); *Early American Jewry*, 2 vols. (Philadelphia: American Jewish Publication Society, 1953); *United States Jewry, 1776–1985*, 4 vols. (Detroit: Wayne State University Press, 1989).

Essential scholarly journals for American Jewish history are *American*

Jewish History (formerly *Publications of the American Jewish Historical Society*) and *American Jewish Archives* (founded by Marcus at that site), which also reprint many documents.

Many important documents are published in Morris U. Schappes, ed., *A Documentary History of the Jews of the United States: 1654–1875*, 3rd ed. (New York: Schocken, 1971); Joseph L. Blau and Salo W. Baron, *The Jews of the United States: A Documentary History, 1790–1840*, 3 vols. (New York: Columbia University Press, 1963); "The Jew and the American Revolution," *American Jewish Archives* 27 (1975), edited by Jacob Marcus; and Daniel J. Elazar, Jonathan D. Sarna, and Rela G. Monson, *A Double Bond: The Constitutional Documents of American Jewry* (Lanham, Md.: University Press of America, 1992);

Excellent general works are the essays collected in Abraham Karp, ed., *The Jewish Experience in America*, vol. 1, *The Colonial Period* (Waltham, Mass.: American Jewish Publication Society, 1969); and Eli Faber, *A Time for Planting: The First Migration, 1654–1820* (Baltimore: Johns Hopkins University Press, 1992). Two works by Frederic Cople Jaher, *A Scapegoat in the New Wilderness: The Origins and Rise of Anti-semitism in America* (Cambridge: Harvard University Press, 1994), and *The Jews and the Nation: Revolution, Emancipation, State Formation, and the Liberal Paradigm in France and America* (Princeton: Princeton University Press, 2002), are the most probing treatments of early American Judaism in the context of American and world history. See also the fine early chapters of Jonathan Sarna, *American Judaism: A History* (New Haven: Yale University Press, 2004). Louis Harap, *The Image of the Jew in American Literature* (Philadelphia: Jewish Publication Society of America, 1974); and Joseph R. Rosenbloom, *A Biographical Dictionary of Early American Jews* (Lexington: University of Kentucky Press, 1960) are excellent treatments of their subjects. Richard Brilliant, *Facing the New World: Jewish Portraits of the Colonial and Federal Era* (New York: Prestel, 1997) provides biographical and cultural information as well as portraits. For the American Revolution, see the collections as well as Samuel Rezneck, *Unrecognized Patriots: The Jews in the American Revolution* (Westport, Conn.: Greenwood Press, 1997).

For European and Caribbean background, see especially Jonathan Israel, *European Jewry in the Age of Mercantilism, 1550–1750*, rev. ed. (Oxford: Clarendon Press, 1989); Todd Endelman, *The Jews of Georgian England,*

1714–1830, rev. ed. (Ann Arbor: University of Michigan Press, 1999); Frank Felsenstein, *Anti-semitic Stereotypes: A Paradigm of Otherness in English Popular Culture, 1660–1830* (Baltimore: Johns Hopkins University Press, 1995); W. D. Rubinstein, *A History of the Jews in the English Speaking World* (New York: St. Martin's 1996); Miriam Bodian, *Hebrews of the Portuguese Nation: Conversos and Community in Early Modern Amsterdam* (Bloomington: Indiana University Press, 1997); Alan F. Benjamin, *Jews of the Dutch Caribbean: Exploring Ethnic Identity on Curaçao* (London: Routledge, 2002); and Wilfred S. Samuel, *The Jewish Colonists on Barbados in the Year 1680* (London: Purnell and Sons, 1936).

Several good works exist on New York: the most comprehensive are David de Sola Pool and Tamar de Sola Pool, *An Old Faith in the New World: Portrait of Shearith Israel, 1654–1954* (New York: Columbia University Press, 1955); and David de Sola Pool, *Portraits Etched in Stone* (New York: Columbia University Press, 1952). Rabbi Marc D. Angel, *Remnant of Israel: A Portrait of America's First Jewish Congregation, Shearith Israel* (New York: Riverside, 2004) has illustrations of all five colonial-era synagogues, although his history concentrates on New York and goes up to the present. Leo Hershkowitz and Isidore S. Meyer, *The Lee Max Freedman Collection of American Jewish Colonial Correspondence: Letters of the Franks Family, 1733–1748* (Waltham, Mass.: American Jewish Historical Society, 1968); and Leo Hershkowitz, ed. *Wills of Early New York Jews (1704–1799)* (New York: American Jewish Historical Society, 1967) are far more than collections of documents: the notes and introductions are treasure troves of information. Jacob Rader Marcus, *The Handsome Young Priest in the Black Gown: The Personal World of Gershom Seixas* (Cincinnati: Hebrew Union College Press, 1970) is an effective portrayal of Seixas and his times.

For Rhode Island, Morris Gutstein, *The Story of the Jews of Newport* (New York: Bloch, 1936) is still valuable despite some errors. Rabbi Dr. Theodore Lewis, "History of the Touro Synagogue," *Bulletin of the Newport Historical Society* 48 (1975): 281–320, is also a fine work. Stanley F. Chyet, *Lopez of Newport: Colonial American Merchant Prince* (Detroit: Wayne State University Press, 1970) is an excellent biography that also treats the history of the community.

The Jewish community in Charleston, South Carolina, enjoys two good older histories and a superb modern scholarly treatment: Barnett Elzas, *The*

Jews of South Carolina from the Earliest Times to the Present Day (Philadelphia: Lippincott, 1905); Charles Reznikoff with Uriah Engelman, *The Jews of Charleston* (Philadelphia: American Jewish Publication Society, 1950); and James William Hagy, *This Happy Land: The Jews of Colonial and Antebellum Charleston* (Tuscaloosa: University of Alabama Press, 1993).

For Georgia, Rabbi Saul Jacob Rubin, *Third to None: The Saga of Savannah Jewry, 1733–1983* (Savannah: Congregation Mikveh Israel, 1983) is a thorough and thoroughly professional work. Two good specific works are B. H. Levy, *Mordecai Sheftall: Jewish Revolutionary Patriot* (Savannah: Georgia Historical Society, 1999); and Kaye Kole, *The Minis Family of Georgia, 1733–1992* (Savannah: Georgia Historical Society, 1992).

A fine, detailed, scholarly history of Philadelphia Jews is Edwin Wolf II and Maxwell Whiteman, *History of the Jews of Philadelphia from Colonial Times to the Age of Jackson* (Philadelphia: American Jewish Publication Society, 1956). Herbert Samuel Morais, *The Jews of Philadelphia* (Philadelphia: Levy-Type Company, 1894) is still useful. David Brener, *The Jews of Lancaster* (Lancaster, Pa.: private printing, 1979) is well supplemented by the transatlantic study of Mark Häberlein and Michaela Schmolz-Häberlein, "Competition and Cooperation: The Ambivalent Relationship between Jews and Christians in Early Modern Germany and Pennsylvania," *Pennsylvania Magazine of History and Biography* 126 (2002): 409–36. The Gratz family has enjoyed two fine biographies: Sidney M. Fish, *Barnard and Michael Gratz* (Lanham, Md.: University Press of America, 1994); and Dianne Ashton, *Rebecca Gratz: Women and Judaism in Antebellum America* (Detroit: Wayne State University Press, 1997).

INDEX

Abendanone, Hyam, 148
Abendanone, Simon, 148
Abendanone family, 153
Abraham, 96
Abrahams, Abraham, 65
Abrahams, Emanuel, 134
Abrahams, Abraham Isaac, 56
Abrams, Widow, 28
academies, women's, 251
Acsha Fielding, 249–53
Acts of Trade and Navigation, 84
Adams, Brooks 259
Adams, Charles Francis II, 259
Adams, Henry, 259
Adams, John, ix, 12, 74, 76, 78, 211, 259
addresses to Washington, 111–12
Adolphus, Isaac and Charity, 50–51, 55
Africa, 21, 89
African Americans, viii, 4, 6, 10, 11, 92, 93, 163, 244, 252, 263, 264
African slaves, 167, 168
Age of Reason (Paine), 9
ages of death of Jews, 144
Aix-la-Chapelle, 177
Alexander, Cosmus, 180
Alexander, James, 43–44
Algerian Jews in South Carolina, 129
Alien and Sedition Acts, 12, 17, 74, 79
Alison, Francis, 216
Allentown, PA, 91
almanac humor, 233
Amatis brothers, 145
American Revolution, viii, ix, 6, 8, 52, 134, 186, 189, 224, 251, 263; and Georgia,

159–68; and and Newport, RI, 104–10; and New York, 62–66, 69, 77; and Pennsylvania, 202–17; and South Carolina, 125–28
Amsterdam, x, 21, 22, 30, 69, 179
Anabaptists in New Amsterdam, 27, 28
Andros, Sir Edmond, 34
Anglican church. *See* Church of England
anti-semitism, 1, 3–7, 9, 13, 17, 18, 49, 50, 73, 74, 105, 189, 190, 217–18, 264; Anglican, 159; Anti-Federalist, viii, 69, 231–32; Baptists, 270; in Brackenridge's *Modern Chivalry*, 253–54; and Thomas Coram, 147; Dutch, 21–23; elite, 130; Federalist, 75, 76, 78–79, 81, 233–34, 237–47; Federalists reject post-1800, 245; in Georgia, 144–48, 152, 159, 166–68, 170, 171; and historians, 259; and Thomas Jefferson, 265; and Jewish use of stereotypes, 58, 219–22; loyalist, viii, ix, 8, 52, 218–20; and Timothy Matlack, 207; modern vs. early modern, 263; and Henry Melchior Mühlenberg, 213–17, 264; in New Amsterdam, 24–27; in New England, 12, 17, 145; in New York, 43–44, 73–74; and James Oglethorpe, 145; in Pennsylvania, 175; Pennsylvania Constitutionalist, 207, 213–17; Pennsylvania German, 192–95, 201, 213–17, 222–24; 257–59; in Pittsburgh, 245–46; political, 6, 17, 191; popular, 5, 17, 192–95, 268; popular in Georgia 144–48; popular, nineteenth century, 157–59; Republican, 73–74, 240,

305